THE ORGANIZER'S MANUAL—What's in it?

"Your imagination is one of the best weapons against a system which uses none."

"Begin *where the people are,* with local manifestations of the larger issues: e.g., with the layoff in a particular shop, not the whole economic recession."

"Meetings that produce nothing but further meetings are perhaps the main organizational disease of the movement."

"A smudgy, semi-legible leaflet implies a subtle lack of respect for your reader and for your own message."

"Most people come to a trouble pad as refugees. They're not looking for a specific kind of help. Therefore, all counseling services should be available upon request and shouldn't be pushed on runaways."

D1253161

THE ORGANIZER'S MANUAL
by The O. M. Collective

A NATIONAL GENERAL COMPANY

THE ORGANIZER'S MANUAL
A Bantam Book / published March 1971
2nd printing
3rd printing

Illustrations by Domingo Barreres

Published simultaneously in the United States and Canada

Bantam Books are published by Bantam Books, Inc., a National
General company. Its trade-mark, consisting of the words "Bantam
Books" and the portrayal of a bantam, is registered in the United
States Patent Office and in other countries. Marca Registrada.
Bantam Books, Inc. 666 Fifth Avenue, New York, N.Y. 10019.

PRINTED IN THE UNITED STATES OF AMERICA

Dedication

To all those who will make a better revolution
than we can prescribe

He who would do good to another must do it in Minute
   Particulars:
General Good is the plea of the scoundrel, hypocrite & flatterer,
For Art & Science cannot exist but in minutely organized
   Particulars
And not in generalizing Demonstrations of the Rational Power.
                                    —William Blake, *Jerusalem*

Supposing a bomb were put under the whole scheme of
things, what would we be after? What feelings do we want
to carry through into the next epoch? What feelings will
carry us through? What is the underlying impulse in us that
will provide the motive power for a new state of things,
when this democratic-industrial-lovey-dovey-darling-take-me-
to-mamma state of things is bust?
   What next?
      —D. H. Lawrence, "Surgery for the Novel—or a Bomb"

Contents

Preface

We, the O.M. Collective, wrote this book so that you, the reader, might go on writing it in practice. In a real sense it is addressed to its own authors, members of the larger collective of all people who want fundamental social change. Where it falls short, your experience may make up for our lack of it. Where it proves useful, use it to write the next chapters of a book about peace and freedom.

Start wherever you are and reach out to others, wherever they are. Begin to make the changes we have all been demanding. Small groups of us, educating ourselves, organizing at the grass-roots level around issues as the people feel them, insisting on our right to control our own lives, creating forms of the new society in the midst of the old—this is our building ground. Out of the process must come a politics of action that can unite all constituencies and bring the people to power.

For this we need skills. We have to be good at holding meetings, negotiating with deans and bosses, writing leaflets, helping people in trouble, demonstrating and dodging tear gas, staying out of jail or getting out, using the establishment's media and political structures against the establishment, and a thousand other things. What to do, how to do it, when and where to do it, even why to do it—this is what *The Organizer's Manual* is about. It is not a rulebook or a set of infallible prescriptions, but we have tried to make it a detailed, practical guide to organizing. Mine it for methods; adapt them to your own situation; improve on them; invent something new and write your own book. The Collective is putting the proceeds from *The Organizer's Manual* back into activity, in projects to spread ideas for self-organization among more people.

The past few years have showed us that we need not rhetoric but self-reliance, not protest alone but positive programs, worked out in their "Minute Particulars." As its modest contribution to meeting that need, the O.M. Collective offers you this pocket reference for getting results.

Foreword

The Organizer's Manual was born of the national student strike of May 1970: of its unexpected strength and its predictable weaknesses.

When the invasion of Cambodia, the Panther May Day in New Haven, and the killings at Kent State, Augusta, and Jackson emptied classrooms at hundreds of colleges and universities, students across the nation gained a new sense of their essential unity that overshadowed most serious divisions over tactics. But the 'student movement' was also made aware of its vulnerability to attack, its lack of information and organization, its tenuous ties with neighborhood and factory, and its urgent need for stronger ties. *The Organizer's Manual* is an evidence of such awareness and a response to it. Conceived in another form during the strike at Yale and Wesleyan and given its present orientation and content by a Boston University student collective, the *Manual* was written as a practical guide for action—to be *used*, not just read. Its message is organization, from the small group to the masses, from the campus to the community. Politically, it seeks the largest common denominator in that commitment to radical social change which defines the activism of the early 1970s.

The tale of its inception and production reads as a sort of case study of the student movement at the beginning of the decade. A young man who has described himself as a "liberal straight" looked from his window upon the May Day marchers under the elms of Old Eli and decided that this new student generation needed the sort of organizing guide that Vietnam Summer's manual and the New England Free Press's community research pamphlet, *Where It's At*, supplied in 1967. A week after Kent State the idea, carried to a Connecticut-wide conference of striking students at Wesleyan University in Middletown, came to temporary port in a professor's office. There, volunteers worked around the clock to mine the move-

ment's literature for organizing ideas, aiming at May 31, 1970,
publication of the collected material. Back in New Haven
after Wesleyan's students had left their campus, the project
was adopted by a dozen devoted typists, and writers who were
preparing it for "underground," photo-offset reproduction at
about the time that Yale's strikers, too, departed for summer
business or pleasure. The original entrepreneur, in pursuit of
his summer studies, packed up about two hundred pages of
notes, drafts, and source materials and in June brought them
to Boston.

At Boston University he discovered some hundred students
who had gone neither home nor to jobs, Europe, or summer
school. Living in and around a "Strike Dorm," they had committed their vacations to working for the aims of the May
strike. Politically more radical and organizationally more experienced than the initiating editors and collectors, the Boston
University strikers were no more monolithic in their thinking
about what the tactics of the movement ought to be. At this
point Bantam Books offered publication "aboveground"—an
option that opened the project to an audience undreamed-of
in "underground," photo-offset circles.

The B.U. strikers and their friends set to work, some thirty
or forty of them, to draw upon their own experiences and those
of others—community people, faculty members, students of
other schools, trade unionists, leaders of the black students'
organization and of a Puerto Rican street gang—anyone who
wanted to help. They began as editors but gradually, as the
previously collected material proved inadequate to the tasks
of today, assumed authorship of a book which they hoped
might help the movement to understand itself. The new
authors moved from the dormitory to an English instructor's
office and, out of collective "brainstorming," wrote a book
about building a movement rooted in small groups and in self-
created alternatives to the structures of the establishment.

In its writing, the radical organizer's manual proved itself
an organizer. The process produced the O.M. Collective which
took on a self-conscious life of its own, always centered on
"the book." It managed to erase invidious distinctions between
editor's work and typist's work and to elicit, not only days of
painful composition, but days of voluntary self-revision from
persons who had never before written a term paper save
under extreme duress. In a small, borrowed New York
apartment, ten of the Collective, advised by a patient if some-

what startled publisher, sat down among its sleeping bags to do most of it over, once again. It is not "done" now. The most of it remains for the authors and for others, for the movement from which it comes, to do in action.

The metamorphoses of *The Organizer's Manual* are signs of the state of a movement that seeks its building ground somewhere between the emptiness of waiting on "peace" candidates and the emptiness of trashing bank windows. Written with no harder political "line" than this, almost every item of organization was nonetheless subjected to intense political debate by the Collective. The direction is outward: from the study group of friends to the mass demonstration, from the limits of middle-class consciousness to a common ground with all people, from talk to action. Given the direction, the question remained, "Organize for what?" It rose to the surface in consideration of how to use the established media and political structures. It bedeviled the section on self-defense. It affected the discussion of nearly every "constituency," not the least being the "Universities" section itself, where "Tear it down!" still seemed a viable option.

If *The Organizer's Manual* has a "message," it rests in its focus upon the organizing process itself. The book was not spun out of an ideology, nor founded upon a systematic theoretical analysis of the present stage of world capitalism, or socialism either. Behind each of these practical, how-to-do-it suggestions—how to run a meeting, a mimeograph machine, a drug-counseling center, a mass rally—lies the assumption that deep-going changes in the social order are imperative and that people must now, in practice, begin to make the changes they desire. The politics of the *Manual* inhere in the process it was designed to further, not in static "goals" or closed "isms." Hence, it cannot essentially transcend the experience of the radical movement of this time. It can, and does, aim to bring together that experience in such a way as to uncover its critical and creative potential for the struggles yet to come. Therefore, where the *Manual* has no "answers" it confines itself to suggestions and approaches, or to an account of how some group, somewhere, tackled a certain problem. This is not only inevitable but as it should be in a book of a collective united not around some prefab program but in an open-ended seeking of ways to effect those radical transformations by which humanity may yet affirm itself.

Students, professors, workers, doctors, tenants, lawyers, organizers, janitors, storekeepers, jailbirds, writers, religionists, scientists, journalists—men and women; most, but not all, very young—have consciously (or a few unknown to themselves) had a hand in *The Organizer's Manual*. From Boston University, Yale, Wesleyan, Harvard, MIT, University of Massachusetts, Lowell State College, UC at Berkeley, Princeton, McGill, Toronto, Columbia, University of Texas at El Paso, a high school in Georgia and another in Wisconsin, and numerous schools forgotten, have come ideas by one route or another. Organizers from street and shop, freedom fighters from the black, Chicano, and Puerto Rican movements, American Indians, Asian Americans, trade unionists, welfare recipients, women in the forefront of the liberation movement: the Collective embraces perhaps a hundred who did something, somewhere, to put together this book in the hope that it might serve the many-sided struggle for a world free of poverty, injustice, and war. Acknowledgment to all these will rest in its usefulness in that cause.

Part A

Principles

I. Organizing

1. Small-Group Organizing

The political function of small-group organizing is to enable individuals to grow, and hopefully to broaden to the point where they are able to work with other individuals or larger groups, building mutual trust while struggling to actualize changes within society.

I. *How the group becomes self-conscious and operative*

A. *An organizer* must have his own head together personally and emotionally, even more than politically, before he attempts to deal with other people and possibly influence their lives. There is no substitute for this. An organizer must also be understanding and sensitive to the problems of those he works with, to enable leadership to develop within the group, and to help the group deal with its own inner conflicts, make decisions effectively, and keep itself together while continuing to grow.

B. *Recruiting* a group can be done by leafleting, by invitation, or by a one-to-one informal discussion-interview. Usually discussion-interview is the best way to organize a small group. Contact people and meet with them individually before arranging the first meeting. This way you will have a better idea of who will attend and what they see as active concerns and issues for change.

Try to recruit five or ten intelligent, committed, hardworking people. If you can't find that many dedicated workers, at least get some warm bodies who feel a sense of obligation. Try to recruit people whose commitment is deep enough so that they will stay with the group instead of drifting off after the first few meetings; political continuity is something the movement must strive for.

3

C. *Planning for the first meeting* is especially crucial because it sets the tone, anticipating what the next meeting will bring. Here, the organizer has a chance to see how the members of the group respond to and interact with one another. Obviously, an agenda should be planned, including some mechanical but, nevertheless, important points:

—Discuss how much time each person could, should, and would put into working for the group.

—Set up a regular meeting time, from two to four hours once a week at least (you can always adjourn early).

—Sketch out a general program and ask for discussion. It is desirable to make the first organized project of the group a short-term one that has a high probability of success. This will give you a chance to get to know each other and filter out your first impressions, and can be used as a basis for attracting others to the movement.

—Suggest to people in the group some specific assignments for the next meeting. This will give a sense of purpose and suggest who in the group will be responsible.

—Evaluate your own resources, the resources of the group and of any opposition. (See "Power Structure Research.")

—At the first meeting, people should discuss their own expectations and politics and goals.

—Try and set aside the first available weekend or a single entire day for a retreat to discuss political objectives. *This conference retreat is essential to a successful organizing attempt.* You should make an attempt to schedule your conference beforehand, since you may be competing with other events. The participants at this conference should also attempt to talk about themselves and about the general assumptions under which the group will operate.

D. *Structure and leadership* is important to a small group. Traditionally, political movements have had strong leadership to direct, crystallize, and even formulate the philosophy of the movement. While the centralized group has the possible advantage of greater efficiency, it also has many serious shortcomings. Leaders can be "bought out" by the establishment and can be disposed of by lengthy court actions, personal pressure, etc. Furthermore, the existence of too strong a leader can encourage power games or factional struggle. For the small group to be successful, as many of the participants as possible must be included in the decision-making process. Rotating the chair after the first couple of meetings helps to develop responsibility and leadership among members. In addition, try sitting in a circle so that each one can see the others and participate easily.

II. *Participation and the decision-making process*

A. *Brainstorming* is an all-purpose technique for getting ten or ten thousand ideas depending on the number of minutes spent and the number of people involved. The basic theory behind brainstorming is that imagination and judgment are two distinct processes in the production of ideas, and that imagination should be given free reign before judgment is brought onto the scene. When the goal is a solution, one wants as many creative ideas as possible. Temporary withholding of evaluation generates the greatest number of ideas.

Brainstorming can be done individually or collectively. It works especially well with groups of five to ten people although it can work for larger groups as well. The leader of the group poses the problem in a way calculated to stimulate thought and permit a wide range of responses. One person should be responsible for jotting down all the ideas that are called out. Brainstormers should note the following:

—Criticism is out. Everyone should suspend judgment until evaluation time.

—Freewheeling is welcome. The wilder the ideas, the better. Everyone should let his imagination soar. It is far easier to tame an idea down than to think one up.

—Hitchhiking is invited. Each person is encouraged to ride on, improve on, add to, divide from, and combine with everyone else's ideas.

—Quantity is wanted. The more ideas the better. Piling up ideas produces an atmosphere that encourages people to be spontaneous.

For best results, brainstorming should be intensive. A time limit should be agreed upon in advance. It can range from five to fifteen minutes. When the brainstorming session is over, the list of ideas should be recopied in readable form and submitted for analysis and judgment. Selection of the best ideas and their polishing can be done later.

B. *Division of opinion, and debates* in a small group should be expected. It is important to realize the advantage of opposition and debate, and not attempt to squash them. You should be prepared to understand your opposition. Listen to what they have to say, and how they are saying it. Try to attack the issue, and not the person who supports it. Avoid making statements like "That's a rotten idea" and "You're crazy!" because that will only give your opponents cause to attack you personally and distract the discussion from the political content. Try to establish both the areas of agreement and disagreement when there is opposition in the group. Finally, remember not to carry discussion too far. If your opponent is tired or in a bad mood, there is always a time when he will be more receptive to your ideas.

You should accept the idea that people will resist change. How much change depends on how hard you are prepared to struggle. Politics is a slow and gradual process. You too have gone through changes. In addition, you must remember that there are times when you will be wrong; you must be prepared to retreat, and analyze and criticize yourself as well as other members of the group. It is a mistake in small groups to act unilaterally to push a program without the the participation of the group. Involve everybody! While you should have a plan in mind, your plan should have some flexibility built into it. As it grows, and as group participation produces new information, you will find the plan itself is modified. Don't let it worry you; make sure that you see the political content of the process which leads to changes in the initial plan.

C. In *deciding on an action*, you should first take into account what your goals are. Then pick the action after a discussion covering the attitudes and opinions of the group members, an analysis of the situation, and an analysis of exigencies, consequences, and alternative actions. Consider what you will do if your action is successful—and what you will do if it is unsuccessful.

D. *Drawing the lessons* from what you have done and how this contributes to your political goals is an important task in small-group organizing. Failures and successes should *both* provide valuable leads for future planning. Keeping a record of what you are doing may also reveal new tactical information for future implementation. In addition it is important to have group members criticize both how they have done their tasks and how the group functions. Above-board attitudes toward evaluation will not only build group solidarity, but will also allow political practice to revise out-moded political theory.

III. *Getting the work done*

A. *Assignments* should be divided up and talked about by the whole group, with the member(s) responsible for report-ing back even if there is a dead end. One method for getting work done is *The List*. You write down everything that must be done, and check it off immediately upon finishing it— something that will guide you through the many things you may repress or forget. If this fails, try bribing yourself.

If there are more than a few days between meetings, it is often important to call people to see what's happening. A quick brainstorm on the phone can keep everybody posted as to what's going down, give new leads where people are stuck, and give you a picture of what the next meeting may bring.

Scheduling of assignments and reports is crucial, not as an authoritarian assertion, but to give a sense of seeing when and how work can and should be done.

B. *Common group problems* usually occur about the third or fourth meeting, as members begin to question the group's effectiveness, or the commitment of individuals. Lateness, absence, and few decisions are the symptoms. Many group problems can be traced to difficulties in the organizer-par-ticipant relationship. To keep a group together the organizer must balance his time between the pursuit of goals and the structure of the organization and the needs of its members. One who worries only about the goals alienates the people, who feel neglected, and an organizer who pays attention exclusively to the infrastructure of the group will not move it forward.

Competent organizers can overcome many doubts and conflicts which tend to arise in all groups. Some pointers are:

—Do not get carried away with your position.
—Be responsible to both the vocal and quiet members of the group. Encourage the more silent members to partic-

ipate as much as possible so that their abilities and desires become more known. Watch both facial and body expressions. Look for disagreement in the expressions of the silent members.

—Talk openly of power struggles, personal interests, and hidden issues with the group. Don't avoid confrontation— bring disagreements out into the open.

—Don't allow yourself to be infected by the despair of others. *Disappointment and despair have disbanded more groups than any other problem. They are contagious and must be dealt with as soon as they arise.* The organizer must remember that his attitude will often permeate the group. He must emphasize the positive successes of the group, no matter how small. Talk out anger and despair honestly and openly.

—Keep meetings orderly, but at the same time be sensitive to the personalities of the participants; assure each one of his equality in the group, and allow each participant to express himself fully and in his own way. *Robert's Rules of Order* may be used to stop conflicts and to speed progress, but take care not to stifle discussion or positive developments. Listen to all participants carefully and question them in order to make their views clearer to yourself and the rest of the group. If the personal interests of a particular member tend to drag out a meeting with irrelevant discussion, try to make the irrelevancy apparent without unduly antagonizing either the entire group or the single member. Humor the innocently disruptive to a point, but cut them off tactfully when necessary.

—Plan specific action projects. Continually monitor progress and keep all members informed of specific accomplishments to date, the roles of each individual, and reasons for the next step. Any project with a lead time of over six months ought to be supplemented with short-term action projects. Even if this delays the long-term work somewhat, the effect on group morale may be very valuable.

IV. *Communications*

A. *The office.* A meeting place is important to any organization as a gathering place for information, a communications center, a place to gather fieldworkers' reports and coordinate work, and a storage and supply center (typewriters to prepare reports, mimeograph equipment for leaflets, etc.). Always put a responsible, competent person in the office; never leave a novice to man it alone. Do not let the office become a counterproductive social hangout. The office is a tool for action, not an accomplishment in itself.

B. *Telephone chains.* A telephone chain or tree is a network of people set up in such a manner that a minimal amount of time and energy is spent in notifying the membership of the group in case of a meeting or an unexpected development. There are many ways to set up such a system so that each member of the group makes one or two calls to contact other members and spread the message further. Once set up the chain or tree should be tested for effectiveness with message drills.

V. *Calling and conducting a public meeting*

Many organizations on the left (with the exception of the cadre parties) have consistently kept their meetings public. An open public meeting usually implies that everyone can decide, evaluate, discuss, and vote on what is to be done. A small group calls a public meeting for a number of reasons: to gain visibility and identity, to plan an action which involves others or to gain support for one, to recruit new members, or merely to propagandize a message. The public meeting is a way for the small group to act as an activating mechanism within the larger group surrounding it. The public meeting is a primary political activity of the small group.

The following are some points to remember when calling and conducting a public meeting.

A. *Publicity.* The purpose and publicizing of a public meeting are interlocking. The publicity should not only attract people who will want to attend but also make known the purposes of the meeting and give exposure to your group and its positions. More people will probably read a leaflet advertising a meeting than will actually attend the meeting.

B. *Agenda.* Prepare an agenda with general headings which allows for discussion on all issues of concern and provides direction for the meeting. It is often wise to open the agenda to discussion, so that additions or revisions may be brought forward early in the meeting, but remember the larger the group, the longer the discussion. Sometimes individuals or groups will present alternate agendas.

The order, content, and direction of the agenda are significant political points. The arrangement of the agenda is a statement of the relative importance of various issues. An important issue placed too late on the agenda can be undermined by obstructionists stalling the meeting and winning their point by attrition. Plan ahead, decide on an agenda that can meet the participants' approval, and try to stick to it.

C. *Chairman.* Choose a chairman who is generally acceptable to the people you expect to attend the meeting. Get someone who will not be too involved in the discussion of any particular issue. Unpopular, incompetent or dictatorial chairmen can doom meetings. Pick women as often as men.

D. *Proposals.* Make proposals short and sweet. Extensive participation in arriving at proposals will mean more of a consensus. The larger the meeting the shorter the proposal, since a large group is more likely to agree on a short statement. Save manifestos for small groups with relative unanimity. Make proposals completely clear to all participants and distribute written copies if possible. Break down large groups into workshops to develop and discuss proposals.

E. *Timing.* Too long a meeting will fizzle out. Determine the extent of participation in the meeting by considering time available, as well as the issues to be discussed, their importance, and the political differences within the group. Assert *Robert's Rules of Order* if the meeting becomes too large, too angry, or is running out of time. The best mechanism for dealing with those who would talk the meeting to death is a time limit for individual speeches. Remind participants that time is budgeted so that everyone who wishes to speak may do so. It helps to have one or two open microphones so that people can speak directly from the floor.

F. *Workshops.* Workshop sessions at large meetings need planning in order to best utilize people who know the issues and can lead discussions. Workshops should be used when the topic to be discussed is complex or your small group feels that a short period of intensive political discussion would lead to a better understanding of the issues. Set a time limit as you break for workshops so everyone will know when to return. Remember to disperse your own small group among the workshops so that you know what's going on.

G. *Factionalism.* You and your group have two tools to deal with factionalism: politically principled discussion and standard parliamentary procedure. Political discussion should be considered first because it usually exposes the root causes of dissent.

Determine who is involved and why. If you think the factionalism is being generated by personality conflicts or feuding cliques, a brief analysis presented to the meeting may isolate the factions before people become bored or angered and leave. If a contradictory political line is being pushed by a small number of disciplined politicos or members of a cadre party, then argue your political principles. If the argument drags and no one is being persuaded anyway institute time limits for individuals or the topic.

If the whole mess gets too far out of hand, the belligerents should be challenged to show that they are not acting like "the Man" and asked to prove how they are contributing to the growth of the movement. Remember smart infiltrators would love to keep people fighting with one another instead of for an issue.

H. *Voting.* "Voting is the menu, not the meal" (Eugene Debs). In a meeting in which every participant has the right to vote, a sense of responsibility and commitment to decisions made is essential if the actions voted on are to be effective— the group must sit at the table and eat the meal. You and your small group should take the lead in making this point absolutely clear.

Know when to call for a vote. Wait too long and you may lose by attrition the strength of a large-group decision. On the other hand, incomplete understanding will bring half-baked actions. You and your small group will develop through experience a feeling about the proper time to call for a vote. Be sensitive to time, mood, dissension, the development of political discussion, the constituency of the meeting, and the understanding of the issue that most participants have.

I. *Planning future action and delegating responsibility.* Meetings that produce nothing but further meetings are perhaps the main organizational disease of the movement. The cure lies in focusing upon specific tasks, even if these delegating responsibility for their accomplishment. It is not undemocratic to pin people down to specific jobs, with times, are only steps toward some larger, future action, and upon places, telephone numbers, and all details made clear. Involve the whole meeting in electing people for such tasks as negotiating, making public statements, and other work de-

manding political judgment. For routine jobs you can let
people volunteer. Plan a follow-up meeting of the whole
body or an open session of your group for reporting back,
evaluation, and next steps. If your large meeting has been
action-oriented, these will not merely be "more endless
meetings," but will, in turn, lead to actions which build the
movement.

VI. *Expansion of a small-group organization; strengths and weaknesses*

Once organized, a well-knit, self-aware small group which
is educated to the issues and problems within its community
has great potential. An effective small group can act as a
"steering committee" for the activities of a larger group
drawn from the community. It can also be a seed from
which other small groups will develop.

In any effective small group there will be members, in
addition to the original organizer, who have a potential
ability for organizing. If the group works properly, as a unit
with shared responsibility and leadership, these potential
organizers should not be stifled by power struggles. After
gaining firsthand experience, they can reach out into the
community and form new, secondary groups directed toward
action on related projects. For example, in university organizing, a small group may include people from different
colleges within the university, who then may go back and
organize small groups in their own colleges.

Secondary small groups may or may not remain directly
affiliated with the original group. They may go off into new
areas and new actions more suited to their particular ability
and the segment of the community in which they will work,
while still remaining within the original political spectrum.
Or their efforts may be more closely directed by the original
small group.

Eventually, through the formation of many groups, both
primary and secondary, people with experience in small-
group activities and an acquired talent for organizing will
come together. When such "organizers" cooperate as a small
group an "organizers' collective" is established. The organizers' collective of experienced people will probably be more
successful in initiating mass campaigns than a small group
of relatively inexperienced people.

In an organization based on small-group components, no member is entirely removed from decision making. Although a few people's opinions may be extremely influential, a large number of people will share responsibility and have an overview of their role. Everyone can relate directly to the small group in which he functions. When people function knowingly and in direct contact with the leadership instead of mechanically under orders from an unseen source, then the chances of a gross error or poor decisions due to the isolation of the leadership are diminished. One might call this "democratic decentralism."

Educational work can be done slowly and extensively in small groups. The members can become politically sophisticated and knowledgeable about issues at a rate which fits their own particular needs. Discipline at actions and in general is more easily maintained in a small group which is thoroughly aware of issues and goals involved. Each small group can act as an affinity group (see "Marches and Rallies") sensitive to what is necessary for the success of campaigns.

The most rapid and effective way of developing new organizers, while engaging in ongoing activity, is through the formation of many small groups. Such groups act as workshops for developing leaders. Sources of new leaders are crucial for the long-term success of a movement.

The main weakness of the small-group form of organization is internal coordination. Decentralized decision making means that many people will take part in each major decision, with normal disagreement, possible inexperience, and the need for thorough debate all complicating the process. This can slow and interfere with the implementation of coordinated effort. But these disadvantages are more than balanced by the advantages of direct member involvement and many-sided debate.

2. Grass-Roots Organizing

Community organizers get involved in communities in one of four basic ways: they are invited by a sponsoring group in the community; they are sent in by a sponsoring or identifiable group outside the community; they come into a community of their own accord; or they are native to the community and want to change or influence certain things.

Frequent targets of people's organizations include: unconcerned, inadequate, or corrupt government officials, public planners, and bureaucratic units; individual oppressors such as landlords and exploitative store or business owners; corporations with exploitative policies; private interest groups and power elites; criminals as defined by law, and criminals who operate within the law; and other sources or symbols of community suffering.

The ultimate aim of organizers should be to help people gain control over the forces which affect their lives. This must be done on a relatively small scale in local areas in order that the people may build a power base from which eventually to control national power in their own interests.

Laying the Foundation

When you begin to work in a community, your first task is to define the issues.

Learn the issues from the people. Go out into the community to analyze the situation and listen to the people. Sit in the local tavern and drink with the men, but mostly listen. Listen to the corner grocery man who is a key to the economic situation in the town. Go to the local playground and talk to the mothers. Talk to the kids who hang out on the corners —they can best gauge the educational and recreational and job opportunities for the young.

Basic research. Go to the local library and read back issues of the community newspaper, and prepare a list of names of people you might wish to contact or whom you might eventually expect to oppose. Gauge the existing community problems and attitudes of the people from the newspaper if you can. Find out who owns the newspaper, the radio stations, TV stations, and other community media.

Find out also as much as you can about who runs the community and how they stay in power. What is their degree of vulnerability? Visit identifiable community leaders, members of the united fund, local ministers, the president of the local bank. Listen and rap with them, and try to discover where their heads are at. Get names of other people who they think you might talk to. Visit local professionals, clergy, teachers, and members of liberal groups and find the good conscientious people. You need this information for two purposes: to find potential high-visibility allies, and to sound out potential enemies

Choosing an Issue

If you see real political potential in a given locality, begin the struggle. Your first issue should be an attainable goal which will provide you with your first victory. It may be as trite as the placement of a new stop sign Your efforts should begin on a positive note.

A good planning exercise is to ask the following questions:

What is the goal of the planned action?
What are your reasons for this goal?
For what reasons might other persons support or contribute to this goal?

Enumerate alternate strategies for achieving this goal.

Estimate the number of people and the kinds of resources which would be needed for each alternative strategy. What facilities, money, free time would be needed to do the job?

After this initial planning stage, make your purpose known around the community. Do leafleting and rapping in churches, schools, bars, barbershops, and on street corners. Collect feedback, work up the suggestions people give and implement them. Develop all your potential sources of support in the specific struggle.

Meetings

When the time is right to begin organizing community manpower, arrange an open meeting. A community member must call the meeting, not an organizer.

The first meeting should be held in a well-known place— a church, school, existing organization or meeting room. Go and ask for permission to use it. Unless you are calling for the start of guerrilla warfare you will probably not be refused, at least not the first time. If you've done your groundwork, a meeting place may come to you in the form of an offer before you even ask

The best way to organize people for any purpose is on a one-to-one basis. Few people respond to a leaflet except in upper-middle-class and student communities You have to invite people person to person and plan around them. It is hard for people to find time to come to a meeting. Besides which, they may be suspicious of this new organization. You and your chosen contacts must talk to as many people as possible, and get the word out on the gossip line. Be ready to provide baby-sitting and transportation if necessary. In bad neighborhoods, offer protection for people going home late.

The most important part of the first meeting is preparation. Go back three or four times to the people who showed interest in becoming leaders. Talk to them about pulling the community together around the issues. You should go over the purposes of the meeting and your own ideas for the agenda with your community contacts. Work especially with the person who is going to chair the meeting.

The meeting should do much more than decide the date for the second get-together. Draw people into the building of the organization and into involvement in the specific struggle by arranging with them tasks to be completed and reported on at the next meeting.

Once the novelty has worn off, continue to give people good reasons for coming to your meetings. Keep the meetings short and offer more than talk. Keep the issues alive and close to the personal interests of the people. Try to keep tangible, though perhaps small, victories coming as well as continuous action and progress on longer-term work.

You might use block parties, Sunday brunches (everyone brings something and you cook it all together), neighborhood movies, etc., as ways to involve new people, break down alienation, and keep the ball rolling.

Grass-Roots Communication

What may seem a disturbingly small percentage of people may realistically be expected to participate in the routine life of a community organization. However, if you have 1 or 2 percent of the community truly committed and working on a regular basis, you should also be able to count upon temporary active support of many more people for a given issue, depending on the issue's relevance.

If you are attempting to reach several hundreds or thousands of people, techniques of mass production and mass communication, money, and an efficient office headquarters become more important. If you are able to use established means of communication and organization (clubs, churches, sympathetic media, etc.), a small staff of activists can spark a wide though perhaps only transient interest in an issue, candidate, piece of controversial legislation, or local crisis. However, the less preorganization and political consciousness the community has to begin with, the less effective an office-based, public relations, mass operation will be.

If you want depth and permanence and lack financial support, you must still organize through one-to-one contact and pavement pounding. Work door to door doing block organizing, recruiting contacts and canvassers as you go. Divide the constituency into natural subunits, of say fifty adults. Seek a contact in each neighborhood section of fifty who will help initiate canvassing or an evening meeting. If you succeed in getting 2 to 5 percent of the people active in a regular fashion you can consider your organization a staggering success at recruitment.

As involvement and peripheral interest increases, newsletter and mass media coverage are increasingly important to maintain communications. If you have the resources and local desire for a newsletter, one should be published regularly. If the legitimate media are willing to cover your events, don't hesitate to avail yourself. Provide them with releases to increase accurate coverage. Any press distortions can be used to demonstrate the biases of the paper and discredit the paper in the eyes of the community.

In the end, however, the important matter is the power of numbers. Can the grass-roots group convince the target system that the group speaks for an impressive segment of the community? While you may not have people ready to take to the streets, how high is public opinion in support of the organization position?

Dealing with the Enemy

Know your enemy. Understand what his strategy is going to be and be able to predict how he might react. You've got to know him as well as you know your own people. Understand him better than he does himself.

When dealing with the enemy, try to get slightly outside his experience in order to get the best of him and beat him. Play by his rules to a certain point. Understand him, and then go just one step further, right beyond the limits of his expectations, where he just can't understand what is happening. You make a fool out of him and destroy him. For example, at a corporation's annual meeting you hold a people's stockholders' meeting on the outside, using people's proxies or voodoo; get your people inside to create a row or to take control. You are using his thing but you are outside his experience. A good action has the quality of a zap and the strength of the people behind it.

Interagency Council

When a number of community organizations already exist within a particular geographic area, an intercommunity, interagency organization can be invaluable. The umbrella organization helps each group find out what each other group is doing, and keeps all groups informed of new programs, opportunities, and threats to community welfare. It enables different organizations to pool resources for mutual benefit, to coordinate instead of duplicate efforts. As it builds communication it can build greater trust among disparate groups. Above all, a coalition organization or "power bank" enables groups with common interests to work together to meet common threats, to redress problems collectively by presenting a united front. For example, in an area involved with urban renewal, it might enable community groups to jointly frame a redevelopment plan to present to government agencies, to supervise all construction that takes place, and to monitor the administration of government funds in the community.

Organizing and Political Awareness

The organizer's job is to help people to *clarify* the problem and to work effectively toward a common goal. What he brings with him in the way of practical knowledge and energy will determine, to a large extent, the degree of his success. People are generally uninformed as to how to go about demanding change or preventing disruption in their communities. Simply making them aware of their own power will bring home questions of broad political importance.

It has been implied that "winning people over" to left-wing politics is the ultimate goal of organizing. But if organizers regard the people they intend to work with as objects of manipulation, then no real understanding can be achieved and no fundamental problems can be solved. The processes of change will be set in motion by honest collaboration between the people and the organizers.

3. Fund Raising

Fund raising is absolutely essential for any significant program, for it serves both to expand programs and to bring in new people. Fund raising is not limited to any one particular technique, and does not require an expert for its success. It is something every local organization can and must do.

Once the organization is launched, the fund-raising pitch should be made, if only by passing a hat near the end of the first organizing meeting to provide an initial financial base from which to expand. A fund-raising committee should be formed. Individual solicitation of prospective large donors should begin at once. An advertisement in the local paper can bring in money as well as interested people, and will give the project greater visibility in the community.

INDIVIDUAL SOLICITATIONS. Nearly all large, national organizations receive 90 percent of their money from 10 percent of their contributors. Consequently they devote the bulk of their fund-raising effort to pursuing members of the potential 10 percent.

The fund raisers should compile a list of the heavy contributors to peace, civil rights, and liberal organizations. Local businessmen, corporate executives, and professionals who have been signers of ads placed in nationally known newspapers or who are affiliated with reformist organizations or caucuses within larger associations should be asked for contributions. (See Directory.) A cover letter from a sympathetic and important person can help for an introduction.

The fund raiser should be polite and should allow the contributor a chance to express his concern and point of view. He should be direct and should not try to hide the fact that he is looking for large sums of money. He should always ask for more than he thinks he can get.

In speaking to these people, it may be helpful to have on hand a copy of the organization's budget showing how much money is needed. Explain what a specific donation could be used for.

After meeting with prospective donors, the fund raisers should send a follow-up letter, thanking them for their contribution or, if none was received, for the chance to talk with them. Formal receipts for all contributions should be sent.

A large contributor becomes potentially most valuable to the organization after he has made his contribution, for he can be instrumental in bringing in other large contributors. Wealthy individuals who are quite friendly to the group should be made members of the fund-raising staff assigned to solicit others.

MAILINGS. To bring in two dollars for every dollar spent is to do well. But mailings, in addition to bringing in money, can interest possible volunteers in working for the group. Mailing lists can be secured from peace, civil rights, and liberal groups. (See "Using the Mail.")

Approach important people to endorse your group and allow their names to be used as honorary members on the letterhead. Fund-raising letters should be brief and to the point (usually no more than one page). The first sentence or two should be strong, and worded to make people continue reading.

Within the letter, be specific; describe fully the activities already in operation and those planned. Be forceful, stress the importance of giving *now*. Letters should be neat. If offset is too expensive, use a carbon-ribbon typewriter and then have an electronic stencil made. If you use a business reply envelope, code it in some fashion, especially if you are using different mailing lists, so that you can analyze the returns.

ADVERTISEMENTS. As with mailings, advertisements rarely bring in more than two dollars for every dollar spent. To run an ad, you might enlist the aid of a professional P.R. man. He can be most helpful in drafting text, in editing, and in getting the ad placed through an agency which will return to you all or part of the 15 percent agency discount. Good layout is essential: since most groups will not be able to afford a full page, you must design an ad which will catch the reader's eye. Select the local paper or papers which have the best circulation and the most liberal position, for they are read by the people who are most likely to contribute to your cause.

Think carefully about when the ad should appear. Sunday

rates are usually higher, but so is the Sunday circulation. Location within the paper is important. Obviously the nearer the front the better, but always go for an outside right-hand page. If you are placed in the centerfold, people may miss you entirely. If an ad returns well, think about running it again, since most papers have reduced rates for second runs of the same ad. If you run the ad in more than one paper, code the coupon of each, so that you can analyze returns.

PLEDGE GROUPS. Once the organization has really got under way, and people begin to develop loyalties to it and its projects, pledge groups become possible. A contributor can be asked to gather some of his friends into a group. Each individual should be asked to give according to his means—say, one to ten dollars a month. A monthly reminder, which could be part of a regular project newsletter, may be necessary. Pledge groups collapse if they are not run regularly.

PARTIES. An informal gathering in someone's living room, supplied with good literature and an articulate speaker, can raise from ten dollars to many thousands, depending on the wealth of your guests. Allow people to socialize for a short while before you start the program. A ten- to fifteen-minute presentation of the aims and activities of the group should then take place, followed by questions. Then, a local person, perhaps your host, should make the pitch.

SPECIAL EVENTS. These include concerts, film showings, speeches by nationally known figures, and theater parties. Special events for fund-raising purposes are worthwhile only if the group expects a large turnout, since they require so much work on the part of the fund-raising staff. The special event can often be an excellent outreach technique. Announcements concerning activities of the local organization can be made before the performance, and the performance itself may convey a political message. (See the relevant parts of *Movement Guide to Fund-Raising*, available from SDS, 1608 W. Madison St., Chicago, Ill. 60612.)

FAIRS. Political fairs can raise several thousands of dollars, especially if a well-known, centrally located area can be obtained for the fairground.

First, seek permission from local officials to use the grounds you have selected. Go prepared with specific information about the size of the anticipated crowd, the time of the event, plans for trash collection, etc. Arrange to pay off-duty policemen to patrol the fairground. Determine whether the city requires you to post a public liability bond. Secure legal assistance, and, if possible, avoid paying the bond. Ask for permission to use the grounds for two days—the scheduled day and a rain date, a week later.

At the fair, get a portable stage or platform for entertainment. Most of the fairground can be filled with refreshment, games, and photograph booths, and booths in which donated articles are sold. Thousands of books and back issues of underground papers can be collected from individuals. Select a large, well-located booth and use it to present literature, free or otherwise, and information on the activities of the local organization. Other local groups should be invited to set up booths of their own.

Publicity: To be successful, the fair must be well publicized in advance. Leaflets, posters, banners, etc., should be used. Balloons with the words PEACE-FAIR, FREEDOM-FAIR, etc., can be obtained, distributed in the thousands before the fair, and sold at the fair. Special leaflets should be produced asking for donations of books, cakes, white elephants, etc., and for people to man the booths. Make sure that the local communications media are notified and kept well informed of the event.

CANVASSING. In order to solicit funds in a public area, i.e., to canvass, it is necessary to check state and local laws first. Most towns require a permit to canvass, and soliciting without one is considered panhandling, an illegal activity. Contact the city clerk or the license bureau. Even if you get the proper permits you may run into hassles. Any cop may try to bust one of your canvassers, so provide each one with a xerox of the ordinance stating that a permit is not required or a copy of the permit. It's not a bad idea to notify the police of your activities in advance.

Shopping centers are both public and private areas. You need both the permission of the town and of the plaza management. (If local chain-store manager says no, try the regional or national office for permission.)

Have a lawyer available to handle any bad scene that comes up. Give your canvassers a phone number to call for assistance. Advise them to pull out in case of trouble and to get the name of the person who asked them to leave, so that the lawyer can deal with him.

FOUNDATION GRANTS. Certain large corporations and

wealthy individuals have established foundations which offer grants to worthy projects for social change. Grants are also made by government agencies. The availability of such money for movement use is a contradiction that must be dealt with carefully. Foundations will often use their contributions as a lever of pressure to exact compromises from a left-wing organization deemed a potential threat to the system. A political organizer utilizing a foundation grant must not allow his tactical alternatives to be limited by his benefactor. In negotiations for the grant, great pains must be taken to assure that a minimum of strings are attached to the money.

Your proposal must be exact, businesslike, and professional. The people who will be evaluating it can spot an exaggerated plea for support or an ambiguous description of your institution.

I. *Preparation*

Study the project you're seeking funds for in detail. Don't rely on secondhand information. Find out how much money is needed, what the project will accomplish, how it will be administered, then make an outline of all the major facts you have gathered.

Identify the foundation you're appealing to. The *Foundation Directory* and the *Foundation News* (published by the Foundation Center in Baltimore) are very good. Try to choose foundations located in your area, and make a detailed study of them at the nearest Foundation Library Center. The main center is in New York City with branches in Washington, D.C., Atlanta, Chicago, Kansas City, Cleveland, and Austin, Texas. (See Bibliography–Directory.)

II. *Preliminary contact*

One person from your group, someone who knows what's going on, should make the initial contact with the foundation to discuss the project and ask if a formal proposal may be submitted. This initial contact should have more material than he expects to use—even a formal proposal, in case it is called for.

III. *Formal application*

A. *Format:* Typewritten, double-spaced, neat and accurate. Don't use a hardbound or fancy cover; a stapled or spiral cover will do.

B. *Content:* Use clear, simple language. Avoid trite phrases or obscure terminology which would make it harder to understand and take a long time to edit.

C. *Length:* This is determined by subject matter, but generally shouldn't be more than ten or twelve pages.

D. *Supporting documents:* This is an appendix that might include a bibliography, a summary of projects, financial data, etc. Keep it short and factual.

E. *Pictures:* Use pictures only when necessary; for example, if the grant is being used for building or remodeling a building, a picture would be helpful.

F. *Budget:* Should include amounts needed for personnel, equipment, supplies, construction, etc., if necessary. If the grant is for less than the total cost of a project, explain where the balance of funds is coming from.

IV. *Follow-through on grants*

Once a grant is received, keep the foundation informed as to the development of your project. This follow-up system will help broaden your base of support with foundations in the future.

Don't give up completely on a particular foundation if they reject your first proposal. Keep the foundation on your mailing list and try again if another project comes up. Many foundations don't usually accept initial proposals from new organizations.

SMALL FUND RAISING. You can raise small amounts of cash through bake sales, dinners, church collections, mixers, and dances; you can gamble or beg; pawn your stereo; steal or borrow; run a soap-box derby; hawk flowers, armbands, buttons, art, used books, posters, postcards, and other handicrafts; print for profit; run a folk or straight auction; establish a household antipiggy bank; collect tithes of allowance, payrolls, and scholarships; donate birthday, graduation, Christmas checks and cash redeemed from gifts; abstain from ————; wash cars; silk-screen symbols on shirts; donate speaker fees and publication proceeds; provide day-care services in the office; run ticket sales and solicitations on the model of chain letters; run benefits.

Pass buckets, hats, helmets, and other appropriate receptacles at meetings and rallies after making a public announcement that now is the time to give. In crowds with sticky fingers have one person watch each bucket as it is passed down rows. Two-thirds of the way into the program, before the climax, and before people begin to get bored and leave, is a good time to make the appeal. A brief halt in the program just for this purpose will minimize the disturbance.

A FINAL NOTE. Always attempt to involve contributors in the organization, thereby strengthening the project with manpower while making money. A donator should be nudged along the road of direct action until he becomes a doer.

II. Self-Education

1. Introduction

Political self-education is a crucial process for anyone interested in doing political organizing. If you don't know your own politics, how they have developed, and how to change your own attitudes or react to them, you may find it difficult to understand others and effect change. Basically, you can divide the question of political self-education into three parts: (1) how to increase your political consciousness; (2) how to make an analysis of your opposition and your society; (3) how to develop the political consciousness of the group you are organizing.

Many people consciously avoid analyzing themselves and relating themselves to their politics, because of internal contradictions between what they think and feel. An introspective analysis of yourself starts with the question "Who am I?" What are my attitudes, opinions, prejudices, and beliefs, how and where did I get them? Your socioeconomic position may be a good base to explore. For example, try to consider yourself in terms of your class: your economic freedom or lack of it; your job or type of school; the social standing of your family in the community. What does an analysis of ethnic background reveal in this context? Consider your family. Did they tell you not to associate with certain types, groups, races of people? Why? Apart from your general background, what events and unique experiences gave you some notions contradictory to basic class ideas you may have been indoctrinated and socialized to accept?

In conjunction with your political introspection, a quiet talk with yourself at the end of each day, reviewing successes, failures, attitudes, and relationships is a constructive activity.

Combining personal education with group criticism and self-criticism is important to self-education.

The second and most important portion of this process is to link one's own individual history and personal views with more general political views and current political struggles. Find a general topic which will lead to a deeper understanding of the issues, background, history, and theory of a problem around which you are going to organize in your own constituency, or which you have discovered in community organizing.

Now, you may want to deal with the third stage of political self-education, namely attempting to apply and organize beyond your own individual knowledge. With a small or large group you may run a teach-in, workshop, study group, or activist research group. The section on "Power Structure Research" and the Bibliography–Directory will provide you with specific leads.

2. Teach-Ins

A good teach-in takes about a month to organize, not so much in actual work time but to set up *where, when,* and *who.* Hold the teach-in in a large hall with adjacent rooms for question-and-answer sessions, and facilities for public-address systems. Push to get the hall for free on the grounds that it is an educational event.

Timing is essential for a successful teach-in. Schedule your event when there is the least competition with other events. Seven to seven thirty in the evening is a good time to begin, as you will not conflict with classes, work, etc., and this early start gives you a better chance of fitting all the speakers in. During the teach-in itself, find out who can stay for how long so you can set up your program appropriately. Arrange for small rooms where people can go and ask questions and discuss what has just been run down. Thus you can avoid having questions tie up your next speaker and at the same time give people who are interested a better chance to further develop their ideas.

Plan as far ahead as possible, especially when recruiting heavies to speak. You should remember that heavies are often difficult to get because they have many requests to speak. Some will no doubt ask a fee, at least for traveling expenses. Even if they can't appear, ask if they can recommend people they think should speak. Of course, the better known your speakers, the larger your turnout.

Tap your local resources as well, and don't be afraid to have one or two people who have never spoken before. Just give them plenty of time to prepare. Those people may then become core speakers for later teach-ins.

You or a member of the organizing group should talk personally with each person who is going to speak. Discuss his particular topic, who else will be speaking on what, and the order of the program, in order to avoid repetition of topics.

During the teach-in, pass the hat to help raise money to offset your expenses. Remember your expenses may include police, insurance for the hall, janitorial expenses, speaker expenses, and travel expenses. Provide also for literature tables to be set up by your group. Allow other groups tables, too, so they are not offended. If you plan a long teach-in, break for entertainment and refreshments if possible. And don't forget to invite the press.

In some cases, you will need principled arguments against opposition or right-wing groups that want to set up in the middle of your teach-in or demand speakers. There are a number of different ways to deal with this. You might put out early notices stating the topics of the teach-in and making clear that it will be from a left-wing point of view. If this jeopardizes your teach-in you can invite some opposition yourself. If they refuse, let people know what reasons they gave so there will be no cries of repression. Sometimes your opposition will wait until the night of the teach-in to create a hassle, often under the banner of the First Amendment. Have a copy of the amendment on hand and read it to everyone. It says, in essence, that Congress shall pass no law prohibiting your right to free speech and assembly. So, if your opponents are advocating that such a motion be passed, they are the ones being unconstitutional, not you. You should point out that no one is stopping them from setting up their own teach-in, nor is there a law saying you should work for your opponents. Of course, don't forget to point out they were aware of this situation and could have done something earlier. If you decide either beforehand or in the process to let them speak, give them early slots in the speaking schedule. Then you can sometimes prevent them from hanging around and disrupting the evening. A good strategy is to follow up one of their speakers with one of your heavies (whom you have fore-warned).

3. Workshops and Study Groups

Workshops are short-term small-group discussions centered around immediate problems and needs. An atmosphere where people feel free to express their ideas candidly and honestly is essential to the success of a workshop. Maximum participation of all people involved will generate new ideas and provide greater understanding of a problem.

Make sure the subject is sufficiently limited to be covered in the time available. Define the topic clearly and state all questions in terms of the problem or need.

Get the basic materials together first. Collect historical and background information. Use primary sources if possible. Have material duplicated and distributed to participants before the workshop begins. If necessary, allow time beforehand for members to read the background material. Getting the information together will help prevent pointless arguments over ascertainable facts.

Have someone in the group take notes on the discussion. If no one objects, use a tape recorder. The best ideas are worthless if they are forgotten immediately after being born.

Play down status distinctions between participants and organizers and try to get everyone involved. Encourage the participants to bring up personal experiences that relate to the problem. Any experts in the group should be urged to contribute their special knowledge. However, they should not be allowed to dominate the discussion. If people feel they have something to gain from helping each other and being helped, they will be more at ease.

Encourage the group to look at the problem objectively and analytically. Redefine and clarify as you go along, relating the problem to larger issues.

After the interest and energy level have reached a low point, review the discussion utilizing notes and individual impressions. Emphasize learning for use. How can the information and ideas from the workshop be put to work for change?

PRACTICAL USES FOR WORKSHOPS

I. *Preparation for actions*

A. PERSONNEL PREPARATION—People who are planning to take part in or lead any sort of direct action should prepare themselves with a number of serious training sessions, preferably led by individuals with experience in confrontation politics. Workshops should fulfill the following functions:

1. *To practice skills.* Prepare the people for action so that mistakes are less likely to occur when actual activity begins.

2. *To understand your opponent.* Empathy with the enemy can be accomplished by determining the factors that will affect him during your action. Such knowledge will better enable you to predict his response to your action.

3. *To build morale.* Workshops will increase the confidence which fellow workers have in one another, confidence which is more valuable in times of stress.

4. *To overcome tensions.* The workshops enable the workers to release tensions constructively which might otherwise have a harmful effect.

5. *To make the working of the group more democratic.* The workshops lead to a fuller comprehension of the activities by a larger number of people. As a result more people can take part in the decision-making process.

B. TACTICAL DECISIONS—Workshops can facilitate tactical decisions for a larger group. They can be used in one or both of the following ways.

1. A workshop with the task of making a tactical decision can break off from a larger group. This subgroup can pursue the problem at hand more quickly and thoroughly than a committee of the whole. Its decision should be presented to the larger body and put to a vote.

2. If its decision is opposed by a substantial minority in the parent group, then everyone concerned should enter into workshops. These should serve to clarify the problems and help achieve some consensus as to what should be done.

II. *Education and consciousness raising*

Workshops are most effective as educational devices if organized immediately after a political happening of major importance. The event should be related to the lives of workshop participants and placed within the framework of a meaningful political analysis. Workshops have been well received after events such as:

1. *The assassination of Martin Luther King, Jr.* His death triggered an emotional response among many whites that made them see for the first time the full ramifications of their personal racism and that of white-dominated Amerika. Workshops aided this process by providing a forum for collective introspection.

2. *Kent State, Jackson State, and Cambodia.* This rapid progression of government-instigated violence opened up many minds to education about the true nature of the American system. In many cases the radicalization process proceeded with equal speed. As a result, many of the workshops did not talk politics, but debated tactics and formed affinity groups in order to learn their politics in the streets.

3. *Ghetto rebellions.* These events have been followed in some areas by white radical workshops that not only discussed the political meaning of black rebellion, but came up with concrete ways in which they could lend support to the struggle.

4. *Campus uprisings and women's liberation.* Discussion groups called by women in the heat of recent campus events have revealed to movement people the male chauvinism to be found on the left. Unfortunately, this is a contradiction that is too well socialized in many of us to be rectified by one or two workshops.

III. *How-to sessions*

Afternoon or weekend workshops are excellent ways to disseminate practical information. Gatherings have been held to advance such specialties and interests as:

1. *Buying clubs and food conspiracies.* How to undermine the businessmen now collecting profits for providing basic human needs.

2. *Radical architecture.* How to design buildings with a workable combination of functionality and aesthetic pleasure.

3. *Communal living.* How and why it's done; exchange of experiences about successes and failures.

4. *New art forms.* Art as a political medium and a daily experience.

5. *Community organizing.*

6. *Alternate media*. Filmies, radio freaks, and underground newspaper people have recently gathered to the mutual pleasure and enlightenment of all.

POLITICAL STUDY GROUPS

While a workshop is necessarily limited by its short duration, a study group can pursue a subject in the depth necessary to develop a general political analysis. It is a learning experience which demands the participation of all members and often develops new verbal abilities and self-confidence. Once study-group members gain a functional theoretical knowledge they can unite around common interests, evolving into a collective to carry out concrete political action.

The first step in forming a study group is matching the right people with a politically relevant subject. People with some common interest or oppression should be recruited. You may prefer to work with friends and acquaintances or organize people at work or school.

Arrange an informal first meeting at which you attempt to decide on a topic around which to base discussions. It should directly relate to the self-interest of all involved, but be conducive to the introduction of an overall political analysis. The women's liberation movement has grown through women's study groups. Other groups can organize around problems such as racism, pollution, Vietnam, and pertinent local issues.

If your people prefer a structured learning experience you should write up a general outline of what you plan to discuss and perhaps come up with a reading list. Try to meet at least once a week at a regular place and time.

The effective study-group organizer does not lead or push the group, but acts as a catalyst to set off the collective learning reaction. Bring people out of themselves and encourage them to articulate what's bothering them. Start at the level of everyday experience. Oppressive personal experiences will provide the major spark to set off the learning and politicization process.

After people discover that they share similar oppressions, an attempt should be made to relate their grievances to a common source. This is probably the most difficult step in the politicizing process. Many people are unwilling to see themselves as victims, unable to control much of their life. An organizer should gear the method of introducing a radical political analysis to the subject being discussed and the speed at which the group is advancing.

Once a study group has pinpointed the source of a problem (e.g., male chauvinism, racism, U.S. imperialism) it can be expanded into an overall analysis to help people better understand why things work as they do. Now that people can see the interrelationships of certain social and political forces, individual frustrations will not as readily lead to self-hatred. Revealed is the inevitability of certain injustices under the contemporary American power structure.

If the study group has been radicalized enough to desire to move politically on concrete issues, it should do so collectively. The energy released within the group should be organized and outwardly directed in order to set other people in motion.

4. Power Structure Research

Real economic and political power in America is centered in the giant corporations. To find out who controls your university or town, these sources should provide a mine of information:

Poor's Register of Corporations, Directors and Executives, in the reference section of most college and city libraries, lists the managers and directors by corporation and also alphabetically. The *Dun and Bradstreet Million-Dollar Directory* also lists corporate executives and directors, and *Who's Who in Commerce and Industry* provides biographical data (education, club membership, home addresses, etc.) of the executives of most big companies.

If you want to learn about a particular corporation or bank or local government, the *Moody's* manuals, published yearly, provide the best readily available source. *Moody's Industrial Manual* gives company histories, lists subsidiary companies in America and abroad, gives fairly detailed financial data, and names executives and directors. There are also *Moody's* manuals for *Utilities* (gas, water, and electric companies), *Banking and Finance* (including insurance and investment companies), and *Municipal and Government* (covering state and local levels, including school boards).

If you want to know whether a company is owned by or owns other companies (which might be producing war material), the *Directory of Corporate Affiliations of Major Corporations* lists divisions, affiliates, and subsidiaries. The *Fortune Plant and Product Directory* lists the locations of all of the plants of major corporations, if you want to find out where to organize for a boycott or strike.

The indexes of the *Wall Street Journal* and the *New York Times* list articles about corporations and can be found in most big libraries. Other sources include business magazines such as *Fortune* (which lists every year the five hundred largest American corporations), *Barron's*, and *Forbes*. A letter to a corporation, hinting that you are thinking of buying stock, will bring a copy of the annual report, with detailed financial information.

The following sources contain valuable guides for power structure research:

Stock Ownership and the Control of Corporations (pamphlet), Don Villarejo, Radical Education Project, P.O. Box 625, Ann Arbor, Mich. 48108, 35¢.

NACLA Research Methodology Guide, North American Congress on Latin America (NACLA), P.O. Box 57, Cathedral Sta., New York, N.Y. 10025, $1.00. Provides an extensive bibliography in two sections: "Researching the Empire" (corporations, government agencies, universities) and "Campus Reconnaissance" (how to investigate campus military contracting).

Researching the Ruling Class

The basic source of researching people in the power structure is *Who's Who in America,* published every two years and available in most libraries. It contains biographies of thousands of leaders, telling you where they went to school, what clubs they belong to, corporate directorships, schools they are trustees of, home addresses, etc. There are also regional volumes of *Who's Who* for the East, Midwest, South and Southwest, and West, one for American women, and an international volume. The East Germans slyly put one out (in German) called *Who's Who in the CIA.*

As noted above, *Poor's* and *Dun and Bradstreet* list the corporate directorships of the power structure. Since lawyers are so important in keeping the power structure in power, here are a few good sources for finding out about lawyers and judges: the *Martindale-Hubbell Law Directory*, which is five big volumes, lists all lawyers and members of law firms. *The Lawyer's Directory* has a useful list of the lawyers for most large corporations, and *The Bar Register* covers "preeminent lawyers" and tells what corporations they represent. The *Directory of American Judges* lists judges both geographically and alphabetically and contains brief biographies.

The vast labyrinth of the federal bureaucracy is neatly compressed in the *U.S. Government Organization Manual*, which covers all three branches and lists agencies and officials, and is published yearly. The *Congressional Directory* gives committee assignments, addresses of local offices, and biographies of all members of Congress, and the *Biographic Register* lists the names and addresses of people in the Department of State and the Foreign Service.

A good guide to the national power structure is the pamphlet *Researching the Governing Class of America*, William Domhoff, New England Free Press, 791 Tremont St., Boston, Mass. 02118, 10¢. Domhoff has also written two books on this subject, *Who Rules America?* (Prentice-Hall, 1967, paperback) and *The Higher Circles* (Random House, 1970, hardback).

The University and the Power Structure

There are more than two thousand colleges and universities in the United States, controlled by approximately fifty thousand trustees. Unfortunately there is no list of these trustees readily available, but college catalogs usually list them, and their corporate connections (the vast majority are business executives or directors) can be researched in *Who's Who* and *Poor's*.

The financial office in most universities will have a treasurer's report available for inspection, and the university portfolio, listing stock, bond, and real-estate holdings, can also be found in the financial office, although it may take some prodding to secure.

Almost all universities and many small colleges do research for the military-industrial complex, and excellent sources to consult include: *The University Military Complex*, NACLA, $1.00; and *Counter-Insurgency Research on Campus Exposed* (pamphlet), Student Committee to End the War in Vietnam,

1029 Vermont Ave., NW, Suite 907, Washington, D.C. 20005, 15¢.

An excellent example of university power structure research is *How Harvard Rules*, New England Free Press, $1.00, which links Harvard's rulers to war, colonialism, and racism. As universities expand, they usually displace working-class people from their neighborhoods; a study of this process is *Cambridge: The Transformation of a Working Class Community—Harvard and M.I.T. Create an Imperial City*, New England Free Press, 15¢.

Research on universities can focus on such questions as these: Who are the trustees? Are they executives or directors of companies which exploit black people, women, and other groups; have investments in countries such as South Africa; produce war material, etc.? Does the university own stock in such companies or hold any Defense Department contracts? What buildings and land does the university own? Is it planning expansion that would displace people from their homes?

Researching the Military-Industrial Complex

Thousands of corporations are involved in the military-industrial complex, many of them as subcontractors or suppliers of parts, and it is difficult to research this area as each war dollar travels farther and farther. The following sources have much valuable information: *100 Companies and Their Subsidiaries Listed According to Net Value of Prime Military Contracts* and *500 Contractors Listed According to Net Value of Military Prime Contract Awards for Research, Development, Test and Evaluation Work*, both Office of Assistant Secretary of Defense for Public Affairs, The Pentagon, Washington, D.C. 20301. *Department of Defense Prime Contract Awards by State* is available from the Office of the Secretary of Defense, Directorate for Statistical Service OASC(C), The Pentagon, and the *Government Contracts Directory*, published by Government Data Publications, is available in most major libraries. The *Wall Street Journal* indexes major defense contracts—how much and what for.

Two groups which have done much research on the ties of major corporations to the military machine and can provide useful research guides are National Action/Research on the Military-Industrial Complex (NARMIC), 160 N. 15th St., Philadelphia, Pa. 19102, (215) LO3–9372; and New University Conference, 622 W. Diversey Pkwy., No. 403A, Chicago, Ill. 60614. An indispensable pamphlet called *Weapons for Counterinsurgency* is available from NARMIC for $1.00, and contains information on chemical and biological warfare, as well as a list of colleges and universities doing CBW research. A good book on the entire field is *The Military-Industrial Complex,* Sidney Lens, United Church Press, 1970, paperback.

Researching the Power Structure in Your Community

The tools for doing local power structure research are not difficult to obtain. *The Care and Feeding of Power Structures* (pamphlet), Jack Minnis, New England Free Press, 10¢, gives many valuable suggestions.

A list of local businesses can be obtained from the local chamber of commerce or library. Executives and directors will be listed in *Poor's Register,* and if not locally controlled, the home office will be found in *Moody's Industrial Manual.* Banks are central to the power structure, and after being located in the yellow pages their financial data and officers and directors can be found in *Moody's Banking and Finance Manual. The Lawyer's Directory* will not only provide a list of local lawyers but also the corporate clients of many of them. Property ownership is central to the power structure: the local tax office will list the owners by street address, although this information is often grudgingly given. Information on planned urban renewal (usually "Negro removal") projects can be secured from the city planning department, and ownership of land and buildings in these areas should be carefully checked.

III. Mass Education and Communication

1. Introduction: Reaching People

Self-education and mass education are two aspects of a single, interacting process. The task of the leaflet writer and canvasser is not to deliver "the correct line" to the people, but to respond to their problems and to help organize the fight for immediate demands in such a way as to transform it into a struggle for a new social order.

The easiest and probably most effective communication is therefore with one's own age, class, and occupational group. Even here, it helps to know how to argue so as to open minds to new ideas rather than close them around old prejudices. How much more essential, then, to know the basic principles of persuasion when, for example, middle-class students address themselves to members of oppressed minorities, industrial workers, and older people generally.

It is not only a question of countering the mass media's daily barrage of propaganda and misinformation, but of helping people to draw from their own experience of oppression the conclusions that will lead to action for change. If this were primarily a matter of glossy P.R. or selling techniques, it would be hopeless. The movement can learn something from the media, but a mimeographed leaflet can't compete with national TV.

The strength of our communication rests in its truth. We, and not the exploiters, warmakers, and pigs, speak to the real situation: to the frustrations and sufferings of the people, to their determination and hope to win a better life.

Fundamental change will not come until masses of people are in motion, demanding it. And people are impelled to move, not by theory or abstract visions, but by recognizing

38

that their immediate conditions have become intolerable and by determining to correct them. Through such struggles—for jobs or community-controlled schools or the release of a political prisoner or the withdrawal from a war—and through drawing the lessons of such struggles, they learn that the ruling system will not and cannot meet, in any basic or permanent way, even their most elementary needs.

It is the central work of the movement to achieve this consciousness and to communicate it to the people at all levels of the struggle. This means addressing ourselves first to immediate, concrete problems; acting and drawing others into action; evaluating victories and defeats in terms of the ultimate perspective, so that we may build a permanent movement that learns from its own mistakes and creatively brings forth new forms of struggle. This must be the aim and content of our communication with ourselves and all people. To further this we can learn some persuasive techniques that will help transform communication into organization and action.

Before you call a public meeting, canvass, write a leaflet, or plan a mass campaign, let the group ask itself questions like these:

Whom are we addressing? (Be precise: not "the workers," "the community," but the workers of what trade and shop, the people of what ethnic, religious, and economic group, in what neighborhood?) What do they know about the issue at hand and how do they feel about it? Are they directly or only indirectly affected? Are they already in motion on the issue or are we trying to make them aware of it? Are we addressing a united group or are there differences and conflicts within it? What traditional attitudes or prejudices are involved? In what terms do the people talk about the issue?

If you don't have answers to all these questions, seek them in the course of the action. Listen more than you talk; be open and alert—and patient. People do not change their minds or adopt new ideas simply because they are *told* to do so. The individual must work things out for himself, in the terms of his partly unique, partly common life experience.

Therefore, begin *where the people are*, with local manifestations of the larger issues: e.g., with the layoff in a particular shop, not the whole economic recession. You are more authentic if you can call the boss or landlord by name and if you know about the local Vietnam casualties than if you lean on phrases like "capitalist exploiters," "oppression," "American imperialism."

People are not mere representatives of a class or race. To treat them as such smacks of manipulation, no matter how essential to their own deepest needs your message is. Respect their interests, beliefs, loyalties. An argument that shows how the Vietnam war harms the U.S. is more persuasive to the patriot than spitting on the flag.

Many workers yearn for consumer gadgets that you may scorn. If they join an anti-inflation demonstration because they can't meet the payments on their color TV, don't romanticize about starvation. You had better be clear which is more important to you—your own anticonsumerist life-style, or the organization of people who may still be reaching for capitalism's goodies.

Don't come on heavy with politics to a man whose mind is on baseball scores. Talk baseball scores and wait for an opening—or save your message for next time, when you are no longer a stranger. Remember that you, too, are a human being and not a mere political phonograph. The easiest, most natural contact with people in speech or writing is politically the most effective, though not always the speediest or most direct.

This suggests an approach to the sticky question of haircuts and clothing styles. Stereotypes being what they are, visible evidences of the new life-style may initially turn off workers and community people who have been brainwashed into feeling menaced by them. If your contact is of the quick, one-shot sort, your appearance may close some minds to your message altogether. But *what* you say and *how* you act will cancel initial doubts if you work consistently and modestly, helping people in their day-to-day struggles.

When you have moved beyond the first-contact stage, you will engage increasingly in argumentation and persuasion. Few people see themselves as abstractly "oppressed" although they are acutely aware of the daily struggle to eat, make a happy home, educate their kids, keep their draft-age boys alive, hold onto some hope for the future—in short, to live like human beings. Starting with the *particular* way each one experiences his oppression, you will deal mostly with countering the lies and evasions which are the stock-in-trade of the schools and the media, attempting to show how the individual's problems are neither isolated nor necessary nor hopeless, if the many join to fight the class system that is their source.

You will get into arguments. The people you meet are not stupid; they have ideas of their own and they will tell you. Let them. Your task is not to "win" an argument, but to provide a sort of catalyst for the development of political awareness—your own and another's. You can't really change another person's mind. You can only provide the occasion, the questions, perhaps some facts, that may help him to change his own. While you should never flatter with false agreement, you will seldom succeed with contradiction. It is not necessary to debate every small point of difference. Try to identify and seize on a point of partial agreement and develop its ramifications. Many people blame their troubles on "corrupt politicians." You can start here with agreement, then go on to the real sources of corruption in society, the ineradicable corruption of the system itself.

To be persuasive, in speech or writing, you must know your audience's attitude toward you and your subject, then adjust your appeal accordingly. Here are some rule-of-thumb approaches:

For the ignorant or the indifferent: The most direct, concrete demonstration by *immediate experience* is best: "Why this is important to you," etc. Facts, events, and straightforward, reasoned arguments go further than emotive appeals.

For the hostile: If possible, let them give their views first. In writing, present the opposing view first, respectfully and fairly. Agree with anything you can. Then answer with facts and logic (*not* invective), point by point, giving a chance for rebuttal where possible. With the person too hostile to listen, your best tactic is simply to preserve your manners and your cool. The way you act may neutralize hostility more than an argument can.

For the doubtful, uncommitted, or partly opposed: Again, listen to their position first. Concentrate on points of agreement and try to develop them, with facts and reason, so as to answer or question the points of disagreement. Assume a common ground, be friendly, don't try to high-pressure people.

For those already convinced and on your side: The point of your persuasion may be to transform belief into action or commitment. Here, in addition to reinforcing the facts, you can use emotive appeals to develop a sense of urgency and solidarity.

Good persuasion and communication add up to common sense and uncommon sensitivity. Know your audience. Know what you are talking about. Use a language the people understand. Respect your audience and yourself as human beings. Concern yourself with the individual and his particular life as the first evidence of your concern for all men and all lives.

2. Publications

a. Leaflets

The leaflet is ordinarily a one-page, one-issue, one-action affair. It can range from the simple "hand poster" advertising a demonstration to the "educational" discussion of an issue, with or without proposals for immediate action. The leaflet planned for street distribution should be laid out and written so that its central idea can be quickly grasped. Even the longer, educational leaflet should be broken up and headed so that its general message is apparent at a glance.

Production. Use, as a rule, letter-size (8½ x 11) paper and double-space. If you single-space, make short paragraphs and double-space between them. Whatever printing method you use, be sure your leaflet is clean and clear. A smudgy, semilegible leaflet implies a subtle lack of respect for your reader and for your own message. Print headlines and outstanding information by hand and leave plenty of white space—the more the better.

Getting your message across. Size of type alone does not create emphasis. The most important parts of your communication should come at the end and the beginning. Be sure that the time and place of any action is clearly stated, even repeated. *Sign* all leaflets with the name and address of the group. People like to know who is talking to them.

Try to head your leaflet with a slogan or phrase that refers directly to the issue or action involved. Use the language of the people you want to reach. Avoid vague phrases like "Fight Unemployment!" The same goes for the body of the leaflet. Use down-to-earth, interest-catching subheads for each paragraph or begin each with a clear, strong topic sentence. Try to stick to *one issue per leaflet* and to develop it concretely, factually, and as simply as possible. Take a single grievance like a price increase and explain, step by step, its connection with the war. Don't try to link up *every* relevant issue at once. Simply to *mention* grievances does not establish their connection with the class struggle as a whole. Avoid grab-bag terms like "imperialism," "ruling class," and "repression," unless you are prepared to nail them down with flesh-and-blood examples.

Timing. Short, frequent leaflets are usually more effective than long, infrequent ones. Try to discuss your first leaflet with the people you gave it to, then respond to their questions or objections in a second. Plan a *series* of leaflets in the same neighborhood, factory, or school, starting with gut issues and developing their broader political ramifications, one at a time. A series of leaflets relating local events and issues to national and international ones can later evolve into a regular newsletter, covering a variety of questions each week.

b. Newsletters

The newsletter can play a role in organizing the group itself, or the wider community, or both at once. At its most primitive it is a single sheet, differing from the leaflet in that it appears periodically and carries a variety of materials, announcements, etc. At its most elaborate it approaches the newspaper, with reports of events and editorial comment, but is usually addressed to a more limited audience.

Whether your newsletter consists of one or many pages, mimeographed or printed, *regularity* of publication is important to build its influence. During a crisis it may appear daily; in a long-term organizing drive perhaps weekly or biweekly.

A newsletter should live up to its name, and this requires news gathering. One or two reporter-editors can get out a simple "house organ" for the group, but a newsletter addressed to a community or a large plant needs many news sources from among the people.

Don't make up for a lack of news by exhortations or long excursions into theory. Better keep it short. Concentrate on the political analysis of local events and issues, linking them with national and world struggles.

Check your news and beware of rumor and garbled facts. To write credibly for a community or a shop, you must know who is who and how things work. If you can't be sure, don't pretend to be an authority. Try to get signed articles from community people and workers themselves.

People are news—and a lot goes on in their lives that is not strictly "political." A well-established community or shop newsletter may include items like marriages, retirements, deaths, and vacation trips. You should, as a rule, get people's permission to use their names or to quote them.

Announcements and advertisements of local events are usually a free service in a newsletter. You can broaden your community base by extending this service to various organizations of the people.

Give your newsletter a name—preferably one that reflects the community. Design a permanent heading; date each issue; always include a masthead to show who is publishing it.

Observe the rules of clarity, cleanliness, and openness, whether you reproduce by mimeo or have it printed. You may use 8½ x 11 or 8½ x 14 paper for a mimeo newsletter and set up your copy in double columns. If you do, its appearance will be greatly improved if you "justify" it. (See "Mechanics.") Break up long columns with line drawings or subheads.

The newsletter may be hand-distributed outside shop gates, on the street, inside the factory, or through community centers, stores, etc. The most effective distribution is usually done by the workers or community people themselves. In any case, try to establish regular spots, as well as regular days and hours, so that your readers will begin to anticipate its appearance. The mailed newsletter is a valuable device for keeping in touch with your own members, as well as with community people, especially in cases where many of them do not attend meetings.

c. Newspapers

Whether your newspaper is addressed to the campus or to a wider community, its effectiveness depends on regularity of publication; access to news and accurate reporting; orientation on particular events and people; a familiar name and format; a lively, well-illustrated, open layout; and above all, a content that raises the level of the struggle by linking immediate with ultimate goals. Since the newspaper ordinarily seeks a larger, more varied audience than the newsletter, it needs a considerably more elaborate organization of office, staff, and funding, and a higher level of journalistic expertise. The people are used to the practices of the establishment press; you should adapt at least some of these to spreading your antiestablishment message.

Content and Style

1. Journalists usually construct the news story on an "inverted pyramid" pattern, the lead paragraph followed by details of descending importance. A reader can thus grasp the central facts at once and an editor can cut an article from the bottom without loss of its essentials.

2. The first paragraph should be short. It should state WHO did WHAT, WHERE, WHEN, HOW—and sometimes WHY. Be concise, but try to avoid a mechanical recital of statistics. Use concrete, graphic language and get the issues up front.

Example: "Mrs. Jane Doe and her six children narrowly escaped eviction into the snow from their home at 1234 Jay Street, Chelsea, on Tuesday, January 20. When Sheriff John Roe arrived with the city van at 9 A.M. he found the steps of the crumbling tenement blocked by Mrs. Doe's neighbors, members of the East End Tenants' Council."

3. Use lots of names and spell them correctly. Quote often and accurately. Check quotations with the people concerned. Let participants in an event see your draft story and suggest improvements. Wherever possible, have a participant write the story himself.

4. If you plan an attack or exposé, check your basic information with several people in a position to know the facts. If the situation is unclear or disputed, say so and print the differing versions of it. All opinions should be properly attributed. If an informant must remain anonymous, you can credit "a member of the Dean's Council" or "an individual placed high in the Pentagon," but try not to overuse this "reliable source" gimmick.

5. Erroneous or distorted facts, sensationalism, gross exaggeration, ad hominem attacks (i.e., attacks on persons rather than issues), and "radical" clichés fail to convince most people and can undermine your credibility. It is your business to expose and counteract such manipulative brainwashing by the commercial press, not to imitate it.

6. The successful newspaper—campus, aboveground, or underground—tends to develop a "personality" that reflects its writers and illustrators, on the one hand, and its readership

on the other. The more the two are fused through sensitive reporting, signed articles and other contributions, "letters to the editor," "letters to the people," and a calendar of community events, the more effective a political instrument your paper will be. Its style and tone can mark it as academic and elitist or as voice of the people, almost apart from its political content. This does not mean that you should "write down" to your audience. Rather, avoid the temptation of many good writers to be cynical or too clever, especially when dumping on the system or its lackeys. Well-aimed invective is a first-rate weapon *if* your reader agrees with its premises; it does not by itself persuade. Avoid "in-group" terms and references unless your paper is addressed only to an "in" readership. Economical, concrete, muscular English prose is best to open the minds of new readers and to break up elitist modes of communication in your own group or staff.

7. Answer attacks with facts and reason while vigorously exposing the lies and distortions of the mass media. Open your columns to your opponent and all who wish to debate with him. A running controversy is a means of education and self-education, and a prime circulation builder. Play fair: do not edit or cut your critic's copy. Prepare a strong, skillful reply and run it beside his attack. A "letters to the editor" column encourages your readers to get in on the act. Don't publish anonymous letters, though you may print a signed letter and withhold the author's name, when he so requests.

8. If you make an error, correct it promptly and apologize, but try not to make errors. You can avoid some hassles (though perhaps not a libel suit) if you use mostly signed articles and print in each issue the statement that the opinions of the authors are not necessarily those of the paper.

9. As you begin to involve contributing writers, you will meet the delicate problem of editing. If a community leader gives you a poorly written article, you must decide whether it can be used as is, or whether its printing may subject him or the paper to ridicule. Confer with the author if you propose major changes or cuts. Try to involve him in the editing process. You can always plead lack of space, but it is usually better to print even an inadequate contribution than to discourage participation. You should work toward having community organizations supply you with their press releases or

designate a reporter to keep in regular touch with your paper. Give extra copies to all contributors.

10. Feature articles and special issues provide means for handling background material, discussing theory, and raising broad political issues in your paper. Through them you can channel to the people the work of research projects or of the experts in your group. You can devote one issue to multiple articles on a single topic or carry a regular feature on each important subject area in every issue. Take care that your research features are not too heavily academic.

11. Apart from your own local news resources, you will need an interchange with the movement as a whole. Subscribe to important activist publications or exchange with them. (See Bibliography.) Reprint material when you have permission or where the copyright allows you to. Be sure to credit the paper and author. Once you can afford it, join Liberation News Service (160 Claremont Ave., New York, N.Y. 10027). Rates vary, but it costs about $15 per month. LNS supplies one or more weekly packets of ready-to-use photos, graphics, and news items collected from the movement as a whole. HIPS (530 Brainards St., Naperville, Ill. 60540) is a high-school press service. Inter-Tribal News (P.O. Box 26, Village Sta., New York, N.Y. 10014) serves underground and hip radio stations.

Staff, Office, Distribution, Funds

1. Staff organization depends largely on the number, ambition, resources, and wishes of the people involved, and the size and frequency of the paper. It takes many people to publish a regular paper. If a small, closed staff attempts all the writing and production, look for the early death of staff or newspaper or both.

2. The larger and more frequent the publication, the more need to specialize and departmentalize. If possible, the whole group should make the paper an extension of its activities, each individual becoming adept at all functions. Though publication requires a division of labor, a rotation of editors, typists, reporters, and street hawkers can train members in all parts of the process and avoid hierarchies. The masthead can carry the names of the editor and contributors responsible for each particular issue, rather than those of a permanent board.

3. If a greater degree of specialization becomes necessary, be sure to have regular meetings to work out group policies and areas of responsibility. There should be no invidious distinction between "editorial," "business," and "technical" staff in a paper dedicated to fighting bureaucracy and class distinctions. The group should meet not only to agree on the contents of the forthcoming issue, but should also hold post mortem sessions to evaluate the journalistic and political quality of the last issue, so that weaknesses ranging from politics to proofreading and distribution can be corrected.

4. Set deadlines for individual stories well in advance of the printing deadline. You will need time for editorial improvements, checking, etc. A close deadline and multiple phone calls help overcome a reporter's tendency to procrastination. Encourage the inexperienced or timid writer by discussing his story with him in advance, offering ideas for the lead, suggesting points of emphasis. Keep folders with filler articles and pictures, in the event a promised story fails to materialize on time.

5. The size and complexity of your office setup will depend on the size of your paper, but in any case it is best to have separately designated spaces for editing, typing, graphics, composing, business, etc. Have a clearly marked tray or box for the receipt of outside articles and notices. You may need multiple phone numbers or an intercom system in a large office. Phones should be manned every day and message taking well organized. Have a bulletin board near the phones.

6. You will need a set of files and a system of ready reference for important phone numbers, community organizations, movement addresses, other papers, etc. Keep a subject file and index of back issues, along with records of the date, number, and cost of each issue and a file of copies. Establish clipping files of articles from and about the underground press, or subscribe to and keep a collection of movement papers for reference.

7. Your method of distribution will depend on the scope and intended audience of your paper. If you can support publication by advertising, subsidy, or membership dues and distribute it free, so much the better. If you must sell it, price it as low as possible. Tell your street hawkers where to pick up bulk packages and send them to designated spots. Check on their sales or distribution: who has leftover copies

and who runs short. The hawker and the paper usually split the proceeds. If you distribute free, check to see that the papers are being taken and read. Ask local stores and organizations to carry a pile on the counter.

8. Solicit subscriptions, starting at just above production and mailing costs. Check your local post office for the rules for a second-class mailing permit. Offer special prices to students, the elderly, GIs, teachers, etc. Solicit sponsorship subscriptions from friends.

9. Check out Internal Revenue Service rules for nonprofit organizations, so as to save certain taxes on supplies, etc. Check with a lawyer on incorporating for mutual protection. Start a bank account where you can cash or deposit checks made out to the organization or the paper.

10. Ads, sales, and subscriptions are the basic means of supporting a paper which is not subsidized by a dues-paying organization. Of these, advertising is the best source of funds. Mail out to prospective advertisers a sheet giving information on circulation, your readers' interests, advertising rates, etc. Learn the competitive rates for similar papers in your area. Be selective: solicit advertising from local businesses that cater to the needs and interests of your readers. You may have to offer a merchant a free ad as a come-on.

11. Don't become so dependent on ads that it affects your style or crowds out your political content. Better ask people to pay for the paper, turn to them for financial support, run fund-raising campaigns, or attempt a less ambitious publication. Be sure to include in every issue your mailing address, phone, circulation figures, advertising rates, and a plea for funds, contributors, and volunteer workers.

Legal Hassles

Printers, because of community pressure or their personal political views, are often reluctant to print an underground. Try this approach: First make an appointment with a printer by phone. Go and see him with the copy. For the first few issues tone down the rhetoric so that he will accept the job. Try to talk to him and explain the material in his terms; the manner in which a printer is approached may be more important than what is actually being said in the paper. Upon refusal to print, you must (1) stop printing, (2) change printers, or (3) sue for breach of contract. (A phone call arranging a time to print the paper is a verbal contract and is legally binding.) But talk to a lawyer first so as not to say something which will void the contract.

The police may step in directly to quash your publication. Unpublished material may be seized (illegally) by police or the printer may turn it over to them. Street hawkers may find themselves arrested for trespass, loitering, disturbing the peace, failure to have a license, obscenity, etc. Have a lawyer available. The American Civil Liberties Union is sympathetic in cases involving freedom of speech and freedom of the press. A political reason for suppressing publication will not stand up in court. Because of the strong Supreme Court decisions, it is difficult to prove a paper obscene, since it must be found so in its entirety, and there is usually some "socially redeeming value" in undergrounds. If your printer is subject to harassment, find out who is behind it and fight back. Even if a suit sets you back for a while, precedents established in a legal hassle will help struggling undergrounds in other parts of the country.

d. Posters

Posters and signs serve two broad purposes in the movement: to announce or advertise actions, meetings, and other events; to keep certain slogans, pictures, quotations, or other political reminders constantly before the eyes of the people and of the group itself.

Design. The sign to advertise a demonstration, meeting, or benefit performance will be posted, presumably, in public places—streets, storefronts, transport stations, walls, etc., where many people pass. It should be designed to catch the eye and deliver its message at a glance.

Include only the *essential information:* a brief slogan indicating the purpose of the event; the event itself (including speakers, etc.); the place; the time; the sponsorship. (If the place is unfamiliar, directions may be added in small type.) Decide in advance what is most important and make it stand out by size of letters or change of colors or placement on page. In general, one or two colors are sufficient. Many bright colors tend to compete for attention. Any illustration should be relevant to the action, simple and eye-catching. Abstract designs should call attention to the words, not compete with them. *Leave lots of empty space around your copy—always.*

Production. The simplest and probably cheapest method of poster printing is by hand with magic markers or broad grease pastels. Once the design and copy is set, you can produce a large number quite fast by an assembly-line technique. Printing block letters is harder for untrained people than italics. A large, clear handwriting is usually more attractive than inexpert printing. Attractive small posters can be made by mimeograph, if you learn the technique of hand printing by stylus on a stencil.

When the copy is large and brief, or when you want to include a simple design (like an explosion flash, a flower, a star or circle, or the silhouette of a building), cut a stencil out of stiff paper with a razor blade or knife. Place the stencil over your poster board and spray with a can of quick-drying paint (available at art stores). When your design is dry, you can print over it, if you wish, with another color.

When you need a quantity of posters and a professional-looking job, silk screen is your best bet. Unless you are blessed with an activist art school nearby where you need only supply the paper, ink, and copy, it will pay you to make the modest outlay required for silk-screening and to have several members train themselves to do it. The complete process, including making the screen itself, can be learned from such paperback manuals as: Biegeleisen and Cohn's *Silk Screen Technique* (Dover); Biegeleisen's *Complete Book of Silk Screen Printing* (Dover); Serle and Clayson's *Silk Screen Printing on Fabric* (Watson)—if you want to expand your artistry to T-shirts, banners, etc.

If you plan to plaster your entire city with posters, get them printed. Block out your copy and choose your lettering from among the printer's fonts and sizes. Be sure to read proof before the run is made. There's nothing like a "typo" in 48-point type on five thousand posters!

Distribution. There are good poster spots and bad, for visibility and for your relations with the public. There are no prescriptions for these save observation, experimentation, and consideration. Make a list of the centers most frequented by the people you want to reach, and the best spots in those centers.

Whether you observe "post no bills" warnings will depend on whom you are trying to reach and what your relationships with the community are. Indiscriminate sign posting can create hostility as well as support, so evaluate the local situation. Ask a storekeeper's permission to use his window and avoid covering up his own display. Don't deface nature or hammer nails into trees. Remove obsolete posters to make way for your new ones.

White glue is expensive but virtually unassailable once it is set. Flour and condensed milk make cheaper tough adhesive. Small signs and stickers can be ordered with the adhesive already on. Scotch tape is expensive, dries out fast, won't hold on rough surfaces. A stapling gun is good for affixing heavy cardboard to wood.

If you plan to paint on walls, a cardboard stencil and a spray can will add dash to a well-phrased slogan—but think twice about using hard-to-remove paints or adhesives for signs which will soon be out of date. Oil-based paints soak into stone or cement and have to be sanded off. Scotch tape will mar interior paint.

e. Mechanics

Every activist should know how to reproduce a leaflet or newsletter by the cheapest, simplest, most available means like ditto and mimeograph. Do not let one or two become slaves to the machine: let the experts train others and pass the job around so that in a crisis any member can step into the breech.

The "ditto" type of reproduction (blue purple) is perhaps the easiest and involves the cheapest machine and supplies (stencil masters, fluid, and paper). A new hand-operated machine will cost $75 and up; electric models run from $400 to $575. Material can be typed or drawn on the stencil master with ball-point pen. Errors can be corrected by scraping the ink off the back of the stencil master with a razor blade, inserting a fresh scrap of the inked backing, and typing over the error. For under one hundred copies, ditto reproduction is adequate, if not elegant. The stencil wears out and becomes too faint to read if you go much beyond a hundred.

The mimeograph machine, which is available in several models and makes at prices running from about $100 to $900 new, has a far greater range than the ditto and, properly handled, can produce clear copies up to one thousand or over on a good stencil. Imported machines are somewhat cheaper than domestic, but if you buy one be sure that you have a steady source for repairs and supplies nearby; many imported machines take a special stencil. If your group cannot afford a new machine, check out the secondhand office-supply houses for both mimeo and ditto machines—but have a mechanic look over anything you plan to buy. Prices should be about half to two-thirds. For large editions, an electric machine is worthwhile, but many an organizing drive has been ground out by willing arms on an old hand-turned machine. If you can't afford any machine at all, ask a sympathetic church, school, or community organization for the use of theirs—and leave it clean and in order when you finish! The approximate cost of operating a mimeo is 20¢ per stencil and $2.50 per ream of paper. Some hints for mimeographing:

1. Cut a mimeo stencil according to the manufacturer's directions, with the typewriter ribbon lowered. Proofread as you go and have correction fluid handy for your errors. Be sure to keep within the limit lines on the stencil.

2. A small collection of styluses, a straightedge, and a plastic stencil of letters and numbers—all available reasonably in office-supply stores—are useful to make line drawings and headlines on the stencil. If you do much stylus work you will need a "light table." Either purchase one or cobble up a homemade model out of a box lined with foil, punched with ventilation holes, and covered with a piece of glass, preferably frosted. Place a 25- to 40-watt bulb inside the box and your stencil on the glass so that the light shines through and lets you see what you're doing.

3. Many newsletters are set up in double columns and are reproduced by mimeograph. Appearance and readability are enhanced by "justifying" the copy so that both margins of the columns are straight, like type. Set your typewriter for thirty-three letters and type up your column on a piece of paper. At the end of each line type an x for each space left unfilled up to thirty-three. Then retype your copy on the stencil, transforming the x's into an equal number of extra spaces distributed between words. A ruled line drawn down the center between columns gives a further professional touch. A proportional space typewriter will "justify" copy without all this bother, of course.

Offset printing is the fastest, most economical method of reproducing large numbers of copies. Find, if possible, a printer who works for the movement; he is apt to be cheaper. Where the movement is strong it can practically keep a printer going.

The offset process involves photographing your copy and projecting the negative onto a lithographic plate for printing. It will therefore look in print very much as it does when it leaves your hand, except that it may be photographically reduced or enlarged. For a leaflet or release, you can simply give the printer copy typed exactly as you wish it to appear. For a more elaborate newsletter, you will need to prepare a layout. Ask the printer for complete instructions.

A *letterpress* shop will set your copy in type, either to be printed in quantity, or to produce proofs which will be pasted down on an offset layout. Line drawings can also be reproduced by letterpress. Remember that typesetting is the most expensive element in any printing operation and that, once the copy is in type, you will be charged extra for any changes that are not printer's errors.

Copy to be set should be clean and correct, typed triple-space, about forty characters per line. The staff should be prepared to read proof before final printing and several should be trained in using the conventional proofreader's correction symbols (see the appendix of Webster's Collegiate Dictionary).

If your group wishes to set up its own printshop, get the advice of a movement pressman or write to: Omega Posters, 711 S. Dearborn St., Rm. 543, Chicago, Ill. 60605. Phone (312) 939–7672.

3. Canvassing

Canvassing, or the organization of systematic one-to-one discussion with people in and around their homes or jobs, is perhaps the most certain way to get to the grass roots, though by no means the easiest or quickest. The fact that it is a long-established method of the old-line parties, census and polltakers, Fuller Brush men, and Jehovah's Witnesses has its advantages and disadvantages. On the one hand, people are accustomed to canvassers; on the other, they may not believe that you simply want to talk issues with them and are not "selling something." In fact, a petition or referendum, a leaflet announcing a meeting, a survey of opinion, a newspaper to give away is usually needed to break the ice and give a point to your visit, even when your main aim is the discussion itself.

Preparation for Canvassing

Perhaps the less the better. Most neophytes are a bit up-tight about knocking on strange doors. "Role Playing" and "Antagonism" sessions are not likely to give them confidence —rather, the reverse. You can practice how to handle thirty types of responses and meet a thirty-first, the first door you knock on. Common sense, courtesy, and commitment to what you are doing are the main requisites.

The inexperienced should go out with the experienced, in teams of two, preferably a woman and a man. If none are experienced, then let the inexperienced plunge ahead together. Making a few mistakes is not fatal. Talk them over afterward and try not to repeat them. Don't expect to ac-complish miracles on one visit. You would not change your politics as a result of a few minutes' conversation with a stranger, so why expect others to? You will mainly hear from people the opinions they hold *now*. In a single visit you may only be able to raise certain questions in their minds.

Know what you are talking about—not just how you feel about it. Fact sheets and other readings, plus workshops and discussions, should prepare canvassers to handle a subject like the Vietnam war *in detail*. This means knowing the government's arguments and how to answer them; knowing *facts* about the war economy and its effect on prices, wages, taxes, employment, education, and social services, i.e., the points where it hits the people. If you are canvassing workers you will need facts and figures on their particular company's part in the complex. The point is not, of course, to spout academic information at everyone you meet. But if you want to answer a forty-year-old Korean vet, who has just lost his job, but who still believes in the domino theory, you'll need better ammunition than some ringing phrases.

Precanvassing sessions, in addition to beefing up general political education, should prepare your group on the compo-sition of the community or plant, the traditional attitudes of the class or ethnic group involved, the local politics and community or trade-union organizations, the current issues and problems that are stirring the people. Get a friendly resident or worker to take part in these sessions, if possible. If you must go "cold," try hanging around stores, bars, and lunch counters a bit to get the feel of the situation. If you have lists of names (voters, etc.), you can probably tell if the neighborhood is predominantly Irish, Polish, Italian, etc. Be aware of probable religious affiliations.

The principal foreign language you may need, both east and west, is Spanish. Use the Spanish speakers in your group for Puerto Rican and Chicano neighborhoods. If no one knows Spanish, get a phrase book and learn a few of the greetings and courtesies. It is a mark of respect that helps to establish rapport, even if you must converse in your own language rather than your host's.

Collect whatever material you need—leaflets, petitions, etc.—in a neat folder or envelope. If you plan to work from a list or cards, it is well to have them readily available, with a pencil for notations, in your pocket. Organize the names in advance by addresses and, where possible, by apartment numbers.

Your appearance matters, but not as much as what you have to say and how you say it. Straight clothing and short hair still go better in most places, but if you can't be yourself except as you are, stay that way. Cleanliness and a comb help a lot.

If your area of operations is distant from your base, ride to it and save your energy for canvassing. Wear comfortable shoes. If your work is inside a large apartment house or project, don't dress too warmly; you will probably not have a chance to take off your coat.

Knocking on Doors

Given a hot issue and a good approach, effective house-to-house canvassing still depends on finding the person you want to see and getting him to open his door. Canvassing everybody in a house is simpler than locating contacts or registered voters, etc., since it eliminates fiddling around with lists, names, and apartment numbers. In either case, here are a few hard-won principles on which to proceed:

A. At *projects* and *large apartment houses:* If the outside door is locked get a kid (or adult, if possible) to let you in. If there are doorbells, get a name on your list (if any) to buzz you in, then visit him first. Or punch any bell and hope for the best. In face of a doorman, *one* name and apartment number is almost essential (invented ones have been known to work).

If you are working from a list of names, you can usually match them with apartment numbers on doorbells or mailboxes. If not, ask anyone you see—in fact, start your canvass with him or her.

Ride in the elevator or walk up to the top floor and work down. (You'll be tireder later.)

B. *Single houses* are easier if you have a list, harder if you don't. Ask kids and neighbors and get names. Keep off the grass and go to the front door.

C. *Knock or ring and wait a decent interval* before repeating. Don't pound on the door like a posse of pigs. If you stumble into a high-decibel family fight, tiptoe quickly away.

D. Many people, perhaps most, won't open the door until you've *identified yourself*. When someone calls "Who is it?" the woman canvasser should answer. Address the householder by his name, if you know it, and give your own. If you use a friendly, confident tone he may think he knows you. If he asks your business, state it generally, emphasizing words likely to catch his interest. Many people will open the door to sheer double-talk, out of curiosity, if your voice sounds friendly. Don't try to discuss anything through a closed door—it's a waste of time from several points of view.

E. *Mean dogs* are canvassers' nightmares. A loose, barking yard dog should be given the steady eye as you advance slowly, hands at sides. The chances are he's a harmless loudmouth, if you're brave. Chained or confined apartment dogs, especially where the people fear robberies, are meant to be dangerous and often are. Wait till the dog's master has OK'd you and restrained him.

F. *Television programs* can be a drag, not only because they blanket your knocking, but because they are competition. If you get no answer when you are pretty sure your knock has been heard, leave and try again. People pulled away from a favorite program are seldom receptive. If you're invited into the middle of a program, you'd better sit it out till your host is ready to talk.

G. Whether you accept *an invitation to step in* or not depends on the focus of your canvass. Obviously, you will have a greater effect if you are able to sit down, exchange a few words on baseball or weather, raise the purpose of your call, listen carefully to your host's opinions, and at least suggest some possible solutions of his problems. You may develop an ally who will fill you in on local issues, introduce you to the neighbors, and join you in action. On the other hand, you may miss a referendum deadline or fail to reach a houseful of aroused tenants while you act as a sounding board for one lonely person. You will have to decide, as the case warrants, whether to stay or politely to disengage yourself. Don't promise to return unless you intend to. Be wary of involvement in personal grievances that can't be handled on the level of organized struggle, and keep out of neighborhood feuds.

H. *If your canvassing aims at house or community organizing,* try to turn it over to the people inside as soon as possible. Perhaps one or two active people will introduce you to others, canvass their neighborhoods, or call small meetings in their apartments.

I. If someone is *aggressively hostile,* you are usually wasting your time if you stick around. Listen briefly. If the man who opens the door seems bent on converting or abusing you, don't bother arguing. Disengage as smoothly as possible. In such cases, your self-control and good humor may be more impressive than any words could be.

J. Try to be sensitive to *the situation of old people* who are often lonely and timid in our big cities and who feel menaced by the young. If you address yourself to their problems and learn to listen courteously, you will find that many older workers and community people are anxious for a contact with you and can bring to the struggle much valuable experience from the organizing days of the thirties.

K. Unless you are forced to cover ground rapidly, as in a petition or election campaign, the best way to canvass is to *work in depth in a single neighborhood.* From the first, keep your ears open to information about schools, local housing hassles, traffic conditions, political lineups, etc. Take notes on your visits—after each one, but *not* in the presence of your host, unless you are frankly taking a survey or poll. Supplement what the people tell you with facts and figures from city hall and from various agencies. Visit the schools if possible. By the time you have become a familiar figure in the neighborhood it will have become familiar to you. You will be then launched in the kind of day-to-day work where you can help raise the level of the immediate demands to a struggle for a fundamental restructuring of society.

At Factory Gates

The techniques of canvassing on or near a job location are obviously different. The soundest method is, of course, day-to-day discussion with one's fellow workers. Next best is to support workers inside who, in turn, keep you supplied with information, news, etc. If you have to start from the outside only, your place and time of approach will depend on answers to questions like: Where and when are the workers at leisure to talk? What sort of surveillance is there and is it dangerous for a worker to be seen talking to you? Can you work on company property or only on public streets? Diners, lunch wagons, and coffee-break wagons are often good locations. Acquaint yourself with the schedule of each shift. Learn who the guards and stooges are, if the situation is tense. Morning factory-gate distribution gets your leaflets into the plant for discussion. In general, lunchtime and breaks are good if you can meet the workers then. In cases where any canvassing around the plant may endanger the workers' jobs, your contact may have to begin with an inside organizer or two who will give you the home addresses of others, whom you can then visit.

4. Information Centers

An information center may be temporary or permanent; aimed at organizing the community or the movement itself; concerned with education or with the coordination of activities, or with a combination of these. At its simplest it may consist of a table of pamphlets, buttons, etc., set up at a mass demonstration or at a street corner during a com-

munity organizing drive. At its most elaborate it may involve
an office or storefront with files, bulletin boards, literature
for distribution or sale, and several telephones. In either
and any case, an effective information center must be accessible and must be manned during the hours that the
people need it. In a crisis, this probably means around the
clock.

A permanent center, especially one that aims to gather
and transmit news of the movement, should be run by a
regular committee, so that each member knows the answers
or knows where to find them quickly. The center should
keep ready files of movement addresses and phones, community organizations, places where people can stay, fact
sheets and pamphlets—especially of the practical, informational sort (e.g., *The Abortion Handbook* by Linda Thurston;
The Poor Man's Housing Almanac by John Marcy. These
can be obtained at cost from the Student Union, Boston
University, 775 Commonwealth Ave., Boston, Mass. 02215).
With adequate space an information center can double as
a reading room and a meeting place. A table of movement
newspapers, a directory of vocations for social change, a
skills and tools bank, a map of the region, a source for
posters, buttons, and news of what's happening—these are
ingredients of a well-equipped center. Above all, its value
to group and community rests on a staff of friendly, devoted,
knowledgeable people who keep the bulletin boards up to
date, know what's going on, and pass the news along.

5. Speakers' Bureaus

A group that sets up a speakers' bureau can perform a
free community service and at the same time extend its own
educational and organizational influence. Many clubs,
churches, schools, youth and women's groups, etc., want
speakers and panel discussionists, but can neither find them
in their own ranks nor afford paid lecturers. With the movement constantly and controversially in the news, more people
than you may suspect are eager to hear from students and
other organizers. Your pool of potential speakers should

therefore include trained members of your own group, as well as sympathetic people of special competence from the university, the churches, the labor unions, the ranks of the professionals, and the community at large. Here are some steps and suggestions for establishing a speakers' bureau:

Basic Organization

First discuss and decide on your objectives. These will depend on your politics, on the major issues of the moment, on the composition and sentiments of the community you wish to serve, and on your group's relation to that community. You may be able to present your political position directly, hence to supply speakers mainly from your own group and its close sympathizers. On the other hand, the situation may require you to work along very broad educational lines. In the latter case, you would probably seek out clergymen, professors, specialists in various fields, community and union leaders—who might not agree with you in toto, but whose opinions and knowledge can help open people's minds. (E.g., a priest who did not fully agree with your analysis of American imperialism might well be an effective advocate of the immediate withdrawal of troops from Southeast Asia.) For debates and panel discussions you could even supply representatives of the establishment view—though this is not as easy as it sounds.

A small committee is sufficient and best for organizing a speakers' bureau. The work mostly consists in making individual contacts and arrangements, attending to a multitude of details, keeping an up-to-date central file. A single devoted person with a telephone can operate the bureau, once it is established. Members of the committee should be able to communicate clearly in speech and writing and to function in a systematic manner.

The committee's job is twofold: to develop a list of people who are competent and willing to speak on issues of major concern, and to discover the community organizations that want to hear them. You can advertise your bureau even before your roster of speakers is complete, but be sure you are "covered" from the beginning, in case you get a quick response. Leaflet your potential "customers" by distribution or mail. Telephone chairmen or program directors of organizations and members whom you know. Offer your service as a contribution to them and to community education.

Speakers

If you plan to depend primarily on your own speakers you may need training sessions, on both the background of issues and the techniques of public speaking. Ask a friendly professor or graduate student to run a short seminar and to suggest appropriate readings. An experienced lecturer or a member of the speech department can help improve a speaker's style even in one or two sessions. If your speaking crew is large enough, its members should specialize in various issues (e.g., the U.S. in Southeast Asia; inflation, taxes, and unemployment; housing, landlordism, and urban renewal; black liberation, etc.), so long as they understand how each relates to the general crisis of the system.

If you expect to use community and university speakers outside your group, be sure you are acquainted with their views and their platform effectiveness. You cannot establish a "political purity" test, so if you decide to ask a pacifist (rather than a Viet Cong supporter) to speak to the local Lions Club on the war, don't try to control what he says or criticize him for not saying something else. Your outright enemies will hardly agree to speak under your auspices. Find out your potential speaker's special competence so as to match him with an audience interested in his topic. The committee member who recruits community volunteers for the speaker's pool should be a person of tact and social presence. Remember, you are asking someone to give of his time and effort free. The chances are he will do so because he believes in your cause, but don't fail to express your appreciation, to be helpful about arrangements, directions, transportation, etc., and to discuss his impressions with him after an engagement.

Keep an up-to-date card file of the names and special competence of your speakers. Requests to speak and the dates of actual speaking engagements should be noted on the file cards, along with pertinent comments or evaluations. As your operation grows, you will need a folder file of brief biographies and perhaps a glossy photo of each speaker, for publicity purposes.

You cannot do much to control your speakers' appearance and level of language, unless they are of your own group. Community speakers are usually fairly "straight," which presents little problem save perhaps with youth groups. If you find that a certain speaker has "turned off" a certain audience, try to find out why, note it on the file, and avoid repeating the mistake. With speakers from your own group discuss the probable composition of the audience and advise accordingly. Long hair will not cancel the effect of a good speech. Some audiences may, indeed, expect a young speaker to appear in feathers and beads. If you agree to play to the stereotype, try to show them that there is an informed and thoughtful head under that thatch of hair.

Programs

Give serious consideration to the debate and the panel discussion as forms for presenting the pros and cons of an issue. Where it is not possible to come on heavily with your full political position, an open discussion can help to open minds. It is not easy, however, to find qualified and willing spokesmen for the establishment. Active military and government men are under some restrictions in talking policy. Try to get conservative professors, retired career military men, ex-politicians, newsmen, etc. You may be surprised to find how few people wish to argue for the government's policies under conditions where they must debate or answer questions.

A dialogue with the audience can often accomplish more than a straight lecture. This means more than simply fielding a few questions. An experienced speaker can, after a brief presentation, get a genuine exchange going with even quite a large audience, but generally it is best to break a big meeting into smaller workshop groups—in which case your speaker will need to bring along a couple of assistants or to recruit them on the spot.

Backup

The chairman of the organization inviting the speaker usually introduces him, but in the case of small or grass-roots groups a speaker may simply identify himself or take along a member of the committee to introduce him. In any event, be sure that all arrangements are clear: that your speaker knows where he is going, when he is expected, what sort of audience he will meet, whom he is to ask for, what he is to talk about. A telephone call within forty-eight hours of the event "confirming" the date is an essential precaution. Nothing ruins your bureau's reputation faster than to leave a community program director to face an audience which awaits your speaker in vain! Actually, speakers should be asked to arrive ten or fifteen minutes early, to allow time for a chat with the chairman of the meeting. Your bureau, and not the speaker himself, should supply the chairman with vital information for his introduction, but chairmen often like to see the speaker first to discuss his approach or to tell him about the interests of the audience.

Your speaker should be supplied with literature—leaflets, pamphlets, even books, on his topic. If the meeting is large or if some of the literature must be sold, an assistant or two should go along to handle this. Be sure you get the consent of the organization before you plan to set up a literature table.

The organization sponsoring the meeting usually arranges advance publicity, but you will probably be called upon to supply information and suggestions. The more service you can render, the more your bureau will be used, since one organization will tell another about it. If you are handling the publicity yourself, through your own leaflets or through releases to the news media, consult appropriate headings in this chapter and "Using Establishment Structures: The Mass Media."

6. Using the Mail

Almost as soon as a small organizing group begins to reach people, it will need to set up a mailing list. Names and addresses of sympathizers should be gathered at public meetings, through canvassing, and through cooperative activities with community organizations. You are in danger of losing contacts almost as soon as you make them if you don't very early in your organizing efforts set up a card file of names, addresses, phone numbers, organizational connections, and any other pertinent information.

When you grow beyond the small-group stage the mail is one of the surest and cheapest ways of keeping in touch with a rapidly expanding membership, keeping friends and supporters aware of your activities, reaching people on crucial issues and actions, and drumming up financial support. Get in the habit of putting return coupons for names, money, and suggested additional names of friends in every piece of literature you send out, or hand out, so that your list can grow geometrically. An ad in a movement paper can bring in still more names.

Compiling the List

If your group and its circle of friends is still small, ask a sympathetic larger organization if you can borrow its mailing list. Some groups, however, are paranoid about letting people see their files. In such cases they may let you give them the envelopes to address, with you paying the costs. Then start your own list with the returns. When you have a sizable list of your own, you will find some movement organizations that will exchange theirs with yours. Be sure to go through such lists for duplications and check to see if the file has been kept up to date. The commercial world does a lively business in mailing lists—as many people's problems with junk mail demonstrate. Don't sell your list or buy anyone else's. Movement organizations working for social change are not in competition and should support one another's efforts without attempting to profit from the help they give.

Organizing for Large Mailings

A large list needs two card files, one alphabetical and one by zip code to facilitate bulk mailing. On each card place name, address, and information on participation in work, fund campaigns, etc. Someone should have charge of the file to add names, to record changed addresses, and once a year to review all the cards so as to purge the file of people who have never responded.

Even moderately big mailings—i.e., ones where you can bundle letters in batches of ten or more for each zip code—

should take advantage of bulk mailing rates. For this and for information on classes of mail, go to your local post office and ask for their booklet of regulations. If your list is too big to address by hand or typewriter, you should consider investment in an addressing machine. The best is a Scriptomatic, which in the large size costs $1,200 new.

To get used equipment, place ads in religious and/or pacifist radical publications, also newspapers like *The Guardian*—in other words, magazines read by older movement people. Ask established groups, churches, or schools to let you use their machines, and offer to pay a small maintenance fee. Then you only need to buy your own blank address plates or cards.

7. Mobile Units

A mobile unit is a happening on wheels packed with people, information, and political mobility. It can serve as an information center, a wandering workshop, a guerrilla theater base, a hassle-free office, a home for nomad organizers.

Buy an old hearse, mail truck, school bus, VW bus, or any reasonable facsimile. Your supplies and housekeeping arrangements will depend on your purposes and range, political and personal. You may want to park regularly at certain busy corners in your city where your well-postered and -painted vehicle will become a symbol of the movement while you distribute its literature and rap with the people. Or you may carry leaflets, films, music, craft stuff, and workshop discussions into remote towns where you are the first they have seen of the movement.

A good-sized mobile unit can carry a mimeograph or ditto machine and supplies, as well as your food, utensils, and bedding. You will travel more happily and carry your message more effectively if you stow your equipment systematically and keep your unit reasonably neat.

Apart from its instant availability for demonstrations and neighborhood campaigns, the mobile unit increases your range in being where the action is and makes you difficult to locate as you go about expanding and linking up the activist network. Make any trip you take a political trip. Keep lists of friends wherever you go and let them know you are coming, whether you plan a mobile unit "blitz" to spark local interest or want advance publicity.

If a town is unfriendly, be careful not to embarrass your contacts; they have to live there long after you have gone. Try wherever possible to involve local people in your discussions or presentations so that you leave behind you a new nucleus from which the movement can grow.

8. Coffeehouses

A coffeehouse can become a center for the political education of young working people, street people, and students; a focal point for mobilization of the movement; a haven for GIs to meet one another and to gain community support for their resistance to daily oppression. To be all these things it must first be a place people like to go to meet people they like. It is a considerable undertaking, fraught with potential landlord and police hassles, but decidedly worth it if your group is large enough and well financed enough to undertake it. Community support in the form of actual participation is the prime condition for success.

Setting Up

Try to get the initial cooperation of local groups like churches and youth clubs. If possible, let them find and choose the place. You will need money for rent and renovation at once, so you should have enough to carry through for several months until fund-raising activities can take over. Buying a house eliminates landlord hassles, but gives the owners some heavy responsibilities. A group in Cambridge limited individual liability by forming a corporation.

Check local zoning ordinances and health and safety regulations. Get from the Government Printing Office or the local Small Business Administration their pamphlets on starting small enterprises. Find out about licenses: live entertainment sometimes requires a separate license. You may need a lawyer. You may also want to take out public liability insurance. If you plan to invest in extensive renovations, get the landlord's written consent and get a lease. This won't, however, save you if the authorities try to close you down as a fire or health hazard or as a public nuisance. Your only real protection lies in the support of the people of the community.

It is therefore *essential* that you understand the local situation before you start. If ethnic tensions, street violence, etc., already exist, your coffeehouse may help to create unity, or it may become a new locus of conflict.

Even if members of your own group make the initial arrangements, try to involve neighborhood people in renovating, decorating, and building tables and benches from secondhand materials. Give your and their imagination a free rein with murals, collages, posters, and a catchy name for the house. Let as much come from the people as possible. If they feel it is their own place, they will be there and you can increase its political content as you work with them.

Day-to-Day Operation

If your coffeehouse advertises particular days and hours, be sure you have enough staff from your own group and the community to open up on time and keep open. Provide coffee; food if possible. Keep charges at a minimum. It is unlikely that a coffeehouse can pay for itself out of normal income. Support it with fund-raising affairs, the sale of posters and crafts, etc.

Avoid liquor and dope. Try to make your rules persuasive rather than coercive, but they had better be clear and firm on this. Excessive noise also gives the authorities an excuse to close you down, so it's worthwhile to tone it down. In any case, you don't want to sacrifice political discussion to mere racket.

Leaflets, pamphlets, posters, books, and records should be on hand for distribution or sale. According to the interests of your supporters, activities may include folk music; chess; athletics; films; draft and drug counseling; discussion groups and classes; workshops in arts and crafts and in leaflet writing and silk screen; Sunday dinners; poetry readings; and always a lot of informal rapping. If you have space enough, a mimeo machine and a poster shop are good for involving your "customers" in speaking to their own community. With a really good setup and the participation of neighborhood mothers, you might start a child-care center, but check health and safety regulations carefully before you try this.

GI Coffeehouses

One of the most needed, and therefore successful, versions of the coffeehouse is the GI coffeehouse. "GI dissent manifests itself across a broad spectrum; the coffeehouses and papers are only the visible center; the invisible bands are sabotage at one end, a quiet but paralyzing disaffection at the other" (Fred Gardner, *Hard Times*, No. 63). A coffeehouse near an armed forces base gives the GI an opportunity to express himself and to work with others against his immediate day-to-day oppression, besides providing an alternative to the clip joints.

The general procedures for setting up a GI coffeehouse are the same as those for a community venture, with a few modifications.

Community and GI involvement from the beginning is *essential*, since it is not only the landlords and town authorities who may try to wipe you out, but the military brass of the post you serve. Try to get clergymen, professionals, and local service organizations to support the venture; you may even get endorsement from local politicians, etc. Have GIs and ex-GIs help you plan it. Let it be staffed mainly with GIs once it gets going.

A place with several rooms is desirable so that simultaneous activities can go on: political workshops, classes (use your university people), films, the publication of a GI newsletter, meetings of the American Servicemen's Union, military counseling (including interviews with shrinks, doctors, and clergymen), folk music, a reading room with political and general literature, etc.

The approach should be broad, including an appeal to many different interests and levels of political awareness. Arranging activities which gradually raise the political level is a sounder method than coming on "heavy" at once. Broad community support is the only way to counter attempts to close you down and punitive measures by the military against your GI patrons. (See *Hard Times*, No. 63, for the defense of the Shelter Half Coffeehouse at Fort Lewis, Washington, by the people of the area.) Keep in touch with other GI coffeehouses —the soldiers will tell you about them—and for further information contact the United States Servicemen's Fund, (212) 677–2290 (135 West 4th St., New York, N.Y. 10012).

9. Films

Film is one of the most effective media available to small groups for the education of their membership and the public. Shown alone or as part of a community meeting or workshop, pictures such as *The Year of the Pig, The War Game, High School, The Survivors,* and *The Salt of the Earth* can initiate political discussion and even inspire action. Since many community groups are unaware that such films exist, you can make their introduction a part of your speakers' bureau program. Discussion will be encouraged if the presentation is preceded by a brief introduction of the issues involved and followed by well-thought-out questions. Discussion leaders should, therefore, see the film in advance.

Single showings or festivals are good money raisers for your political activities. The cost of most noncommercial films is low enough so that even a modest admission charge can reap a surplus. Unless you plan frequent showings, buying a projector is a luxury. Many individuals, churches, schools, and audio-visual departments own 16-mm projectors and will lend them to you. Failing this, you can rent one when you need it from a camera store. Two or three of your members should be trained as projectionists, if you do not already have a film buff in your midst.

Many campuses and communities boast talented moviemakers, amateur, student, and semiprofessional, and the private collection of film libraries is a growing hobby. Try to make contact with such people. Encourage them to make films of events such as demonstrations and marches, and of conditions in the communities of your region. For those who wish to learn filmmaking, Edward Pincus's *Guide for Film-Makers* (Signet, 1969) and *Creative Film Making* (Collier, 1969) are good all-around texts. Ask a skilled filmmaker to start a workshop in your group.

You can rent noncommercial films for prices ranging from $10 to $75. Some old commercial films are almost as cheap, but the most significant ones and the more recent films are likely to start at about $75 a showing. If your school or college has an audio-visual department, borrow its catalogs. Some excellent films, such as those of the Canadian Film Board and BBC, are available through conventional companies. (You can also call the Canadian and British consulates about outlets for these films.) The best catalog for feature-length films is the *Feature Film General Guide*, EFLA Publishers, obtainable through Walter Reade Organization, 241 E. 34th St., New York, N.Y. 10016. Best for general shorts is *Contemporary Films*, McGraw-Hill, 330 W. 42d St., New York, N.Y. 10036.

For radical films there are several "Newsreel" distribution headquarters:

Atlanta Newsreel
P.O. Box 5432, E Sta.
Atlanta, Ga. 30307
(404) 373–7903

New York Newsreel
322 Seventh Ave.
New York, N.Y. 10001
(212) 565–4930

Boston Newsreel
595 Massachusetts Ave.
Cambridge, Mass. 02139
(617) 864–2600

San Francisco Newsreel
451 Cortland Ave.
San Francisco, Calif. 94110
(415) 826–2989

Chicago Newsreel
2440 N. Lincoln Ave.
Chicago, Ill. 60614
(312) 248–2018

For radical films including the "Newsreel" productions contact American Documentary Films at 336 W. 84th St., New York, N.Y. 10024, (212) 779–7440; or at 379 Bay St., San Francisco, Calif. 94133, (415) 982–7475.

All regional offices of the American Friends Service Committee supply films on Vietnam, War and Peace, War and Conscience, Poverty and Prejudice, Marches, Boycotts, The Nuclear Age. They charge only $4.

For both political and just plain far-out films: Grove Press, 214 Mercer St., New York, N.Y. 10012. (Grove is also the repository for the "Old Cinema 16" collection, which has many political films from the fifties and early sixties. Prices on this collection are unfortunately high.)

The Museum of Modern Art, 11 W. 53d St., New York, N.Y. 10019, has the most extensive collection of 16-mm films around (especially good for background material).

Inquire of all movement organizations whether or not they

have a film rental library. Also contact local radical or underground newspapers and local or regional headquarters of the movement.

Additional sources:

Anti-Defamation League of B'Nai B'Rith
72 Franklin St.
Boston, Mass. 02110
(617) 542–4977

Film Industry for Peace
817 Broadway, Rm. 1506
New York, N.Y. 10003

Films for Social Change
5122 Waterman Blvd.
St. Louis, Mo. 63108

Massachusetts "Pax"
65A Winthrop St.
Cambridge, Mass. 02138
(617) 491–0650

New York Cinetract Co.
40 E. 7th St.
New York, N.Y. 10003
(212) 598–2406, 2409, 2413, 2414

Shell Oil Co., Film Library
450 N. Meridian St.
Indianapolis, Ind. 46204 (esp. "The Mekong")

Wholesome Film Center
22 Melrose St.
Boston, Mass. 02116
(617) 426–0155

10. Guerrilla Theater

Although it has antecedents at least as ancient as the Roman mimes, guerrilla theater emerged as a self-conscious form of political education out of mass demonstrations of the late sixties like the Pentagon in '67 and Paris in '68. It is theater performed not in theaters but in the streets; not by actors but by political activists; not, as a rule, before expectant customers but before passers-by.

With as many definitions of guerrilla theater abroad as there are troupes, the common denominator is political impact. From the crude reenactment of a single incident to the fairly sophisticated scenario linking issues with sources and solutions, guerrilla production aims at "gut" reaction rather than at intellectual persuasion. Hence it relies less on verbal symbols than on physical: violent gesture, slapstick, horseplay, ritual dance, music, noise; grotesque, exaggerated, shocking masks, props, and costumes. Such dialogue as accompanies the action may be similarly extreme, comical, and vulgar; the words may be sung or chanted.

The political strategy of guerrilla theater is the awakening of the people to the rule of brutality and injustice behind the illusions fostered by the establishment and its media. Its primary tactic is shock, used so as to shake confidence in the status quo and to set people doubting the official fairy tales of a class society. A group that plans to make guerrilla theater a regular part of its political arsenal should first acquaint itself with the theory and practice of established troupes and clarify its own theatrical and political objectives. For a successful troupe, the two are inseparable.

The aim of guerrilla theater (perhaps of all theater) is to create a metaphor or symbolic revelation of reality that will force people to see and to think about the world in new ways. The metaphor seizes upon the *essence* of everyday events and, through exaggeration, distortion, and change of context, strips them of their familiar aspects—"blows them up" to expose the shocking truths within. Its purpose is neither to shake people up for the mere "hell of it," nor to create panic and hostility. A performance that masks itself as an actual occurrence is normally neither good theater nor good politics. When people feel personally threatened they react defensively, i.e., conservatively. When they find that they have been upset by a hoax they are usually angry. Neither fear nor anger tends to open minds. Nor does a confusion of representation with reality permit the audience to penetrate beyond the individual and accidental to some universal truth beneath the surface of the action.

The successful metaphor stands on its own feet, not as a threat to the viewer's primitive sense of self-preservation, but as a challenge to the security of his whole intellectual-emotional socialization. He is forced to question his image of the world, which is the first stage of radicalization. When Father Daniel Berrigan drenched the Catonsville draft files with blood he created a theatrical metaphor of the war more shocking than the casualty lists themselves.

Forming the Troupe

The primary resource is *people*—to brainstorm ideas; think up scenarios and act them out; make masks and costumes; paint scenery and placards; collect junk and transform it into theatrical props. Don't wait to find an "experienced" crew; create one. Use the members' special talents without limiting their functions. A guerrilla troupe works best with jacks-of-all-trades.

Beginning with people and place, your own group and the community, effective use of your resources will depend upon your analysis of the concrete situation before you. The scenario for a strike mass meeting can assume an audience already in motion, hence employ language and symbolic action quite different from the piece designed to awaken a neighborhood to a new issue. Ideally, even the personnel of the troupe should differ, for your aim is a theater in which workers play for workers, students for students, Puerto Ricans for Puerto Ricans, blacks for blacks—about their own world and how to change it.

You probably won't need a playwright, but you can't get along without a sharp focus on a single political objective and a fund of ideas about how to put it "onstage." Hold a brainstorming session and let the group create the "play." Even a longer, more complex scenario should unfold as a series of theatrical cartoons rather than emphasize a story line. Sketch a minimal outline of action and dialogue, but leave room for your performers to improvise. The French students of Vincennes were able to spark hour-long street-corner discussions with a cast of four archetypal characters (Third World Peasant, Revolutionary Peasant, Ugly White Man, Capitalist Army Officer or Policeman) in a repertoire of two-minute slapstick improvisations. As sources of inspiration for more elaborate productions, consult the Bibliography for works which include sample scenarios and commedia dell'arte techniques. Adapt freely from old and modern drama: Molière, Büchner, Jarry, the dadaists and expressionists, Brecht, etc.

Equipping the Troupe for Action

A permanent group of players (as against one organized for a single demonstration) needs a workshop–rehearsal place and warehouse. Try to find a loft, garage, barn, or storefront that combines all these and can even double as a small theater. When you buy basic materials, think how you can use them over and over. Inventiveness, not a big inventory, is the key to guerrilla versatility and mobility.

If you plan performances in parks and playgrounds or expect to hit the countryside (see "Mobile Units") you might invest in a portable stage made in demountable sections.

A painted backdrop can be strung on a pole hung between goalposts. Scenery should be minimal, simple, bold, symbolic; music loud, popular, even naïve (folk, rock, children's songs, circus marches, etc.). Sound effects can include everything from bells and drums to the barking dogs and police sirens of the neighborhood.

Street-corner guerrilla theater takes the city for its backdrop and makes the most of it. Props and costumes—grotesque, striking, symbolic and easily transportable or expendable—are almost the whole arsenal of effects for the street corner. Masks, placards, stilts, bullhorns, gongs and whistles, balloons, confetti, food, animals, symbolic objects (weapons, blood, whips, clubs, tools, papier-mâché computers and missiles, etc.)—these are the sort of props you may use. Costumes should be outrageous, or should clearly identify the character (the Landlord, Nixon, the VC Peasant, Uncle Sam). An appropriate hat, mask, pair of glasses, or loose garment thrown over street clothes can transform you. If you operate without a permit, design masks and costumes for quick change, in the event you must split and disappear in the crowd.

Choosing an Audience

Since guerrilla theater can be performed almost anyplace, the places you select become a part of your political statement. Except when you perform by invitation or for political friends, be prepared for any eventuality—in order fully to use your opportunities or to defend your troupe if necessary. If you are focused on reaching people, you will usually seek locations where the audience is neither strongly on your side nor strongly against you. Most groups do, of course, play before movement gatherings to raise spirits and funds. Some groups have also invaded hostile territory (board meetings, graduations, ROTC exercises, Wall Street). It is a question how much this frightens the power structure, but if you undertake it, know in advance where the nearest exits are and prepare a very short script. The usual, and usually most fruitful, arena for guerrilla theater is what may be called the "neutral" or "mixed" place, which it is your purpose to transform into a friendly place.

If police interference is likely, try the system developed by French students in the post-'68 period of repression. While four or five actors perform, have a half-dozen more kneel in a circle around them to clear a small playing space, another group leafleting, and several standing by in the crowd. If all goes well, these will help initiate a discussion after the "play." If the police come, the supporting group can create diversions (arguments, stupid questions, fainting fits, chases, sudden bursts of music—whatever works) while the actors get out of costume (or into transforming costumes) and split in several directions. A ready vehicle is useful. Plan where you will meet in such an event—and open the show again on another corner.

Keep your pockets clean when performing. If you do get arrested, let it be for political work.

The presence of the media at a guerrilla production sometimes reduces blatant police harassment. If it doesn't, try to use them to publicize your group and the reasons why it is attacked.

If "disturbance of the peace" is a gimmick frequently used against you, try silent pantomime. Here, especially, you must depend on visual means—masks, costumes, props, gestures, placards, and leaflets to make your point. This will not, of course, take care of "unlawful assemblage" or "blocking a public thoroughfare." Your only real protection lies in community support.

Such support, and your own effectiveness, are greatly enhanced if you can include the audience's friends and relatives in your cast. Repeated performances in a single neighborhood are therefore better for building a base than onetime blitzes in transient downtown areas. When you begin to "belong" to a community, both heckling and police attacks tend to disappear.

This article is indebted for some information and ideas to prepublication copies of materials to appear in Erika Munk's forthcoming *Guerrilla Theater* (Bantam Books), particularly the writings of R. G. Davis of the San Francisco Mime Troupe.

11. Zaps

A zap is symbolic shock therapy aimed against the status quo. A zap pits irrationality against hardened rationality. Zaps undermine the confidence and composure of the self-satisfied and complacent. They break old patterns of predictability and offer new avenues of communication.

A zap is contradictory. It can be humorous in content but deadly serious in intent. Anyone who comes into viewing, hearing, smelling, tasting, or feeling distance can be zapped.

Spread ZAP graffiti around. Carry an ink marker and gummed graffiti labels with you everywhere. Use every available space to your advantage. Put political quotes on popcorn boxes and in right-wing books.

Experiment with political definitions and timely slogans. Print up "wanted" posters of your most dangerous opponents.

Mailed Zaps: Send roaches to slumlords.—Send dirt back along with bills to major pollutants.—Don't put stamps on bills at all. Postage will be due from receiver.

War Zaps: In your spare time, call the Pentagon, collect, and ask to speak to someone in the Intercommunication Center. Ask how the war's going.—Process draft forms using your dog's name.

Money-Economy Zaps: Give away free: money, posters, beer, etc.—Burn money.—Design dollar-bill toilet paper and distribute it.

Ecological Zaps: Wear gas masks in the streets.—If you can guarantee shipping and adequate grazing area, the government will supply you with your own buffalo (keeps the herds at a controllable level). Park it in front of the Department of Interior in D.C.—Call Hickel and ask for a personal, guided tour of his newly interior-decorated office (well, that is his job, no?). You'd like to see his $55-per-yard carpet.— Call your local polluter and ask where you can purchase packaged, government-inspected air.

Miscellaneous Zaps: When filling out a job application (or other form), in the blank that asks for Race_____, write in Human!; where it asks for Sex_____, write Yes.—Call your TV station around 3:00 A.M. and tell them you were watching the test pattern on TV and ask them why they took it off. Tell them it works! Ask them who or what they are testing.—Sneak into a convention of liberal politicians. Cut the cord from the mike and insert a jack into the tape deck. Insert a recording of farts; or a recording of Country Joe and the Fish singing "Be the first in your block to have your son come home in a box."

IV. Alternate Structures

1. Introduction: Vocations for Social Change

Community-based service programs provide an important alternative to depersonalized, overly bureaucratized, centrally administered programs. Staffed and run by local residents, they can bring people together to overcome common problems and meet common needs. Out of such programs communities can build a strong community power base.

There is no single way to overcome local problems. And no single way to radicalize people. However, a community dealing functionally with common issues will become politically aware. Public-service programs are one way to educate people about alternative, nonestablishment solutions to their problems. If the alternatives are right, people will accept them.

The examples that follow in this section must be taken as guidelines. Structure and practical action will grow within the community as it comes to grips with its problems.

To note especially: Vocations for Social Change (VSC). Getting in touch with them should be one step in the education of any organizer planning to use this section for effective community action.

"VSC is a decentralized clearing house for persons struggling with one basic question: How can one earn a living in America . . . and at the same time ensure that his social impact is going to effect basic humanistic change in our social, political and economic institutions?" (from VSC newsletter).

VSC publishes a monthly newsletter with job openings in groups working for social change; proposals for projects which need help getting started; lists of places to get education or apprenticeships in skills for social change; articles on topics related to social change; and lists of people looking for meaningful jobs.

Members of the VSC group are available as source people, and will come to lecture, teach, or visit your community if you can pay for them. They attempt to decentralize VSC by helping to set up local newsletters and counselors, as well as local projects dedicated to social change. Their address is: Vocations for Social Change, Inc., Canyon, Calif. 94516, phone (415) 376–7743.

VSC is interested in receiving listings of available jobs, people available for jobs, and any interesting information related to social change jobs, or educational opportunities. Their newsletter can be obtained with a contribution, or through a person in your local area. Write to them for details.

2. Medical Clinics

The existence of a free community clinic is a concrete statement against the deficiencies of American public medicine: its overcentralization, lack of commitment, depersonalized care, and unresponsiveness to the total picture of community life. Locally organized clinics often have strong support because they are built by community people directly around community needs. Outside organizers setting up a free clinic should make special effort to understand the nature of the neighborhood and involve local residents in all aspects of the project. Eventually other groups may develop around the clinic to deal with community problems and larger issues.

Setting Up

The clinic can be located in a storefront, unused doctor's office, or mobile unit. Mobile units are outreach facilities, usually spending several months in different locations around the community. Out on the streets, the mobile unit can fit itself directly into the neighborhood and reach large numbers of people. New York branches of the Black Panther party canvass their communities giving blood tests for anemia, eye and ear exams, routine dental checks, and lead-poisoning tests for children. Limited space and facilities make mobile units more a base for treating short-term and acute problems than for preventive care. A stationary clinic is better able to handle preventive medicine, educational programs, testing, and lab work. If funds and staff allow, a mobile unit could be used to extend the reach of a storefront health program. A single mobile clinic should try to make arrangements with larger clinics to back up its program.

Funding

Funding for salaries, equipment, and supplies can come from private donations, church and civic groups, the sponsoring agency (if there is one), or grants. It is best to seek grants from private foundations rather than from the government. Government funding involves strings, bureaucratic nit-picking, heavy competition for limited amounts of money, and hassles with the local power hierarchy. If the clinic remains independent of larger agencies, it can often deal more easily with a wider range of community problems. Autonomy avoids the power struggles and competition for money that go on within umbrella agencies, hampering the clinic's freedom to work with various local groups.

Legal Protection

Keep in touch with a good lawyer, and take the necessary steps to protect the clinic against lawsuits. Many free clinic patients may be minors, who for various reasons (drug problems, pregnancy, VD, etc.) may not want their parents involved. Treating them without parental consent runs the risk of suit from the parents. But if you are good to the kids and provide them with competent care, there is little likelihood of pressure from parents.

Malpractice suits are a problem for any medical facility. The possibility is always there. The clinic doctor should be covered by malpractice insurance for his own protection as well as the clinic's. The AMA provides a special insurance package that is cheaper than private coverage, but doctors must join the AMA in order to qualify. Clinic facilities should also be covered with both theft and accident insurance.

Staff

The permanent staff should include a doctor, at least one registered nurse, more if possible, and community organizers to help coordinate programs. A free clinic often has to deal with a large number of patients in a very short space of time. This cuts down on individual attention and limits the doctor's ability to develop a rapport with the patients. Staffing the clinic with local volunteers can help develop stronger community ties and provide a basis for training, while giving the medical staff more time for patients. Seek the aid of medical and nursing students to supplement the permanent staff. Many routine testing procedures can be done by student nurses. Try to arrange referral and backup with local MDs for special problems that can't be handled at the clinic.

Services and Programs

The high price of prescription drugs often prevents patients from getting the medication they need. Keep standard medications on hand. Buy tetracycline, penicillin, vitamins, etc., in bulk and give them away free. Use the generic formula when writing prescriptions; name brands are more expensive. Make use of Medicaid whenever possible. For patients who aren't covered, consider using Medicaid prescription blanks and having them borrow a card from a neighbor. Every effort should be made to help people avoid the exorbitant cost of drugs and medicines.

Drug companies send free samples to doctors every month or so. They can be used to supplement the clinic's supply of medicine, but they come too irregularly to be depended upon.

When issuing contraceptives, make sure women understand the different methods available. Evaluate and explain all methods honestly before prescribing or suggesting any one. Have a good supply of birth-control pills, and dispense them for free. If possible, arrange for a gynecologist to come in on a part-time basis to fit diaphragms and coils, otherwise refer women to a better-equipped clinic.

In most cases, the main services a free clinic can provide regarding abortions are guidance, counseling, and referral. Most states still refuse women the right to decide for themselves whether or not they will bear a child. Those states which have liberalized laws specify that abortion must be done in hospitals. Where abortion is legal, the clinic can refer women to hospitals, and help them find ways to finance the abortion or have it done for free.

Prenatal care is usually not feasible in a small clinic. The clinic can diagnose pregnancy, treat women for short-term problems, and help with dietary planning. Notes and prescriptions for diet programs can be used to help welfare recipients get food supplements.

Transportation for getting patients to and from the clinic

and making house calls is a necessary service. If funding allows, buy a station wagon or VW bus; otherwise, try to arrange an informal network with volunteers and staff members who have cars.

Educational programs should become a part of community-based health programs. Set up health and first-aid classes, drug education groups; train welfare mothers in nutrition and new skills. Such programs are sometimes difficult to maintain, especially through mobile clinics, but the community organizer on the staff can aid in coordinating programs and extending them back to the community. The organizer with a knowledge of the community can bring people to the clinic, and work with groups that may develop around the programs. For example, bring ex-junkies in to work with the clinic and help with drug abuse or rehabilitation programs.

If facilities allow, local residents can train as aides, secretaries, lab assistants, etc. Paramedical training serves a double function: it opens skilled jobs to the previously unskilled and helps to break the myth of medical exclusiveness by spreading basic skills throughout the community.

Additional services might include physical exams for working papers, notes for the draft, bailing people out of jail, connections with Manpower and Job Corps to help find jobs for local residents.

3. Youth Services

a. Drug Counseling

Drug abuse is generally treated as a criminal offense or, in more enlightened circles, as an individual's emotional problem. In practice, this kind of treatment has failed because prisons and most counseling services don't deal with drug abuse as a social problem within a political context, as well as an emotional problem. To date, only transference techniques have been successful in treating drug dependents. Clinics substitute methadone for smack. The Black Muslims substitute a political ideology for drugs. Mutual emotional self-support groups like Synanon substitute group strength for individual strength. But each of these produces a dependence as great as the original one.

In this society, everyone is striving for emotional and material security, an escape from boredom, and "happiness." Larger and larger sectors of our society are turning to drugs to fill these needs. More and more people are lying in their own vomit, convulsing from withdrawal symptoms. Younger and younger people are dying from overdoses. We are indoctrinated with the myth that relative material security has been reached and that emotional security means the absence of insecurities. Realistically, the human condition is filled with insecurities and uncertainties which we must learn to embrace. Boredom results from a deep-seated sense of alienation. The poor quality of relationships in a highly competitive society, the lack of control over our lives, the absence of creativity and spontaneity, and the mechanical nature of work leads to feeling bored with our friends and our jobs. Society's answer to boredom is play. We watch TV. We listen to music. We get vicarious highs from watching professional sports. We fuck. We take drugs.

No drug deals with the fundamental causes of depression or anxiety. Drugs might generate healthy internal perceptions, revelations, and releases from tension. However, drug abuse can lead to a total dream state, allowing our corrupt status quo to keep the people in a state of servitude. "Drug politics" suggests that counseling services must develop small-group situations where the people relate to each other as individuals and deal with their relationships to their environment.

Your small group of drug counselors will have to first deal politically with the drug question, which includes developing a campaign against repressive drug laws and irresponsible drug advertising. There is an implicit danger in waging this campaign. You will be making powerful enemies who, on a multitude of legal technicalities, may be able to close you down. Until you are firmly entrenched in the community the campaign may have to be a soft-sell affair. However, this doesn't mean to fight repressive laws only with moral liberal arguments; attack them on principled political grounds.

Drug Education

All the counselors will need a thorough drug education. Medical personnel, dealers, users' personal experiences, and street people are excellent resources. Most people, including users, are ignorant about drugs and use drugs unsafely. Many users don't know that if STP and thorazine are dropped together, you can kiss your ass good-bye. Counselors must be prepared to teach and lecture to the community on safe drug usage and drugs in the political context. Counselors must know how to handle overdose and withdrawal victims and set up an emergency service for them. Counselors must know the drug lingo: dropping, skin popping, shooting, ODs, spikes, cutting, bumming out, etc. They must know the generic names of drugs, but more importantly their street names: angel's dust, magic pumpkin, big H, boo, hog, smack, orange wedges, sunshine. They must know the long- and short-term effects of common drugs. A good source is R. Linegeman's *Drugs from A to Z, A Dictionary* (McGraw-Hill, $2.95).

A good drug education also includes knowing where to refer people for help the counseling service can't offer. In Boston, for example, experience has shown that the Whittier Clinic handles ODs very well and that Massachusetts General is the worst place to send people on bad trips. This kind of general information should be available for anyone coming to the counseling service.

Backup

Professional backup, when used intelligently, can be of great value. Foremost, your professionals can defend the program if a reactionary group or the pigs in the community attack you. They can also be invaluable in fund raising. Associating other community leaders with the service can have the same effect. Professional medical backup is useful for general advice and treatment for the physically sick. Drug abusers have a high susceptibility to disease, particularly shooters who may contract hepatitis or mononucleosis. Doctors can also prescribe drugs such as methadone and medical treatments which you probably can't provide. Social workers may be able (through the system's channels) to help with family problems. Shrinks can help those people who are so flipped out or so far into their fantasies that you can't deal with them. However, if a person is referred to a shrink or a doctor, the counseling service can't wash its hands of him or her. Because psychiatry and medicine are primarily concerned with "curing" people to the extent that they are functional, and because the "professionals" rarely relate drug abuse to social conditions, their prescriptions only partly help.

Legal Stuff

Legal hassles are multifold with drug counseling. Zoning variances for facilities may be needed, especially if you intend to allow people to sleep in at the center. A workable relationship with the police is vital. If you get busted regularly, you may be shut down. If the pigs stake out your center to discover drug users for later busts, no one will come to your doors. Good community rapport and support is the only way to prevent repression. You may find yourself dealing with local governments. If you can get money with a minimum of strings from a government agency—local, state, or federal— political attack and pig harassment may be minimized. Organizers should promote the program constantly, educate the community, and fund-raise. Consult and retain an attorney. Know the laws that affect you. A legal-aid program should be available to people in the program in the event they are busted.

Reaching People

Media publicity like newspaper copy, radio advertising and talk shows, leafleting, and local speaking engagements is standard. Street recruiting is more difficult but may be the only way to reach people who are ashamed to ask for help or who irrationally conclude they don't have problems. Counselors shouldn't make people feel guilty about coming for help. Where the counseling service is located a large, general people's room with an open-door policy should be available so people can float around without being intimidated by questions. If practical, this room should be open around the clock. Coffee and food should be provided. People may want to talk informally with counselors or people already in a program, before getting involved to find out what's coming down. The program should offer structured group meetings as well as informal unstructured situations.

Most people will be paranoid about entering a drug program. They fear lecturing, being manipulated, being busted, and admitting their problems. A formal private meeting between the counselor and the new member may be useful but isn't essential. The counselor should deal openly with the member's fears, carefully explaining the confidential nature of the program, its goals, and what is expected of members. The counselor should keep minimal records (if any) including name, address, phone, a friend's phone number, and any miscellaneous data that seems pertinent. He should try to determine if the programs the service offers will be beneficial to the prospective member. If they are not applicable to the new person, maybe referral suggestions can be made. If the person is to join the program, the counselor must try to determine with which group the person will be most compatible.

In a structured or informal gathering the counselor acts as a discussion leader. He adds focus and direction to the meetings and ensures full participation by everyone. He controls the group's direction to the extent that the political inferences of drug problems are discussed in juxtaposition to individual problems. The best meetings are unplanned and just happen with the people there at the time. Planned meetings may be no good at all for many people since they will not be able to cope with the responsibility of keeping commitments.

Extra Special Problems

So far we have made no distinction between organizing techniques for different types of drugs. Hard drugs like cocaine and heroin have the added problem of addiction with which to reckon. They also present an extra special problem: the Mafia is virtually the sole distributor of these drugs in the U.S. of A. It is highly unlikely that such a public-opinion-conscious organization as the Mafia would move against a service program. It is more unlikely that a drug counseling service will make even a minute dent in Mafia profits. However, this year an organizer from a collective in the Bronx, working in a drug program, was murdered without apparent motive. We do not mean to inject paranoia, only a note of caution.

b. Trouble Pads

The barbaric programs concocted by the establishment for the "benefit" of runaways mangle creative minds, deepen growing disillusionment, and perpetuate emotional problems. In most states a runaway under twenty-one cannot get counseling or medical attention without parental consent, unless he or she is a medical emergency. Parents in New York (which is like most states) have three ways to deal with their runaway children:

1. They can ignore the constant running away.
2. They can call the police, which results in the child going to a state mental institution or children's shelter which is a prison for kids.
3. They can send the child to special boarding school or a residence if they are wealthy—the cost ranges from $11,000 to $20,000 a year. In New York, if a youth has a history of hard-drug use, homicidal or suicidal tendencies, he or she will not be admitted to a residence! What are these institutions for anyway?

The kids in trouble pads say they're runaways because they couldn't communicate with their parents. Some felt they were being overprotected and weren't allowed or trusted enough to handle responsibility. Others were put up on mommy and daddy's highest paragon-of-virtue pedestal and felt undue guilt when they erred in the slightest way. Others were without family because they were driven from home, abandoned, or the parent or guardian died. Most of the kids know they have sexual hang-ups that caused or compounded their problems. If these problems don't sound severe consider that many of them turn to hard drugs after running away. One youth in the East Village said when he couldn't score junk he would shoot water. Anything to get a spike in his arm. They hated being told by parents, "We know best—I was your age once . . ." As one wise runaway commented about the East Village youth, "His parents were never his age."

A trouble pad provides temporary and crisis counseling to runaways and street kids. It should have a freely structured atmosphere that is conducive to open discussion. A people's room will help. (See "Drug Counseling.") A trouble pad is an alternate family structure where runaways should feel happy and secure with a cooperative group. Programs should be structured around counseling, recreation, and work to enable runaways to work out solutions to their own problems.

An ideal solution would be a residence where people could live for longer periods of time. They could work intensely with each other and the counselors to deal with their problems. Residences could house many diverse services. But a residence would be expensive to run. You face problems of who to admit and for how long. Your own bureaucracy would necessarily be complicated. Just feeding a large number of people is difficult.

Even in a temporary pad, a referral service should be available. Keep on hand phone numbers and addresses of Planned Parenthood offices, clinics that do pregnancy tests, draft, drug, job, and abortion counseling services. Most people come to a trouble pad as refugees. They're not looking for a specific kind of help. Therefore, all counseling services should be available upon request and shouldn't be pushed on runaways.

Since many runaways are minors from the upper middle class, legal hassles may be heavy. In California, where there are large numbers of runaways, a minor is legally emancipated if he or she is away from home longer than twenty-four hours. This means he can receive counseling or medical treatment without parental consent. Organizers might support this type of legislation in other states.

Priorities

We do advocate establishing trouble pads. They can deal with the immediate problems of runaways and may be a good place for political activity. However, the drug situation is totally uncontrolled. Drug abusers may number in the millions. In practice, trouble pads and other service organizations are rendered ineffective because they are forced to deal with large numbers of drug-dependent people who can't get help anywhere else. Drug counseling is the most important service radicals can offer the "orphans" of this country.

4. Storefront Learning Centers

A storefront learning center provides an alternative educational experience for the entire community—the children, their parents, the volunteer "teachers," and the regular public-school teachers. It serves as an adjunct to the public school by providing a tutoring service for students having trouble keeping up with the pace in the classroom; and it offers a true alternative to the authoritarian, overly structured classroom by providing a free environment where the child can create his own learning situation on an individual or small-group level. Here the child learns the subjects of his own choice, at his own speed, by experimenting with everything around him and constructing his own teaching tools. Children are inherently creative and curious and will learn about whatever interests them, given the chance.

There is no distinction between "teacher" and "student." All those in the learning center are free to participate in any project and assume whatever roles they wish. Adults learn from the children, children from the adults. Parents are encouraged to come and learn, too. If one of the center's volunteers wishes to visit a parent, he (she) does so; if parents wish to join in the activity of the center, they are welcome. It is as if the center were the next-door neighbor's home, only more exciting and educational. No formality is observed—people are free to come over and "visit" and "play" whenever they wish.

Setting up a center is a complex operation and the more you try and do, the more complex the problems will be. (See Bibliography–Directory.) If you are not already a part of the community in which you plan to set up the center, you should contact some respected person there—minister, housewife, etc., and work through him or her at first. Organize a small steering committee of those interested and discuss the project with them. It will do you no good to set up a center with service no one wants, no matter how strongly you may feel they "need" them.

Your choice of the building is the first and most important step. Attempt to get a building donated—check for unoccupied buildings owned by the city. Here is a checklist of things to consider:

1) You want a place easily accessible to the neighborhood kids, in a safe block without too much traffic.
2) Try to find a building with large rooms and lots of sunlight. Anything from an apartment to a warehouse or a storefront will do, but with lots of floor space.
3) Research the building codes, and health and safety laws in your city. You can be shut down for a missing fire extinguisher. It's worth a day's work at city hall to make sure you're legal.
4) Also check out liability insurance. Is it necessary? Just

what will it cover? Does your landlord already have it on the building?

5) Make sure the neighbors will tolerate loud noise.
6) Invite the whole community to make the center their own. Clean, paint, build together, have a party to get the place ready.

The next thing to consider is your equipment. Try to get as much as you can free, from individuals, stores, schools, the manufacturers themselves (offer to test out their new toys for them). Ask the children what they want in the center, also. Suggestions:

1) Tables and chairs are good, but you don't need too many. Kids often work better on open floor space—perhaps some mattresses to cushion the floor will be enough. Above all children need room to run around.
2) Have a never-ending supply of paper, paints, crayons, clay, blocks, etc.
3) Science equipment need not be complex, the basics will do —a gerbil, fish tank, plants, magnets, a microscope, etc.
4) Have lots of handicraft tools—sewing and knitting materials, carpentry tools, a pottery wheel.
5) Provide all kinds of games and toys—balls, marbles, cards, board games.
6) Make a mechanical toy from an old typewriter, or a toaster with the plug and cord removed for the kids to take apart and "fix."
7) Collect any old clothes to be used as costumes for dress-up.
8) Start a library of books of all kinds. Maybe the public library will donate some of its old, worn books.

The subject matter you offer for tutoring and the kind of equipment you get will depend on your staff's abilities and your community's desires. It is a good idea to hold a short meeting every week to make suggestions on new equipment, new subject matter to be made available, etc. If you become interested in a new thing, don't be afraid to offer it to the kids before you are an "expert" in it. What better way to learn a new skill than with a few other people who are at the same level of understanding as you are?

The kind of services you provide will determine the hours

you stay open. If you run a preschool you may find the morning best, avoiding the afternoon nap hassles. Otherwise, you may find your service needed nine-to-five every day. If you are only a drop-in center your scheduling can be loose—all you need is staff on hand to keep an eye on the kids.

A drop-in center is the easiest way to start—it requires little scheduling or complex plans. After that you may wish to have more organized activities. For example, plan day trips to parks, museums, etc. Plan for these about a week in advance and encourage the parents to join you. You may wish to schedule special projects, too, like painting a mural on the center's walls. The Store Front Learning Center in Boston, started by Jonathan Kozol, planted a vegetable and flower garden in the lot across the street. This requires a great deal of energy and advanced planning but provides an entirely new experience for most city youngsters, brightens up the neighborhood, and lets the children know the satisfaction of eating food grown with their own hands.

If you plan to function also as an adjunct to the local public school you may need to schedule your time more precisely. Individual tutoring of formal "school" subjects requires that both people show up at the same time and place. The center in Boston has also opened its doors to public-school teachers, in a program where the teacher brings her class over to the center during the school day. It will require a research effort on your part to find out what the principal's feelings are, which teachers to approach, will the school board try to hassle you, how about the kids' parents.

A program of this sort can be very rewarding, because you are not only giving the student a chance to break away, but you are helping his teacher to learn a new form of education and to see the results firsthand with her own class. You may find the teacher very reluctant at first to accept her role as just another "student," but she may come to understand the worth of a nonauthoritarian directorship role. You might also consider holding workshops and study groups for the public-school teachers to discuss your kind of educative experience.

Your main job should be with the children of the community, however. They are very honest—if they don't like you, they won't come back. If this happens, hold a meeting with them and listen seriously to their criticism. Here are some general rules for dealing with the kids:

1) Be a person. Children don't respond to teaching machines.
2) Be honest. If you're angry show it, kids understand, just let them know why.
3) Don't approach the center as work, it's a way of life.
4) Be a child, learn with the kids, don't be above them.

5. Tenants' Unions

Tenants' unions usually begin as primarily defensive organizations to fight rent raises, evictions, and landlord refusal to repair. Out of such struggles they can emerge as effective instruments of political pressure for rent control and building-code enforcement; for community participation in urban planning; even for the organization of such alternatives to landlord housing as cooperatives. A community tenants' union may develop out of the organization of a single apartment house, or of the tenants of a single landlord in many houses, or on a neighborhood basis. Organizing a successful community tenant union demands understanding of inner-city problems and knowledge of the means by which substandard living conditions are perpetuated. It can break down passive acceptance of substandard conditions, provide a substantial base of community power and education, and a feeling of community interdependence. It can create alternative sources, governance procedures, alliance efforts, and funding programs.

As much work as possible should be handled in small-group sessions. It may aid communication and coordination to arrange local groups according to landlord or territory. For militant demonstrations, eviction resistance, and self-protection, the small groups should stick together. Mass meetings can be held to discuss and vote on major policy issues and problems.

Rent strikes are often an excellent way to force response from recalcitrant landlords. To stage a legal rent strike the tenants' group must go through the courts and prove illegal actions by the landlord. The court appoints a receiver for the rents and the money accumulated is spent on property repairs. Illegal rent strikes mean more work in the community than in the courts. Organize door to door, circulating strike pledges and information. Since the courts will rule against you, find legal delays to use during eviction resistance. Despite the hassles, illegal rent strikes can be a source of valuable publicity and put privileged interests on trial.

Legal assistance is necessary to any well-functioning tenants' group. If a lawyer is not part of the group, contact free legal defense projects, law students and professors, or the National Lawyers Guild. Do extensive research on the laws governing landlord-tenant relations, and learn what local ordinances apply to tenant problems. Know what actions you can take against unresponsive landlords. If possible set up a telephone advice center, informing community people of their rights, warning them of landlords to avoid, and referring them to special help. A newsletter is another way to spread this information through the community and keep residents aware of actions by the union.

Research on landlords, politicians, and other local issues serves a vital educational function. Once the group knows the background of landlords, politicians, and relevant government activity it becomes easier to handle issues and decide what course to take. One Boston tenant group, after putting their research together, brought a local slumlord before his temple's rabbinical court, which ordered him to make repairs. When no repairs were made, the tenants initiated a rent strike that finally forced the landlord to sell his buildings to the community cooperative formed by the strikers. A federal grant helped to finance the purchase.

Funds are a prerequisite for any ongoing tenant organization. If a tenant union is successful in gaining funds then it can begin to provide for projects in addition to tenant programs. In distributing funds, care should be taken to avoid waste. Assess who needs what, and what the priority projects are. Initial funding can come from membership contributions, but be prepared to hit churches, federal and local agencies, and student governments. Check around the community— one contact leads to another.

Every community control group should be aware of other organizations in the area. Set up alliances exchanging advice, support, and resources. Consider the possibilities of coordination committees, although different conditions and objectives often mean coalitions should be loose. Any plans for working together with different interest groups must evolve from understanding of their problems and position, and respect for their programs.

Community control efforts are long-range propositions. If time is short, don't plan for action more complicated than rent strikes against specific landlords, and collective bargaining programs. If you are aiming for rent control or community cooperative housing, plan for a long-term commitment and a lot of hard work.

6. Organizing Economic Alternatives

At present, consumer protection is band-aid help for a massive social hemorrhage. The political analysis in most existing consumer protection groups is weak or nonexistent. Ralph Nader and other lesser-knowns have pioneered the field and are involved with large existing operations. Organizing radical caucuses within these existing organizations may be a better tactic than initiating new organizations because of the difficult and voluminous technical material to deal with.

Cooperatives in various forms may eliminate many of the problems consumer protection groups are trying to solve by offering alternate methods for consumption. They could serve as transitional institutions that could help a mass movement fundamentally change the existing capitalist economy to a Socialist one.

Consumer Protection Groups

Community action organizations and other local service groups are good starting places in looking for members. Since most consumer protection material is technical, good resource information and people are also needed. They can be recruited from Legal Aid offices, consumer protection departments in the attorney general's office, law schools (both professors and students), and libraries. Larger businesses may loan executives as a public-relations gesture. Their expertise will help, but remember their biases. The group members' personal buying experiences are also valuable.

One consumer group set the following outline for its goals:

1. To discuss the types of problems confronting the consumer. To educate each other to recognize the pitfalls. To point out that we all are vulnerable.

2. To frame suggestions and make demands on business and government.

3. To learn to use the methods and remedies now available to full advantage.

4. To develop a set of resources for the consumer's help and information.

The majority of consumer problems occur in relatively few classifications. Some of the most common:

Bait Advertising—the ad describes a product at a very reasonable price but when you go to buy it the product is not available, or the salesman degrades it and tries to sell you a higher-priced item.

Guarantees and Warranties—where the consumer by signing a contract has fewer rights than he would under the uniform commercial code without signing; or where the guarantee is not specific as to the customer's and seller's rights and responsibilities.

Mail Fraud—where the consumer may pay for items in response to a direct mail ad and never receive the merchandise or a refund; or where a chain letter is used to elicit money from the consumer.

Rebuilt Goods—where used or reconditioned merchandise or parts are sold as new material and at the same price as new material.

Packaging, Labeling, and Pricing Problems—where it is very difficult for the consumer to determine the most economical purchase because of (1) excessive air space in the package, (2) confusing fractional weights, (3) selling products by weight that are consumed by volume or vice versa, (4) keeping package size and price constant while the net contents are being reduced.

Referral Selling—where you buy an expensive item or contract for home repairs with the understanding the cost will be reduced by using your item as a demonstrator. You will receive a fee for each sale prompted by your demonstration. Usually your whole neighborhood is flooded so you can't get any referral sales.

Unordered Merchandise—merchandise is sent to your home without your asking for it. Then a bill is sent for it and they expect you to pay. Sometimes even threatening letters or collectors arrive.

Credit Sales or Installment Lending—where the buyer isn't aware of extra charges such as finance charges, length of time to run and payment size, and any liens or chattel mortgages giving the seller rights to the merchandise that the consumer bought.

Collection of Debts—where the consumer may not understand what is expected of him, or how to reach an agreement with the lender, or what constitutes harsh or unreasonable collection practices or illegal harassment.

Repossession and Resale—of items purchased under the sales contracts and defaulted on. Where the consumer doesn't know how to avoid extra costs, his right to redeem the merchandise or his right to require the sale of the merchandise with the money of the sale applied to his debt, or that he must be notified if a sale is to take place on his merchandise.

Third-Party Problems—involving the buyer, the seller, and the finance company or bank.

Unconscionable and Adhesion Contract—where the consumer has made a bargain that no person in his right mind could make, or any fair or honest man would accept. Contracts that are one-sided, take-it-or-leave-it, or that are agreements to make agreements and provide for excessive damages, or that are standard form contracts may be considered unconscionable.

These consumer problems are covered in some of the books listed in the Bibliography–Directory or under "Consumer" and/or "Consumer Protection" in most local libraries.

Help for Consumers
Better Business Bureau; Legal Aid—Lawyers Referral

Service—Bar Association; labor unions. State agencies: attorney general; Commission of Insurance; banks; Department of Public Utilities; Weights and Measures; Consumer Affairs Bureau. Federal agencies: Federal Housing Agency; Veterans Administration; credit unions; family service agencies; Federal Trade Commission; postal authorities—postal fraud; Food and Drug Administration; United States Department of Agriculture; President's Committee on Consumer Interests.

Organizing Economic Alternatives

The capitalist system is not geared to meeting many of the people's needs. Blacks, Puerto Ricans, poor whites, inner-city dwellers, and minority groups in general feel the lack of services more acutely than other classes in the society. Generally, the movement's response to their economic deprivation has been to make demands upon the establishment for higher welfare payments, more jobs, technical training, and better education to get more jobs, etc. These demands are politically sound and must be a focal point of our efforts to build a mass movement. However, an alternative suggestion is to provide in a more direct manner the commodities that the vast majority of inner-city dwellers need.

There are four methods for organizing economic alternatives we will discuss here: buying clubs, cooperatives, credit unions, and direct charge cooperatives. They are all based on the premise that it is advisable and possible for low-income people to solve their own economic problems with their purchasing power collectively. Organizers participating in these programs are faced with two initial problems. 1. Since cooperatives are mass-based organizations the membership may come from numerous socioeconomic groups. It is generally easier to organize cooperatives from people of the same class background, because their product needs should be similar, and relationships are natural and cordial. 2. The organizer's immediate peer group may be different from those people's whom he intends to organize. There may be an element of suspicion when a young person tries to organize older people into cooperatives, but we can all define ourselves as consumers, which is our common denominator in this situation.

Cooperatives can be a functional model for an improved economic system. We are striving to abolish the exploitation of workers and transform ourselves to free and independent human beings. We must function without profit, middlemen, and corruption. Products must be distributed according to need—i.e., useful products. It is not necessary to produce, distribute, and sell twenty-seven kinds of hair spray and not have enough productive facilities remaining to supply cheap food, mass transit, etc. People should have food just because they need it to survive. We will not engage in distributing products for conspicuous consumption.

Buying Clubs

The first aim of a buying club is to act as a method of organizing consumers toward the goal of a community cooperative organization. Buying clubs should start as small organizations. Six-member clubs seem to work well. The final size of the club is discretionary, but don't enlarge too fast.

Build strong and slowly. Talk to each other about yourselves, your needs for a buying club, actual possible savings and future projections. Responsibility should be taken by club members for recruiting new members, taking orders, collecting money, supervising distribution of goods and purchases, keeping records and distribution of educational materials. Everyone should understand fully as much of the operation of the club as possible. Two people should be assigned to each task. Rotate all responsibilities, and arrange the rotation so that an experienced person and a novice are working in the same area, allowing for a continuous, smooth operation. The knowledgeable group will have better brainstorming sessions and less boring meetings. The more versatile individual members are, the more cohesive the group. Keep away from specialization and hierarchy which alienates people from the product, themselves, and their brothers and sisters in the cooperative and in the movement.

Choosing good products to work with requires careful research and analysis. Good produce stock includes perishables like eggs, as they are in good demand with big savings possibilities.

Single product distribution will facilitate solving early mechanical problems you may encounter: bookkeeping, money collection, analysis of the market, distribution, etc. A buying club with a single product distribution can demonstrate effectively the value of cooperative buying and working together. If this vital lesson is missed and confidence in the club is lacking, future actions will be abortive. The product analysis should be oriented to a mass buying situation. For instance, it may be known that in a low-income project of 10,000 residents the consumption of eggs is, on the average, about one egg per person every other day. This would result in a demand of 5,000 eggs or 416 dozen per day. In the average week, over 2,900 dozen eggs are consumed. For any product the consumption rate, i.e., the number of people who need it in a given area, market price, and your price must be known in advance.

Other questions to be answered: Is the product easily transportable? If not, can you transport it anyway? Can you buy the product cheaply enough to undersell the chains?

Front money or operating capital is obviously necessary for the successful functioning of the buying club. Stay away from banks and all other means of private financing. If the club is to work, front money must be obtained by taking cash with the order from the member and using the combined cash to buy for a known demand. Since trust is involved, members must decide what is an appropriate time between when they turn over their money to the buyers and when the product is delivered. Two or three days generally is sufficient.

Don't count on developing credit where you are buying the merchandise. It may actually hamper the group later when it expands and larger orders are made. Your creditors will probably again demand cash which would put stress and undue turmoil on the group. Cash on the line is crucial.

A first task for the club (before negotiating with wholesalers) is to survey local stores. Find the best dealer for several potential products and buy collectively from him. Don't forget to celebrate. Maybe you can eat what you get, together.

Warning: The danger in buying clubs is that they can dead-end with no further programs developing. A buying club is not an end in itself.

Cooperatives

A cooperative is a buying club of buying clubs. The purpose of a cooperative is to act as:

1. a central purchasing agent.
2. a wholesaler for the buying clubs.
3. a distributor of education materials to the members of the buying clubs.
4. a central bookkeeper-agent through which excess capital is accumulated.

Each buying club elects voting representatives to cooperative meetings. New representatives should be elected periodically. An alternative is mass meetings with all members of a buying club having voting rights.

Cooperative operations require storage space. Empty warehouses or storefronts (depending on location) sometimes can be a steal. A lease as long-term as possible is recommended. Once you are successful, landlords tend toward greed. High rents could force you out of the community entirely, as all landlords will try to jack you up. In addition to standard office equipment, the operation may require adding machines, cash registers, and a safe. If possible, buy officeware with cash; if not, buy on time. Avoid renting equipment. It will be a continual overhead, eating into your pocket. To maximize savings, be flexible and experiment with new methods of buying and selling, handling money, ordering and stocking. Systematically investigate all the wholesalers in the area. Their location, prices, and political attitudes should be considered.

A coop can be conducive to bringing people together for community and political action, as well as for economic savings. An effective community cooperative serves as a focus for those organizing the community around larger issues. A strong cooperative can be instrumental in forming community identity and consciousness.

How much to mark up the goods over the price paid by a coop requires in-depth analysis. Too many cooperatives envision themselves as miracle stores that sell at lower prices. Coops do sell products at lower prices, but they will go out of business if they cannot cover their own overhead. Coops which fail through "success" become community versions of capitalist discount stores.

Credit Unions

A small markup coupled with a high volume allows the accumulation of relatively large amounts of capital which can be put in a credit union, established to handle the individual and group finances of the members. All transactions should be recorded in the books of the central cooperative.

The accumulated capital can be used to help finance the introduction of new products, community-owned and -operated businesses. A credit union can also facilitate working back into production, distribution, and ownership by the people of basic resources, and owning and controlling the retail facilities necessary to get the goods and services to the people.

Direct Charge Coops

A direct charge coop is a store where everything is sold at cost. A nominal membership fee of five or ten dollars is standard. Overhead and improvement costs are calculated for a three-month period. The members each pay an equal amount to the coop to cover these costs. Grocery stores of this type have sold twice as much food as retail outlets with equivalent floor space.

7. Altering the Environment

One of the fundamentals of the American system has always been the idea that the right to make a living is sacred. As long as you don't infringe on anyone else's life, liberty, or property, you can make money in any way you see fit. The natural resources of our country are legally there for the taking. And the pioneer myth of man against the wilderness has given an aura of God-given right and even moral duty to our careless use and outright plunder of the land.

The question of ecology, carried to its logical conclusions, brings the entire American system into question and raises doubts about principles which have always been accepted as good by everyone. The economic practices of big business obviously cannot continue if we are to survive. The implications of the ecology action movement are as radical as any "political" movement going. In fact, environmental crisis is perhaps the best issue through which to educate many people. It is clear that the present system has gotten us into this mess. It is clear that the problem is critical and must be dealt with. And it is a problem which can be attacked on many different levels by everyone, from housewife to businessman to politician to farmer. Everyone is affected and everyone knows it.

Action by Organizations

Ecology action organizations should provide the following services to the community: a regularly distributed newsletter on what has to be done and what has been done; grievances and discussion meetings and community projects. Scout troops, women's clubs, school groups, etc., are good places to plant suggestions for projects.

Within the organization itself, utilize a storefront office as a place from which to (1) publish research; (2) keep a file on local polluters; (3) document the legislative records of local congressmen and representatives to see if they match recent eco-rhetoric; (4) publicize an environmental hot line which gives the phone numbers of government agencies in your area to contact about instances of pollution; (5) lobby for legislation banning the internal-combustion engine and funding good efficient mass transportation; (6) start an ecology food store which specializes in organic food, returnable containers, and minimal packaging; (7) in conjunction with the food store, establish an ecology counseling service which develops with people ways to run an ecologically sound household; (8) send out speakers, movies, and literature; (9) distribute birth-control information and devices (check the legality so you know the situation). Demand that abortions and birth-control devices be provided free; (10) organize boycotts against local or national firms which insist on operating without regard to the environment; (11) send out guerrilla theater groups to hold mock funerals for rivers and other dying resources or hold parades for clean air complete with balloons, gas masks, drums, and coughing participants; (12) initiate campaigns to return all bottles, cans, and excess packaging to stores. Ask that it all be sent back to the manufacturer; (13) watch over, and fight when appropriate, "urban renewal" zoning, highway and airport projects, university and corporate expansion into surrounding neighborhoods; (14) set up "people's parks" in abandoned lots; conduct neighborhood cleanups (with community consent and participation).

If you need money, raise it in appropriate ways: with ecology fairs and parades, bicycle repairs and organic food sales, and the like.

Personal Ecology Actions: A Few Suggestions

Don't use nonbiodegradable detergents—use baking soda mixed with soap flakes, or commercial biodegradable detergents.

Don't use paper and plastic things—use real dishes, cloth towels, handkerchiefs, etc.

Don't use too much heat—it's bad for your health, and

you're using up one of our most precious natural resources. If you're chilly, put on a sweater.

Don't use too much water—wash two loads of clothes in the same water, put a brick in the toilet tank, shower less often, or with a friend, and take showers, *not* baths.

Don't use too much electricity—turn off all lights not in use, dry clothes on a line, use no electrical gadgets.

Don't use your car every time you go out—buy a bicycle for health and thrift.

Don't throw out nonreturnable, nonbiodegradable containers—recycle them as storage jars, flowerpots, mixing containers, etc.

Don't eat crap food—learn to grow your own in gardens, bowls, pots, windowsills, and under ultraviolet light.

Stop smoking—make a personal commitment to stop polluting your own body and the air.

Learn how to fix any mechanical equipment you depend on, and share your technological skills with others. Don't let the machine rule you.

Limit your family. If you want children, adopt.

These are just a few possibilities. One of the important things about the ecology movement is that people are going to have to change their basic life-styles, economic as well as social. Cooperation rather than competition must be stressed. With a move toward new life-styles, creative action is unlimited.

Back to the Land

Some groups are looking to rural communes as a solution to the life-style, political, and ecological problems. If yours is one of them, a couple of cautionary notes may save a few years of frustrating failure.

1. Farming is tough, underpaid, skilled work: don't do it unless you have people with some practical skills (or money) that can support your group during your trials.

2. Farming beyond subsistence level needs a big investment, e.g., $250,000 for equipment.

3. Don't go experimenting with the environment; you may mess up that and even worse. Consult your local farmers and USDA officials for some advice and recommendations.

4. Remember you can't create reality outside of reality. Nor can you expect to recreate the past.

Perhaps the best advice is to start small, e.g., gardens

plus a few animals you know how to take care of—say chickens and one cow. Talk with your local vets and get all the USDA publications on any farming extensions you plan. A good contribution your rural commune can make is put people up while they are resting from city actions. Be serious; don't bother to buy semi-desert, steep hills, or ruined land. Even with fairly good land, it takes skill, talent, and experience to improve the soil. Ignorance will mean a hungry couple of years.

V. Taking Action

1. Strategy and Tactics

Organizations live on action and die in committee. Campaigns are not only the mechanisms for obtaining issue-oriented goals, they are the very lifeblood of a movement—the very essence of political education.

The better a campaign is mounted, the greater the lessons to be drawn. If you enter into a campaign blindly, your eyes may remain closed to the wisdom which can come from the experience. The campaign must be organized not merely to maximize success and minimize failure, but even more importantly, to provide a frame within which the very crucial lessons can be seen clearly.

Since the course of every campaign depends on a number of variables—issues, targets and their vulnerability, the degree of your group's organization, the political climate, financial resources, mass support, etc.—no one scheme for organizing a campaign can fit all possibilities. The plan presented here is designed primarily to be used with the small-group organizing scenario presented in the first chapter of this book.

Realistically, most campaigns won't start with a group of experienced organizers. For our purposes we will assume that one organizer has formed a small group of relatively inexperienced people and that they will wage the campaign. These people will have to concentrate on their own self-education as well as on the campaign. In order to recruit other small groups, they will have to rely heavily on calling for actions which get people involved, since their organizing skills are still underdeveloped.

Issues

Issues make themselves: they arise out of contradictions and oppression which are always present, and must only be chosen. Once your small group has sounded out the community, the criteria for picking the issues and demands should be:

1. How well do they relate to the community's most pressing problems?

2. How can they be used to expand general political consciousness?

3. How easily do they lend themselves to the development of other issues?

4. How knowledgeable is your group in the area in which the issue is classified?

Do not try to build support around an abstract theme. Pick clear, obvious issues; and always look at the issues in light of a long-range movement for radical change.

The Manifesto

The manifesto is a brief statement of your group's views and an explanation of your political analysis, your policies, goals, and intentions. A manifesto fixes the issues in the organizer's mind and forces everyone to deal with concrete arguments rather than generalities. During the drafting of the document, everyone should brainstorm the political arguments, pro and con, that will be the central issues of the campaign. Anticipating the arguments will enable everyone to debate the issues more effectively. The manifesto should be published or reproduced and sold or given away at political tables, at demonstrations, and at all actions. Organizers should have copies with them at all times to give to people.

Starting a Campaign

To start a campaign, call a public meeting and present the demands and goals in your manifesto. If you can induce the press to come, give them a prepared statement of the demands. Otherwise your demands will have to be given directly to your opposition (if they attend your rally), or to people who will take it to them.

Timing is essential to both starting and continuing a campaign. Your campaign must build momentum if it is to be successful. If you plan to involve street or community people, start when the weather is conducive to outside activities. Or start when a regularly scheduled event will naturally focus concern on your campaign, e.g., a month before elections, but watch out for cooptation. Of course, don't hesitate to press forward if nothing is going on and there are people who seem willing to participate.

The campaign should be both goal-oriented and educational for both participants and observers. Your strategy should allow for continuous actions generating publicity and/or discussion: street distribution of informative leaflets, door-to-door canvassing, etc.

You must also arrange your tactics in a time sequence for maximum effect. Do not schedule a mass demonstration to open a campaign, since chances are it will fulfill everyone's need for action at one time and it will be difficult to get people back to work again. One big rally can turn into a funeral service for a movement if everyone goes home drained of his enthusiasm. Start with small actions which relate directly to the issue and the opposition. Early direct confrontation will raise campaign fervor and zeal.

Throughout your campaign test cases for readily attainable goals should be continued simultaneously with more long-range efforts. These will give your people something to do while the lengthy operations jell, keep morale up, and serve for agitprop.

Test Cases and Tactical Decisions

Under usual conditions the selection of test cases is the basic strategic problem in carrying out a campaign. An initial test case should be directed at an easily attainable goal, and perhaps at only one segment of the target structure. Formulate a demand which you pretty much know will be agreed to when pressure is applied. For example, in a campaign against U.S. militarism and imperialism, the first test case demand at a university might be keeping military recruiters off campus. The action you take in such a test case will depend on the particular circumstances. You might try a simple presentation of your demand by a group of students, leafleting, informative picketing, or symbolic actions. If your university administration is as repressive as most, you would probably go on to use such tactics as a rally, obstructive picketing, or a sit-in. The propaganda aspect of your actions should be given great attention since you will need more support when you escalate your demands.

A successful first test case, handled properly with regard to the issues and people involved, should boost the morale of your group, attract new sympathizers, and help in the organizations of new small groups and campaigns. It may also cause division in the ranks of your opposition and make the contradictions in their position clear. If your first test case fails or if you think you are still too weak to go on to a higher level of the campaign, then consider another test case with an easily attainable goal. Of course, the possibility that rapid escalation of the struggle will be more effective in building an enthusiastic campaign must be taken into account; it is sometimes worth sacrificing careful, gradual development to dramatic effect.

The secondary (long-range, difficult) test case requires greater commitment and a greater base of support. It will be more crucial in terms of basic political principle and will probably involve a nonnegotiable demand. Much is at stake so actions must be carefully chosen. If you employ a sit-in, for example, make sure that your sit-in cannot be ignored, since an unsuccessful sit-in may require escape, and escape may require concession. In the case of a fast you may be forced to compromise or starve to death.

Carrying our previous model campaign further, a secondary test case might be a demand for the abolition of ROTC. Your movement should be stronger by this time because of successful agitprop and previous test cases. At this stage of the campaign you should do things like staging rallies and marches, large-scale picketing, sit-ins, strikes, and boycotts. (See following section, "Some Actions.") Present your demands from a position of real or apparent strength.

If your secondary test case fails, despair and disappointment may move in and you may lose some support and morale. A good small-group structure, however, should help a great deal to overcome such setbacks. Try to rebuild a stronger movement around new test cases, or retry the old test case.

If your more difficult test case is successful (make sure you give it enough *time* to become successful—maybe even several months), then you can move on to work for other long-range goals and launch new and more difficult campaigns. Prepare a new manifesto if you have to. You may move vertically to stronger, more crucial demands or horizontally to more extensive campaigns aimed at other segments of the structure under attack.

For example, you might demand an end to university war research or you might move into the communities surrounding the campus and work for draft resistance and GI rights.

Remember, a bulldozer can knock down a brick wall. But, if you don't have a bulldozer or the ability to run one then the best way to tear down the wall is brick by brick. A successful test case is one brick removed from the wall of the status quo. An unsuccessful test case teaches you a more effective way to remove bricks. Either way you can't lose. If you are lucky and a little smart you might take out just the right bricks to tumble that wall.

Making Demands and Negotiating

As your group begins to implement your manifesto, you will increasingly find yourself engaged in formulating and negotiating demands. This process is of prime importance, not only for wringing such concessions as you can out of the establishment, but also for developing consciousness and solidarity. What demands you will make, to whom you will present them, are questions that can be answered only in terms of your actual situation.

In making demands you should recognize ahead of time that you may have to compromise, so ask for double what you want. Be sure the group and its supporters recognize this, so that they will estimate the victory correctly if you come off with half. The process of drawing up the demands, electing spokesmen, hearing reports of the negotiators, and accepting or rejecting the terms is one that should involve an ever-widening circle of people, even though it begins with a small group.

Nonnegotiable demands are those which involve political principles upon which there can be no compromise, e.g., ridding the campus of ROTC, freedom to demonstrate. They are raised not to win some crumb from the bureaucracy, but to challenge the whole system of rule that the bureaucracy serves. They are nonetheless demands that you seriously organize to win and that can be won as masses of people make them their own. A nonnegotiable demand should be centered upon an issue that strikes at the heart of the power structure. Its full implications must be clear so that everyone understands why it cannot be compromised and why it will probably be met with hysterical opposition.

With negotiable demands, the *appearance* of strength is as important as actual strength. Nonnegotiable demands are more of an all-or-nothing affair. If your first action (say a two-hour sit-in) doesn't work, you will constantly have to escalate the actions until the opposition capitulates. Since the actions may become heavy when fighting for nonnegotiable demands, the politics *must* be up front. The organizer shouldn't manipulate the constituency by calling for high-risk actions (e.g., a militant picket line) when the people aren't aware of the implications.

Below are some suggestions and points to remember in making demands and negotiating:

1. Be sure of your demands. Research them thoroughly and try to come up with the best possible statement of what you want. If necessary, ask for preliminary negotiations in order to determine how your demands should be stated and presented. Make sure these early negotiations are well publicized. Anticipate your opponent's arguments and be prepared to meet and counter them. Never accept any information from your opponent without verification. Try never to have to accept information from your opponent.

2. Refuse to negotiate with any individual or group that does not have the power to accede to your demands. Don't accept "lower-level" negotiations.

3. Find out about the people you will be negotiating with. Prepare a file on these negotiators. Get information from both their friends and enemies.

4. Try to negotiate on your own turf. Otherwise, settle for neutral territory. Sometimes flooding your opponent's waiting room or office with your people offsets meeting on his ground. Be careful he doesn't think it is a sit-in, unless you think it might be or ought to be.

5. Bring as many people as you can to the negotiations. Try to make sure that some of your people are strangers to your opponents, as this will tend to make the other side uneasy.

6. Be cynical and skeptical. Don't be fooled by opponents who are "nice."

7. Stick to the demands you are presenting. Other negotiations may be set up later for other issues.

8. Ask for more than you want, so that you can show flexibility and reasonableness by apparent compromise. By the same token, you can have part of your delegation escalate demands so that *you* look reasonable in contrast and can lead the opposition down a primrose path.

9. Watch out for attempts to divide and conquer your delegation. Don't hesitate to divide and conquer the opposition, especially if you sense some sympathizers on their side.

10. Form your delegation with people of different personality and appearance. Confuse the opposition: have your freaks talk straight and your straights talk freaky.

11. If you see people are getting into a bind, call a recess and discuss the situation with your delegation.

12. Never negotiate for time-consuming "committees," "commissions," or "appropriate channels."

13. If you are winning, allow your opponent to save face.

14. If your opponents are using negotiations to grind you down, do zaps. Start continuous free substitution for "sick" negotiators and make them feel like they are negotiating with a parade, or put out a leaflet saying that you offered to negotiate for the whole world, but your opponents were unreasonable and refused to negotiate.

Attitude

Every power structure worth its salt has built-in mechanisms to oppose change. Anyone who desires change must mount defenses against these repressive mechanisms. But there is a danger that defense may become mere reaction. When a campaign is based primarily on reaction it can be controlled by the forces you oppose. They will come to know exactly how you will respond to their tactics, and therefore are in a position to make you do exactly what they want you to do. If you have a campaign based on issues and analysis, stick to it. Don't do anything which may subvert your well-thought-out goals. The best defense is a good offense.

Relating to a Larger Movement

While you are waging the campaign you can't be insensitive to what's going on elsewhere. Events like Kent State and the invasion of Cambodia may preempt your program. If your campaign is based on a broad radical critique of society, it should be easy to show solidarity with your brothers and sisters around the country.

You may want to go further and change the nature of the campaign to deal with pressing national problems, coordinating with a nationwide effort. You might add national demands to your own or revise the manifesto to include new goals and issues. Guest speakers from around the country could be invited to talk on national issues. A general exchange of ideas with the rest of the country breaks down the feeling of the isolated community. People will be more dedicated if they are part of a large strong movement.

2. Some Actions

a. Marches and Rallies

Marches and rallies are mass actions involving relatively large numbers of people. Because of their size, these actions should be extensively planned in advance. The large mobilization rallies require long-range, full-time planning. Information about such mass demonstrations is not within the scope of this book. Smaller-scale marches and rallies (100 to 5,000 people) can and will be used by organizers who have built a small-group movement and are ready for mass action.

Preparation

Once you have decided to hold a march or rally you must determine where to hold it. Choose locations for a rally, or for the starting and terminal points of a march, which are well known, easily found, and easily reached by car or public transportation. Estimate the number of people you want or expect to attend and choose your location accordingly. If you arrange for a small place for your rally and get a large number of people you will have the problem of overcrowding; if the area is too large your crowd will seem small or "swallowed up." This also holds true for a march. Don't schedule a small-scale march on a boulevard or a large march on a small street. However, if you expect the police to act against you, give yourself room to get away.

Make absolutely sure well in advance of your action that you can use the area. You do not want an aborted action which will leave potential supporters underwhelmed with your effectiveness.

Make sure you will have the necessary materials ready. Platforms, sound equipment, banners, leaflets, etc., should be ready and checked. Speakers should be firmly committed and standby speakers should be ready in the event the unexpected happens.

Arrange marches and rallies according to a schedule and try to stick to it. Balance the scheduling of a march between considerations of maximum effect and the distance which people can reasonably be expected to march. Make sure you know just about how long it will take your groups to cover their march distances so that a rally planned for the end of the march will come off on time.

Prepare contingency scenarios for your demonstrations in the event of inclement weather, under- or overestimated crowd, police actions, counterdemonstrations, etc. Brainstorm such eventualities and possible alternate plans.

Arrange for refreshment for people who come to the action, if necessary or if possible. Chances are that your action will not be large enough to require provision of sanitary equipment, food, extensive transportation arrangements, or communication hookups. However, if you expect a very large crowd, are planning a lengthy program, or if your action is being held a considerable distance from where the participants live or away from available facilities, these things should be considered. A relatively extensive communications system should be arranged for marches, especially if they are to be large and long.

In many instances it is necessary to obtain a permit to hold a public gathering from the town or city clerk or the agency which has jurisdiction over the place where you hope to stage your actions. Sometimes a police permit is required. Different municipalities have different rules governing the requirements for assembling groups of various size. Permits are not necessary for sidewalk demonstrations. Singing, chanting, and stopping of traffic on side streets do not make a march a breach of the peace. However, a street march is much harder to defend legally without a permit. It may violate parade or traffic ordinances. If a parade permit has been refused, and the march is peaceful, it is probably not disorderly conduct. Unfortunately the snarled traffic which results from your taking to the streets probably will result in a confrontation with the police.

Make copies of the necessary permits or the local ordinance permitting you to hold your event. Members or marshals of the sponsoring organization should have these ready to show police who may attempt to stop the action on the notion that it is an illegal gathering.

If the local power structure is especially reactionary or oppressive, it may not be politically wise to recognize the legitimacy of their rule by requesting their permission to gather. In such cases, your strength in numbers and sheer determination will hopefully suffice in lieu of a permit. But expect trouble.

In all mass actions the convenience of the people should be considered. If you rally on the sidewalk, leave a space open for pedestrians. If you march, be sure to leave enough room for traffic, even if you have a parade permit. Inconveniencing a tired worker trying to get home from work can only result in his alienation from your movement.

It is imperative to have sympathetic lawyers or law students on hand as legal observers to offer immediate legal advice and act as expert eyewitnesses in court. Photographers should also be present to record police brutality for the media and for legal actions.

If the political scene in your area is extremely volatile, or if you have the slightest premonition of violence, bring medically equipped personnel. Expect the worst, no matter what your politics or tactics may be.

Designate articulate and knowledgeable members of your group to leaflet and rap with individuals in the vicinity of the demonstration. Your main purpose in holding a demonstration is educational. Let people know what is going on and why.

Crowd Control

In order to prevent a demonstration of any size from turning into a mob scene it is necessary to formulate some method of crowd control. Coordination between demonstration participants also functions to give your demonstration a degree of togetherness, thus enhancing its image in the media and effect on bystanders. If violence should erupt, street organization will permit you to act promptly in line with your politics and the tactical circumstances.

At this stage in the political struggle, two basic and somewhat opposed methods have evolved which permit coordination of demonstration participants: the marshal system and affinity groups.

The marshal system enables the sponsoring group to have a degree of centralized control over its demonstration. This system is objectionable to many movement people, who feel that marshals will inevitably force politics on demonstration participants by way of limited tactical alternatives. Small-scale demonstrations are usually easily managed and coordinated and so marshals will probably only be used to any great extent in emergency situations. In all cases, marshals should be trained in the arts of nonviolence. They should be briefed on all the information that anyone involved in the action may need.

The anticipated size and character of the demonstration largely determines the number and nature of marshals trained and their dress. At large mobilization-type rallies marshals should look quasi-official—if for no other reason than to make them recognizable. But at modest-size demonstrations marshals should appear unauthoritarian and unofficial so as not to look like "minicops" or "peace pigs."

Marshals are more useful in marches than at rallies, since marches require more extensive coordination. They are needed in proportion to the size of the crowd, the duration of the event, the size of the territory to be covered, the degree of militancy of the crowd, and the likelihood of confrontation with the authorities.

Recruit marshals from all sectors of people expected to attend. They should reflect a cross section of expected participants. Blacks and women are particularly successful as marshals. Most demonstrators hesitate to bait black marshals or exhibit male chauvinist arrogance.

Affinity groups are to many people's minds both safer and more politically acceptable than the marshal system for organizing participants at a demonstration. The function of the affinity group is to deal with any anticipated problems with people coming and the pigs.

Affinity groups consist of four to six people who have met prior to the demonstration and plan to "run together" in the demonstration itself. The entire demonstration does not have to be broken down into affinity groups. Enough affinity groups should be formed to provide a visible example of order in planned actions and in emergency situations.

The group should discuss what it plans to do at the demonstration, keeping in mind all eventualities. Affinity groups usually attempt to maintain cohesiveness by not attempting to do more than any one member of the group is willing to do. The person who assumes leadership of an affinity group must be one who is trusted by all group members so that he can direct them easily and quickly in emergencies.

Marshals usually prove to be less politically useful than affinity groups. Because they are authorized to keep a demonstration to a plan, marshals tend to become authoritarian and inhibit spontaneity. This reduces the political impact of a demonstration. Affinity groups, on the other hand, because of their decentralization tend to allow greater spontaneity while still keeping the demonstration orderly. Affinity groups also provide greater tactical flexibility in responding to violent situations. Direction is more externally applied by marshals, while affinity groups, if formed correctly, tend to move in collective cooperation.

Violence and Trashing

Unplanned violence may have several sources. Paid police provocateurs can initiate and encourage destructive tactics to give repressive forces an opportunity to destroy your movement or knock in a few heads. They are dangerous because they try to encourage others to join in the violence and are often successful. "Plate-glass revolutionaries" come to your demonstration to act out their fantasies and release pent-up frustrations, or because they believe that their tactics are politically desirable, because increasing pig repression will effectively radicalize the movement and the rest of the society. Normally peaceful members of your group may be pushed into violent reaction by an overt, unprovoked, violent action against a few trashers.

Regardless of who initiates violence, if it is not widespread at first it will become so. Those who are to keep order must act quickly. Marshals and affinity groups deal with violent situations in slightly different ways.

The first thing a marshal must remember in talking a crowd into leaving the vicinity of the approaching violence is that people don't like having orders shouted at them. A short comment on the political irrelevancy of the violence coupled with a statement that the crowd is merely participating in the "ego trip" of a trasher can be effective. This should be complemented with physically cordoning off those engaged in violent action and gently moving back the crowd. Help others to remain cool and to leave quickly.

Affinity groups function by just moving away from violent action themselves. If enough people start to leave then others will follow. If the crowd is composed of affinity groups, or at least interspersed with them, then their obvious movement away will encourage everyone else, except the provocateurs, to do likewise.

A violent joy seeker can sometimes be discouraged by confronting him with his purpose. Go up to him and ask: "Are you a brother or a pig?" If he says, "Fuck off!" do so; you'll never get anywhere. If he says he is not a pig ask him why he is acting like one. If you break the spell of violence and get him to respond, he may calm down. If he doesn't, give up and try to get the crowd away.

In the thirty seconds it takes to commit violence, no one can determine the motives or political position of those doing the act. Provocateurs, militant trashers, and joy seekers all throw rocks. All are to be considered enemies if they are performing an act which is counter to the goals of your group.

b. Pickets

The fights of the trade unions have established picketing as a most effective tactic for a wide variety of situations.

Picketing is generally considered to be an exercise of free speech. You should check local laws, but in most cases no permits are required.

Regardless of the type of picket line, or your purpose in setting one up, there are some general rules to follow:

1. You should keep moving; it is required by law. It makes your line look better and less sloppy, and enables you to keep your ranks closed.

2. If you picket all day, try to have enough people to organize second and third shifts for the relief of tired walkers. This is also important if you expect arrest, since you will have a second group to take the place of the arrested.

3. If you picket in the winter, early in the morning, or for long periods of time you should set up a coffee kitchen.

4. You should have songs or chants to sing on the line. This keeps you from getting bored, and the rhythm helps keep the line neat.

5. You should not block all of the sidewalk. Make an elongated ellipse, or just have one line which goes back and forth.

6. You should carry signs or wear sandwich boards in order to inform passersby of the reason for your picket. It is advisable to mount your signs on cardboard tubes, because if you use a wooden stick, you may be busted for carrying a weapon. Of course if you feel you will need the stick, use it; if not, avoid the possible bust. Sandwich boards are good because they leave your arms and hands free.

7. You may wish to leaflet while picketing. Have leafleters stand separate from the line, so they can stop and talk while they hand out leaflets without jamming up the line or stopping it.

Informative picketing is done with leafleting and highly visible signs. A boycott picket can be informative. The picket line is set up at a store, factory, office, etc., to make people aware that a certain product, manufacturer, service, etc., is being boycotted because of a labor dispute, pollution, war complicity, etc. Signs and leaflets should clearly state the issue involved and the details of the boycott.

Obstructive pickets are militant. They are designed to keep people from passing, by force if necessary. In labor struggles, obstructive picket lines are used to keep scabs out of factories. They are also used in war protest to disrupt the movement of military men or material. Of course, obstructive pickets are illegal, so you better expect to get busted if you try one.

Political picketing may be informative or obstructive. A baby-carriage line in front of a welfare office and marchers in front of a fascist foreign embassy are examples of political pickets. These pickets are primarily symbolic and thus, informative. The antiwar picket cited above is an example of an obstructive political picket.

A *counterpicket* is used against the pickets of groups you oppose. If a "patriotic" veterans' group is picketing in favor of extending the Indochina war, then you may want to organize a picket to picket them. Make sure the degree of commitment is high among your picketeers, because a counterpicket is one of the best ways to provoke a fistfight.

Picket lines can also be used as a defense measure. If you are holding a vigil or sit-in on the street, and the police are approaching to hassle you, spontaneously regroup, form a line, take out signs from under your coats, and start to march. They can't bust you for unlawful assembly or blocking the right of way if you are picketing.

c. Sit-Ins

The sit-in, or live-in, comes to the student and community organizing movements from the Indian independence struggle and such great battles of the workers as the automobile and five-and-dime "sit-down strikes" of the thirties, repeated in the occupation of plants like Renault by French workers in 1968. It offers the tactical advantage that the defenders of a fortress have but, like a siege, it can be broken. (Witness Harvard, 1968.) It has the virtue of constituting an attack upon the sanctity of private property, hence of symbolizing the fight to put human concerns above considerations of profit and law.

A sit-in at a university administration building, city housing department, or court differs from the sit-down strike in that its success does not depend upon stopping "production." The actual paralysis of an establishment agency is not usually its real objective. Although sit-ins have enforced immediate, limited demands and wrung concessions from welfare departments and schools, their thrust is primarily educational and symbolic—a means to publicize and dramatize an intolerable situation, rally the people to its correction, and force the opposition to declare itself publicly. Over the past fifteen years, welfare mothers, evicted tenants, victims of highway demolitions, protesters against polluting industries and airports, draft resisters, courtroom demonstrators, and high-school and college students have sat in various appropriate places for long or short periods with varying results. From Gandhi and others through Martin Luther King the southern movement of the fifties and early sixties learned numerous forms of the sit-in and invented some more of its own. It was the basic method by which the restaurants of Route 40 were desegregated and the Florida and Maryland trespass laws challenged and found unconstitutional. Since 1965, major sit-ins encompassing demands from free speech to abolishing ROTC to instituting black studies to the firing of a racist professor have taken place at Berkeley, Columbia, Harvard, Cornell, the French universities, and Sir George Williams in Montreal, to name only a few.

1. Surprise is an important element in a sit-in—even for gaining access to the building you plan to occupy. The place itself should be selected because it is the opposition's stronghold, or because it is symbolic of the issues, or because your occupation of it will create maximum disruption of its normal operations. You can sometimes start a sit-in by taking a delegation in on "legitimate" business and then refusing to leave, additional forces meantime filtering in by twos and threes. Since university administrations send spies to student meetings, organizers should consider how to plan a sit-in at a mass rally without giving the opposition time to get ready for it. One way is to discuss everything but the precise time and/or place and call a quick rally for later when, at the appointed time, you can gather your forces and march upon your target.

2. Sit-ins should begin in daylight. At night you can't tell who is in a building. If the police are there first, save it for another day or someone may get killed. In the daytime you probably won't have to break locks to enter, but if you think you will, take along a pry bar and do a neat job. Self-indulgent trashing or plain sloppiness not only divert attention from your cause in the public mind, but tend to lower the morale of the militant group itself.

3. The same goes for hassling secretaries and for ripping off books, supplies, etc. The wage workers are not the cause of your problems, even when they stick with their bosses. As to administrators themselves, decide whether you will let them and their staff stay or not. If not, escort them safely to the door and put guards there to prevent their return. To avoid violence two conditions are essential: (1) having the building filled with your people and (2) having your people committed to act unitedly and with such discipline and restraint as all will have discussed and agreed to, even before you enter the building. Sheer numbers won't necessarily enable you to hold the building against attack, but they tend to discourage attack.

4. If there are important files in the office you occupy, your group should discuss and agree on your policy toward them. Student sit-ins that uncover proof of faculty-administration CIA connections, war contracts, and other such establishment hanky-panky (as at Harvard in '68) do a service to the movement. On the other hand, indiscriminate reading of student and faculty files violates the right of individual

privacy. One possible procedure is to know what you are looking for; select likely targets and the right files, and reject the temptation to peek into personal records that could only provide tidbits for gossip. If there is a reproducing machine handy, collect your information without actually stealing from the files. Take the copies out to a safe place, in case you get busted later.

5. Decide in advance whether you are conducting a limited demonstration sit-in or intend to hold the place until your demands are met. In the former case, announce your intentions in advance, so that your departure will not appear to be a failure of nerve.

6. If there has been time for advance planning you should have individuals and committees ready for various specific tasks; if not, hold a meeting as soon as possible and get organized. You will need people for guard duty, cleanup, food preparation, medical aid, communications and liaison, etc. Organize sleeping shifts. For a long stay, plan for political workshops, speakers from the outside, music, guerrilla theater, etc.

7. Think ahead about supplies and take them in with you if you plan to remain awhile. A walkie-talkie and a transistor radio are important for communications with the outside, especially if the electricity and telephone are shut off. (If the phone is on a switchboard be very cautious in using it, anyway.) If you think your opposition will go to extremes, take in candles and oil lamps and draw an emergency supply of water right after you enter. Be sure that food is brought in early and start rationing it at once, if you think your connections with people outside are likely to be cut.

8. Plan in advance what you will do if the police are called to clear the building. Your course will depend partly on the numbers and militancy of your group and the physical layout of the building, but above all on your degree of support from the rest of the community. Unless you have really solid and active outside backing, don't try to hold a building against a police attack, and perhaps not even then. They have the firepower and the movement can't afford to sacrifice people to no avail. Outside supporters should keep up a steady pressure on your opposition to open negotiations and not to call in the pigs. Keep your politics up front and discourage tendencies to work off frustrations by trashing. A disciplined action will strengthen the hand of your allies and develop

the sort of support you will need if, in spite of everything, you are arrested or otherwise penalized.

9. From the time you start the sit-in you should call on your opposition to make a public statement as to where they stand on your demands. The chances are that the mass media will cover any such action, so be sure to have a competent press release writer on hand and try to get your position before the public and keep it there. Have publicity people and negotiators both inside and out. The results of any negotiations should be brought before mass meetings of supporters outside as well as the sit-in group itself, and any agreement should have the consent of both. The building should not be vacated nor any agreement made without a complete amnesty for all who took part in the action. When you leave, whether by prior agreement or because you have won, make your departure a further demonstration for your demands by marching out with slogans, songs, and signs. Try to transform even a police bust into a political statement to the people, though this is hard because the police prefer the cover of darkness.

d. Student Strikes

Student strikes against universities have begun to manifest explicitly what is still only implicit in most workers' strikes against corporations—the essentially antimonopoly, antiwar thrust of *any* demand for economic or political or, indeed, educational reform today, no matter how small. Lacking the European workers' tradition of mass political strikes against the government, American workers may not for a time yet draw the full conclusions necessary to transform their fight against war taxes and war inflation into an assault on the war-breeding system itself. It is safe to say that most American workers, blue-collar and white-collar alike, at this moment do not understand campus explosions such as that which greeted Nixon's invasion of Cambodia, nor do they approve of them—let alone recognize that the students' fight expresses indirectly their own deepest class interest. This situation can change rapidly and, indeed, is changing as the unending war pushes up prices, taxes, and unemployment rolls, cuts public services, and provides the rationale for muzzling public protest. Students, striking or not, can hasten or retard this process, without which a fundamental transformation of the social order can hardly be expected.

This would suggest that a student strike, whatever its precipitating causes, should be regarded as a political action directed not simply against the university, but toward its metamorphosis into an institution of the people. Hence, the double slogan: "Close it down! Open it up!" When this is understood—first of all by students themselves—the media will have more difficulty persuading the working people that campus strikers are spoiled suburban brats who don't appreciate their advantages.

Strike Demands

Workers may "win" a strike for higher wages (a basically defensive struggle) and return to work without having challenged the private profit system or even the oppressive nature of the corporation concerned. A student strike, however, even one set off by some relatively minor or temporary frustration, can and should be raised to a political level: to an attack upon the university's servitude to the corporations, its indifference to the welfare of its community both on and off campus, its toleration of academic habits so mind-dissolving that, far from fitting students to cope with life in this era, they subvert even the socialization they are designed to effect. In this context, the formulation of the strike demands is decisive. The most conscious and active group should try to raise issues like the rehiring of a professor or the halting of university "slum clearance" evictions to the level of demands for the reorientation and restructuring of the university itself.

All demands of a political strike are, in a sense, "nonnegotiable"—both because they involve principles and long-range goals and because the institution struck against (in this case the university) has not the power fully to grant them, even if it were willing to. Because a demand is "nonnegotiable" does not mean that it cannot be won. You should never enter a strike except to win. Upon your demands depends the possibility of transforming "Close it down" into "Open it up"—to new ideas, new policies, and new structures.

A student strike often occurs more or less spontaneously, in response to some event that signalizes a new stage in a growing series of repressions (e.g., France, 1968; U.S.A., 1970). Such a strike may be voted at a hastily called mass rally or even begin without a formal strike call. The immediate demands, whether addressed to the specific event, the overall situation, or both, emerge with the first picket signs and shouted slogans. Behind them, of course, lies a whole history of grievances and of organization around them. The planned and prepared strike usually represents, as does the sit-in with which it may be combined, the culminating sanction adopted when negotiations and more limited forms of mass pressure have failed to achieve results. In the case of the spontaneous strike triggered by broad political issues (e.g., the war, the persecution of the Panthers, etc.), the activist group has often the task of developing concrete, detailed demands to implement the general ones for its particular campus. In the local-issue strike, where the demands have already been worked out through innumerable meetings, leaflet and press discussions, and perhaps negotiations, the group should now raise them in a political context that includes the aim of changing the university itself. Thus, an issue involving the tenure of a radical professor which has bogged down in negotiations should, at the strike stage, become a demand for student participation in the whole system of hiring and firing faculty.

A walkout that closes down a university creates a new relationship of forces within it. Heretofore apathetic students are set in motion in spite of themselves and thus are open to political education as never before. Activist students work around the clock, on "strike time," in which the process of radicalization is geometrically speeded up. The faculty, individually and as a body, must choose whether to stick with the trustees and administration or to join their students. Administrations themselves may split on what policy to follow, once it is no longer possible to cover up the mass disaffection with the usual platitudes. In the course of their duties, secretaries, custodians, dorm directors, and security men will be forced to take a stand. The establishment press, TV, and radio will swoop down upon the campus for statements, news, and pictures.

A strike heightens every contradiction within the university and between it and the larger community. Alliances with faculty, staff, and community, capable of redirecting the university, can be built around the demands if the strikers properly understand their own goals. Polarizations can also take place—between student factions, professors and students, university workers and students, community people and students—that can isolate the militants and put the most intransigent elements of the administration more firmly in the saddle.

Unless activist students decide to abandon the university entirely, which they may someday do, "closing it down" can only be a prelude to winning the real objectives of a strike against the university. When and if the place tries to reopen, students can close it again and even make further reopenings impossible, as in recent Japanese experience. This is one way of using the university as a lever for forcing broad political demands upon the government. In certain situations it may be the only way that students can make their weight felt on a national or international scale. It will hardly achieve an immediate restructuring of the university, however. For this the students have to remain together as students, which means on campus, and use the university's present facilities and structures to effect changes in them and to reach the nonacademic community with the overriding issues of war and repression as they affect everyone.

"Open it up" means more than demanding that the dormitories keep going or the student union be made available as a strike headquarters. It can mean an opening up of negotiations (with or without faculty collaboration) on such questions as university war research, investments, and expansion plans. It can give rise to such new forms as free classes for the community; strike dorms; students or student-faculty security patrols; the employment of research facilities to gather information on urgent issues (e.g., the Lemberg Institute on Violence at Brandeis, the Quincy House War Room at Harvard); student-run classes in dormitories, lounges, and on the lawns; "free seminars" of faculty and students on how to improve teaching and learning; community and national coordination centers; alternate structures such as neighborhood free clinics, legal aid, drug counseling; revision of the university calendar in recognition of students' political commitments; the actual implementation of educational innovations, black studies programs, etc.; the initiation of student participation in all phases of the university's operations. These possibilities are not mere projections. The U.S. national student strike of May 1970 saw the initiation of at least some of these new departures at Princeton, Brandeis, Boston University, Berkeley, Stanford, University of Pennsylvania, Harvard, Yale, Columbia, MIT, Trinity, University of Rochester, University of North Carolina, Johns Hopkins, Queens College, and a host of others.

Strike Organization

A sudden explosion of protest such as occurred on May 4–5, 1970, after the Cambodia invasion, May Day in New Haven, and the Kent State killings can close down the university without much prior organization. Opening it to the new possibilities of the situation, however, takes not only well-conceived demands but people to back them up. One of the pitfalls of a student strike is the tendency of manpower and militancy to fall off when the "Close it down" phase is over. At the height of the strike hundreds or thousands of students will take part in formulating, debating, and pressing demands that they are not willing to implement, once they have been won. A grudging administration will be quick to take advantage of a slack response to its concessions. There is no quick remedy for this problem, but you can prepare to cope with it by building in advance a broad network of politically educated small groups. Organizers should also recognize the letdown period as normal, so that they do not feel that the strike has fallen apart when many erstwhile militants go back to classes, or skiing, or home.

Preparation

All major policy decisions, including the strike vote itself, should be taken at open-mike meetings, after a full report by the leading committee. Centrally called meetings should, if possible, be supplemented with dorm meetings, separate college meetings, etc. Since action is the objective, it is important that such meetings not be allowed to bog down in hassles over subsidiary tactics. Prepare an agenda that focuses on the action; limit the time of speeches; perhaps divide into workshops for implementing the proposals; above all, try to give the meeting clear information and a coherent political perspective. A student strike, because of its chaotic potential, demands of the participants a high degree of discipline. It is therefore essential that the maximum number of students participate in policy decisions on trashing; use of force toward nonstrikers; attitude toward the faculty, staff, and security force; need for marshals; behavior if the police arrive en masse; etc. If the student governing body has previously been negotiating on the strike issues, it should be authorized anew and augmented, if possible, by additional members. The basic strike committees should be recruited by volunteering and/or election. As many as possible should leave the mass meeting with a specific job to do.

Coordination

Whether you elect a central strike committee or leave coordination and negotiations in the hands of the student government or some other existing group, the leading strike body should represent the many working committees that the action requires: information and communication, security, funds, picketing, strike newsletter, publicity (contact with the media), publications, education (workshops, seminars, fact sheets, etc.), speakers, faculty and staff liaison, community liaison, contact with other colleges and high schools, medical aid, legal aid, transportation, and probably more. This beehive must be coordinated so that at any moment it can act unitedly. Therefore, some centralization is necessary. One model that has proved workable is a delegated body made up of committee chairman or elected representatives, including strike negotiators and student government members. Since this adds up to a fairly large body of active people, its meetings, which may be daily, should be kept as short as possible. A small steering committee can be elected to collect and clear information, prepare agendas, and otherwise free the central committee from a mass of detail, so that it can concentrate on major political and organizational questions. The working committees should avoid switching delegates to the central body since to do so breaks continuity and causes time to be lost in reviewing past decisions.

Set up a central strike office at once. Coordination of effort and communication of information are the first things the strike committee must guarantee. If possible, your office should have several rooms so that various activities can go forward at once: committee meetings, mimeographing, poster making, dispatching of pickets and canvassers, etc. If you can't liberate enough space for all this, place some of the technical functions like mimeographing elsewhere, as close as possible. The strike office should be well supplied with phones, but unless you have a separate room for it, place your crucial communications center elsewhere. Have a phone, more than one if possible, for incoming calls only. (If you can get a switchboard setup, better yet.) This number should be publicized in every leaflet and meeting, and given to other schools and organizations. Additional phones should be used for outgoing calls. Get as many as possible since you may need, in a crisis, to start a telephone chain or contact dozens of people in a few minutes. The communications committee should be a steady crew and large enough so that the phones are manned around the clock. Supply cots or sleeping bags in the center for the off-duty shift and be sure the crew is fed. The committee should have bulletin-board lists and file cards of all important numbers—organizers, committee members, picket captains, cooperating faculty, administrators, university security, supporters in other universities and schools, etc., etc. If many long-distance calls are to be made, try to get Wide Area Telephone Service (WATS) or use the university's. In addition to its central file of numbers, the information center keeps an up-to-the-minute calendar of everything that is going on or is planned: rallies, committee meetings, workshops and seminars, special mobilizations and delegations, calls for pickets or canvassers, etc.

Funding

Develop a fund-raising committee at once, but don't leave it alone with the job. If the strike has been prepared in advance, you should have a strike fund ready when it starts. (See "Fund Raising.") If it is spontaneous, appeal to the general sense of urgency and solidarity to get money from student government and other activities, individual faculty members, staff, and students, sympathizers in the community, etc. Ask for donations of money or goods (food, etc.) from stores near the campus (they make plenty from the students). Try to use the university's facilities as fully as possible: vehicles, phones, bulk mailing rates, meeting places, radio station, audio-visual labs and supplies, paper, reproducing machines, public relations contacts, etc. Friendly secretaries, underadministrators, and faculty members can be a big help here. Stay in the dorms and insist that they continue to serve food. Take over the kitchens and serve it yourself. Make the university fund you, if you can.

Communication

Along with a communications center, a daily (even twice- or three-times-daily) strike bulletin or newsletter is essential to pull the whole complex action together. Even if the regular student newspaper is functioning as a strike organ, you will need a quicker and more constant way of transmitting news, discussing political issues, proposing next steps, etc. Anyone who wants to publish his ideas in the newsletter should have a chance to do so. Never mind if viewpoints disagree: have people sign their articles and let controversy rage. This is the very stuff of political education. Set up your newsletter committee and its mimeograph in a room of its own and publicize its location. (In a big strike have other machines available in various places, for the leaflets that various groups will publish, and for emergencies.) Set up a poster workshop complete with cardboard, magic markers, crayons, paint, and silk screen. If you have no trained poster makers, try to get your fine-arts students or a nearby art school to donate their skills.

Publicity

How the public media treat you will depend primarily on the general political climate and the specific issues of your strike. However, even if they abuse you, don't dismiss the possibility of getting some reflection of your position through them to the public. Universities are sensitive about their public image. If you can counter their (and the media's) attempt to portray you as destructive lunatics by getting your grievances and demands before the whole community, you can use their concern with P.R. against them. Set up a publicity committee, preferably including members who have worked with the student press and who have experience in writing press releases, organizing press conferences, speaking on radio, etc. Take care, especially in a tense situation, that the central committee or, on policy questions, an all-strikers' mass meeting, OK's any press release that goes out in the name of the strike. Press conferences should be attended by a number of strikers. At moments of crisis, especially, strikers should be cautioned against making statements to reporters or even talking freely with television cameramen, etc. They should be warned that many of the latter will urge them to acts of trashing, violence, or plain crazy behavior, in order to get what they consider "newsworthy" shots. If strikers are invited to appear on TV the central coordinating committee or a larger meeting should decide who should go. In all contacts with the mass media keep your demands up front; use the occasion to stress the political content of the strike; challenge the university to meet the serious issues around which you are fighting.

Security

Even in an apparently peaceful situation the possibility of busts, police violence, the intervention of troops, and the provocation of government infiltrators should not be dismissed. Your first security guarantee is, of course, the solidarity of the strikers themselves and their awareness of the political significance of what they are doing. Policy toward trashing, violence, and defensive violence should be thoroughly thrashed out at large meetings so that strikers place themselves under voluntary discipline and self-discipline. Otherwise they, and the strike itself, may be victimized by the irresponsible acts of individuals, whether enthusiasts or provocateurs, acting against the will of the whole. In the "Open it up" stage of a strike, trashing, false alarms, and violence are generally inappropriate, since the political aim is to put the university in the hands of the people, not to wreck it. Even in the "Close it down" stage, damage should be avoided if possible, since it is you who will have to live with it when you make the place your own. The same goes for using physical force on nonstrikers; they will be around later, and probably less radicalized than before.

Even if strikers themselves are wholly peaceful, you cannot be sure that your headquarters, information center, picket lines, demonstrations, and living and eating places on or off campus will not be attacked. General alertness and an efficient twenty-four-hour communication center are absolutely necessary. The information committee should make a habit of checking reports of possibly dangerous situations before passing them on. If there has been trouble or trouble is expected, car and foot patrols, especially at night, are in order. At Boston University, the pigs were kept out of the campus area by a peace patrol of students and faculty members after a series of false alarms and fires and a police invasion threatened to close the place completely. In tense situations which may involve mass police mobilizations or troop movements, place inconspicuous watchers in tall buildings or in cars near station houses, armories, and army bases. Equip them with walkie-talkies or have them call in if a convoy leaves its base headed your way. At Yale (around

May Day, 1970) strikers learned of the movement of the Eighty-second Airborne into Massachusetts about eight hours before the national guard headquarters knew of it. All the techniques of self-defense in mass actions—affinity groups, medical and legal aid committees, etc.—should be in readiness, and general instructions on self-defense, first aid, behavior under arrest, etc., issued to all strikers.

Opening It Up

Don't wait until you have won your demands to start liberating the place. Students won't return to their classes if you offer them better ones. Start workshops, seminars, guerrilla theater groups, everywhere—in classrooms and dorms and out on the grass, as at Columbia in 1968. Have students, faculty members, community people learn and teach together. Bring people from other schools to meet with you and send your people to theirs. Organize free classes for the neighborhood adults and kids and demand that the university make these a permanent program. Develop the kind of imaginative programs that you would like to see all year, then demand that they be continued.

e. Harassments

A harassment is a short-term pressure tactic. It should be linked with your group's specific goal or demand. You should first demonstrate to your opposition and everyone who is "neutral" or ignorant of the problem that you have attempted other "channels" but have had no success in negotiating your demands.

Research the most vulnerable part of your opponent's organization. Then find a short, sweet, and effective harassment that will quickly force the boss's hand. Some that have been used are the phone-in, lie-in, swim-in (where appropriate), sit-in, walk-in, and mail-in. Be sure to explain to the working people in the organization the real purpose of your action, so that alienation of those who surround your target is minimal, especially since you may be creating extra shitwork for them.

An economic harassment especially effective against merchandisers is to have a large number of people bring back what they bought one or two days before.

The Panthers performed a politically effective harassment of the police. They tailed the police cars every night on their runs through the community. This reversal of the standard order proved to be an effective self-defense measure. The pigs couldn't come down hard on anyone because they were being followed so closely by the Panthers. It also had a psychological impact. It made the pigs paranoid and gave them a taste of what it was like to be on the other end of their own brand of harassment.

A well-publicized harassment can also be a powerful symbolic action educating people to your issue. Fashion your effort so that your community and the organization you are pressuring can see the political and economic rationale for your tactics.

f. Symbolic Actions

Vigils

A vigil is a rally, picket line, sit-in, etc., intended to symbolize your issue and your commitment. It aims not at physical confrontation, but at intellectual and emotional confrontation. Direct action by the opponent is not warranted or expected.

A silent march with each participant carrying a candle to represent a soldier killed in battle is a vigil. Other examples would be a group of people in front of the White House singing hymns, or a group sitting silently in front of a draft board, each member holding a draft card with blood dripping from it. A prayer service in a conspicuous public place adjacent to your opponent's territory is also a vigil. Since a vigil is directed specifically at the conscience, all participants should be disciplined enough to maintain the serious nature of this type of action.

Hartels

This is a technique developed by Gandhi. It calls for large numbers of people to stay home for certain periods of time. It is best used for community or local issues where empty streets and stores in one particular neighborhood are obvious indications of your base of support. It is only effective on a large scale and thus requires a great deal of participation. Leafleting, canvassing, and mass meetings should be used to prepare the community. The decision as to the length of the hartel will be dependent on your evaluation of commitment in your community. It is better to call for a hartel of one hour and have everyone adhere to it than to try to be dramatic and call a six-hour hartel and have people drifting out of their homes after two or three hours.

Reverse Strikes

Overwork or obstructive conscientiousness effects a reverse strike. Work stops because everyone does too much. For example, the air-traffic controllers wished to emphasize severe understaffing in their profession, so they started to follow every air-traffic-control rule on the books. This use of efficiency to protest inefficiency and danger effectively slowed down and snarled traffic throughout the United States. When every safety procedure was followed to the letter, there weren't enough people to handle all the work and this made the air-control situation perfectly clear.

This method is very effective in a bureaucracy. Most bureaucracies "show" progress only because everyone ignores a large number of the procedural rules and requirements of his job. Often, if these rules are followed to the letter by every employee, work will grind to a halt in a flood of excess paperwork. If every executive filed as many copies of his memos as he was supposed to, there would be nothing but memo files in every office in the country. This action is effective in demonstrating specific issues of mismanagement by government or corporations or as a symbolic expression of distaste for their policies or functions.

Fasts

A fast is a highly disciplined activity and requires a great deal of understanding and commitment by its participants. A fast can be a very effective action, but it is useless unless it is well publicized. For this reason it is often most effective when well-known figures take part. Both extensive publicity and the visibility of your participants are most important. A tactical fast is not simply ceasing to eat. It must be carefully planned and executed. Both preparation for the fast and the actual fast should be conducted with constant medical supervision. A good doctor can tell you how long you can and should hold your fast and how to prepare your system for the shock. Set a reasonable limit. You are not out to prove your superhuman endurance nor do you want to destroy the impact of the fast by having to give up before you publicly stated you would. The fast is a moral statement of your commitment and is designed to force people into an examination of their conscience.

Refusing Honors

Refusing awards or renouncing past ones can be an individual action or an organized effort. An individual act will have little effect unless it is well publicized and is directed against a specific target, the presenters of the honor. When an individual renounces or refuses an honor, he should do so with all possible fanfare and a clearly worded statement explaining that it is a protest against the presenting organization's contribution to an objectionable state of affairs. A press conference is a good idea. A well-known, respected personage is most effective with this tactic. If there is no well-known figure involved, massive participation may have as good an impact on the media, and hence on the public. An example would be an entire graduating class refusing their diplomas because the school does war research.

g. Boycotts

The boycott has proven to be an effective tool for winning demands from businesses and government, and raising the political consciousness of the public. It is a tactic with a long history among disenchanted people and involves a direct act of refusal and denial.

Lenin, advocating a boycott of the Duma in 1906, stressed the importance of an active boycott: "The boycott should serve to extend and intensify agitation and should not become passive." An active boycott is one where there are people picketing, constant publicity, and acts of defiance.

The size of a boycott is determined by the particular political situation. A nationwide boycott is hard to initiate, costs a great deal of money, and is likely to fail. A boycott in a local community is more likely to be effective because of its more manageable size and the relation which can be made to the immediate concerns of the people involved.

There have been innumerable court battles over the use of boycotts. Be aware of the laws in your state and community concerning them. Know what hassles you may be getting into and have legal assistance ready.

The boycott is an economic tool, and is most effective

when it upsets a competitive balance. Most products, stores, and industries have peak seasons; learn when they are and time your boycott to knock the profit out of the peak. The most common peak seasons for retail trade are August–September (back to school); late October–New Year (Christmas season—the big one); and the six weeks prior to Easter.

Even if your boycott is not successful, the nature of your demand and the political tie-ins may educate the people about the issue you are fighting for.

Boycotts may be a direct tactic employed to attain specific goals. The grape boycott organized by Cesar Chavez was such an action, aimed at forcing certain growers to accept union representation for migrant workers. This kind of action is a direct and dramatic attack on profit operations.

Symbolic boycotts are used to show immediate strength or potential power. The Spring 1970 Strike Committee's boycott of Coca-Cola and Philip Morris was such a boycott. Though these items were not directly related to war, a successful boycott would have indicated the ability of dissenters to disrupt more relevant corporations.

A boycott must usually be sustained for quite a while. Plan your resources carefully. A few pickets every day would probably be better than a mass demonstration, but a sizable showing the first day can gain some extra publicity. Try to keep your target area narrow or specific so that efforts may be effectively directed.

A boycott can be made more effective and politically significant if you can provide services for the people in lieu of those boycotted. Alternate goods and services should be provided, free of charge if possible, or at minimal cost. Besides putting extra pressure on the target, free transportation to a competitive facility in low-income areas breaks local boredom and increases economic mobility. Involve as many people as possible in serving others. Boycotting exploitative markets in the ghetto and either providing alternate, cooperative markets (such as Operation Breadbasket in Chicago) or transportation to outside stores can do more than overcome economic problems. It can build a sense of power and self-determination in a community and be a foundation for inter-community cooperation.

Publicity is the key to the success of the boycott. Letter writing, leaflets, posters, demonstrations, bumper stickers, pickets, mass media, etc., may all be used to tell people about the boycott and ask for their help.

Distribute boycott pledges in appropriate areas. These will provide a way for people to make a firm commitment to the action. They will also give you a direct measure of sympathy and will serve as a publicity handout.

The threat of a boycott, itself, may be a powerful weapon; use it as a lever in preliminary negotiations. Present your demands to the offending organization and allow a fixed amount of time for an answer before proceeding with the boycott.

You should always have easy access to the people you are boycotting. Know when they are hurting and know when to put on the pressure.

If you mount a successful boycott and win your demands, congratulations. Now boycott your victim's competition. Utilize the base of support you have created in order to escalate your demands.

h. Tax Resistance

Tax resistance is a direct and clear expression of dissatisfaction with government policy and a tactic which can be centrally coordinated as a national mass action. Tax resistance organizations have been formed throughout the United States to assist people who wish to withhold taxes in protest and to provide coordination for such activity.

If you decide to withhold federal tax money, you might check with the local war resisters' league as to what risk is involved and what to expect. (See Bibliography–Directory.) The government will probably handle failure to pay tax money like any delinquent account. They may garnish your bank account, put a lien on your holdings or earnings, or confiscate property for auction.

In some cities, war resisters' leagues may have set up escrow accounts to which you may contribute the tax money you withhold and share collective control over its use and the use of accrued interest with other tax resisters. Thus, money may go to help people live, rather than to kill. If the IRS brings action against you, and you would like your withheld money back, it will be returned.

The 10 percent federal excise tax on your phone bill

(passed in 1966 as a direct subsidy for the Indochina war) can be left unpaid with no interruption in service. You may withhold the tax as itemized, or withhold 10 percent of your total bill if it is not itemized. Notify the phone company each and every time you withhold the tax and state your reason for doing so. (The War Tax Resistance has pretyped IBM cards available for this purpose which can be enclosed with your bill.) The tax doesn't go to the phone company, so they won't give you any trouble or disturb your service. Eventually they will notify Washington.

Once the phone company notifies the IRS, it is out of their hands. The IRS will use their typical harassment techniques—letter, telephone, and visit. Indicate your position or ignore them. Chances are they won't bother you too much since it costs a great deal more to collect the phone tax than it's worth. They may eventually get it from your bank account or earnings. So far, there have been no reported busts for phone-tax resistance.

Joining with a war resisters' league in the above activity makes for a unified mass action directed at a very specific goal. It also channels money to worthy projects and links individuals in a larger movement.

VI. Defense

1. Legal Protection

Legal Precautions for Actions

Establishment legal structures have built-in guarantees against injustice and arbitrary treatment which may be used by activists. Many times these guarantees will not work unless you make them work. In the case of arrest stemming from mass confrontation, your rights will usually be ignored. Even if you know the law and protest illegal treatment, it is often your word against that of the policeman, jailer, or judge. Nevertheless, you can very often obtain better treatment by reminding your arresting officer that you know when *he* is breaking the law.

Pocket lawyers (legal information sheets) should be provided to all members of your group before embarking on any activity which could lead to arrest or legal difficulties. They can be prepared in cooperation with lawyers, law students, and such organizations as the American Civil Liberties Union, the National Lawyers Guild, and student and professional legal assistance groups. The following sample should be checked by a local lawyer to see that all of the information in it applies to your locality.

SAMPLE POCKET LAWYER

IF YOU ARE STOPPED OR ARRESTED:

1. Do not run away.
2. Ask why you were stopped. (The policeman does not have to answer.)
3. Remain silent. Remember: *Anything* you say may be held against you. Give only your name and address.
4. If the police officer is not in uniform, ask for his identi-

fication. You cannot be legally arrested unless he properly identifies himself.

5. Resisting arrest is: going limp, running away, calling to a crowd to help you, or talking back to police. This is a separate crime of which you can be later convicted, *even if you are found innocent of the original crime.*

6. Police do not have the right to search your car or home without a warrant, probable cause, or your consent. If you refuse to give consent, try to do so in front of witnesses. It is then up to the police to show cause. You can, however, be frisked.

IF YOU ARE TAKEN TO A POLICE STATION:

1. Police must either release you here or book you (charge you with a crime). Booking usually takes between an hour and three hours, but if you've been arrested in a large group it will take much longer.

2. As soon as you have been booked, you have the right to two phone calls: one to a lawyer, relative, or friend; the other to a bail bondsman. If you don't have dimes the police must give them to you.

3. In the event that your lawyer can't be reached, ask to have a lawyer assigned to you. You can always change to your own lawyer when he arrives.

4. If you don't have money to hire a lawyer, the state must get you a lawyer without charge. If you don't have a lawyer, and don't want a court-appointed one, call the Legal Aid Society or American Civil Liberties Union nearest you.

5. Demand medical attention if you are sick or hurt.

6. The police may search you, either on arrest or at the station house. Ask for an itemization of all things taken from you. As a preventive step always make sure to have nothing on you which may incriminate you if arrested.

7. Again, refuse to sign or say anything until your lawyer arrives.

8. The police may photograph and fingerprint you, but may not put you in a lineup until your lawyer arrives.

9. You will be held in custody until arraignment (formal charge by a judge). You must be brought to court within twenty-four to forty-eight hours of your arrest, or at the first court session after that, if a weekend or holiday supervenes. You should be told of your rights at the arraignment. You have a right to consult counsel before arraignment, either your

own lawyer or a lawyer present in the court. You *must* have a lawyer at this point. If no lawyer is made available, say "I OBJECT TO THIS PROCEEDING" and make sure it gets into the record.

10. You should be allowed to post bail or pay a bondsman's fee. If you cannot afford it, you may request the judge to lower the bail or remove it, but he does not have to. You may be released on your own recognizance, i.e., on your own pledge to return for your hearing.

In addition, a good pocket lawyer should also include:

1. A phone number to call for legal help or information.

2. What to expect under the conditions which prevail in the particular area in which you are working.

3. Specific local information on how to make bail (include names and phone numbers of sympathetic local bondsmen), and the possibilities of release through personal recognizance.

4. Specific information on charges and penalties pertaining to your locality.

5. Advice about identifying the arresting officer and possible witnesses.

6. Information on legal medical aid. (See "Medical Aid.")

Legal Observers

Legal observers for demonstrations and other mass actions provide neutral witness to incidents, arrests, violations of rights, etc. They also gather names, addresses, and impressions from witnesses and participants. Legal observers may provide legal information, e.g., legal defense numbers, or arrange initial support for arrestees. Recruit legal observers through movement law groups, law students, the American Civil Liberties Union, etc. (See Bibliography—Directory.)

Legal observers should be stationed at police headquarters and the jail to watch the treatment of demonstrators and to mobilize legal defense. They should also establish the identity or description of police involved in the arrest.

If conditions permit, a legal observer may attempt to watch an arrestee being taken from the scene to the jail. His presence may inhibit any tendencies toward violence and prevarication on the part of police.

Insignia for easy identification by demonstrators and police should be provided. If possible, police acknowledgment of the legal presence should be sought.

Observers work in conjunction with legal defenders, who will provide the actual assistance and advice for the arrestee. Legal observers should be provided with phone numbers and walkie-talkie or other communications media to report regularly, to call for additional observers, or to summon medical help. The need for numerous telephone lines and dimes should be anticipated.

Points for legal observers to remember:

1. Record as much information as possible. Periodically fill out report forms and return them to observer headquarters when you finish your tour of duty. Minimal report form includes . . .

Date, time, place.
Type of incident.
Person involved. (Identify as thoroughly as possible.)
Police involved. (Badge number and/or name.)
Apparent charge.
Witnesses: name, phone number, address.
Description of incident, including judgment as to fault, appropriateness of force used, etc.
Observer's signature.

2. Above all, do not do anything which would put yourself in danger of harm or arrest, or which would prejudice your effectiveness as an observer. Your duties do not include crowd control, actual assistance, or vainglorious heroics.

Defense Funds

Every organization that anticipates confrontations with the law should consider setting up a legal-defense fund. Legal-defense funds can be ongoing collections for an organization's varied legal expenses, or can focus around a specific trial.

Contingency plans for emergency funding should be developed early, preferably before any overt actions are taken. Preparations to cover legal fees, fines, bail money, or bail bondsman payments (15 to 20 percent more expensive than bail money) might also include gathering names of individuals willing to post bail. Established insurance companies will sometimes write liability insurance policies with specific clauses that cover legal defense and provisions for bail. If the particular venture permits, this might be a helpful precaution.

A trial-centered legal-defense fund raises money and psychological support for the victim of repression and his family. The publicity surrounding a defense fund creates the opportunity to counter mass-media distortion or omissions, alert people to injustices relating to the court system, and educate them about the particular issues involved and about movement ideals. It can form a base from which to organize, inside the courtroom and out, and support demonstrations to ensure a fair trial. It can politicize lawyers and law students and encourage their involvement in the legal-defense preparation.

All arrangements should be made with *approval of the defendant and his lawyer* so as not to damage his defense or go against his personal wishes.

Make information available through newspapers, pamphlets, and speaking engagements. Contact other groups which might be able to offer assistance. Open a bank account for depositing checks made out to the fund—e.g., "Free Bobby Defense Fund."

Money may be raised by straightforward appeals for contributions to cover legal expenses; by gimmicks such as selling "tickets" to the courtroom "show"; by soliciting in conjunction with a petition drive; and by charging speakers' fees. Speakers might include defendants themselves (once out on bail), friends, wives, husbands, witnesses, movement people speaking on their behalf.

Political Trials

The following is part of a proposal passed by the Political and Legal Defense Workshop of the Student Mobilization Committee (reprinted from "How to Defend the Antiwar Movement," *The Student Mobilizer*, March 1970).

A political trial is one in which individuals are publicly tried because they hold ideas which challenge some or all of the assumptions underlying the right of the power structure to rule.

The U.S. courts are designed to appear as impartial bodies mediating between different interest groups. When the defendant has attacked the status quo institutions which are directly related to and supportive of the judiciary system, however, it too becomes a repressive force.

The key to understanding a political trial is to recognize that it is a battle of opposing ideas. Essentially, when activists are on trial, they are engaging in a struggle for the right to hold dissenting views in spite of phony charges they usually face like "criminal anarchy" or "conspiracy to riot." The issues at stake are basic democratic rights—the right to free speech, free assembly, freedom of the press—rights which are included in the First Amendment of the Constitution but which must be continually fought for against the attempts by the ruling class to infringe upon their free exercise by the citizenry.

The democratic rights in the Bill of Rights were and have been maintained only through protracted struggle. These rights are always in danger of being eroded. It is the job of movement activists to use a political trial as an opportunity to demonstrate to the masses of Americans that civil liberties are being threatened, as a means of defeating any attempts by the ruling powers to deny us those rights. This can be done in three ways.

First, it can be done by building a broad, united public defense on the basis of the defendants' democratic rights as outlined in the Bill of Rights. We must explain that if any sector of society or any individual can be denied civil liberties, then any one of us can be.

Second, it can be done at the trial itself when every effort can be made to show that the defendants' ideas are the real target and the charges are merely a smokescreen for the attempt to stifle dissenting views.

Third, the defendants can use the courtroom as a forum to explain the ideas the power structure is attempting to suppress. Since the attack is an attempt to prevent the defendant from expressing his ideas, his doing so in the trial itself both undermines the attack and helps focus on the trial's real purpose. . . .

Some people think that because the courts help maintain the illusion of justice in the country and because the majority of people still believe in the judicial system, any victory won from the courts only perpetuates these illusions. Therefore the only proper action is to denounce the court. It is true that the courts operate behind a facade of "justice," but legal victories provide two important gains for the movement. One is the vital fight to continue activity. This is a real victory for those faced with a power structure that would, if it could, throw us all in jail. The second gain for the movement is that legal victories encourage people, and, like all other political victories, help to strengthen the confidence of the American masses in their own power and ability to wage successful struggles for social change.

2. Medical Aid

Health Precautions for Actions

A "Pocket Medic" with basic street-medicine advice and phone numbers and locations of health facilities, movement doctors, and emergency transportation should be printed up and distributed free beginning a few days before the event. Cooperating radio stations and underground newspapers may also convey this essential medical information. Public training sessions in street medicine may be scheduled. Everyone involved in the action should be urged to study and follow the relevant advice, and to inscribe emergency phone numbers on their skin.

Pocket medics should be tailored where possible to the specific situation anticipated. A good pocket medic includes the following information:

1. An explanation of what the pocket medic is for.
2. What preparations to make before coming to the demonstration.
3. What kinds of physical and psychological threats to health may develop at a confrontation, and how one may act to protect oneself and others.
4. How to recognize and deal with medical emergencies.
5. How to recognize street medics, how to phone, find, get transportation to first-aid stations and medical centers.

The sample which follows is meant as a supplement to, rather than a substitute for, a professional movement or Red Cross first-aid course, practice, and experience. If you plan to reproduce or summarize any part of it, go over it with a physician. Do research into the kinds of chemicals likely to be used by your local police or militia.

SAMPLE POCKET MEDIC

As repression increases, we must think and act to defend ourselves from reactionary violence. Besides organizing affinity groups for mutual support, we must learn to care for each other when injured. While medics with medical kits and some training may be present, everyone must know essential preventive and therapeutic street medicine. If you remember just a few basic things, you can be a tremendous help in confrontations where gassing or more serious trouble is happening.

PRECAUTIONS TO TAKE; COME PREPARED

1. Get a tetanus shot if you have never been immunized. Get a tetanus toxoid booster every two years. Lockjaw (tetanus) resulting from wounds can be fatal. If you didn't get the injection before being injured, see a doctor for a booster shot as soon as possible afterward.

2. Wear protective clothing to defend against chemical and physical injury when anticipated. Wear high-buttoned shirts, tight sleeves and cuffs, laced heavy shoes, a belt, jockstrap or cups, bra which is not tight, a helmet or helmet liner, and carry airtight goggles. If you can't do without glasses, strap shatterproof glasses to your head.

Do *not* wear contact lenses as they trap gases against the eye and can cause serious irritation to the cornea and eventual blindness. As the cornea itself has no nerve endings, you will not feel the irritation.

Do *not* wear earrings, loose straps, or anything around the neck which could be pulled to hurt or choke you. Do *not* wear false teeth: you can choke on them if unconscious.

3. EVERYONE should know the addresses and phone numbers of medical stations and centers in the area.

4. Do carry or wear identification cards or tags if you have any drug allergies, a known illness, or medications which you must take, e.g., "I am a diabetic on insulin," "I am allergic to

penicillin." Carry labeled medications and doctor's prescription for drugs you must take regularly. It is illegal for labeled drugs to be confiscated. If they are, it is grounds for a lawsuit.

5. Do not carry your address book or notebooks which might be helpful to the pigs.

6. Do not carry scissors, even in a first-aid kit. You could be busted for carrying a concealed weapon.

7. Supplies:

a. Heavy magazine or newspaper to use as splint foil.

b. Square foot or more of clean cloth for use as bandage, tourniquet.

c. Wet cloth in a plastic bag, soaked in water or lemon juice, or vinegar for gas mask.

d. Easily used water containers, canteens, plastic squeeze bottle, dropper bottle.

e. Roll of ½-inch adhesive tape.

f. Sterile 4-x-4-inch gauze pads for bleeding gas protection.

g. Eye drops.

h. Band-aids.

i. Plastic bag of wet cotton balls to rinse wounds or squeeze water into eyes (do *not* touch or rub eyes with cotton).

GENERAL BRIEFING FOR FIELD SITUATION

1. BE CALM. If impossible, fake it. Help people keep their cool. Don't scream at people. Tell them to walk, not run. Gesture people to slow down. Reassure them that if they keep calm, they'll make it. Crowds panic easily. Calm the people to prevent needless injury.

2. PROTECT THE INJURED from crowds, trampling, abuse. Approach a person in trouble or blinded slowly and with a calm voice. Tell him who you are and what you will do if he wants your help. Recruit bystanders to keep the crowd back. Evaluate the situation. Send for help.

3. DON'T MOVE A SERIOUSLY INJURED PERSON UNLESS NECESSARY. You need an expert evaluation of his injury, and skill and manpower, to move a seriously injured person. Careless handling can cause much harm to the victim. Stay with the injured if necessary to prevent amateur interference. Dispatch someone for professional help immediately.

4. DON'T WASTE TIME OR SUPPLIES, especially with large crowds, heavy gassing, a lot of violence of long duration. Ration supplies and efforts according to the needs of the situa-

tion. Give the seriously injured most of your attention. Get professional help to them.

TEAR GAS. Tear gases come in a wide variety of canisters and grenades which should not be handled. They are hot and can explode. Tear gas can also be sprayed by pepper fog machines. CN tear gas is weak and used most commonly. CS tear gas is strong and has particles in it.

Effects. CN and CS cause tearing and burning of the eyes, respiratory tract irritation, occasionally nausea and vomiting, headaches, and a mild burning sensation of exposed skin. People with asthma or allergies may have great difficulty breathing when gassed. High concentrations have caused death.

Prevention. (1) Escape. (2) Apply an antitear-gas facial before the action begins to neutralize the gas: Mix eight to ten eggs with one cup of water and a tablespoon of baking soda. Beat very well. Spread mixture around face and eyes. (3) Wear airtight goggles and gas mask, or a cloth soaked in water or vinegar. Don't put vinegar on the face.

Treatment. Rinse eyes repeatedly with water, normal saline, or dilute boric acid, using droppers, squirt bottles, or squeezing wet cotton balls. Wash from the inside near the nose to the outside. Get someone with clean hands to help you keep your eyes open. It hurts more when the water hits, but it's necessary to irrigate out the chemical as fast as possible. After rinsing, use commercial eyedrops like Murine. Do not rub eyes. Shed gassed clothing and get into fresh air as soon as possible.

Gas may be rinsed or dabbed from exposed skin. Mineral oil applied to the skin for a minute and then wiped off with alcohol wipes may help, after exposure. Keep alcohol away from eyes. Vaseline is not advised as a preparation before battle with gas.

MACE. Mace is a close-range chemical incapacitator. It is dispensed as a liquid stream or spray from propellant canisters held by hand. Mace is not yet available as a crowd-control device but is used on small groups or individuals.

Effects. Mace causes temporary blindness and severe eye pain; in high concentrations, skin irritation and respiratory difficulty. Convulsions can occur if sprayed into the mouth. Eye damage due to Mace can lead to blindness.

Prevention. For eyes, ski goggles; for skin, vaseline only if applied prior to Macing and wiped off *immediately* after, or you will be burned even worse. Mouth, keep it shut.

Treatment. Irrigate eyes with dilute solution of boric acid or irrigate copiously with water for ten to twenty minutes, AS SOON AS POSSIBLE. DO NOT RUB YOUR EYES. Use nonprescription eye drops to alleviate pain. Rinse skin with gentle wiping. If pain or blurred vision persists, see a doctor.

PHYSICAL INJURIES

BRUISES, Strong blows to chest or abdomen may cause internal injuries and bleeding. Blows on chest may result in rib fractures whose symptoms are painful or difficult breathing or coughing up blood. Blows to the abdomen may produce such symptoms as persistent abdominal pain, nausea, vomiting, pain in either shoulder, shock. Blood in the urine after a blow to the back or sides suggests a kidney injury. If any of these symptoms occur, seek medical attention immediately.

HEAD WOUNDS. For simple lacerations and bleeding, apply firm, direct pressure to the wound for ten minutes or more until bleeding stops. If the blow or pain is severe, or if unconsciousness or disorientation occurred with the blow, go to a medical station or center for evaluation to rule out concussion, fracture, or intercranial bleeding. Occasionally, what appears to be a slight injury to the head may get worse hours or days after the injury. Warning signs of possible increased injury to the brain include unusual behavior, sleepiness, stupor, difficulty in arousing from sleep; imbalance, stumbling, paralysis of a limb; unusual eye movements; vomiting with or without nausea; severe headache not relieved by aspirin; fever, shaking chills; bleeding from nose or ears. If any of these signs or symptoms are noted, contact a doctor and get to a hospital emergency room at once.

WOUNDS. To stop bleeding apply firm, direct pressure on the wound with a clean bandage or cloth or with your hand if a compress is not available. If possible get the injured person to help with own care by holding the compress. In cases of severe bleeding where arteries are cut and blood spurting and uncontrolled by direct pressure, a tourniquet may be necessary. Tie a belt or handkerchief above the bleeding area of a limb, and keep tightening as the bleeding stops.

Do not loosen the tourniquet as bleeding stops because more blood loss and shock will occur. As soon as possible get the injured person to a doctor or hospital. Write down on the skin (forehead) of the victim the time the tourniquet was applied so the doctor knows how much time he has to treat the limb.

In head wounds, if the skull is broken and bleeding is uncontrolled by pressure, press the artery on one side of the neck at a time. Do not apply a tourniquet to the neck. Get immediate medical attention.

SHOCK. Shock is a life-threatening complication of trauma, physical or even emotional, which involves a profound disturbance to the circulatory system. Without adequate treatment, shock can lead to permanent damage of vital organs or even death. Signs of shock include cold and clammy pale skin, chills, nausea and vomiting, rapid and shallow breathing, rapid weak pulse, dilated pupils, nervousness or unconsciousness, usually associated with injury and blood loss (which may be internal).

Once respiration is assured and major bleeding stopped, treat shock.

1. If the person is conscious he should be on his back with his torso flat. In the absence of head injury the legs should be elevated at least twelve to eighteen inches.

2. Conserve body heat with blankets, coats, or newspapers placed both under and over the person. Remove cold, wet clothing when possible and convenient without exposing person to cold.

3. Loosen tight clothing, belts, collars, bras.

4. Use ammonia inhalants to keep person conscious.

5. Keep person quiet, warm, and comfortable but do not give oral liquids, food, or medication without professional approval. Liquid and foods can seriously complicate an emergency.

6. If a person is unconscious and in shock, he should be placed on his stomach with his face to the side, and his body on an incline with the head down where possible. Check to see his airway is clear. Extend jaw and neck. Make sure tongue is not swallowed back; if is, pull it forward. Clear mouth of obstructions. Follow previous instructions.

7. Reduce pain wherever possible (e.g., splint a fracture), because pain increases shock.

8. Fainting is a mild form of shock with temporary loss of consciousness due to loss of blood or decrease of blood pressure to the brain. Elevate feet and loosen clothing, and massage stomach to restore blood supply to the head.

BULLET WOUNDS. Get the victim to professional medical attention immediately. Do not try to remove the bullet. Treat bullet wounds like other bleeding injuries with a clean bandage and direct pressure.

With chest wounds make an airtight bandage with adhesive tape over the wound to keep air from being sucked in which will further collapse the lung and compromise breathing. Use vaseline gauze, blood-soaked gauze, a baggie, or plastic wrap as bandages. Keep the person lying on his wounded side.

MEDICAL-LEGAL CONSIDERATIONS

Wounds from violence. Doctors in every state are required by law to report immediately by phone and in writing to the police any gunshot wound, knife wound, or other act of violence even if self-inflicted. However, a victim of such wounds is under no legal requirement to report the cause of the injury to any authority, *including the doctor.*

Medical rights in jail or custody. If you are arrested, the state assumes care for you in toto and you have a legal right to demand and receive prompt medical attention. But cops and jail guards may be very slow to call a doctor at the request of a prisoner. If allowed your telephone call on arrest, have your lawyer or bondsman call a movement doctor. Report the nature of your injury or illness and the identity, when possible, of the authorities denying care. If the authorities confiscate your medications, demand them back and demand to see a doctor.

Advantages of having a personal physician. Your doctor will not be risking a job with the state by demanding treatment or hospitalization, or by testifying to your injuries later on. His attention and *loud* promise to return to check on you can prevent beatings and brutality while you are in custody.

In-hospital rights and precautions. You have a legal right to information on your medical record. It may be important for you to obtain a signed copy of the doctor's reports which document your injuries or illness. You may need this information to prepare legal defense or to launch a suit against the police or a medical institution. Demand full documentation of your injuries, including X rays, photographs, and lab tests.

Malpractice. Medical staff have been known to provide inferior medical attention to political undesirables. Get the name of the doctor, intern, or house-staff member who is treating you, particularly if you are receiving care in the emergency room for injuries sustained in confrontation. Demand local anesthetic prior to getting stitches. Demand a urine test for blood if you have been clubbed on the back. If refused, threaten a suit for malpractice. No hospital can refuse to treat an emergency because of inability to pay. The police should not be allowed to interfere with your receipt of medical care. Do not let them take you from the emergency room until you have been fully treated and results from all tests have returned.

Mental detention. In most states, on the word of a physician that your mental state constitutes a danger to yourself and others, you can be held for seventy-two hours for "observation." This tactic has been employed to give police time to build a case against you, or merely as a measure of harassment or repression. If this occurs, demand to see a lawyer and doctor of your choosing. Request a hearing on your commitment as soon as possible, and persist in this request until it is fulfilled.

Organizing Medical Presence

Manpower. Nurses, medical and dental students, doctors, ex-medical corpsmen, people with training and experience in first aid, street medicine, and marshaling techniques are the movement's medics. If you are starting from scratch to develop manpower, contact a nearby chapter of a movement medical organization such as Medical Committee for Human Rights, Student Health Organization, Physicians' Forum, or an independent medical center group. (See Bibliography–Directory.)

Medics may receive training in formal classes given by the Red Cross and U.S. government, in movement training sessions, or as apprentices to medics in the streets. All attempts should be made to pass on information and skills to the people, so they can protect themselves.

Deployment. Street medics may work as teams, matching experienced with less experienced individuals. Depending on the demonstration and police practices, people should decide whether or not medics should wear identifying insignia or clothing, and whether they should participate in the action itself. In violent situations, medics have been singled out by pigs and beaten; also medics have inadvertently attracted police attention and led them to make arrests of patients. On the other hand, medics who are visibly available and recognizable can help reassure a person who has been injured.

If feasible, place medic observers in emergency rooms, jails, and detention areas to document the treatment of demonstrators by police and hospital staff, and also to forestall abuse.

First-aid stations. First-aid stations with varying degrees of sophistication in people, supplies and facilities may be established to back up roving medics and provide a publicly known source of medical support. If possible, each station should have a licensed doctor or nurse in attendance. Space for first-aid stations may be a donated storefront, a church basement, or a tent outdoors. In the latter case, permits for using public property may be necessary, apart from the demonstration permit. Where possible, the aid station should have access to running water.

The territory and shifts of medics may be coordinated from first-aid stations or central headquarters to provide thorough coverage throughout the theater of action. A communications system (telephones, walkie-talkies, or runners) should be worked out so that medics can be assigned to trouble spots or get qualified help to the seriously injured. Circulating medic teams should report in at regular periods to restock or be relieved.

Transportation. Station wagons and microbuses when available are preferable to sedans as ambulances or roving medical units. They may be stocked with extra supplies, blankets, and stretcher. The driver should always be accompanied by one or more medics who can treat patients on the way to the first-aid station or nearest medical center.

3. Group Security and Self-Defense

One key to good group self-defense and security is group tightness and self-knowledge. Adequate defense scenarios are generally easy to plan and difficult to execute because group members are unaware of each other's weaknesses or potential behavior under stress.

The second key is discipline. Individualism destroys self-defense plans and generally gets people hurt. In street actions, affinity groups seem to work well if leaders are followed loyally by all the members of the group. Even when the leadership makes a wrong decision, the result may not be catastrophic if everyone follows. Part of the ethics of group self-defense is *not* to take risks for other people and *not* to advocate anything you would not do yourself.

Your group should have different defense scenarios to meet different needs. Be flexible. Defense, by definition, is a reaction. If you overreact, you go beyond defense. Therefore, use the least amount of force necessary to deal with any particular situation. Militant self-defense can sometimes be destructive to your ultimate goals. For example, if your group is walking a picket line and the defense plan is to leave peacefully when the pigs arrive, then one well-placed punch could cause a riot with ensuing injuries and reduced group effectiveness.

A great many people are taking karate instruction. Most karate classes are heavily ritualistic, which may be a waste of time. Karate, although effective for self-defense, may not meet the needs of affinity groups or street fighters. Make sure the instruction you are getting is what you need.

There are a number of useful guidelines that may save your plans from defeat and prevent infiltration: Check out all rumors and verify your information. Find out who saw, heard, said—what, when, where. Assume surveillance. It may be wise to use post-office boxes instead of personal addresses. If you give someone information that incriminates you or your group, be sure that person "needs to know." The best security is to work and live closely with those in your group, especially those who contribute most to policy decisions.

Snoops, Infiltrators, and Provocateurs

Of the forty substantive witnesses who testified in the government's case at the Chicago conspiracy trial, thirty-five were police agents or infiltrators.

Often agents are placed well in advance of the commission of any supposedly illegal activities. Some agents have several jobs—intelligence gathering, provocation, and entrapment; while others are merely snoops, not seeking to redirect or influence the policy of an organization. Some work full-time with a particular group. Some agents appear only, but consistently, just before and during major local and national actions.

The agent is often the most militant and aggressive in suggesting illegal activities, but usually fails to provide any political justification for them. Be suspicious of members of a group who remain reluctant to get involved in theoretical discussions even after heavy attendance at meetings or conferences. Some provocateurs try to create dissension and further the trend toward illegal action by discrediting leaders who will not be pushed into action without good political justification.

Agents often try to win confidence by supplying you with illegal drugs or guns. Be suspicious if his professed financial state contradicts such "gifts." Be suspicious also of leading questions related to planned actions. To be legally culpable for the actions of a group you must advocate such actions. Agents try to collect statements proving that you "personally incited to riot," to use in eventual prosecution.

The most famous provocateur in the country is Tommy the Traveler. Tommy knew the exact situations and the names of student radicals on every campus he "visited," but no one was suspicious. At Columbia in 1968 he tried to talk Rudd into escalating his tactics, and even led a building take-over. In Chicago in the summer of '68 he urged people to kill pigs. At Cornell in the spring of '69 he supplied guns to the black students. At Wisconsin in the spring of '69 he participated in the fire bombings. Fourteen were arrested in the wake of his provocation. He also appeared at Buffalo, and Washington, and Hobart, and, and, and . . .

Some agents only gather information; they are hard to spot. They can give themselves away by a misplaced interest in your membership lists, fund-raising contacts, or friends.

An agent will often avoid encounters with political friends when "off duty," and keep his private life secret. He can sometimes be discovered through a straightforward call to your local credit bureau for a credit check. This can reveal the real employer of your suspect. Some agents must disappear or make long-distance phone calls regularly to check in.

When arrested, agents are not usually upset or uncomfortable around the police or the paddy wagon. They may be shoved and hit less, if at all, and once at the station may be separated from the rest of the group.

Once you know someone is an agent, you can control the information to which he has access and even feed him false information, for a limited period of time. Since he can easily verify information, the agent will catch on quickly. Expose him and tighten up your security. Remember, he will soon be replaced by another.

Telephone Privacy

If you think your phone is bugged, be paranoid and act accordingly, but don't let "them" know that you know. Let them think that they are getting inside information, because if they realize that you're on to them, they will find another way to cop info.

Don't use real names or refer to specific places, times, dates, etc. Use "he," "she," "it." Give people nicknames which refer to peculiarities that only your group is aware of—Minder-Binder, Frickles, Ma. Work out a code where if you tell someone to meet you at five o'clock, that means three hours later, etc. Don't mention dope on the phone; why give them an *easy* way to get you?

You might consider getting a second phone with an unlisted number. Better yet, go to a phone booth. Don't use the phone at all when there's really serious business to take care of. One way to circumvent the problem of bugged phones is to use one of three modes of short-wave radio.

1. The most bug-proof method is also the most difficult, namely CW short-wave equipment which operates via Morse code. Each transceiver (transmitter-receiver) will cost from $50 to $200 depending on power (range) and operating conveniences. This system is almost completely bug-proof, you can tune the dial to a different operating frequency at any time, and it is capable of great range (hundreds or even thousands of miles), but it is very inconvenient in that every user must know Morse.

2. Voice-operated (SSB) short-wave is like the above but more expensive ($100 to $500 per transceiver). It is the most convenient and versatile of the three methods, has long range, and is almost bug-proof if you change frequencies often. There is a slight danger of being accidentally overheard by a short-wave hobbyist, so avoid revolutionary talk; if you are really paranoid, use code names and/or a foreign language if possible. Both of the standard short-wave methods, incidentally,

involve getting a license from the FCC; the license exam tests your knowledge of electronics, equipment, relevant laws, and Morse code. Fortunately only one member of your group need get the license; others can operate (illegally of course, but the offense is unprovable) using his call letters with only minimal operating instructions.

3. The cheapest and easiest approach is "citizens' band" radio, which requires no license and no knowledge of electronics. It is voice communication, and it varies from $10 for a walkie-talkie with a quarter-mile range up to $150 for a transceiver with a twenty-mile range. However, in CB there are only twenty-three available frequencies, which makes bugging a little less difficult (but still harder than bugging a phone) and makes accidental overhearing more likely than with standard short-wave. Change frequencies often, avoid blatant rhetoric, and use code names.

VII. Using Establishment Structures

1. Cautionary Introduction

Some of you will find this section useful, some will not. It depends on where you are at politically and where you hope to go. We cannot afford to waste revolutionary energy in nonproductive or counterproductive tactics, no matter how ideologically appealing they may be. So the selection of tactics must be pragmatic—based on a hard judgment of what will advance our collective goals. Some of you will find that you can work most effectively within the established structures, while others work best around or underneath them.

If you choose to use existing structures, it is important that you be always consciously aware that the power structure will attempt to coopt your work, to erect a facade of rhetoric and apparent action as a substitute for real change. Many of the establishment structures discussed in this section function as "safety valves" designed to get people to let off steam about their grievances without forcing meaningful improvement.

Don't underestimate your opponent. Beware especially of liberals who are very helpful as long as the changes you want are superficial or affect someone else's profits and power status, but who resist with many rationalizations any effort to reduce the exploitative power they themselves hold over people.

2. The Mass Media

News Operations
The key to making full use of the news media is to know what makes news and how the various media treat news items.

Study both the content and the style of electronic and print journalists. You have to be able to translate both your group's ideology and actions into language which will appeal to media editors and through them to the public. Very significant stories have been ignored because they were poorly presented to the editors.

To be "newsworthy" a story must have an element which is either new, surprising, creative, significant, or of special local interest. The media like numbers, so try to find interesting statistics. They like unusual things which will strike people's fancy, so brainstorm; a new idea could gain more constructive publicity than a dozen sit-ins. They like pointed quotes, so quote people—even yourself. If you can find something in your story which is a "first," you've got news.

A news story usually must be built on an event, preferably one featuring local community people and institutions. A news story must describe specific occurrences, must quote specific statements, and must name specific people, places, and actions.

Timing is important in using the news. When you see a news story which is relevant to your group's activity, use it as a peg to hang your own story on. Issue a press release immediately which tells of your related work or quotes a public statement by a member of your organization commenting (either critically or with praise) on the initial news item. Tie actions to your statements when you can; for example send statements not only to the press but also to appropriate officials.

If your organization is criticized, harassed, framed, or busted, get your side of the story out immediately. (The police often issue reports within minutes.) Don't wait to send a written press release; phone the press with your statement. Be cool; be accurate; be factual, not argumentative; don't confess guilt, but don't lie. Give the facts, and then give your charges.

The press secretary. Every continuing organization should have a press secretary—a member who is highly articulate, is fully informed about all of the group's activities, has a nose for what makes news, and can prepare all news releases and other contacts with the news media. His responsibilities include (in addition to writing news releases) getting to know some editors and reporters, learning how the media operate, notifying the media of events which deserve coverage (such as boycotts or demonstrations), and setting up press conferences. He should issue press releases to report on all events which appear to be newsworthy but were not important enough to attract reporters (such as the beginning or settlement of a rent strike, a public statement by an organization representative).

The news release. The news release, or press release, is a news story written by you (rather than by a reporter) and supplied to the media, who may at their option use it directly, edit it and then use it, or ignore it entirely. Since you write the story, you can make sure that it includes all the important elements and gives them their proper emphasis. To create a favorable impression among media editors, make sure that you send out only news releases with usable news, not reams of propaganda. If you want a release to reflect an ideological point of view, quote statements by group or community members to make the point. Nonquoted material should be straight factual reporting of events.

The format of the news release is straightforward. Use mimeo paper (preferably 8½ x 14 to make it harder to misplace) with your organization's letterhead at the top. At the top type FOR FURTHER INFORMATION followed by your press secretary's name and phone. Then give the release time ("For immediate release" or "For release after 10:00 A.M. Monday June 8" for example). Then come the headline, the dateline (normally the date when the news release is written), and the body of the story. (For advice on writing the story, see "Mass Education and Communications: Newspapers.") Type "more" at the bottom of each page except the last, and put your organization name and press secretary number at the top of each page.

All news releases should be distributed to the editor at small papers, the city editor at large papers, the assignment editor at radio or TV stations, and also the specific department editors and beat reporters who are relevant to the story's content, such as the political editor, city hall columnist, real-estate editor, sports reporter, and social columnist. Send releases to *all* local papers and broadcast stations, not just to the big ones; include suburban stations and weekly newspapers. For lists of the media in your area, see *The Working Press of the Nation* and *Ayer's Dictionary* at the library and the listings in the Yellow Pages under "Newspapers," "Radio Stations," and "Television Stations."

The press conference. A press conference is an event you

hold to notify the press, all together and in person, of something especially significant—the formation of a project, a major policy statement, the announcement that a national figure will give his support to your project, etc. The format of the press conference ranges from a statement to a gang of reporters on the front steps (either your own steps or those of the agency you're battling) to a full-scale production in a rented hall or hotel ballroom with TV lights, multiple speakers, and security guards to handle the crowds.

Announcing a press conference does not guarantee full attendance by reporters, nor does it ensure publication or broadcast for your statement. To improve your odds, check these rules. Use press conferences sparingly, for major news only. Establish credibility with reporters and editors in advance by always sending them competent and newsworthy press releases. Your press secretary should get on the good side of media editors by visiting them and learning their preferences in the handling of photographs, press release distribution, etc. Learn the deadlines of all your local media and try to schedule your press conferences accordingly (normally early Saturday afternoon for Sunday papers, early morning for the afternoon dailies, early afternoon for the radio-TV evening news and morning papers, two days before publication for weeklies).

If possible, notify the media about the conference at least twenty-four hours in advance by means of a short press release; the release should include a short note at the top beneath the press secretary's phone number, saying that the purpose of the release is to announce a press conference. Find some reason to call the editors and reporters a few hours before the conference to remind them about it.

Start the conference on time. Begin by distributing (to everyone simultaneously) "press packs" containing the text of the statement, relevant background, a brief press-release summary, and data on your speaker if he is special. After the speaker reads the statement, request questions. Be prepared with solid answers to likely questions, plus factual documentation if appropriate.

Television and Radio

Except for word-of-mouth, the electronic media are the prime source of information, ideas, and politics for the majority of the population. (Polls show that only 10 to 15 percent of the adult population read newspapers or newsmagazines closely.) Moreover, because of its immediacy, its visual impact, and the size of its audiences, television can be a more effective medium for turning people's heads than print media or street demonstrations.

So it is important that the movement become active in the electronic media, to force them to serve the people better and also to use them to spread ideas, inform people, and gain publicity. It is not smart to cop out and ignore radio and TV. They are among the most flexible, available, and useful of the established institutions. Media usage is a major form of power, and it would be foolish to let the system have uncontested control of so important a tool.

As with any other kind of organizing, begin with self-education. Learn how the media are motivated and structured, how to infiltrate or attack them, and how to exploit them for the benefit of the people. For a brief basic survey, read "What Do We Do About Television?" by Nicholas Johnson (an FCC commissioner) in the July 11, 1970, issue of the *Saturday Review;* in addition to a good deal of solid information, the article includes broadcasters' license renewal dates, the names and addresses of a few citizens organizations, and other useful references. Also check the sources listed on pp. 19–20 of the *NACLA Research Methodology Guide.*

While you prepare to use television as a medium, consider also using it as a target. Organizing against a local station, whether to force improvements or to challenge its license, has several useful purposes. It can force broadcasters to provide programming which is more relevant to the oppressed minorities which together constitute much of their audiences.

Try to organize a constituency which is being ignored or harmed by present programming policy. Picket a station, stage mass demonstrations, and boycott the station's advertisers. At the outset students may be most effective as catalysts, to get a movement going by learning about community needs and grievances, suggesting to community leaders how television can be made to serve the community, and convincing them that organized community action can create change. Once a movement gets going, student groups can provide valuable help by swelling mass demonstrations, helping man picket lines, printing and distributing publicity leaflets, and broadening sponsor boycotts. When making your demands on the station manager, specify exactly what kinds of programming the community needs; make sure that the demands receive maximum publicity; and emphasize that programs produced for oppressed communities should be produced by members of the community.

Organized community pressure on the Federal Communications Commission can be a surprisingly effective way to force a radio or TV station to better serve the community's real needs, especially if you arouse community support for a challenge of the broadcaster's license. For a model example of how student and community groups can put together the data required for an effective license challenge, get *Television Today: The End of Communication and the Death of the Community*. (See Bibliography–Directory.)

However useful organizing against broadcasters is, in the long run the movement must become directly involved in using radio and TV to serve and communicate with people. Currently the market in television for independently produced programs is expanding at a terrific rate, and this situation presents unprecedented opportunities for community involvement in TV programming. The rapid expansion in the number of broadcast channels (due to UHF and especially to the advent of community cable CATV), combined with the decreasing fraction of programming provided by networks and the broadcaster's burden of filling five hundred hours per month, are the causes of the increased availability of TV time. We must now organize the communities to demand public use of the new channels and pressure the stations to make the facilities available, and then get into producing the right kinds of programming ourselves.

Even now there are a number of ways in which we can use radio and TV to broadcast ideas and information. For example, broadcasters give air time to "responsible spokesmen" to express opposing views in response to broadcast editorials. (For Media Ithaca's free pamphlet *Clearing the Air*, which explains various ways in which citizens can obtain free air time, see Bibliography–Directory.)

Don't be deterred from producing a radio or TV program by fear of the technical sophistication of the electronic media. Advice on technical details can always be obtained, and the broadcast engineers are there to handle anything complex, so the producer is left free to concentrate mainly on content and presentation. Get a 16-mm camera, a tape recorder and microphone, or a Sony videotape system, and start capturing the reality that the establishment producers ignore. Get equipment into the hands of ghetto dwellers, welfare mothers, factory workers, prison inmates, even cops!—and use your imagination to employ the recorded reality trip for maximum impact. Take advantage of the visual impact of TV. Don't make the ego-tripping mistake of staring a camera at a speaker's face. Capture visual (or, in radio, aural) images which carry your message.

Most radio or television stations are still basically establishment businesses dedicated to making a profit, so don't waste yourself trying to produce programs of blatantly radical ideology and revolutionary rhetoric unless you have a noncommercial broadcaster for them. To be effective, put together either imaginative documentaries or, better, solid community service programming manned by members of the community.

Programming topics could include ghetto news ignored by the media; consumer education; health information; exposés of pollution, consumer frauds, and bad or dangerous products; publicizing city facilities and services which are available to all but which ghetto residents tend not to hear about; general legal advice; and any other service for the oppressed communities. In any broadcast, supply your audience with a reaction route—relevant phone numbers, addresses, canvassing, demonstration plans, etc. Exploit the talk-show format both as a means of spreading awareness of issues and as a way of learning from your audience.

On the whole, more radical discussions and presentations can be broadcast on radio than on TV. This is partly due to the spread of noncommercial listener-sponsored radio stations in major cities. For example, WBUR-FM in Boston (partly university-sponsored and partly listener-sponsored) broadcasts underground news, creates radical documentaries, and produces "The Drum," a nightly program by and for the third world. Another successful station is operated by the Aquarian Research Foundation in Philadelphia, and there are several member stations of the Pacifica radio network around the country (such as WBAI in New York).

In order to make efficient use of movement resources, tape

recordings of good programs should be made available for exchange among other movement-oriented stations. A distribution center for radio tapes is Radio Free People in New York. (See Bibliography–Directory.) Also, as a result of the 1970 Goddard College Alternative Media Conference, a collective video bank is being established for the exchange of videotapes and video equipment.

Other Media Opportunities

Use your imagination to take advantage of numerous other ways in which the established communications media can be used to benefit the community and publicize your work. For example, the letters-to-the-editor column of a newspaper is a free medium, and many papers use it for the expression of opposing views. Similarly, radio and television stations which broadcast editorials normally will make free time available for replies or substantive criticism. Many stations broadcast public-service announcements, through which you might be able to publicize meetings. And feel free at any time to call editors and suggest (with reasoned arguments) specific subjects which deserve investigative reporting or editorial coverage.

3. Political Structures

a. Campaigns

In view of the certainty that the election of even the most progressive candidate will not bring about the radical restructuring of the economic and governmental systems, which is our real goal, can political campaigning be valid and worthwhile? If your answer is no, then clearly you should devote your energy to whichever form of constructive radical action you do believe in. But there are some reasons to support a "yes" answer.

1. Even now, sick as the system is, the oppressed classes would be at least slightly better off if some of the people in power were concerned with their needs.

2. Regardless of whether your candidate is elected, a political campaign can have considerable educational value.

The established communications media are much more willing to publicize the views of registered candidates than those of antielectoral movement leaders. Use this establishment bias for the people's benefit.

3. The organization and public communication tasks of the movement require money, and there are many sources of funds which are available to registered political candidacies but denied to other citizen movements. This bias should be used by promoting appropriate reformist candidates as focuses of fund-raising activity and then employing the campaign to organize oppressed constituencies.

4. Any political campaign involves setting up a headquarters, raising funds, establishing communications tools and procedures, conducting canvassing, and handling the people-interaction problems of organizing. So an active political campaign can, if its members and sponsors are willing, move en masse into the community after election day and serve as the nucleus of a continuing movement to organize the oppressed constituencies in your area. A particularly good aspect of campaigns is their tendency to attract people from various segments of the community—professionals, media insiders, factory workers, welfare mothers, students—introducing them to each other for work in a common cause, erasing some of the superficial barriers to mutual understanding, and establishing a sense of community.

Campaigns of "peace candidates" and "radicals within the system" are often set up by the regular political parties. While their style may not be your own, local party workers usually have the kind of experience needed to deliver the vote in their community. When an organized effort already exists to back a candidate you support, get involved in his campaign in the way you can personally be most effective.

Before you start your own campaign, consider what it is you want to achieve. Do you want to elect a candidate not supported by any existing group experienced in campaigning? Do you want to obtain a forum through which to air an issue? Do you want to use the electoral processes as a means of organizing an area to pressure for change? Obviously, your tactics should be selected accordingly.

The essentials of a political campaign—filing for candidacy, setting up a campaign headquarters, recruiting volunteers and funds, planning publicity and canvassing—require enough

legal and practical know-how to fill a book as large again as
this. Consult the Bibliography–Directory—and try to find
some *experienced* people to head your campaign.

b. Voter Registration

It is easy for people who have adequate food, housing,
and health care to look upon registration and voting as
cooperation with a corrupt establishment. But many people
depend on that corrupt establishment for these things as
well as for schools, sanitation, public works, etc. One way
these people can gain the political muscle to obtain better
treatment is through the power of the vote. More extensive
voter registration among urban and rural poor and minority
groups can lead to greater community control and political
self-awareness.

Voter registration drives give activists the opportunity to
learn firsthand about the communities they canvass for
potential registrants, and to practice canvassing techniques
useful for other campaigns later. They provide the occasion
for talking to large numbers of people about political involvement.

Voter registration drives take a great deal of planning,
and depending on the size of your drive, you might want to
begin to organize as much as six months before election day.
Laws governing voter registration vary from state to state
and are presently in a state of turmoil. It is essential to keep
abreast of the most recent developments. The local branch
of the League of Women Voters is a good source for this
information; most League branches can send you a printed
pamphlet explaining the laws in your area.

Coordinate your efforts with community groups. They
are known by the people, and can provide manpower and
the best advice on how to publicize the campaign. Invite
the leaders of local organizations to meet in a neutral place
and evaluate the resources you can muster together (people,
money, special skills, etc.). Committees might be set up to
handle background information gathering, canvassing, leafleting, posters, mobile units, etc.

A successful voter registration campaign will result if you
make registration as easy as possible for the community you

are working in. It will be necessary to cut through much bureaucratic red tape, and to gain certain technical concessions from local public officials. Cooperative public officials can (1) lengthen periods for registration; (2) increase the number of registration places in "high-traffic" areas like schools and shopping centers; (3) set up hours convenient for the largest number of people; (4) schedule registration dates as near to election day as possible; (5) supply equipment such as mobile units, sound trucks, tables, voter lists, residence lists, voting machines for use in demonstrations, and registrars; (6) deputize community people to act as additional registrars.

Canvassing pairs should reflect the ethnic makeup of the community. Whenever possible, try to have local volunteers call on the people they already know personally. While a person-to-person approach that reaches every door in the community is best, telephone canvassing and street-corner tables may also prove helpful.

Coordinate training sessions for canvassers with local groups supplying volunteers. Canvassers should be thoroughly familiar with the legal and administrative requirements for registration and voting, and must be prepared to explain them in the simplest language possible. These include requirements relating to age, residency, literacy, and police record. (Anyone who has been convicted of a felony is often ineligible for suffrage.) These qualifications prohibit substantial numbers of adults from voting in certain areas, and might be reevaluated if more people studied their repercussions.

Canvassers should carry with them an educational leaflet they can leave at every door. This should include information about the mechanics of voting, a sample ballot, the hours, days, and address of registration and voting places, and the number to call for more information.

Canvassers should also carry data forms for each person with spaces to record whether he has registered or will register, needs transportation and/or baby-sitters, and is willing to work on the drive. If there are members of the family who are too young to register for this election but who will meet the age requirement for the next one, it is helpful to note down their names for reference in future registration drives.

Approach for Canvassers

Tell each potential registrant exactly why you are asking him to register. Stress the fact that you are there as fellow citizens who want better things for the community.

You are likely to encounter both psychological and mechanical barriers among potential registrants, especially among urban minority groups. Psychological barriers include timidity, fear, lack of concern, feelings of futility, etc. Other barriers might include the problems of making two trips to the voting place—one to register and another to vote, the time and money it takes to get there, and the inconvenience of the registration hours.

(*Note:* Appreciation is due to the League of Women Voters of New York for their help on this section. See the League's pamphlet *Voting Is People Power* for additional information. Available from League of Women Voters Education Fund, 1200 17th St., NW, Washington, D.C. 20036, 25¢.)

c. Letter Campaigns

A mass letter-writing campaign is designed to pressure local, state, and national legislators, administrators, and celebrities to take a specific stand on a particular issue.

Letters should be personal, well informed, neat, and most of all, frequent. Know your legislator's record and the committees on which he serves; let him know you're familiar with his past actions and positions. One good source for this information might be your local newspaper; another is the local League of Women Voters. Get in touch with the League for information on upcoming bills and amendments. Know the issues thoroughly, and clearly organize the arguments for the position you would like to see him adopt. Identify legislation by bill number, give specific arguments, and ask, "Will you support 'X' amendment," and "If not, why not?"

When writing to legislators, identify yourself as a constituent, voter, taxpayer, active citizen (member of "X" committee or organization). Write legibly or type, be brief, use your own words and stationery, and be sure to include your address and a signature he can read. Write early in the session if you have some ideas you'd like him to incorporate into a bill that's about to come up. For proper forms of address, consult the appendix of a collegiate dictionary such as Webster's Seventh.

Double the effect of all letters by making at least two carbon copies. Send one to President Nixon and one to the editor of the local paper (include "cc Richard Nixon"). Don't forget "congratulatory" letters to legislators who have recently taken actions you admire in the face of considerable opposition and controversy.

Group Activity

Assemble in a large room typewriters, paper, envelopes, stamps, pens, names and addresses of people to be written to, and sample letters to spark people's imaginations. Publicize time and place of event through local media.

Another alternative is setting up tables on street corners and encouraging people to write a quick note then and there. Be equipped with paper, pens, names and addresses; stress to passersby that it only takes a minute, and that you'll take care of posting the letters yourselves. This technique is especially effective right after a major event has taken place.

At Home

Distribute letter-campaign kits door to door (while canvassing, perhaps), at shopping centers, churches, etc. These should include sample letters, names and addresses of people to be written to, and a statement of the importance of writing. Also publicize through local media.

d. Referenda

The referendum is a procedure for bringing a particular issue or question to a public vote; it is an especially effective tactic on a local level, and can be run on state and national levels as well.

Referenda can (1) *stimulate thought about the issues*. The campaign creates the opportunity to inject lots of informational material into the community and have it discussed with interest. Only issues are involved here—not candidates' personalities. (2) *Get lots of people involved*. The referendum campaign is a good opportunity to mobilize supporters and offer them useful activity. Many people prefer to work around traditional electoral methods; this is a chance for these people to work actively for shared goals. The campaign can build a sense of solidarity needed for future activities, and can also help raise funds. (3) *Reflect the people's feelings on a specific issue.* Where there is latent or blatant opposition to a government policy, a referendum can be a valuable instrument for making this discontent known. Results of the referendum are concrete, official, and easily publicized. (4) *Pressure individuals and groups to introduce political change.* Referenda can be written in such a way as to be binding on a public body.

Steps

1. Consult an attorney. Learn about specific local legal requirements in regard to referenda. A certain number of signatures will probably be required to get the question on the ballot. Know how these signatures must be gathered and muster the manpower to gather them. Get many *more* signatures than the number required by law.

2. Analyze the community. The prevailing opinions on the issues involved will condition the way you word the question. A mildly worded question might demand a majority in favor if it is to be called a success. A more radical stance might demand a smaller favorable response to be termed successful.

3. Publicize the referendum. Establish a speakers' bureau and information center. Use local press and radio as well as leaflets, buttons, and bumper stickers. Send out press releases periodically. (See "The Mass Media.")

4. Get supporters out to the polls, and make sure they understand the procedure involved in registering a favorable vote.

5. Publicize the results.

e. Lobbying

Lobbying is the direct personal presentation of your views to your government representatives. It is best done not by scattered gadflies, but by an organized constituency aroused over a specific issue.

The effectiveness of your lobby depends partly on your representative's being impressed by the fact that people feel strongly enough about an issue to make the trip to Washington (or the State House). The easier it is for the lobbyist to make the trip, the more likely it is that he will be ignored. "Easy-living students" may be less effective lobbyists than groups of working mothers, factory workers, busy housewives, soldiers on short leave, etc. The advent of the eighteen-year-old vote, however, makes it necessary for legislators to be more responsive to student lobbying. Some practical guidelines for lobbyists:

1. *Know your legislators' records.* Get in touch with the League of Women Voters in your area to find out what his past positions have been on various issues. If your time in Washington or at the State House is limited, concentrate on those legislators not yet strongly committed to one side or the other, who seem to show some potential for change. If you have time, talk with those already on your side to encourage them and to get advice on how to approach the others. Don't take up their time or yours convincing them to adopt positions they've already taken.

2. *Try to arrange a specific appointment.* Have a representative of your group call in advance to find out when your congressman or senator will be able to meet with you. The delegations of college students who went to Washington in May 1970 to lobby against the war and the president's move into Cambodia were able to meet personally with a large number of congressmen and senators by arranging appointments in advance. Sometimes you will be unable to see your legislator in person; it is just as important to speak with his assistants.

3. *Emphasize shared concern.* You are likely to be most effective talking to legislators from your home state or district. Discuss the effect of national policies on local industries and community life. Emphasize the extent to which others in the constituency share your concern.

4. *Know the facts.* Know what you believe, and why you believe it. Don't let the power and prestige of a senator change your mind. The individuals and organizations who devote considerable time and money to lobbying also provide an important service to the legislators: they supply them and their offices with needed information. Bring your legislator articles, studies, and research that support your point of view. Supply him with statistics and data that make him better informed while making your argument more convincing. This is especially relevant when the issues involved are local ones and the information deals with areas your legislator is not likely to have researched thoroughly already.

5. *Your best arguments are your own.* Your legislator will be most interested in your personal relationship to the issues. Support logic and facts with obvious emotional commitment.

6. *Organize your arguments clearly.* Present your most effective arguments first; the legislator may have time for only a short interview.

7. *Be prepared with pointed questions.* Make them specific, but not offensive.

8. *Be specific in your requests.* Urge your legislator to support specific bills (know their official numbers) dealing with particular issues and policies. You might ask him to cosponsor these bills as well as vote for them.

9. *Try to keep your visit short.*

10. *Don't be discouraged.* You probably will not "win" any arguments with your legislator. You can have an effect without its being readily apparent: changes of position are usually announced publicly at press conferences, not privately.

Part B

Constituencies

Introduction

The present conditions of life will be changed as the people
unite in a determination to change them. So far we have dealt
with principles of organization and political education without regard to the particular ways in which various sectors of
the population experience the crisis of the system. The following section addresses itself to issues and organizing procedures
among the major constituencies of the people's movement—
defined by common interests and outlook based on age, sex,
race or national origin, occupation, and special forms of oppression. Mostly written by and for members of the constituencies themselves, the articles of this part seek to clarify the
position and problems of each group and to place its particular
demands in the context of a united struggle for the liberation
of all the people.

I. High Schools

The phenomenon of political participation, so new to most college campuses, is descending into the high schools. Students, whose only concerns at this age are supposed to be cars, football, and the opposite sex, are now demanding control over their educational environment.

This political awakening on the part of high-school students may prove to be the primary factor leading to the ultimate breakdown of the American educational system as we know it. High schools have traditionally served as a final staging area for the channeling of young people into their predetermined roles in the economic system and its resulting class structure. Unrest at this educational level poses a serious and immediate threat to this country's power structure, which can be expected strongly to resist any demands for significant change.

The *inside* activist can locate those of a like mind through friends and organizations already involved in some way with social issues. Such groups include student government, student publications, and political and current-events discussion clubs.

The *outside* agitator-organizer should become acquainted with the active students and their friends, and learn about the school, its atmosphere and problems. For the students are, of course, the most reliable source of information about what really goes on in the school. Unless the community is likely to be extremely receptive, avoid suspicion that you are trying to influence students. Let the students come to you.

Both inside and outside organizers should study the sociopolitical climate of the community and the educational system. Sympathetic liberal adults can be of great help as resource people.

The following are a series of questions, the answers to which will help the serious organizer determine the weak points in a local school system:

How long do members serve on the board? Are they elected or appointed . . . if appointed, by whom?

Is the Board of Education mostly a rubber stamp for the school administration or does it really exercise control over important policy matters? Attend meetings or check minutes.

What is the structure of the school administration? Who is the superintendent of schools, how is he appointed, and to whom is he responsible? How centralized is decision making and authority?

Who is in charge of and what is the procedure for the appointment of principals, teachers, and other personnel? What are the procedures for "removing" such school personnel?

Who teaches what? What percentage of the teachers in each school do not have full certification to teach? What percentage of teachers and administrators are members of minority groups?

Are the teachers unionized? If so, is the union affiliated with the American Federation of Teachers?

Immediate demands are, of course, determined by salient local issues and the general level of political consciousness of a given student body. Keep in mind that radicalization usually begins with an awareness of an oppression occurring in daily life.

Students may wish to explain a planned action to their parents. There are cases of disciplinary action against students being revoked because of parents' protest and support of student demands.

Contact local peace or social action groups (AFSC, SMC, SCLC, NAACP, ADA, etc.) and enlist their support and perhaps a promise of financial aid.

Legal aid and advice should be obtained. Learn what local laws are relevant to your planned actions. Elicit a promise of aid from the local ACLU or a sympathetic lawyer in case of arrests or expulsion from school.

A high-school political movement is most effectively built, at least in the initial stages, around a demand for student control over some facet of life at school. Although the student vs. high-school authority is the primary contradiction to be dealt with, the form which its resulting conflict takes is determined by the socioeconomic makeup of the student body.

Suburban-type High Schools

Relatively sophisticated political issues can often be raised in schools dominated by the college-bound children of the secure middle and upper classes. In such communities where parents are well educated and politically liberal, a natural base of support exists for demands concerning individual freedom and student control of their environment.

1. *Free Speech*—Because some reactionary school administrations insist on maintaining censorship over school publications, and veto power over outside speakers, the violation of constitutional guarantees can provide the impetus for a student movement. Demands for free speech often bring to the surface contradictions in the local power structure between would-be liberals and those who insist on more repressive means of control.

2. *The U.S. War on Indochina*—Because many students may have been exposed to the antiwar movement through their parents and older brothers and sisters, involving them in a school-based antiwar organization may offer an opportunity to build the political education of all involved. Workshops and teach-ins can be conducted on war-related issues such as U.S. imperialism. Organizers should concentrate their educational efforts around the question of why the liberal politics of many parents has failed to halt the U.S. war effort.

3. *The Draft*—The most effective way to organize around this issue in any school is to demand a competent draft counselor to explain the alternatives available to military service.

4. *Appearance Regulations*—Rules such as those governing hair length have been successfully fought in many schools by individual court actions. In order to make such issues politically relevant, they should be *collective struggles*, with all segments of the student body involved. Don't simply demand that guys be allowed to have long hair, insist also that girls be allowed to wear pants. When you win this much, push for the abolishment of *all* dress codes.

5. *Student Government Power*—In most schools the administration in the person of the principal has veto power over any significant action taken by the student government. A political movement, initiated by student government representatives, can be formed around the demand for a student government responsible only to the student body which elected it. Ideally, such a government would have freedom

to spend its budget as it sees fit, and enjoy more than just an advisory role in academic and disciplinary matters.

6. *Women's Liberation*—High school may be an opportune time and place for women to educate each other about the nature of their particular oppression. During the high school years, male chauvinism is probably more open than it is in later years after young men have acquired a degree of sophistication. This factor, combined with the fact that women generally mature faster than men at this age, make high-school women very open to ideas concerning their special plight. Consciousness raising could focus on the dating game (waiting for the boy to call, "paying back" his financial outlay with sexual favors, social ostracism if the girl doesn't conform), as well as on sex-based tracking at school, which shunts girls to home ec and typing classes, and keeps them out of shop, preengineering courses, etc. A simple issue like beauty contests could also be a good starting point.

7. *How the System Uses Sports*—Politically advanced student bodies may be ready to be educated about the function of sports in preparing people to enter the capitalist economy. However, the idea that sports exist mainly to foster the spirit of competition between interest groups may fall on many deaf ears. The suggestion that opposing teams switch half of their players before a game will not be readily accepted until the proper political groundwork has been laid.

Technical High Schools

The tracking system is the major vice at these schools. It functions to stifle creativity and emphasize only those abilities that the local economy needs.

In these schools, economic and disciplinary oppression is real in the daily lives of the students. The organizer should prepare to act around more concrete issues than the virtual abstractions that are often relevant to a suburban high school. What follows is a list of issues, by no means all-inclusive, that may apply to schools filled with the children of exploited economic and racial groups.

1. *Pigs in the School*—Many urban high schools are analogous to "pacified hamlets" in Vietnam. Armed pigs patrol the halls and the doors to the outside are locked throughout the school day. ID cards are required, and per-

mission is necessary to travel in the hall while classes are in session.

An excellent first demand for a political movement is the expulsion of all pigs.

2. *Peer Pigs*—Many schools have systems of student "safety patrols" which turn student against student. These patrols report other students for such infractions as smoking and cutting classes. Student activists should confront members of this patrol and work toward a total boycott of the patrol system.

3. *Smoking Regulations*—A major grievance in many high schools. This is best attacked by showing the hypocrisy of banning student smoking while the faculty has private lounges especially for such a pastime.

4. *Drug Counseling and Sex Education*—Glaringly non-existent at many urban schools. If the administration refuses to comply with student demands for these programs, students should obtain the help of sympathetic parents or college students and set up their *own* programs. Successful alternate structures are an excellent political education and impetus to further collective action.

5. *Racism*—A source of open conflict between students in many urban high schools. When tensions are great the organizer may find this to be a nearly impossible issue to deal with. Intrastudent education is probably the best way to bring together a student body divided against itself along racial lines.

Student-run assemblies and discussion groups should be organized which bring out the role of racism in keeping students pitted against each other instead of against the school administration. Students must be made to see that they have a common enemy that uses racism to prevent them from struggling together. When this point is clear, it will be easy to draw a parallel between racism in the school and its function in society at large.

In many high schools, it may be necessary to deal with the problem of racism before other issues can be tackled.

6. *Community Control of Schools*—A fight that can only be undertaken with strong parental leadership. This is one issue where students are often relegated to a supporting role. A widely based community organization is necessary for the success of such a battle.

Dealing with the Administration

Political conflicts with principals can get very heavy, very fast. Students are sometimes suspended, teachers are dismissed "for academic reasons," and parents are called in.

Attempts should be made to enlist teacher and/or parental aid. Both can give a school administration a helpful push.

Do not assume at the outset that the principal is your enemy: he may be a liberal who will grant your initial demands. Use such a preliminary success to whet student enthusiasm for your movement, and then escalate your demands.

At this stage, negotiations are in order. While negotiating you should be doing everything possible to build your base of support. Teach-ins and in-class discussions may be useful.

If negotiations break down, you may have to shift to more extreme tactics. Confrontation or disobedience of administration edicts is an extreme step and necessitates the wise use of all means of publicity to dramatize your legal and/or moral justification for taking action. *Strike quickly*, before they break down your movement by intimidation.

Dealing with the Faculty

Most high-school movements bypass the faculty. In so doing they neglect an important source of potential backing.

Teachers often feel threatened by demands such as curriculum changes and faculty hiring by student committee. If they fear you, they may work against you.

Rapport should be established with teachers early in your movement. Reveal to them your aims and show your willingness to work with and for them. First, talk to a few teachers individually or in small groups. Then choose a spokesman or a small group of students to speak at a local teachers' association or faculty meeting. Use this opportunity to explain the nature of and the reasons behind your demands. Ask them for suggestions, and suggest in turn ways in which they can help through faculty resolutions, teach-ins, open class discussions on relevant issues, etc.

Dealing with the Community

It must be remembered that high-school students usually live at home with their parents and are more closely tied to the community than are their college comrades. This makes it difficult for a high-school political movement to survive if the local community is openly hostile to it.

Students should make every effort to explain their demands to the community. If outright support cannot be engendered, you may at least be able to prevent reinforcement of the repression brought down by school administrators.

Make the Struggle City- and/or Statewide

High-school activists sharing common city or regional school boards should communicate and attempt to coordinate their efforts. If one city school is on strike, the leader can be transferred across town. When all city high schools are on strike, repressive measures are much more difficult.

Newsletters and meetings can be used to keep organizers in various city schools in touch with each other and aware of local political happenings. Efforts should also be made to contact college activists. As awareness of common oppression increases, it may become feasible to coordinate radical actions throughout the secondary and college educational systems in certain regions.

A Final Note

It should again be emphasized that the issue around which to organize depends entirely on the local conditions of the high school. The organizer should study his constituency and plan a program accordingly. The "systemic" approach to organizing, trying to relate such phenomena as dress codes, administration censorship of the school newspaper, the draft, and the war, is probably the best framework in which to work. As the man once said, it don't matter what spoke you start with, you always get to the hub of the wheel.

II. Universities

Introduction

The educational institutions of a society are an index to its underlying assumptions and values, since their primary function is the transmission of one generation's vision of the good life to the next. By the same token, the currents of change often become visible in the schools and universities before they are discernible elsewhere. Student radicalism has a history dating back eight hundred years, at least to the heresies at the young Sorbonne. It is hardly remarkable, therefore, that the general crisis of world capitalism has produced in the universities of the world a crisis of confidence in that system and in its assumptions about human life. And it is not surprising that the young generation's demand for radical social change begins in a demand to restructure the university.

This might seem a case of attacking the symptoms of the disease before the cause, were it not for the peculiar relationship that the modern university bears to the economic substructure of the social order it was created to serve. A prime support of the ruling class, it nonetheless has a "gravedigger" potential. Education in the sense of "liberal arts" anciently meant studies befitting *free men,* a small minority who were thus prepared to rule over the many peasant craftsmen, trained only in practical skills. A technological civilization must educate vastly greater numbers of nominally "free men" as managers, specialists, researchists, administrators, persuaders, expediters, etc., to effectuate the rule of a still smaller minority of monopoly capitalists over the mass of producers. Even the skills of the latter increasingly require training that goes far beyond narrow technique and invades the realm of the "liberal arts." Witness the clamor everywhere: Finish high school! You can't get a good job unless you go to college!

Free public education in the United States is largely a

result of capitalism's ineluctable dependence upon such an "educated" work force. The advance of industrial technology (and of its ability to amass wealth and power) requires the continual production of new, inventive minds: mathematicians, biologists, economists, psychologists, and political theorists—even historians and artists, since every aspect of past and present, linked as they are to the future, must be brought under control.

To create this "product" the technological society maintains a vast system of schools and supports the notion that a large part of its youth (in the U.S. about half) shall postpone entering the labor market while they engage in studies similar to those that were once reserved for "free" men. To the horror of the corporate and academic elite who run the show, the "product" has begun to learn its lessons too well—to turn its studious gaze upon the institutions themselves and its inquiring mind upon what it means to be "free."

Thus, as the crisis of the system deepens, the university emerges as one of its inevitable contradictions. Children of the managerial and technical middle class, living the best life the "American dream" has to offer, sometime in the 1960s began to transform their leisure, their affluence, and their academic exposure to new ideas and alternate social structures into a penetrating critique of the institutions which had nurtured them. Humanism in the classroom, research for slaughter in the lab. Economics to end third world famine, in the lecture hall built with income from United Fruit. Sociology and architecture to save the inner city, while the university evicted its tenants, ignored the poor at its gates, and admitted "without discrimination" any black who could pay his way. "Freedom of inquiry" and "intellectual adventure" in classes of five hundred graded by an electric eye. This appalling performance had been going on for a long time, and for a long time few seemed to notice. Why was it brought home to students with such force only in recent years?

Two generations ago D. H. Lawrence speculated:

Supposing a bomb were put under the whole scheme of things, what would we be after? What feelings do we want to carry through into the next epoch? What feelings will carry us through? What is the underlying impulse in us that will provide the motive power for a new state of things, when this democratic-industrial-lovey-dovey-darling-take-me-to-mamma state of things is bust?
What next?

In the 1960s Lawrence's bomb went off. It was, perhaps, a real bomb at Hiroshima that began it, followed by the McCarthy period's unveiling of establishment hypocrisy about civil liberties and personal freedom, and the collapse of liberalism in the face of this. Then came the nicely balanced mix of condescending approval and savage resistance that greeted the black liberation movement. Above all, there was the ultimate, blatant cynicism of the Vietnam war. All these, against a background of empty suburban prosperity and the the bankrupt imaginations of those who had let it happen, conspired to create the "bust," of which the radical student movement is only one visible and vocal expression. The middle-class young, raised on the liberal fairy tale of a wonderful system whose basic intentions were good—needing only a little time and energy to correct its small flaws—discovered it wasn't like that at all. They marched in the South and they marched against war, and they found out that the fairy tale was a lie. They asked the people who were supposed to know—their parents, their professors, their elected representatives. They not only failed to get answers; they were told to shut up. So, from Berkeley to Boston, from Columbia to the Sorbonne, they set off the bomb.

The blacks, the Chicanos, the Puerto Ricans, and other minorities had no fairy tale to recover from, for they had always lived outside the dream. The radical student movement of the sixties was born in the South, at the black colleges, in the fifties.

The demise of the American dream has left a gaping hole in the American psyche. "What feelings do we want to carry through into the next epoch? What feelings will carry us through?" The students, at the forefront in the exposure of that hole, must now fill it. This is why what happens at the universities in the seventies has much to do with how we will live our lives in this late century. This is why organization for the new order must begin here and now.

University Organization: Proposals and Demands

The overall objective of the student movement is simply to restructure the university. In the midst of fighting for innumerable subsidiary demands, this inclusive aim should be kept up front. Radical students seek, within the present system, changes in the university which can transform it from a stronghold of the power structure into an arena for the struggle against it. They have begun to insist that institutions of higher learning in the United States reexamine their positions with respect to three major relationships: (1) the power structure itself, as it is manifested in government and in corporate business; (2) the communities in which they are located; and (3) the people who, individually and collectively, constitute the university itself.

1. As regards university complicity with the political and corporate power structure, the main objectives have been and are:

—An end to ROTC and military recruitment on campus.

—An end to war research and to other government and corporation work in which academic expertise is employed to develop weapons or to further colonialism abroad and exploitation at home.

—A redistribution of university investments so that endowment funds are not used to support the most savage forms of enslavement and profiteering. Under the present economic system it is probably not possible to do away with all investments in capitalist enterprises. However, it is possible to distinguish between industries that produce for the needs of life and those that market death in one form or another. Attacks focused on such symbols of oppression as Dow Chemical, United Fruit, and General Electric have helped to expose the callous indifference of educators toward their corporate ties, and opened the way for demands that university funds be invested in socially constructive ventures.

—Adoption of a public position by trustees, administrators, and faculty members against the war, political repression, racism and colonialism, pollution for profit, etc. Words are not actions, but without such minimal verbal commitment there is not even leverage for action. The schools will furthermore be expected to resist the government's threat to use its taxing power to emasculate political activity on the campuses.

2. In regard to the university's relationship with its "home" community, students demand a degree of responsibility that has been lacking up to now:

—Institutional expansion must not make refugees of the neighbors. As landlord, the university is expected to practice the enlightened sociology and the respect for law that is preached in its classrooms.

—The university is being asked to turn its face outward, to listen to the problems of the people around it and to make available its resources of personnel, property, and skills for the health, legal protection, and education of the community. It is time to close the gap between theory and practice by taking the class out of the classroom, the course out of the catalog. Law and psychology, economics and history, are needed in the neighborhood to fight landlordism and price gouging, to improve schools and hospitals, to help oppressed minorities to recover and preserve their cultural heritage.

3. Within the university itself students demand with growing insistence the actual freedom of choice that they are presumably being trained to exercise. At most institutions (the larger ones certainly) administrative/academic hierarchies are obsolete in the light of the tasks of the time. The old holies, grades and credits, are absurdly inappropriate ways to evaluate the life-centered learning that must now go on. Departmental territorialism continues to fragment the students' view of a world that someone is soon going to have to see *whole* if it is going to survive. In rejecting the status quo, activists are abandoning the abstract slogan of "power" for a multitude of innovative proposals designed actually to give the student control over his own education. These fall into three interrelated categories:

—Students demand a part in decision making, from trustee to department level, in matters academic, judicial, and administrative—and on more than a token basis. This implies a new conception of who runs the university for whom. Meaningful participation would include some sort of review of major decisions by the whole student body.

—They claim a hand in planning the curriculum, structuring courses, proposing subjects, working out alternatives to grades and credits. Since students must live while they study, along with these come demands for control over housing and food regulations.

—They want to help restore the university to its original ideal—to make it a meeting place of minds in search of wisdom, rather than a factory for the production of machines to serve the machine. This means replacement of the "multiversity" concept with imaginative student-faculty experiments in small classes, workshops, inter-disciplinary studies, abolition of departments, inde-pendent study, community classes, black-run programs for blacks, student teaching, etc. And this, in turn, de-pends on the students' participating in employment and tenure decisions, which determine what sort of faculty they will have to work with.

Any school that means what it hires scientists, philosophers, and humanists to say ought to meet this determined, if groping, effort with honest collaboration. Those that do not (and perhaps many will not) are not likely to meet their obligations to society as a whole, to the community around them, or to the young generation that now must gain power to make changes and knowledge to decide what changes it wants to make. If this happens, the university—among the most fragile of our contradictory institutions—may be the first of them to collapse. The demand to restructure the uni-versity is, as base, the demand that the university save itself.

Organizing Students: Grass Roots in the University
1. The school calendar is your time frame. Except at moments of overriding crisis (as in the spring of 1970), major actions are rarely successful in examination periods, and vacations tend to break the rhythm of organization. Proposals for major academic or administrative changes may easily take one to three years to become effective, even if nobody is dragging his feet. Student organizers must, therefore, look ahead: use academic interims for evaluating past actions and planning future ones; concern yourself with the calendar and demand its change if it impedes learning and organizing; prepare to pursue campaigns for major innovations over more than one academic year, so that you don't have to begin anew after a vacation; if possible keep some of your group on hand during the summer so as to start fall organizing on registration day.

2. While the university's rate of change is slow, the passage of a student "generation" is incredibly swift. The more you organize around major, long-range goals, the more serious the problem of natural attrition among the organizers. It can be met only by conscious, organized attention to the recruitment of freshmen from the day they step on campus.

Members of your group should arrive early, for orientation week, with your own antiorientation (or disorientation) program. Meetings, raps, leaflets, guided tours of campus and community, social events, guerrilla theater should acquaint the newcomer with an "extracurricular activity" that the dean is not likely to mention. Friendliness and helpfulness, rather than heavy politics, are in order at this stage. Let your information center, newsletter, and "need" line become the new students' resource for tips on professors, ways to juggle requirements, information on birth control, abortions, apartments, etc. Help the younger students discover their own interests and talents; then consciously train them for the various jobs of the movement. Involve sophomores and juniors in negotations and in student positions on committees, so that they gain experience in dealing with administrators and faculty members who will be there when you have gone.

3. The problem of continuity can also be tackled through bringing graduate students into the movement and through making alliances with community people. Grad students who have been active elsewhere are valuable sources of new ideas and methods. Since many are teaching fellows, they provide a link with the faculty. They can be a bridge to the community, as well, since they usually live off-campus. Your group should address itself to their special problems and demands, which usually center around semistarvation and degree requirements so stultifying that they practically unfit a man to be a teacher, or anything else. Local residents are likely to remain even longer than grad students, and they have an immediate stake in the struggle to make the university responsible to the community, but when you graduate do not leave them without contacts in your group. The neighborhood needs active student support in facing a superlandlord like the university.

4. Another bridge to the more permanent community is the university staff. The word is used for everyone from the head secretary and the boss-electrician to the part-time typist, the waitress, the janitor, and the security guard. "Staff" is no more monolithic in its attitude toward student activism than it is in pay, status, or function. Conditions vary between institutions, but the exploitation of the minorities and the unskilled,

and the pay differential between men and women, is about the same as in society at large. The university's role as an employer is an important aspect of its relationship with the local people. A radical student group that is serious about reaching the community should begin at home by supporting staff members in their attempts to improve their situation. First, acquaint yourself with the facts: wage scales, working conditions, fringe benefits, seniority provisions, bargaining rights, etc., as they apply to various categories of university workers. You will probably find that the white-collar staff has little experience of union organization and, despite many grievances, is not easy to organize. The building and grounds workers, maintenance people, and cafeteria employees are apt to be more militant. If you can't organize secretaries, at least make friends with them and let them feel your support. Talk with the workers, but spend most of your time listening to them. If they are engaged in a struggle for better conditions, find out from *them* how best you can support them. Your role will often be the mobilization of your fellow students to observe the workers' picket lines, put pressure on the administration, etc. The chances are that the workers don't need your advice about what demands to make or how to negotiate for them. If you insist on giving it, you will only help build the stereotype of the arrogant student who thinks that college has made him smarter than the workers. You can prove your support day-by-day, by the sort of consideration that lightens their labor. A serious member of the movement does not pass the counterman in the cafeteria or the janitor in the hall as if they were part of the furniture, nor does he (as some worker-student alliance enthusiasts have done at Boston University) leave a meeting hall or a dormitory room looking like a disaster area.

5. Part of the self-education of a student organizing group should consist in a fairly systematic study of the structure of the university itself. This is important for at least three reasons: First, if you plan to make an issue of the trustees' corporate connections, or the chemistry department's services to the Pentagon, you will need to know a lot of facts before you can change them. Second, if you present your demands to the wrong committee or concentrate your pressure on a man who has no power, you practically ask for stalling and buck

passing. Third, the university's facilities are, at least in theory, there for the benefit of the students; if you don't know what is available and what your rights are (and what you can make your right), you will fail to utilize for the movement the "contradictions" represented in the university. The larger and more complex your institution, the more essential it is to devote several workshop sessions to researching its finances, outlining its hierarchy, analyzing the springs of power in terms of administration and faculty, understanding the procedures governing tenure and promotion, and making inventory of all the spaces, machines, services, and supplies of which you may be able to avail yourself. A faculty, administrative, or even graduate-student ally is a great help here, but you can make headway by studying trustees' and treasurers' reports and budgets, master plans, faculty manuals, judicial regulations, residence-hall rulebooks, and even the general catalog. No manual or catalog will, of course, tell you how to use the university environment creatively: to build your alternative structures within it; to insist that it serve your purposes in every way you can think of; to form alliances with those in a position to help you; to discover the points where waste occurs and support your organization with what they throw away. In the practice of these principles of survival you will become expert with experience.

The Student Establishment: Governments and Newspapers

If your college or university runs true to the usual form, the first time you make a demand you will be asked for your credentials and will meet administrative hesitation to deal with anyone but a duly constituted "student government." Of course, you yourself should be ready to show the one credential that counts, a mass of students behind your demand, before you go in to negotiate. As for the administration's preference for talking only with elected student officials, it ought to be resisted on general principles. However, your cause gains strength when it becomes the cause of the student governing body, which presumably represents the largest constituency in the university. The backing of the recognized body usually puts at the disposal of the movement an office, an organizational apparatus, funding, and sometimes a newspaper, all of which are needed not only to win concessions but to make practical use of what is won.

The sound way to transform a timid, liberal, do-nothing student government into an instrument for radical change is to enter the elections with your candidates and your program. Transform the campaign into a forum for the airing of grievances, the proposal of solutions, the planning of alternate structures and services of which the students are in need.

In the event your school is represented by a captive "company union" body it may be legitimate and even necessary for the mass of students to boycott the elections as a fraud, to make restructuring the student government its first demand, and even to use extra-"legal" methods to break the control of the administration's stooges. One general principle holds in such cases: the overwhelming majority of the students should be in motion demanding a representative student government, for if you act without them, by coup d'etat, you are not likely to be able to consolidate your victory in a program of radical new structures.

Whatever the precise organizational form, the arena of student government operations now embraces three main areas, all of which require an exercise of power, a scale of financing, and a level of executive expertise inconceivable a few years ago.

First, the government functions of the body are constantly being extended, as students insist upon control over their own lives. As administrative and faculty boards make room for permanent student members, and as temporary committees (some charged with such far-reaching work as the selection of a president or the formulation of a judiciary system) include students, the demands upon elected officers and the effective power that they wield are vastly increased. So, too, is the possibility of cooption and the necessity for constant interchange, on a grass-roots, small-group basis, as well as at mass meetings, with the student body. Paranoia about cooption can sometimes impair your chances of winning real concessions. On the other hand, it is no exaggeration to say that almost all administrators and a lot of faculty members will try it, almost unconsciously. A sound theoretical understanding of the questions involved, common sense about the possibilities of your situation, and above all, regular reporting and discussions of your work with students of any and all political tendencies are essential antidotes.

Second, student governments or their subcommittees increasingly find themselves at the negotiating table, thrashing out student demands with university trustees, presidents, deans of students, and whatnot.

How you conduct these sessions, whether you bargain for concessions or deliver ultimatums, will depend upon the issues and whether you consider your demands "negotiable" or not. Win or lose, you can turn almost any negotiation into an educational-organizational victory and can guard against falling into bureaucratic traps by keeping the channels to the entire student body constantly open for reports, discussions, criticisms, and suggestions.

Third, as student governments have become radicalized and responsive to the unfulfilled needs of the students, they have begun to set up services that the university has either refused to bother with or handled badly. Your small organizing group could initiate some of these or demand them of the student government if it has not moved. Once elected to office, you will have the organizational and financial means to establish radical alternate structures to meet immediate problems and provide models for further changes. Some, already operating at one school or another, are: a birth-control clinic, a cooperative book exchange, a student tenant union and apartment service, an information service on abortions, birth control, and VD, a drug counseling referral center, draft counseling, a medical cadre, a day-care center, a coffeehouse, a bulk food-buying cooperative, a legal aid program, a bail fund, seminars and free classes, Afro-American centers and classes, self-defense lessons, a twenty-four-hour telephone line for problems ranging from lost kittens and lost lecture notes to illness, loneliness, and worse.

As with the student governing body, your group's attitude toward the student newspaper and/or closed-circuit radio station will depend on whether or not these media are speaking to the issues. If the situation is so repressive that you cannot, by the normal methods, transform the school newspaper into an organ that fights for change, then you had better start your own. Even if you can only afford a mimeographed news-letter, it will gain a mass readership if it speaks to the students' needs. Don't hesitate to criticize the inadequacies of the established paper, but unless the editors are out-and-out administration apologists, try to win them to a more militant position rather than insisting on a polarization. If you are able to gain editorship of the school paper, use your position responsibly to create an all-student forum around the important issues; the same with the radio station.

Organizing Faculty Participation and Support

Students and faculty, together, *are* the university. To the extent they become polarized, the university ceases to be. Education, beneath all the heavy trimmings, is still "a good man on the other end of a log." Not all professors recognize that their only role is to act as one of these good men—nor do all students see themselves as the other. If either jumps off, the class is over. In recent times both have been guilty of abandoning the log, but faculty members first and worst. Their abdication is of much longer standing than the present crisis.

Not suddenly, but over many years, and especially with the expansion of higher education after World War II, administrators and their bureaucracies have usurped the professors' prerogatives in educational policy making. Because teachers did not organize and fight *every time* the budgeteers raised the size of their classes, *every time* the trustees made a corporation man their dean, *every time* the department head prescribed meaningless examinations on meaningless textbooks, *every time* the master planners built a shoddy prison and called it a dormitory, *every time* the admissions committee abdicated to the self-appointed St. Peters of Princeton—because they did not scream bloody murder *every time* the student's interests were subverted—because of this, the computers and their corporate servants took over, with glacial inevitability.

However much Joe McCarthy's know-nothing attack on radical scholarship was a cause of the collapse of the faculties and however much a result, the fact remains that the teachers of the fifties and early sixties (with a few, brave exceptions) barricaded themselves behind "professionalism" to engage in a narcissistic game called "publish or perish," while the corporations, the Pentagon, and the venal, routine minds that serve them were permitted to transform the schools into production lines for war matériel. Indeed, the professors helped them to do it. It is easier to spout facts to five hundred than to probe the meaning of facts with fifteen. Today's older faculty participated in this abdication of principle; the ones who are fortyish are its products; the young ones, thirty and under, were in college when students were beginning to march.

Faculties are not monoliths. Tremendous hassles are going on inside, political as well as academic, and student tactics should aim to take advantage of this. The tenure system being what it is, the younger men cannot always carry your resolution. If you fail to recognize this and let disappointment or impatience prevail over an informed analysis of the actual relationship of forces, you will tie the hands of your staunch allies and throw your potential, still vacillating supporters into the arms of the reactionaries. The faculty members of most institutions, especially the very large ones, have less power than students think. It was given away to the businessmen, bit by bit, and can only be regained by a united front of students and younger faculty (and a few older exceptions) in a fight to restructure the university.

To equate the entire faculty with the administration is a strategic error as dangerous as trusting the entire faculty. In demanding major changes in the way your school operates, you will normally try to drive a wedge between the faculty as a whole and a reactionary administration. Your purposes thus broadly coincide with the interest of all those teachers who believe that an educational institution ought to be run by educators and those being educated. This includes many professors you would hardly call radical: liberals, dedicated teachers with no strong political leanings, a few power manipulators, and a sizable backlog of men and women who are simply sick of IBM cards and memos from the vice-president. If you are serious about winning you will have to work with a lot of people with whom you don't entirely agree —perhaps agree only on the point that has brought you together. You will have to suffer through a lot of stupidities without showing your anguish too openly. You will have to teach your teachers, criticize them freely and permit them to criticize you. Above all, you will have to learn constant vigilance, so that some liberal "friend," upon getting the concession that he wants, cannot hoodwink you into thinking it is your whole pie, or isolate you from your other allies by branding you "unreasonable."

In this general framework, call on faculty members to help you in the three main areas where they can be very useful: public support for your position on the big, national issues; concrete assistance in proposals to change the university; use of special skills in services to you and to the community. Here are some procedures worth considering:

1. Keep faculty members informed of what you are doing. Don't assume they know; they often do not. Make sure they receive your newsletter or newspaper and address special leaflets or letters to them explaining your position and demands when you want their support. It is best to take a reasonable, moderate tone and to be accurate in your facts. Invite faculty members (or selected ones) to your meetings, or offer to hold a teach-in *for* them, at which they can learn about your full program, ask questions, etc. Encourage willing professors to meet small study groups outside of class hours. Invite them to live awhile in your dorm! Invite them to write articles for your newspaper or newsletter. Don't try to censor them, but don't hesitate to debate with them if you feel like it.

2. Address faculty meetings, committees, etc., on your problems and proposals for action. You will normally need an invitation, so ask a friendly professor to get you invited. Show up with a reasonable number and let all prepare to participate. Avoid shouting matches, even if you are heckled. By remaining cool and sticking to your point you can isolate the types who just can't stand listening to students except in "recitations."

3. If you are invited to sit on one of the standing or ad hoc faculty committees, attend the meetings even if they bore you—and try to make them less boring. This does not necessarily mean waking them up with guerrilla theater (though that has been done with some success). It means, first, learning what the business is about and how it affects the students, then using your opportunity to propose innovations.

4. Know the rank of your faculty allies. Some have more "muscle" than others. If your best friends are among the nontenured junior faculty, as is usually the case, don't ask them to do things for you that may get them fired, unless the situation really demands it (in which case, if they are fully with you, you won't have to ask). Stand by those who do stick their necks out, if you want others to do so—and pass the word along to the next student "generation." Political reprisals against activist professors often come two or three years later, under the cloak of "academic" reasons.

5. The whole matter of hiring, firing, promotion, and tenure in the academic world is a can of worms. It seems absurd and inherently arrogant for a departmental committee of older professors to guarantee any man a lifetime position in which he may be teaching *your* children long after the committee members are dead. On the other hand, tenure was won in a struggle to give the professor something like trade-union security and to ensure his freedom of speech. Tread warily when you attack tenure. Few wholeheartedly approve of the academic "ladder" where it is "up or out," with tenure as the prize for good behavior—especially since the climb is usually measured by publications and rigid degree requirements, with little weight given to teaching ability or rapport with students. However, no one really knows what to replace it with. Student groups should study this problem thoroughly and try to come up with something. Activists should not limit themselves to protesting firings but should let the departments hear evaluations of all professors. Try various methods of polling the students on both the course and the teacher. Be sure to get a fair sampling—from most of the students in more than one course of a particular professor. Judgments made on the opinion of too few can create serious injustices in either direction.

6. The official support of a faculty body in demonstrations, strikes, sit-ins, and community mass actions lends strength to your cause and sometimes helps you interest the media. If it is hard to get, don't waste too much time on it. Ask individual professors to speak and identify themselves. Dressing the faculty in caps and gowns at large demonstrations, especially in cases where the police are itching to attack students (Columbia, 1964), has proved effective. If you ask a professor to speak, give him the same freedom you would give another student, even if you don't agree with all that he says. If a faculty member is arrested in your demonstration, give him the same support you give students—and keep alert for future reprisals by the university.

7. Faculty expertise can be used in at least three ways. First, your close allies are sources of information about advance plans and power hassles within the institution. If you want to keep hearing the inside news, keep their confidence. Second, a fairly large number will, if asked, participate

in teach-ins, workshops, and study groups, especially in their own field of competence. In schools where direct political action is difficult, this may be the main way faculty members can participate in your movement. You, in turn, can help train them in better communicating with students and translating theory into practice. Get them out of the classrooms and into your dorms, dining halls, strike offices, etc. Third, as you begin to work with the surrounding community, look upon your doctors, lawyers, political scientists, language teachers, experts in black history, and artists as a rich resource that you can offer to the people, so long as they, and you, keep learning from one another and from the people themselves.

Dealing with Administrations

Unlike the faculty, no section of the administration can be assumed to share the students' desire for major innovative change in the university. When you find an individual official who has awakened to the fact that the school is for students, support his hand and make the most of his help, but for the most part you will have to deal with the administration in terms of demands and negotiations. This is especially true of political and community issues such as ROTC and university expansion. In the case of questions like student-run classes, the abolition of grades, or changes in the judiciary system, you may be asked to send representatives to an ad hoc or permanent committee to "work it out." You should take full advantage of student membership in administrative bodies and demand this as a right if your school does not permit it. This does not, however, eliminate the need for formulating demands, organizing the mass of the students behind them, and keeping everyone fully informed of what is going on. How you proceed depends on the issues and on whether you are presenting negotiable or nonnegotiable demands. Here, however, are some generally applicable suggestions:

1. When your demands have been formulated and ratified by the students, present them in writing to the officer or the chairman of the committee that can act on them. In the case of committees, supply all members with copies. If appropriate, send further copies to any interested parties,

like the president of the university or the trustees. If you have reason to expect skulduggery, send your demands by registered mail, return receipt requested.

2. If you are invited to a private or informal discussion with administrators, insist that other students be allowed to attend. This does not necessarily mean bringing a mass delegation. Save that for the escalated action after you have met resistance. Prepare everyone who goes to speak factually and to answer questions. To be moderate and courteous at this initial stage strengthens rather than weakens your cause. Your command of facts makes it harder for the administrators arbitrarily to refuse you and easier for you to expose them if they do. You may even be able to split their ranks and draw some liberal elements to your side. If you listen more than you talk at these early sessions you may pick up hints of administration in-fighting that you can use to advantage. This assumes that you are negotiating with the idea of getting actual results. If your tactic is primarily to demonstrate and expose, it is not necessary to tread so gently, even at first. However, it is important to develop some sophistication in dealing with university officers about anything: if the president invites you to dinner, you ought to be able to go without fearing cooption. If you don't feel able to tell when you are being coopted, you'd better not be a negotiator.

3. Stalling, buck passing, and fussing about protocol and "channels" is routine administration procedure, even in non-controversial matters. Therefore, set a date by which you expect a reply, and try to make it stick. If you really want results, don't ask the impossible, but force them to treat your demands as a priority. Long-range, complex proposals can be broken down into steps, with dates attached to each. Except in crisis situations, "either-or" deadlines are best saved until you have met a refusal or you see that they are trying to sink you in the subcommittee swamp. When you issue an ultimatum be sure you have something to back it up with.

4. If well-formulated written demands, a factual, polite presentation of them, a reasonable deadline, and evidence of widespread student support produce no results, get busy on the next steps. Through leaflets, newspaper, radio, etc.,

let the entire university community, especially the students, faculty, and working staff, know the state of affairs. Through mass meetings and workshops, draw everyone possible into planning further actions. Such broad consultation should take place *before* and *after* every stage of the campaign, which might run something like this:

a. Resubmit your demands, in stronger terms, with a new and shorter deadline. Send a mass delegation to present them this time.

b. If this brings no result, escalate to the demonstration stage, constantly drawing in more students. Picket administration buildings or hold a mass meeting in front of the president's house. Invade and disrupt the meeting of the committee or board involved. Avoid violence or destruction and keep your slogans directed toward the issues, not administrative personalities. To avoid getting busted, don't announce your plans far in advance and keep the demonstration short. Or try guerrilla theater. A faculty council freaked out at one large university when a silent, masked parade circled the polished table where it was busily avoiding some important issues. Make your protest pointed, symbolic, and related to your demand, so that it helps to educate your own people and makes it harder for the opposition to shrug it off. If your struggle involves the community, be sure that community people are among your spokesmen and part of your group. Through press releases and press conferences inform the local media of your problem and position, preferably before the demonstration stage, so that it is harder for them to portray your actions as "just more student unrest."

c. If the administration breaks up your demonstrations with the police or simply refuses to respond, you can now turn to a sit-in, a strike, or both. Neither should be undertaken unless a large number of students (and/or community people) are in motion behind the demands and a still larger number are concerned and sympathetic. You must have a militant core to organize, act as spokesmen, and face the major risks involved (i.e., arrest, expulsion, bodily injury), but if a small militant group takes it upon itself to act for an apathetic or uninformed student body, it is committing both a tactical and a strategic error. A serious action against the university's private property or its normal operations is a great educational and radicalizing experience for everyone who participates: to approach it lightly or in the spirit of revolutionary elitism is to negate its long-range effects for the movement, not to mention probably losing the immediate battle. Don't rely on the judgment of your small group alone when estimating whether the situation is ripe for such an action. Call mass meetings, more than one if there is time, dormitory meetings, cafeteria meetings, workshops. Try to get expression of sentiment from the less radical sections of the university. Test out your faculty and staff. Turn the newspaper into a forum of opinion, criticism, proposals. If the students respond negatively or languidly and fail to attend the meetings, you should probably go on organizing, attempting to open or reopen negotiations, and mounting ever larger and more imaginative demonstrations until your people are in motion. If, when you call mass meetings, you see a lot of students there who don't usually attend radical gatherings, it is a good sign that the issue has caught on and it may be time to plan an action more substantial than delegations and rallies. (See "Taking Action: Sit-Ins, Student Strikes.")

UNIVERSITY AND COMMUNITY: CHOICES FOR SURVIVAL

Movements for social change within the university form, as a rule, around issues arising from the need for educational renovation and innovation and the need for a new relationship between university and community, local and national. Ultimately, these concerns are one. Students are asking that their schools convert from the production of managerial and technical system servers to the nurturing of human beings who may yet save humanity from the system. They are insisting that the university make a new choice of what "community" it will serve. They ask for commitment to people rather than to corporations. This is the full content of the demand for "relevance." To meet it, universities will have not only to question their definitions of teaching and learning but to decide where their loyalties lie.

If it proves impossible for the university to take a stand against the life-denying forces of present-day society, then the university itself may be impossible. The students and, from an opposite quarter, the communities are sounding the tocsin. The university's peril arises from the fact that its critics are presently at odds. The public's long-standing resentment of the tax-exempt institutional landlord and redeveloper is now bolstered by its resentment of the unruly middle-class student. To save itself, the university must help to bring its students and its community together, which means to become more responsive to both. If it fails to do so, then both will likely be in at the kill.

At the moment this may seem no great loss. Yet each has an interest in the survival or, better, the creation of centers where men and women of all classes, ages, skills, and talents may freely seek ways out of contemporary chaos toward a new order of existence. Granted that the universities are not now such centers, will it be easier, or even possible, to create the necessary forms when policemen have taken over the classrooms or when there are no classrooms? This is the most serious question posed by the politically motivated uproar over "campus unrest," as well as by that unrest itself.

To split and confuse the opposition to the war and its social cost, a reactionary government has cultivated the misunderstanding between the concerned public and the concerned students. That this may jeopardize the very existence of the university, the Nixons and Agnews probably know. The university has been one of the first targets of every modern totalitarian regime. This fact speaks not only to the university's vulnerability (partly a result of its own ambivalence and cowardice), but also to its potential as a threat to the status quo, hence as a force in the search for a new order. The salvation of the American university in the 1970s would seem to depend upon its ability to realize this potential. The breach between it and the public will not be closed by compromise with know-nothing reactionism, or by public-relations campaigns to improve its "image," or by more projects in which communities are treated like guinea pigs. In general terms, the university must begin to put its resources of knowledge and manpower at the disposal of the people in a genuinely collaborative effort to find ways out of the present crisis. Institutionally, this means an end to the myth of scholarly neutrality which has served as cover for complicity in war, colonialism, planned poverty, and environmental devastation. Educationally, it means a willingness to test its teaching and research, content and method, by the criteria of human needs and human aspirations.

Even given the willingness, neither administrators nor professors nor, for that matter, students and people outside know how, practically, to change a "system" of which they are all the products. But coping with the obvious difficulties (financial, legal, political) can wait upon discovering direction. Actually, the first steps are simple and inexpensive. Students, nonstudents, and teacher drop-outs are already taking some of them, as evidence by the countrywide proliferation of "free" schools and universities. Ephemeral and hand-to-mouth as many of these may be, they are springing up faster than they are folding up and have already provided both motive power and models for experimental programs and colleges within the system itself. (See Bibliography–Directory.)

Based in college communities, the "free" university's impulse is outward, toward the people whose interests the established schools have practically ignored. As the "free university" movement penetrates the workers' communities and the ghettos, however, its organizers are uncovering some pitfalls. Community people, like students, want something better than they have had—the best, in fact. They tend, however, to define the best rather differently than students do. Inner-city dwellers, suffering the urban blight of schools, housing, and community services, often seem less alienated from contemporary society and from the university than students brought up in green suburbs—possibly because they still aspire to these. When the "free school" organizer, seeing this, learns to ask the community what it wants rather than to present it with what he thinks it ought to want, he may find himself replacing "Third World Liberation Movements" with "English for the Spanish-Speaking," or "Exploring New Life-Styles" with "Budgeting for the Home." In meeting such requests, as he should, he may presently realize that he is merely supplementing what the evening high schools and neighborhood centers already do moderately well. As he struggles to define the role of the "free university," he may be tempted to make either or both of two condescending assumptions: on the one hand, that freewheeling discussion groups centered on current struggles are all the community needs or wants to become "radicalized"; on the other, that bread-and-butter courses in practical skills are all that poor people can really be interested in.

To settle on either assumption is to treat people as if they were class stereotypes, sharing none of the students' own complex interests in and feelings about the world, save those that concern economic and political survival. This is, in fact, to negate the real "revolutionary" potential of a student and nonstudent alliance. The "free university" organizer will therefore probably need the aid of his professors (those who are up to it) and of all the advanced students, independent experts, community leaders, etc., that he can marshal, to make sure that the educational content is not diluted, but expanded, deepened, and made fully "relevant."

The fact is, most college students have discovered their alienation from modern society in college. The ecologist who gives his class a life prospect of thirty years, the political scientist who fills these years with famines and wars—these are providing new perspectives on the "success" of parents who pay the tuitions. The student's response is necessarily a divided one: on the one hand, moral outrage against a system which denies his own advantages to most of the people; on the other, guilty revulsion against the very canons of the "success" which produced his advantages. Hence the students' "political" demand that the poor and oppressed be permitted to enjoy those material benefits which students "culturally" reject for themselves.

Since this inner contradiction is hardly recognized by the students themselves, it is small wonder that working people sometimes find student dissent and student "counterculture" next to incomprehensible. But university people do not comprehend the communities too well, either. Mutual understanding can come when the communities are offered, through whatever structures prove appropriate, the best educational experiences that the students have had, and much better. This will surely need the collaboration of every element of the university, first of all the faculty, which will have to (and, in the process, can learn to) change its ways. Teachers and students can neither use the community merely as an experimental laboratory for trying out new educational structures, nor as a life-giving source of revolutionary attitudes and activities. The liberating forms cannot come out of romantic revolutionism or an urge to expiate the sin of being middle-class. They might come, and soon, if students, community people, university faculties and administrations would determine that each has a vital stake in the process and would open themselves to learning from one another in the course of a common effort. What can happen when one or another group forgets that vital stake, the following case history will illustrate.

The Communiversity: An Unfinished Parable

When the students of Boston University joined the national strike of May 1970, they demanded and were granted a University-sponsored student-administered program of free evening classes for the people of Greater Boston. With only minimal help from the faculty, students worked out details with the University Council, set up an office, recruited volunteer teachers (professors, students, independent professional people, community organizers), issued a course catalog, arranged for publicity and, on June 8, opened the Communiversity, complete with child-care center, coffee hour, fifty course offerings, no fees, no requirements, and no registration procedures, to all who wished to attend. An estimated three thousand per week did so, in two-hour classes which met once a week during a five-week semester. (Some continued much longer as student-led discussion groups.) Most were held in University classrooms and some required large lecture halls. The thirteen courses offered at community locations were generally smaller, but at least half of them were successful. Each class decided on its own procedures, usually open structures of lecture and free discussion or division into small groups.

The student body, gathered in less than two weeks through leafleting, canvassing, and announcements through the media, was composed of about half university students and half community people, mostly middle-class and white collar, quite a number middle-aged. The program did not, in its first, hastily organized semester, attract many people from the inner city, save for some from the black community who participated in courses like "Black History," and a group of American Indians who attended a course devoted to their situation.

The subjects offered can be roughly distinguished as political, cultural, and those involving "survival skills." Each course, in its own way, tended to provide a radical, though nondoctrinaire, critique of present society. Some, like "White Rule in Africa," "American Foreign Policy," "The Why of

War," "The History of Women in America," "Genetics and the Population Explosion," offered a general "political" orientation, while others, like "The Draft Law," "Inadequate Medical Care," "Juvenile Delinquency," and "The Teacher and Social Change," focused on particular problems. "Cultural" courses included "Language and Relations between People," "Literature of the Counter-Culture," "The Biblical Roots of Dissent," "The Generation Gap." "Survival skills" ranged from "Consumer Protection," "Grass-Roots Organizing," and "Landlord-Tenant Relationships" to "Basic Sewing," "Leaflet Writing," and "High-School Mathematics." Course titles and descriptions were generally proposed by the teachers, since there was not time thoroughly to canvass the communities about what subjects they would find most useful. Such a canvass in preparation for the Communiversity's fall semester turned up, for example, a widespread demand for English for the Spanish-speaking. The student organizers recognized that the direct involvement of the leaders of community organizations in choosing, planning, publicizing, and teaching the courses was essential to the project. They succeeded in scheduling half of the fall's fifty-eight courses in various neighborhood centers.

As plans went forward for the autumn, a subcommittee of the University Council, the body which had approved the project at the time of the strike, proposed that the Communiversity agree to a number of restrictions if it planned to continue operating in University classrooms. Two of these, especially, betrayed an almost total misconception of the meaning and purpose of the Communiversity. In recommending that the leadership be limited to students registered at B.U. the subcommittee negated the Communiversity's prime objective, i.e., to build a genuinely collaborative community-university educational structure. In effect, it announced the University's intention to exercise unilateral control. Similarly, a plan to subject the credentials of Communiversity faculty to review by a university regulatory body apparently sought veto power over what would be taught and by whom. The student organizers rejected these restrictions and began to look for space outside B.U. classrooms. In the face of this resistance the subcommittee dropped its proposed regulations. It was agreed that the Communiversity should function independently of the University and, like any other student activity, be permitted to use available classroom facilities. The name of Boston University was dropped from the fall course catalog. . . . Victory.

The question is, *for whom?* The students were right to resist restrictions which would have undermined the Communiversity's community base and destroyed its freedom to experiment. But they lost, nonetheless. In not demanding and fighting for continued University support and sponsorship, they lost what had been won by the May strike, when the University had been forced to acknowledge its institutional responsibility to the community and to support its students' attempts at educational innovations. Administrators and faculty members lost an opportunity to experience new relationships with community people and with students. The University's withdrawal represented a failure of nerve at a moment when the survival of universities may depend upon just such common efforts at attacking common problems. The community lost not only the benefits of resources and expertise that students cannot supply, but the chance to develop an expanding collaboration with an institution that hitherto had shared very little with it. It would seem that no one involved had a clear political understanding of what he was about.

Organizational Suggestions

For those who plan to set up a "free university" on a fairly large scale, with or without university assistance, here are some hints, gleaned mainly from the Boston University experience.

Especially during the school year, a large group of students, faculty members, and community people will be required to initiate and administer a "free education for the people" program, with a division of labor among a number of working committees. The most important of these are:

Office: phones, files, correspondence; regular hours, probably five days a week.

Curriculum and Teacher Recruitment: two cooperating committees, one to handle university liaison; the other to work with community organizations in planning, staffing, and scheduling classes. (This is the most important of all the committees.)

Class Assistance: members to attend each course to assist teachers and students in developing open structures and to provide "feedback."

Publicity: two committees, one to publish and distribute (mail, canvassing, etc.) each semester's course catalog, and perhaps to issue a weekly newsletter for the student body; the other to deal with the mass media.

Child Care: members to arrange for a suitable place and equipment and to cover the center during class hours.

Membership and Social: to arrange for a coffee hour at classes and for occasional social and cultural events.

Funds (unless the university or student government finances the undertaking): to conduct a continuing program of fund raising, seek foundation grants, etc.

The establishment of such working committees would not, of course, automatically provide a policy-making base. If community people are to be involved in genuine planning and leadership, policy decisions cannot be left to a vague "collective" of active students, nor can one assume (as did the organizers at B.U.) that maximum democracy resides in mass-meeting governance. What works well on the campus may not be appropriate to involve people engaged in various occupations all over a large city. To encourage and ensure community participation, some sort of delegated body is probably best. Representation of the working committees, of the teachers, of the community centers sponsoring classes, and of the classes themselves would provide numerous categories that include community people, as well as university students and faculty, and would probably create a body larger than were any of the Communiversity's "mass meetings."

Whatever the precise forms, so long as a clear policy of broadly delegated responsibility and power is maintained, with community participation and consultation at every step, the possibilities of the Communiversity concept are tremendous. The universities as such should follow the initiative of the students and open themselves as "communiversities" to their neighbors. If they will not, or until they do, students, with their friends of the faculty and the community, should go ahead on their own.

III. Ethnic and Racial Groups

Introduction

In the era of worldwide revolution against colonialism, the long-ignored demands of the major ethnic and racial minorities in the United States for an equal place in the nation's life become challenges to the system of monopoly capitalism itself. The fight against racism that once saw full integration and equality as its goal has been transformed into a struggle for national self-determination within the borders of the U.S. and, as such, is allied with liberation movements of the peoples of the third world, from Vietnam to Peru. The black people and, in their particular ways, the Chicanos, Puerto Ricans, and American Indians, have begun to recognize that their status in the United States is essentially that of colonized peoples. Thus even their day-to-day battles for bread and housing and education and justice are in fact, as Malcolm X and Eldridge Cleaver have shown, battles against the same power that burns Vietnamese villages, rings the globe with military bases, and fills the third world with its counterrevolutionary spies.

The white majority within the United States shares a common enemy with the colonized peoples at home and abroad. From the superprofits of colonialism the rulers of the "mother country" bribe the white worker, even while they send his son to war and threaten to replace him with the "cheap labor" of the very people whose impoverishment is the basis of his marginally better position. When the great mass of the exploited, the white workers and hard-pressed middle class of the U.S., understand this and recognize the liberation movements of blacks, Puerto Ricans, Chicanos—and Vietnamese and Bolivians—as the advance guard of their own struggles for a better life, only then will they be able to break the yoke of racism to unite against the common enemy.

The articles of this section were written by a collective of black students at Boston University; a black student leader at the Massachusetts State College at Lowell; Mexican-American organizers in El Paso, Texas; and on the basis of lengthy interviews with a member of the Puerto Rican Young Lords Organization, and with American Indians and Asian Americans. They are designed to acquaint all concerned persons with the ongoing movements, the problems and the issues. They are written not to call the white activist into the ghettos to help, but to urge him to go out among his own people to carry on the difficult fight against racial, national, and class prejudice, a fight which must be won, and soon, if a new order is to be born.

1. Blacks

THE BLACK STUDENT IN UNIVERSITY AND COMMUNITY

The black student in the white university is in a frustrating and often confusing position. Many of the problems that he will have in getting himself and his brothers and sisters on campus and in community together will seem overwhelming.

The artificial white atmosphere in which he is placed will affect all of his social and political actions, whether he likes it or not. He is part of a special breed of blacks. His presence on the compus is more often than not a compromise between the violent threats of angry black America and the conscience and fear of the white American power structure. He will probably be pampered and cared for by the university more than the white students around him. Most of his bills and expenses may be taken care of by the school.

The racism and oppression that he feels will be more on a mental than a physical level. He will understand the oppression of his people, not only in terms of experience, but also as general theory. Yet during his stay in that situation, he is faced, in terms of everyday living, with the need to understand who he is, why he is where he is, and how his situation relates to the black struggle of liberation. Each university setting will present its own unique problems.

The setting will also determine what kinds of action he can take toward liberation.

GETTING TOGETHER ON CAMPUS. In attempting to get himself together, it is important that he understand the brothers and sisters with whom he will have experiences on the campus.

In most cases the black student in the white university will come from a strong black middle-class background. This "middle-class" status will only mean that his parents probably aspire to the position, not necessarily the physical presence, of white middle-class America. Unlike his parents, his generation has grown up with an internal sense of black awareness. His search will be to understand what that awareness is to mean. Attempting to discover his identity will be one of the factors of his frustrations.

Often he will be confronted on campus with a smaller group of black students from the lower class. He will find that this group will have many different and unfamiliar values and norms. Strangely enough, the strongest pressure for conformity will come from this smaller number of lower-class black students. And in order to appear "together" the majority of black students may have to adopt these norms and values.

The black man-woman situation at the university is another factor that has to be examined in attempting to get together as individuals or groups. Both sexes must be able to sit down and analyze the situation that confronts them on the campus. Shall they live the stereotype or create new relationships?

Other important factors are the number of black students in the university and their ratio to the number of white students, the geographic location of the university in relation to the black community, the "status" attached to the university itself.

The problem of black awareness requires that the student be careful not to fall into the self-set trap of "enemy stereotypes." He will look to the community for clues as to how he should act. However, in the black community there is a culture and an "anticulture," anticulture being that part of black people's behavior which merely constitutes a reaction to white oppression. It is essential that the individual black student analyze the condition of his community and determine that which is real and relevant to liberation and that which is counterrevolutionary and merely the result of oppression. He must learn to utilize that which is good and truly black and beautiful and to destroy those elements of black culture which destroy his people.

For example, the presence of narcotics in the black community is the result of exploitation—a desperate attempt to escape exploitation. We understand the ill effects of narcotics on any human being, thus it is foolish for black students to adopt the use of hard drugs, thinking that it is a norm of black culture and something that whitey doesn't understand. Similarly with the consumption of cheap wine. Brothers and sisters on the corner drink the wine as a means of getting away from the "white tray." We understand how this wine destroys the body and the mind. For black students to adopt the habit of drinking cheap wine as a part of black culture is to fall into the trick bag of living stereotypes of the "anti-culture," mistaking it for black culture. The black student should work to show his brothers and sisters in the community the reasons for and effects of "anticulture," rather than adopting it for himself.

The black student should not only learn the manner in which American capitalists exploit the black community—by pushing the sale of expensive clothes or big cars, for example—he should clearly show that he is not a victim of that exploitation. Industry has even attempted to exploit black awareness by selling Afro clothes and other African culture items. The black student must understand such tactics and then deal with them properly.

The problems on the "integrated" college campus now are very different from those in the past. A decade ago the black student was often preoccupied with proving his worthiness and equality with his white colleagues. This is no longer true. Black students are more confident of their ability and of the beauty of their blackness. They have stopped attempting to educate white students to the "race problem" and recognize that its solution rests with themselves and not with white America.

The role of white radical left students must coincide with this changing attitude of black students. White radical leftists have two important tasks. First, they must educate themselves about the problems confronting black people in America. Second, they must shoulder the task of educating other whites about these problems. They can no longer expect black students to be involved with either task. In any kind of action or protest against racism and white oppression, white leftists must be willing to accept a subservient role to black organization and leadership. The fact that the toughest situation for whites to face (whether they be from the right or new left) is to take orders from black people indicates the depth of American racism. White new left students must recognize that their presence is no longer desired in the black community. If the whites desire change, they must first strive to clean up the sickness of their own race.

The attitude of the black community on this issue should not be that of hatred or black racism. The simple fact is that a struggle for liberation is fought and won only by those whose liberation is at stake. Part of that liberation is the very willingness to take leadership in the struggle.

ACADEMIC FOCUS. It is essential that the black student make a careful analysis of the education that he is receiving. If the educational institution serves only to preserve the society which created it, the norms and values of that society will be preserved. If the student is given only skills and expertise, he will merely keep the same old society functioning. The tasks of nation building require that the black student's education go much further.

Is there any difference in the educational objectives of white America and black America? Are there two educations similar and complementary, or quite different and contradictory? Why does white America want the black student in school and why does black America want him there? If the goals of each prove to be different and contradictory, can a situation be created in the white university where the black student can preserve and build black, rather than white, America? If he finds that, traditionally, the educated black has not been able to help his community, then how can he discover in education the tools for real change?

One of the chief priorities of the black students must remain academic work. In order to place black people in a position to wage a physical struggle of liberation or to defend themselves from oppression and exploitation, it is first essential to have people with skills and expertise. Indeed, black students must concentrate on the technical skills offered at the university. Engineers, biologists, administrators, medical specialists, agriculture specialists, architects are only a few of the various professions needed for liberation. Now is the time to take advantage of the training that is offered.

But it is very important to understand that all subjects and fields are related to liberation. Subject areas in the humanities, such as Afro-American studies, are important, but to the serious black student this subject material is part of his extra studies only. The concentration on other fields (math, science, technical skills) that can be learned in the white university should be "schoolwork."

The important added task of black students should be to bring new concepts of education into the white university which will allow all subject matter to be taught from a black perspective. New concepts of education should be developed to allow the black student to gain an educational experience which will teach him to preserve and build black America, rather than maintain the American white power structure. Black students should build and support programs for the black community, not only for their own sake but because this can be the very essence of black education—the source and generator of the new concepts.

TACTICS. In working toward their goals black students should avoid open confrontation whenever possible. The days of building take-over and sit-down protest are over. Through nonviolent civil disobedience students merely place themselves in a position to be very easily attacked by the repressive forces of the white power structure. For an example, when students illegally occupy a building, the university seeks an injunction to order to have the students removed. Failure of the students to obey the injunction sets off a series of reactions by the law-enforcement agencies. The students at some point will be removed from the building, jailed for failing to comply with the injunction, and marked as "radicals." They will then be carefully watched by the intelligence agencies and thus their mobility and ability to maneuver is destroyed. Their presence in any future action, violent or nonviolent, threatens the effectiveness of those who plan to carry the action out. The same is true for disruptive protest marches or rallies. The university will call in university police agencies, followed by municipal police, followed by state police, national guard and, if necessary, national troops and, at some point along the line, the disruptive protest will be stopped. The situations at Jackson State and Kent State should never be repeated.

Black students must develop other methods of struggle which do not necessarily involve mass open confrontation. Instead, an attempt should be made to develop tactics which legally disrupt the operational processes of the university as a means of winning goals. Jamming the university communication network by having hundreds of students dial vital numbers at the same time, or infiltration of the university structure by employment of blacks are only two of the kinds of methods that should be developed to pressure the university and win demands. Because of the continuing repression by the white power structure, students must employ legal "hit-and-run" tactics and utilize the element of surprise in promoting changes in the concept of university education in a racist white society.

COMMUNITY INVOLVEMENT. Community involvement is very important for a number of reasons. First, there are immediate needs of black people which must be met now. Black students can meet many of these needs. Second, community action places the black student constantly in a position where he can see and experience the blunt end of American racism from which he is somewhat protected on the campus. Third, the black student finds out how he can apply his learned skills to serve black people in the community. Fourth, experience in the black community will test the quality of his education and be a source of clues for its change.

Before attempting to aid the black community, one should study its class structure, examine the existing agencies, evaluate how effective they are in providing services and programs for the black community, and find out from the people what kinds of programs and services they need and want.

There are several different class structures within the black community. The dominance or influence of one class over the others will depend on the individual community. There are very few upper-class blacks anywhere. Their power and influence is small. Their wealth, which comes from white America, has usually been fully tapped. In the growing black middle class, there are two rather distinct elements. The established middle class is usually made up of older-generation blacks who have gained some degree of black political awareness only in recent years. For the most part, this class still seeks assimilation into middle-class white America. A physical assimilation is no longer a major priority, but rather assimilation in terms of values and economics. The established middle class has little power in American society or over the masses of blacks living in America. It derives its status and power only from its relationship with the white power structure. But the established black middle class can be utilized to provide resources needed for programs and services. It will cooperate in providing both financial and manpower resources, mainly manpower. Many black church members who are active in the community can be found in this class and the black middle-class church can be utilized to provide needed resources for programs and services. The established black middle class is chiefly in need of political education. Programs and services designed to give instruction in political ideology and in Afro-American humanities can be very effective in promoting its striving toward black liberation.

Another element of the black middle class is the "hustler." Members of this class survive through small-time crime, both organized and unorganized. Pimps, prostitutes, numbers racketeers, gamblers, narcotics pushers, and gangsters are all members of this class. In *Negro* America, the status and position of respect of the middle-class hustler was extremely high. The masses of lower-class blacks aspired to become members of the hustler middle class, rather than of the established middle class. This class accepts little of American values and norms other than economic success and success to the "hustler" is defined by big cars and very expensive clothes.

Unfortunately, the black middle-class hustler is seldom careful as to whether he exploits white or black America. To many members of this class, political awareness is only another means of making money. In terms of resources for programs and services, little can be expected from this class and little will be received.

The middle-class hustler is in great need of political education. Should an effective means of providing that education be discovered, this class could provide dynamic resources for the struggle of black liberation. Should political education of the middle-class hustler continue to prove futile, then this class more than any other will have to be destroyed as quickly and permanently as the white oppressor. Its presence can no longer be tolerated in the black community.

The masses of blacks still remain in the black lower class. This class will be able to offer the least in terms of resources. This class is more in need of political education and organization than any other in the black community. The members of the black lower class bear the full weight of white American racism and economic exploitation. Most of the programs and services offered should be designed to meet the immediate needs of these people.

The lower-class masses of blacks will be the most difficult to work with. Apathy toward politics and organization is great. For most of their time, their energies and efforts are directed toward basic survival. Because of its lack of power this class is open to exploitation and oppression by the white American power structure and, for that matter, by other classes of the black social structure. Voiceless and angry, the black lower-class masses will ultimately determine the success or failure of the liberation struggle. The most frightening fact is that they are now lacking leadership and direction.

It is too late for the black intelligentsia to argue about the virtues of competing ideologies. The most effective and winning ideology will be the one which is capable of meeting the immediate needs of the black lower-class masses. Should the time bomb of their discontent explode before such leadership and direction is provided, then it will probably mean that the destructive frustration and outburst will be met and checked by the military might of the American white power structure. But should that leadership emerge, all of the military strength of America will not be able to stop the determined masses of blacks from winning the struggle of liberation.

FALSE DIRECTIONS. There are a number of agencies in the community which black student organizers should attempt to detect. These agencies are detrimental to the liberation struggle and should be exposed and destroyed.

In an age of growing black awareness, the "pork-chop black nationalist" can have his heyday. He hides under a facade of black nationalism, yet far from being committed to the liberation struggle his agencies are exploiters of black people. The white power structure, usually the liberal elements, has helped create and support this element in the black community. The "pork-chop nationalist" often receives funding from the government to provide services. Rather than using the funds to provide effective programs, the "pork-chop nationalist" pockets most of the funds for himself. The people of the community can sense the phoniness of the "pork-chop nationalist." He will be destroyed by the black community itself.

Another kind of agency in the community, usually created and supported by the conservative elements of the white power structure, is that designed to establish a black capitalist class. It should be obvious that the oppression caused by the capitalist economic system is the same whether it is administered by whites or Negroes. Black capitalism may result in double exploitation since it must produce enough profits to fill the pockets of both the Negro and the white masters who pull the strings.

The days of American and European capitalism are numbered. The nonwhite nations of the world are beginning to pull themselves together in order to wage a united struggle against the forces of neocolonialism and European colonialism. For black Americans to join the capitalist power structure would mean waging a struggle against their African and Asian brothers and sisters. The failure of the "black capitalist" movement is inevitable. The masses of blacks have refused to support its establishment. It is essential that political education be given to ensure its failure.

COMMUNITY ORGANIZING. In many instances, agencies in the black community will be established by the government and receive funding. These agencies may appear to be functioning in the manner of the "pork-chop black nationalist" or as the "black capitalist" in order to get the funding. In actuality, they may have the support of the community and provide effective programs and services.

The easiest method of determining the effectiveness of community agencies is by talking with brothers and sisters on the street. They will know whether an agency is effective or not. By talking with the people in the community, black student organizers will be able to determine what kind of programs and services the people need and want.

One of the most effective means of organizing the black community is to solicit the aid of those who live there. This is not an easy job, especially when attempting to organize the lower-class blacks. Many brothers and sisters from this class have been constantly used and exploited. They will be afraid to help. They may also be so involved with basic survival for themselves and their families that they do not have the time to help. Their attitude will be pessimistic toward the programs you attempt to start. They are used to failure. But these brothers and sisters are far from ignorant. If you can show them how the programs you are attempting will help them to meet their immediate needs, then you have a good chance of gaining their active support.

Another means of selling your programs to the people is by working with the children. Your presence will excite the beautiful and curious minds of little brothers and sisters in the community. The stifling and fatal atmosphere of the public schools has not yet destroyed their imagination. These children, like their parents, will be quick to detect condescension and paternalistic attitudes. The youth of the black community are forced to mature rapidly in order to survive.

Flyers and short news bulletins are not effective in speaking to the black community people. They are used to being led down false paths with letters, notices, etc. They will not be motivated to participate in the programs unless they are personally contacted. Many black communities have radio stations or community programs. Use them whenever it is possible.

The above methods of gaining support and assistance in starting programs are only a few of many. The individual community will produce different methods of motivation. Part of the task of providing services and programs involves discovering the methods of involving people in them.

PROGRAMS FOR ACTION. There are a vast number of services and projects which black students can start and run. One important project would be to establish information centers: to collect data on the operations of existing agencies in the community; to evaluate these agencies; to refer people to them. The information center could provide facts about where community members could find the greatest purchasing power for their dollars. It could help people take care of problems in dealing with the white power structure. For example, students from the center might go with a mother to the welfare agency to question the validity of the actions of a particular social worker.

It is important that self-sufficient programs be created. For example, rather than merely renting a house for an information center, an attempt should be made to purchase the property. In this way the existence of the center does not depend on continuous charity. To raise funds, offer real and tangible services to community people or others, e.g., haircuts or parties. Or students might live in the building which houses their program. The funds they would usually pay for dormitory living could go toward the purchase price.

The use of parties and rallies is a good method of getting people familiar with your programs and building enthusiasm for them. Since good times are few and far between, this is a means of meeting the immediate needs of the people. Make some education a part of the party; the people will be susceptible to new ideas and new programs.

As mentioned earlier, the middle-class black church is another avenue for getting programs accepted in the community. Many members will be willing to volunteer time and energy to help get the programs off the ground. The black middle-class church is usually conservative. The politicization of the black church members will be slow and will require patience, but by using moderate techniques, it can be accomplished.

To solicit the aid of lower-class black church members will be very difficult. The religious philosophy of the church will usually restrain the members from participating in political activities. The emphasis is more likely to center on religious activities in the church.

The organizers should attempt to know and use the language of the black community. This will eliminate much of the fear of "strange intruders" into the community and will increase the credibility of the program.

Black students can volunteer their services in helping existing agencies. Usually the most effective agencies are those which lack the adequate finances to hire expertise and manpower. For example, students might be able to solicit funds from the university or full student body to aid breakfast or clothing programs being administered by existing community agencies. Black students can help organize a voter registration campaign—a year-round drive, rather than a crash campaign connected with a particular election.

Another political task that can be undertaken is the creation of emergency mobilization groups. There are many situations where a large group of community people may need to congregate immediately. For example, if a number of blacks are arrested on trumped-up charges, the ability of a large group of people to mobilize at a certain police station at once could be decisive in whether the victims would meet with police brutality or fair treatment. The mobilization group could also be helpful in aiding people who are being evicted or forced to move, by having telephone numbers of other members and providing prearranged transportation. As the mobilization group grows, it would then be possible to break into smaller units which would be committed to emergency situations, and which might organize themselves into time shifts or simply be on call.

Black students can also start self-help groups in housing projects. Many project families live in constant fear of their neighbors and tend to keep to themselves, which keeps them from learning to work together. Organize baby-sitting services, sanitary teams, and other basic need programs. The people can begin to organize their own food programs, patrol against criminals in the community, and provide transportation services by forming car pools.

The creation of vigilante committees in the black community by black students is a further way of meeting the immediate needs of the people. School administrators, teachers, cops, etc., find it difficult to "slack off on the job" when carefully and systematically observed by community people who vow to report them to their superiors and the public press.

The black community is in need of courses and instruction to help them understand and cope with racism and exploitation, while trying to deal with their basic economic problems: how to protect themselves against hustlers in the streets; how to act when arrested; how to repair and maintain homes and property; where to learn about sex education, birth control methods, and maternal care. Day-care centers; drug and alcohol abuse clinics; telephone personal counseling services; and self-defense instruction in karate and rifle are other projects black students can organize.

Only after the immediate needs of the people are being dealt with will the black community be willing to accept programs designed for political education and organization.

If the basic needs programs are effective, the community may then be persuaded that programs for larger political purposes may also be worth its effort.

It is essential that the black student give his best effort to his work in the black community. His effort there will certainly shape and qualify the success or failure of the black liberation struggle. And his experience in that struggle will certainly shape and qualify the education he wants from the university—it may even shape and qualify the education he gets.

THE WHITE ORGANIZER IN THE
BLACK COMMUNITY

Before committing yourself to organizing in the black community, it would be wise to consider some obvious but often ignored facts. First, you may not be the revolutionary, organizer, or even the person you think you are. The cliché of the "ego-tripping" white radical did not arise out of a vacuum. (Such "tripping," it might be added, is not confined to whites.) Secondly, there is, among movement organizers, a zealousness much like that of religious missionaries. Revolutionary zeal often fosters a "savior complex" which has a negative influence on the organizer's interaction with the community. A third factor, stemming possibly from the messianic self-image, is the feeling that your truth is the only truth. This commonly held, but rarely acknowledged, view can make communication virtually impossible. It might be very rewarding to devise some method (e.g., role playing) of periodically testing your receptiveness to the views of others. Finally, you should be aware that your decision to organize in the black community does not obligate anyone in that community to like, respect, or work with you. The organizer who relies on the community to satisfy his psychological needs for support and approval should not expect to be very successful.

The question of motivation also deserves some reflection. It would be absurd to insist that organizers be motivated by unadulterated altruism. But it does not seem unfair to ask that they not be driven by a need for the expiation of guilt feelings. Past alliances between blacks and whites provide ample evidence of the negative consequences of excessive guilt feelings on the part of whites. The blacks in those situations displayed an understandably opportunistic bent. The whites, as might be expected, soon tired of being misused. Both groups ended up as losers.

None of the above can be considered encouraging. Revolutionary optimism must be tempered by a conscious awareness of some often unpleasant realities. There are, of course, many positive aspects to working with any group of people. The organizer who earns the respect and friendship of the black constituency can count on his fair share of joyful camaraderie. If you seek this kind of response, however, there is a need for some positive preparation on your part. Apart from the soul-searching already suggested, a close look at the community to be organized should be very helpful. The role of the organizer should be to help the constituency solve its problems—not to solve what he thinks are its problems. Learn how it defines its troubles before you have lost your objectivity.

Focusing on the lower economic end of the very diverse black community, what is most impressive is the similarity in attitudes and thinking to those of middle America—this, in spite of the contradictions which daily bombard them. The often-discussed black self-hatred derives much of its impetus from the coexistence of middle-class morality and lower-class behavior. Lower-class blacks have the same aspirations as their middle-class brothers, but are much more aware of the futility of even trying to act white. These brothers bear the brunt of this oppressive system. They are therefore much more receptive to organization. Black revolutionary groups have depended heavily on these "brothers off the block" in their efforts to organize the black community. White organizers should be forewarned that many of the brothers are not yet sufficiently politicized to accept their struggle on any but a black versus white level.

The Black Panther party for self-defense has been in the forefront of the struggle in terms of political education and organization. It also has the distinction of being willing to work with white radicals. The Panther party's feeling about organization is that whites should organize other whites. They restrict their organizational efforts to the black community and ask that their white allies reciprocate in kind.

The Black Muslims differ from the Panther party in their refusal to work with whites. Muslim rhetoric is harsh and heavily black-supremacist. It is interesting to note that most of the revolutionary brothers and sisters borrow freely from both Panther party and Muslim interpretations of the struggle. It seems evident that nothing is to be gained by attempts of whites to organize in any area where Panther party or Muslim contingents are in evidence.

The most important advice for any organizer in the black community is be yourself. Honesty is important to black people. We have had our fill of white saviors and father surrogates. We do not need your dogma or your self-sacrifice —we need results. If you are sensitive to our needs, and not hung up on your own, you are welcome.

2. Mexican Americans (Chicanos)

The second-largest minority group in the U.S. has been largely ignored until the mid-1960s. Chicanos, among the first to settle the lands north of the Rio Grande, have suffered injustices at the hands of white America ever since "manifest destiny" drove U.S. troops down to win their land "for the union and people."

Over one-third of the 5 million Mexican Americans living in Texas, California, Colorado, New Mexico, and Arizona live below the $3,000-a-year poverty level. Mexican Americans have the lowest median education in the country, and are subjected to schools that fail to deal effectively with language and cultural differences. In the "barrios" where most make their homes, employment is low, jobs that exist are often the most poorly paid, and living conditions are abominable. Living conditions are just as bad in the "campos" where many Chicanos work as migrant farm laborers, and opportunities for education are even fewer. Chicanos are freqeuntly abused physically and verbally by law-enforcement officers, arrested on insufficient grounds, deprived of proper use of bail and of adequate legal representation, and underrepresented on juries.

Conditions persist due to a combination of "gringo" racism and neglect, and to the Chicano's failure, until recently, to organize to control the forces that control his life.

The most recent generation of Chicanos has seen a new pride in the richness of Chicano culture, an awareness of the scope of his problems, a rise in militancy, and an increasing readiness to view political organizing as a means of bettering the conditions of "la Raza." The most active groups today are those with the most radical positions. While in the "barrio," at the university, and in the agricultural fields Chicano activism has been growing steadily, a sense of alienation from politics rooted deeply in Chicano culture continues to be the greatest barrier to political organizing. Any attempt to organize Chicanos must address itself to the Chicano's brand of political apathy.

The "hacienda," the church, the family, and the political culture have all been significant influences on the Chicano's attitudes, and must be viewed in relation to each other. Under the arbitrary and harsh peonage system of slavery on Mexico's "haciendas," the predecessors of today's Chicanos were forced to relinquish all control over their lives to powerful "hacendados"; they learned that authority was something best left alone. Those who crossed the border to escape the violence and pillaging of the Mexican Revolution came with little clothing, little food, no money, less education, and fewer skills. The church, whose mysticism offered them an escape from their sordid existence, perpetuated a "Sea por Dios," or "God wills it" attitude, encouraging a passive submission to destiny and to existing authority in both reliigous and secular realms. In the fatalistic view of many Chicanos, God meant them to be a suffering people whose final reward lies in the heavens. The Mexican-American family, in which the father reigns supreme, has further strengthened a tradition of unquestioning submission to authority. The Chicano's contact with government has involved an acceptance of the system's finished products, his only inputs being payment of taxes, labor, allegiance to his country, and compliance with authoritarian decisions. A long history of political exploitation has made the Chicano distrust leaders outside the family or the church.

The Chicano organizer in the "barrio" must help his community realize that organized groups of people have the power to control the forces that now control their lives. A deep understanding of the history and culture, Mexican, American, and Mexican-American, that has molded his people's political mind is a prerequisite. The information presented here is merely a guideline; check the Bibliography–Directory for further references.

The most effective means of countering his people's alienation from politics are: (1) cultivating the personal trust of individuals in the community, (2) showing people that gaining power through political action works by choosing projects that will successfully deal with concrete, immediate problems, and (3) using pride in the positive aspects of Chicano culture as the rallying point for political action.

1. A challenger of traditionally unquestioned authority will be listened to only if he is trusted and respected. This trust must be cultivated personally, on a one-to-one basis. Only Chicanos should attempt to organize Chicanos. The Chicano is finally experiencing the phenomenon of leaders who intimately understand Chicano values and who truly share the aspirations of their followers. Because of the nature of the dominant role the "Anglo" (white man) has played in the lives of most Mexican Americans, Chicanos have come to resent Anglo attempts to infiltrate the ghetto; the trend is toward a rejection of "white father" figures. White organizers would have difficulty establishing the kind of personal trust necessary for successful organizing.

Middle-class Chicanos are often mistrusted by "barrio" youths. Their role in "barrio" organizing has been negligible, although they have had considerable success organizing "Chicano studies" at universities. As the Mexican-American community has received more national attention, and as more "barrio" Chicanos have entered the university, Chicano college groups have recently become more active in local affairs. A deep understanding of Chicano values and a sincere commitment in terms of time and effort can bridge initial gaps of trust for middle-class Chicano organizers.

A Chicano organizing in a "barrio" that is not his own must be prepared to deal with the suspicions every outsider meets. The Mexican American's tendency toward introspection makes him hesitant to express his feelings and grievances to anyone not considered part of the community. Since Chicanos are especially suspicious of outsiders who attempt to integrate themselves into the community too quickly, the organizer must be ready to make a long-term commitment.

2. The organizer should at first deal exclusively with specific local problems and should concentrate on developing a cohesive local organization. Since situations vary from one

"barrio" to another, the organizer must evaluate the specific situation using historical and contemporary data, and from there chart the most appropriate plan of action.

Organizing might be approached in a grass-roots fashion or by working with small core groups. Tenants' unions, cooperatives, and buying clubs are good means of getting the people together. Many "barrio" groups have successfully brought pressure to bear on government authorities and others actively concerned with questions of housing, police actions, discrimination in city and county jails, and other issues. As success has given these groups confidence in their collective power, some have tended to employ more "confrontation politics."

Organize drug rehabilitation clinics and draft counseling centers. (Over 60 percent of Anglo youths receive deferments as compared with only 4 percent of Chicano youths.) Set up youth organizations that run job and school placement services. Encourage Chicano youths to expose themselves to new educational and social experiences outside the community which can give them the skills they need to help solve their people's problems. Programs might be set up with cooperative universities to help meet young Chicanos' educational needs. Pressure local school boards to offer instruction in basic skills (arithmetic, reading, etc.) in Spanish as well as English. Establish community newspapers that inform Chicanos of their rights, and centers to which they can report incidents of police harassment. Collect literature on Chicano activism in other communities and on a national level, and make it available at an information center.

3. Chicanos have responded to oppression and discrimination by withdrawing almost completely from Anglo society into the confines of the "barrio." This self-imposed isolation has reinforced communal values. Recently a new type of cultural pride has begun to manifest itself within the "barrios." At secondary schools and on college campuses, young militants have organized courses in "Chicano studies" designed to open up storehouses of buried information, and stimulate discussion about the potential for a united Mexican-American movement. The "barrio" organizer should help his people develop pride in "la Raza," their language, and their culture. Pride in a shared culture provides the basis for greater co-operation with other Chicano groups. As "barrio" groups gain confidence in their own stability and power, they

become more willing to give up some autonomy to further larger Chicano movements.

The "Plan Espiritual de Aztlan," drawn up in 1969, holds that Chicanos comprise "a Nation, a union of free pueblos, Aztlan . . . The struggle must be the control of the barrios, campos, pueblos, lands, economy, Chicano culture, and Chicano political life." This appeal to nationalism has served as a symbolic rallying point in the emergence of a united Chicano political party. "La Raza Unida," the Chicano party, has succeeded in electing candidates on the state and local levels all over the Southwest. "Barrio" organizers should encourage the community to run local candidates of their own and to support "La Raza Unida" candidates on a state level. As Chicano activism increases on local, state, and national levels, the potential for alignment with non-Chicano movements will also increase.

ORGANIZATIONS: See Bibliography—Directory for addresses.

Mexican-American Narcotic Organization (MANO): rehabilitation of addicts, staffed by addicts themselves.

Brown Berets: militant "barrio" group known for political and armed fight against police harassment.

Mexican-American Youth Association (MAYA): "barrio" group involved in finding school and job opportunities.

Movimiento Estudiantil Chicano de Aztlan (MECHA): university-oriented group involved in recruitment, scholarship funds, and academic issues.

Lucha ("struggle"): narcotic rehabilitation in California.

Mexican-American Youth Organization (MAYO): "barrio" youth group.

Mexican-American Political Association (MAPA): in California, political party analogous to "La Raza Unida," running candidates in state elections; also name of student groups on college campuses.

Crusade for Justice: Denver-based catalyst group with affiliates all over the Southwest. Involved in extensive educational programs designed to cultivate political and social awareness and pride in Mexican history and culture. Clearinghouse of Chicano activities throughout the Southwest.

IN THE "CAMPOS": The five-year-long successful grape strike led by Cesar Chavez made many Americans aware of the Chicano migrant's plight for the first time. Chicano migrants in other agricultural industries (potatoes, lettuce, etc.) are planning further boycotts and strikes around issues including: better working conditions, higher wages, payment on payday (as required by law), overtime, back overtime, adequate medical and unemployment compensation.

CHICANO PEACE MOVEMENT: An active Chicano peace movement has dramatized the fact that the number of Chicanos fighting in Vietnam is highly disproportionate to the percentage of Chicanos in the total population. The Chicano March for Peace, the National Chicano Moratorium, and workshops and rallies all over the Southwest have demonstrated that the Chicano is anxious to get out of Vietnam and bring his struggle home. *Viva la Raza—con safo!*

3. Puerto Ricans

The people of Puerto Rico are victims twice over of North American monopoly capitalism. Since 1898, when the island was invaded by U.S. troops led by General Nile and taken from its semiautonomous status under Spain to be subjected to direct military rule, Puerto Rico has been a colony of the United States. Although a series of liberalizing reforms, made over the years largely in response to the independence movement, have resulted in commonwealth status for Puerto Rico and U.S. citizenship for its inhabitants, the plight of Puerto Ricans is not substantially different from that of other third world peoples. The vulnerable one-crop economy (sugar) into which the island was forced at the time of World War I has been replaced, since about 1948, by a more varied agriculture and by the development of a number of light industries. Nonetheless, overpopulation, insufficient work, and poverty have driven some 1½ million Puerto Ricans to the United States as permanent residents. Tens of thousands more migrate back and forth each year to plant and harvest crops in the East and Middle West. On the farms and in the cities they suffer the double exploitation that corporate business reserves for ethnic and racial minorities and so, again, fall victims of a system that founds its wealth and power on the impoverishment of the colonized peoples.

Dwellers in the ghetto and on its fringes, the Puerto Ricans, like the blacks, bear the brunt of the "urban crisis." The landlord, the welfare investigator, the loan shark, the job agent, the sweatshop employer, and every sort of hustler and racketeer take full advantage of the new arrival's unfamiliarity with the language and the laws. Unemployment, or employment only at menial wages, not only keeps the family poor (many must support members back in Puerto Rico), but operates to weaken the family structure itself. The welfare system and the fact that there are more jobs available (at bottom rates) for women than for men, create a situation which undermines the traditions of machismo and paternal authority, and tends to make the mother the dominant influence in the family. It is not unusual for the father to leave the family or to live apart so that his wife can receive welfare. While in Puerto Rico husband, wife, and children may have worked together on a small family-owned farm, in New York father and mother will hold jobs separately while the children try to cope with alien, overcrowded schools, give up, drop out (half of them by the tenth grade), and, too young and unskilled to find employment, begin to live on the streets. There, the process works itself out with deadly predictability in a high incidence of addiction and crime. Yet it is among these young "street people" that a new feeling of national pride is arising, and with it a new political and class consciousness, and the organizations of struggle to implement these.

Such leadership as has come from middle-class elements among Puerto Ricans—politicians of the established parties, agency administrators, business people, and white-collar employees of large corporations—has not been directed toward giving the disoriented youth a sense of identity with their cultural heritage. It stresses, rather (as do the public schools), the rewards of forgetting that heritage, replacing Spanish with English, and setting one's sights upon those goods which are the American equivalent of the good life. Presented with television's glossy packaging of Americanism in the midst of a sordid slum, it is not surprising that children soon begin to speak of new arrivals from Puerto Rico as jibaros (hicks), to find their parents' moral standards old-fashioned, and among themselves to use the language of their new, more sophisticated world. But the "American dream" is not for them. Having rejected Puerto Rico, they find themselves rejected by America because they are Puerto Ricans.

Out of this impasse came street gangs like the Young Lords, who began in Chicago in 1959. And into it has come the junkie on the corner, who speaks Spanish and is not ashamed to be a Puerto Rican because, whatever else, he has never got hooked on trying to be a "real American." Some youngsters, seeing this, have sought Puerto Rican identity in addiction. Street gangs like the Young Lords are seeking and finding it in political struggle.

The youthful street gangs of all oppressed communities are consciously or unconsciously organs of protest and struggle. They are training corps in which their members learn discipline and solidarity, not to mention some of the more technical requisites of assault and defense against the city which has made them outcasts. A sense of identity and pride grows with the constant testing of manhood in situations of peril, secrecy, and martyrdom. The gang itself becomes the almost sole source of personal identity and its welfare the ultimate sanction for the individual's acts. It is not, however, the powerful enemy, the source of poverty and racism, that suffers its depredations, but rather the vulnerable community that is its home. For the young Puerto Rican, his community had come to symbolize the contradiction between the "white American" success to which he had been taught and tempted to aspire, and the place that society has actually reserved for the Puerto Rican—even if he speaks only in English and laughs at his parents' old-country ways. Only the junkie was not hung up about being Puerto Rican. He was free of the bind, but he wasn't changing it, either.

For the gang to turn its attack toward the power that thrives on the people's hopelessness required some loyalty beyond the gang itself, some sense of "us" that could include all the victims of that power. After almost ten years of mainly apolitical activity on the streets of Chicago, the Young Lords, in about 1968 or '69, donned the beret that symbolized their political coming-of-age. They were quickly folowed by the Young Lords of New York and by other gangs in the major centers. The new source of identity was national pride in the Puerto Rican heritage and dedication to the Puerto Rican people, both here and in the island; the new direction of the attack centered on organizing these people to win control over their lives. Without warning the Young Lords of Chicago in 1969 appeared at a housing and urban renewal meeting, took over, and forced the inclusion of blacks and Puerto Ricans on the policy-making board. Later, as the police went out to hunt them down, the group captured the station house and used it for a workshop meeting with the people on neighborhood problems. A sit-in at the McCormick Theological Seminary, an aloof institution living behind fences in the Puerto Rican community, won a private grant of $600,000 toward low-income housing. A church, run by middle-class Americans and some anti-Castro Cubans, was taken over by the Young Lords; the Cubans fled, but the Americans, awakening somewhat to their responsibilities, have continued to work with the new people's center. Joining the Panthers and poor white people in the Rainbow Coalition, the Young Lords and their supporters have succeeded in setting up a free health center, a free breakfast program for the children, a free clothing distribution center, and a drug counseling service. These achievements have unleashed from the Chicago political regime a campaign of terror of which Fred Hampton, one of the Coalition's founders, was a victim in December 1969.

With the Puerto Rican youth, as with the black, the well-spring of the movement which makes possible such coalitions of the especially oppressed is a revolutionary upsurge of pride in nation, culture, and people. Parallel with the black youth's affirmation of the African heritage and the retrieval of black history is the Puerto Rican's effort to repair broken ties with the Hispanic sources of Puerto Rican culture and with the island's chronicles of struggle. This expresses itself, first, in a return to, and new attention to, speaking and writing Spanish. Some youth have become aware of the corrupted state into which the Puerto Rican's Spanish has fallen, especially in the past three-quarter century of U.S. rule. They are responding to the call of groups in this country like Aspira to study Castilian and thus to regain the standard language. If this tendency develops it may have consequences more far-reaching than linguistic ones alone. The Spanish oral tradition is exceptionally rich and vast, with a tenacious, uniform quality which remains intact from East Harlem to Patagonia and which translates an authoritative code of behavior, a formal conception of the family, and a set of moral assumptions very different from those prevailing in Anglo-Saxon North America. Its revival among the revolutionary-minded youth of the ghetto can help to reunite the generations, and the U.S.-born with the island-born, and thus can become a source of strength in the struggle ahead. (There is already evidence of this in the Young Lords' concern for elderly tenants and welfare mothers, their attention to the home-village-based social clubs, their respect for—without belief in—the Pentecostal movement and that mixture of Catholicism and voodoo known as *santamera*, or *bruheria*.) Further, to retrieve the linguistic tradition which unites the Hispanic-African-Indian cultures and peoples of Latin America is a step toward uniting the movements of Puerto Ricans and of Dominicans, Costa Ricans, etc., who share their ghettos in New York and Chicago with those of the students in Puerto Rico, and both with the movements everywhere below the border which are rising to resist U.S. domination.

The independence movement is growing apace in Puerto Rico—five major organizations among the radical students who are, as in the U.S., primarily middle class. Many are products of private Catholic schools rather than the "Americanizing" public institutions and their main strength, though it is spreading, is centered in the University of Puerto Rico at Rio Piedras, near San Juan. As in the U.S., they are trying to go out into the communities of city and countryside to organize the people around immediate demands linked with nationalist aspirations. Although the Nationalist party as such is not very strong, the name of its founder and leader, Don Pedro Albizu Campos, is invoked by all independence groups. This movement has the support of the militants in the U.S., who nonetheless believe that the people here cannot determine the lives of the people of Puerto Rico.

Independence is a particularly complex question for Puerto Ricans, whose U.S. citizenship facilitates their continued migration north to somewhat expanded economic opportunities. Yet, they find in the urban areas of the East and Middle West that theirs is not the citizenship enjoyed by the native North American. The island, even for many in the second generation, remains the home where one cannot live for long, but for which one saves and hopes. The middle class in Puerto Rico, freed of federal income taxes and able to come and go at will, on the whole supports the present situation or urges that Puerto Rico's interests would be better served by its admission to the union as a full-fledged state. Needless to say, middle-class complaints about underrepresentation are not carried so far as to support the anti-ROTC, antiwar demonstrations of the students at Rio Piedras, though many individuals of all classes resent the draft of Puerto Ricans and the presence of some thirteen U.S. military bases on the island. Actual organization against U.S. militarism is little developed. National sentiment and national interest, as is usual with the colonized bourgeoisie, are canceled by immediate economic self-interest. In the United States, the *alcahuetes* ("Toms") offer themselves as token Puerto Ricans to the establishment parties, sing the songs of statehood or the status quo, and advertise the rewards of "Americanization" just as if ghetto Puerto Ricans were equal citizens.

By facing the truth that they are not, young Puerto Ricans in the U.S. are laying the basis for further and broader coalitions with the black people and other exploited groups and even with the student movement. The urban areas in which they live harbor a more mixed population than do most of the black ghettos. Cubans, Dominicans, blacks, American Indians, Arabs, Italians, and Jews, trapped in the slums by racial discrimination or poverty, live side by side with Puerto Ricans. They are uniting on struggles around bread-and-butter issues and in these the students can give a helping hand. The possibilities for work by non-Puerto Ricans among the Puerto Ricans as such are more limited.

Student organizers probably should concentrate on informing themselves, keeping in touch with the Puerto Rican organizations, and giving whatever support is requested. This may often be financial or legal, but will chiefly mean work among other elements in the population to counteract the racist and antiforeign prejudice which has greeted the Puerto Ricans ever since they began to come north in numbers. The immediate, day-to-day struggles in the ghetto revolve around rents, repairs, heat and hot water, urban renewal, employment, welfare, health services, protection from police and judicial oppression, and improvements in the schools. The time may soon come to raise a demand that urban schools should teach Spanish from the primary levels up. The non-Puerto Rican organizer should focus on coordination with the community to bring pressure on government agencies and politicians who thus far have failed to meet the problems that the influx from the island has brought with it. This goes for the commonwealth's Migrant Division itself. Aid to Puerto Ricans in setting up alternate structures, such as those initiated by the Rainbow Coalition, can be offered, using the expertise and the facilities of the universities. An important point of attack is in the universities and colleges themselves, where campaigns should be mounted for scholarships to Puerto Ricans and programs for the study of Puerto Rico and its culture.

The student organizer should not try to work in the ghetto unless he speaks Spanish really well and has a deep understanding of Hispanic cultural attitudes. The formal structure of the Latin American's social life, the importance of certain ceremonial courtesies, their attitude toward time, so different from the Anglo-Saxon's—all these must be absorbed into one's behavior, not merely learned abstractly. Beyond this acculturation, the organizer would need specifically to understand the role of various groupings in the community (e.g., the Pentecostal churches, the home-based social clubs), and to understand the subtle differences in approach to island-born as compared with U.S.-born Puerto Ricans. If this is not possible for most student organizers, they should not therefore feel that there is nothing they can do. The politically aware student activist is needed to work among the non-Puerto Ricans and whites who are the majority, to convince them to support the struggles of the minorities, and to help them to understand that these struggles are in their own deepest interest.

4. American Indians

Buttons and bumper stickers proclaiming "Indian Power!" and asserting that "Custer had it coming" symbolize an Indian militancy hardly seen since the last resisters were forced to lay down their guns some three-quarters of a century ago. More—they signalize a new Indian consciousness that transcends the old tribal differences and animosities which once aided the white man in his conquest of the land. It is embodied in the occupation of Alcatraz by a multitribal band of about one hundred; in the three-year-old United Native Americans, which claims a membership of about 12,000; and in the National Congress of American Indians, which represents almost all of the reservation population of some 400,000.

From symbolic acts (e.g., some Washington Indians' closing of a littered beach to tourists, the Passamaquoddies' exacting of tolls from motorists, four Dartmouth students' successful protest against an Indian-garbed mascot) tribes have moved to active resistance in defense of threatened lands and rights. In Washington, Tulalips have gone to jail for deliberate violation of fishing regulations which reduced them, according to one woman spokesman, to "savages with no more rights than a bear." In Alaska, 55,000 Indians, Eskimos, and Aleuts have claimed title to 90 percent of the state's land, which they intend to keep tied up in court until their rights are recognized. Urban Indians, of whom there are some 200,000, scattered for the most part in low-income white neighborhoods and on ghetto fringes, are also developing forms of organization, as their ample representation at the national convention of the National Congress of American Indians in Albuquerque last year shows.

"Integrity, not integration" expresses the direction of the Indians' drive toward self-determination, as it describes the thrust of black, Puerto Rican, and Chicano liberation movements. The specific content of the Indian struggle differs from these, however, in some important respects. Tribal traditions, which are the sources of social and cultural identity, still work against a national Indian consciousness, despite growing unity in action. Unlike other minorities, the Indians occupy a specially defined legal status in the nation, with a federal bureau assigned to its maintenance and protection. And as precarious as their possession of it has proved, they have a land base of their own. These three unique features of the "Indian question"—tribal identity, Bureau of Indian Affairs supervision, and territorial integrity—have intermeshed during the past hundred years of U.S.-Indian relations to create a contemporary situation of considerable complexity. Although Indian people differ among themselves on positive programs, there is something like unanimity on two negative demands: *no termination,* and *an end to BIA domination of Indian life.* A major source of the complexity of the present movement, and of the difficulty outsiders have in understanding it, lies in the fact that these two demands partly contradict each other. Yet both are absolutely essential if the Indian is to gain control over his own life.

"Termination" is the policy adopted by the federal government in 1954, initiated (without Indian participation, naturally) by the reactionary Senator Watkins of Utah as a solution of the "Indian problem." Under the pretense of "freeing" the Indian from the "second-class citizenship" in which his tribal rights supposedly involved him, the termination policy meant not only an end to BIA supervision but to long-standing commitments by the United States to protect its Indian tribes. (Actually, the Indian had, since 1924, enjoyed in law a dual citizenship, with both constitutional and tribal rights.) The rationale, if not the method, was that of the infamous allotment system adopted in 1887, which forced private land ownership on the reservations and thus reduced self-sufficient tribal communities to extreme pauperism and cultural disintegration. By the 1920s, the very existence of the Indian people was threatened; their land base, in the process, was reduced from 138 million to 55 million acres. With the reversal of this policy by the Indian Reorganization Act of 1934, the gradual repurchase of tribal lands had begun to revive tribal life when termination threatened it with total annihilation. This, of course, was the purpose of the policy, for to get rid of the Indian as a "problem" one must first get rid of the tribe which is the seat of his cultural heritage and identity. That this particular form of genocide could be sold to the public as "emancipation" bespeaks not only the well-known oppressiveness with which the BIA exercises its trusteeship, but the integrationist climate that surrounded the early Civil Rights movement. The results of termination, for those tribes which became its victims, ranged from total economic disaster to dispersal to disappearance. The Menominees of Wisconsin, a forest tribe whose sawmill not only provided employment but supported schools, a hospital, and other social services, have, since the reservation was closed down in 1961, lost their jobs, community services, part of their lands, and, virtually, their tribal identity. Termination is still a threat and if it has not been implemented in recent years it is because of the practically unanimous resistance of the Indians and the NCAI.

The failures, corruptions, bureaucratic stupidities, and racist practices which have characterized BIA operations for most of its history are so well known that their continuance is a measure of public indifference to the sufferings of the Indians. Charged with protecting tribal lands and traditional ways, the BIA has connived at robbing the tribes and at teaching contempt for Indian culture. From birth to death the reservation Indian's life is under the absolute dictatorship of a bureaucracy (one BIA employee for every eighteen reservation Indians) that can take control of his property or his children, choose his occupation, or anything else it decides is "for his own good." What "good" the BIA has wrought, a few figures can illustrate: The Indian's life expectancy is forty-six years, compared with seventy-one for whites. Four-fifths of Indian males have less than five years of schooling, and the dropout rate remains twice the national average. Unemployment ranges from 20 to 80 percent. At least 70 percent of the housing is substandard; a large proportion of families carry water from a distance. The people have little incentive to improve conditions, even when they have the means, since almost any project bogs down in years of BIA red tape. The BIA boarding school and the public schools systematically teach a racist history that dismisses the child's people as "dirty savages" in a "vastly inferior culture." The teen-age suicide rate among Indians is three times the national average, on some reservations ten times. Alcoholism (a problem among urban as well as reservation Indians) is the commonest form of escape for young and old alike.

Among newly militant Indians, there is opinion for a ten-year phasing-out of the BIA, with distribution of its quarter-billion-dollar budget directly to the tribes. Others, hating the BIA no less but fearing termination more, call for replacement of its white personnel with Indians and a complete overhauling of the bureau, with a view to placing all decisions about Indian affairs in Indian hands. The reservations, if not thrown to the wolves of taxation and competition, can become viable communities. Already a few, through tribal initiative and some help from antipoverty funds and private industry, have begun to develop self-supporting economies and a greater measure of self-government; e.g., the Lummi of Washington and the Gila River Pima-Maricopa.

Among those who have chosen the city there is an increasing number of well-educated young Indians whose voices are among the clearest now being raised for "integrity, not integration." Writers and speakers like Vine Deloria, Lehman Brightman, and N. Scott Momaday are reaching a national audience with a demand for self-determination and for an end to white America's racist contempt of Indian culture. They are awakening a new sensitivity toward the exploitation of Indian crafts, the misuse of Indian religious symbols, the caricaturing of Indian chiefs in advertising, and, above all, the movie and television stereotype of the Indian as savage enemy or stupid animal.

Such sensitivity represents the very least support that the white radical movement can offer the Indian liberation struggle. Publicity and actions (boycotts, picket lines) against businesses, television stations, and advertisers, etc., that persist in peddling racist stereotypes of the Indian are needed in every part of the country. Protests against textbooks that teach contempt for the American aborigine can be mounted by students and teachers in schools from first grade through college. Facts about the Indian liberation movement and about the culture of the tribes are needed to counteract the pervasive lies of the past. Teach-ins on a large scale, with Indian speakers if possible, and a continuing program of workshops and seminars should be planned in high schools and universities. Pressure should go on administrations to institute Indian studies, to hire Indian instructors, and to develop scholarship programs for Indian students. At the least, appropriate departments can be made to offer courses in American Indian history, religion, and culture.

The Indian people do not need or want white students to organize them, either in the city or on the reservation. They can, as can all who suffer from the conditions in the inner city, use support in daily struggles against unemployment, slums, and discrimination. Because of the Indian's legal status under the BIA, he can also use political support on a national scale and (especially in the twenty-six reservation states) on a state and local scale. This means, in general, insisting through elected representatives, etc., that the Indians be permitted to decide upon all matters that affect their lives.

Contemporary America, as people who form communes and wear beaded belts seem obscurely to realize, is in need of what the first American has never forgotten. The Indian, unlike the white man, has always regarded the land as sacred, the very source of his communal life. His respect for nature, and for his fellow human being, once helped to make him prey to a civilization that throve on wasteful exploitation and violence toward both. That civilization no longer thrives— or rather, the human being, even the white man, can no longer thrive within it. The Indian way has outlasted it, in spite of all. The revival and further preservation of that way may well be a condition for the revival and preservation of truly human life in this country.

IV. Women

ORGANIZING WOMEN

Structure of the Women's Movement

In the past few years, the women's movement has been
growing at a phenomenal rate. Essentially, women's lib
consists of small, locally based and locally initiated groups
of women. There is no real national coordination, and many
women in the movement are trying to avoid it. Local groups
allow women to deal with the specific manifestations of their
oppression in ways appropriate to them. There is a wide
informal network of communication through newsletters,
journals, conferences, and personal contacts. Various groups
do come together to implement strategy and tactics on
specific issues.

Political Positions Within the Movement

The political positions held by women's groups cover a
broad spectrum.

There is at least one national organization, the National
Organization for Women (NOW), started by Betty Friedan,
which has a number of local chapters throughout the country.
NOW is basically middle-class in membership and oriented
toward legal reform within the system (abortion law repeal,
equal pay, etc.).

Some groups see the women's movement as an integral
part of the broader struggle being waged by all oppressed
groups. The basic assumption is that the capitalist structure
is the basis of oppression, and change to a worldwide socialist
structure is a necessary (but not sufficient) condition for
liberation.

Some groups, while recognizing the validity of this analysis, are more "feminist" in their orientation toward tactics
and refuse to work with any male-dominated group.

Still other groups are more concerned with sexual politics

and have rejected the viability of any type of relationship with men. Some of these women advocate homosexuality as the only rewarding and equal relationship.

Two Levels of Organizing

Organizing women must proceed on two levels: psychological and political.

The psychological level is important in order to counteract the devastating effects of cultural conditioning, to give women the confidence to work actively to change their lives.

The political level is equally important, for it is the social, economic, legal, and political structures which create the conditions of oppression. Until these are changed, no woman will have the full freedom to act in her own interests.

Common Problems in Organizing Women

A major problem in organizing women is their lack of consciousness as a group, which is created and reinforced by the cultural conditions of being women in a world dominated by men.

Certain attitudes and beliefs follow naturally from this condition; in most cases, these attitudes cannot be changed overnight, but it is most important to be aware of them, and explicitly raise them with women, before they will be able to come together effectively on their own behalf.

Women's alienation from women. Men and women are taught and shown in a thousand ways, both blunt and subtle, that women are inferior to men: they are not capable of competing with men physically or intellectually; they are not very interesting or stimulating and therefore are not to be taken seriously. A woman's only important goal in life is to get married and have children; she lives to please men, her success is defined by the attributes of the man she is able to catch in marriage, and she is doomed forever after to live vicariously through the lives of her husband and children, never to have a life of her own, never to know herself, her needs and capabilities. Since the definitions of social reality are all created by men and learned by both men and women, it is not surprising, therefore, to find that women regard other women with as much scorn as do the men. Women are accustomed to viewing other women as competitors for men's attention only.

Woman's alienation from herself. The socializing process

which defines women as inferior affects not only a woman's definition of other women but also a woman's definition of herself. The self-contempt which results is destructive to the healthy growth of personality; it produces all sorts of defense mechanisms which interfere with good relationships and also produces a lack of self-confidence in positive action. It inhibits the atmosphere of trust which must develop within any women's group before action is possible.

The threat of liberation. Many women regard women's liberation as a real threat to their feminine identity, an identity defined by society and internalized by most women. Until this threat can be to some extent countered, a woman will not even consider going to a women's meeting. Also, many women encounter ridicule from family and friends, both male and female. This animosity arises both from lack of understanding and a fear of any change in societal roles. It is important for an organizer as well as the group to be supportive and help women gain the confidence to withstand these attacks.

The media have also distorted many aspects of the women's liberation movement. It focuses on the most extreme positions and tactics to the almost total exclusion of what the majority of women in women's lib are in fact thinking and doing. Such extremism is frightening and often incomprehensible to women who have not yet begun to break out of their oppression. It becomes very easy, then, for women to be alienated from the movement and to avoid dealing with the issues that are being raised.

Basic Goals

Although women's groups may vary in their political analyses, there are three underlying, fundamental, long-range goals to which they must agree in order to build a mass women's movement:

First, women must make their present lives more bearable. That means organizing to attack immediate social and economic problems.

Second, women must reeducate themselves. Once women learn the mechanisms of their oppression, they will then learn how to deal with it.

Third, women must realize that they are in a double bind: while many of the problems women face have their roots in the present power structure, we must also counteract male supremacy. However necessary political revolution may be, women must realize that it will not necessarily alter their low cultural and psychological status (as it has not in Cuba). The liberation of women demands more than their changing basic institutions of society. It demands altering consciousness and finding new methods of social organization.

Cardinal Points for the Organizer

Before you attempt to organize other women, you should recognize and come to grips with your own oppression in political terms. Working from your own oppression gives you a gut sense of solidarity with your sisters and avoids the uncomfortable feeling of being manipulative or seeing yourself as a "do-gooder."

You should work or live in the office or community you attempt to organize. Making contact comes easily—on the job at lunch or during coffee breaks; in a community at the supermarket, in parks, at PTA meetings. Once you have established contacts you should hold sessions to begin to talk about your common problems. Your first contacts and discussions are crucial, for this is where you will either gain or lose the respect of the other women. Take interest in all their concerns and interests, and create an atmosphere of openness and trust.

With many women the most ineffective approach you can take is to plunge in with some abstract theoretical argument about women's oppression and exploitation in a capitalist society, or to advocate alternative life-styles like communal living. While you may feel these ideas are entirely valid, strategically you accomplish nothing more than alienating potential group members. Focus on concrete issues through which they can readily see the justification for change: day-care centers for mothers, discrimination in wages and promotion for working women, and so forth.

Whenever possible, the idea of group action should come from the other women, not from yourself. Coming together to discuss issues is a significant action in itself. You should sense where the potential leadership in the group lies, but do not encourage domination of the group by a strong woman leader as it may inhibit growth of other members by reinforcing old patterns of quiet acquiescence to a "masculine" will. Liberation must give each woman a chance to learn to make decisions and think for herself.

Another aspect of leader domination to be avoided is the destruction of the foundations of security in a woman's life before she is strong enough to replace it with something else. You may consider the security which comes from dependence on a man to be a tenuous one at best, but for many women it is all they have. They can only shift the focus of their strength and identity at their own speed, and any effort to "force" this change is doomed to failure.

"Consciousness raising" moves step by step from the exploration of personal grievances to genuine political action. Encourage women to bring up the "trivial" things which bother them. For example, many wives will not initially be able to relate to the fact that they have little identity of their own, that they live through and in subordination to the lives of their husbands. They may, however, be aware of feeling bored with their daily routine of housework, of feeling frustrated at staying home all day. When women can come together and begin to verbalize their problems they very quickly realize that they are not alone in their difficulties.

The organizer's expertise and contact with the larger women's movement is essential. Bring in other women with expertise, radical schoolteachers, women trained in karate. Gradually, the women in the group can move into contact with actions taking place in other parts of the country and increase involvement with women in other groups.

CONSTITUENCIES

Working Women

Women do not consider themselves, nor are they treated, as legitimate workers. Rather, they are there to serve, to assist, to do shitwork—despite the fact that nearly 50 percent of all women work, and they comprise about 40 percent of the nation's work force. They get less pay for equal work. They do not have access to many of the jobs open to men.

They are educated—or not encouraged to seek an education at all—accordingly. They are given the dull, repetitive, meaningless jobs. They are among the first to be fired, and the last to be promoted. There is little pride or sense of worth wrought from most jobs that women are forced to resort to. A woman doubts her own abilities and potential, lacking the confidence to seek more rewarding vocations. Likewise, she is not encouraged to develop herself in certain areas, considered as "man's work."

Women doing office work have little control over what they do and little opportunity to learn from their work, since they are seldom given responsibility or explanations of what they are doing. There is little chance for them to enter management training programs. Even women who make it out of a typist pool usually go no farther than being a secretary. They are industry's version of the housewife. Stewardesses are an excellent example of a second type of job open to women—one that takes little "smarts" but is considered "glamorous."

Blue-collar women who hold down jobs in factories and plants are often used to maintain the unemployment level in a competitive economic system. When they are not needed, they are sent back to home and family, often at the sacrifice of much-needed income.

The most important issues are economic: higher salaries, better working conditions, job security, unemployment compensation, equal pay with men, job opportunities, day-care centers, free family planning programs and health clinics, wage differentials, discrimination in hiring and promotions, and on-the-job training programs.

Professional women. Professional women are not as vulnerable to economic sanctions as are nonprofessional women, though they still face a degree of nepotism and discrimination in their jobs. Greater leeway is often possible in their actions. However, many professional women are not consciously alienated from the structures in which they operate. They see themselves as having "made it" in a man's world and feel that continuing to make it, i.e., keeping the men's respect, is possible only by sticking to the rules of the game as defined by men.

Professional women can best be organized by initially focusing on an issue of professional relevance but indirectly related to their position as women. Gradually work around to issues directly affecting their personal lives as women. The process may also work in reverse. Some women are attracted to women's groups out of specific personal grievances, and once involved, become radicalized.

Housewives

The primary task of an organizer is to present to the housewife the fact that she is one of many. Unlike workers or students she is isolated from her sisters, her function being to maintain the small unit of the family; her field of action is the home. The organizer must bring to the housewife's attention that her field of action is the whole community and neighborhood. She is the one who spends twenty-four hours a day in it, using the streets and parks, taking her children to school, shopping in the neighborhood stores. It is in these basic activities that her potential power in the society and her importance to the movement lie.

ACTIONS

Aggressive action is important to counter the conviction that women must not initiate, control, or have power in any way.

Even before the women in your group are ready to initiate their own actions, they can take part in larger regional and local actions, such as boycotts of products whose advertising is degrading to women, campaigns for abortion on demand, etc. Take part in women's marches and rallies in your city.

Smaller projects will result from the specific issues that arise in consciousness raising. Some examples would be to picket obvious manifestations of sexism, such as local beauty contests, Playboy clubs, topless bars, or pornographic movies.

Another project would be work stoppage in the home, at the factory, or at the office. This type of short-term strike—maybe one hour on the assembly line, two or three days in the home—is effective because it emphasizes the amount of work women actually do. If housewives refuse to cook and clean for several days, their husbands will realize their dependence on them.

Women should let the fashion industry know what they think of being treated like dumb sheep who will follow any fad. Refuse to change styles every year just to support the garment industry, picket stores that will only stock the "latest" style, demand that all lengths of skirts be available.

Women's groups should also organize study groups to study women's history, self-defense, and things like nutrition and child psychology.

Actions for Working Women

1. When possible distribute leaflets and petitions to expose problems, to inform other workers, and to keep issues viable.

2. Share each other's work loads, don't compete with one another; this strengthens unity and keeps up group spirit.

3. Form a telephone chain to keep everyone informed on internal and under-the-table activities.

4. Have "sick days" when everyone calls in sick and abstains from work. (Effective when you have a specific demand(s) in mind.)

5. Management will often attempt to break up women's movements by offering special favors to particular members (a small promotion, a raise, a vacation); or in some cases will find excuses to fire certain leaders of the group. Maintain solidarity with your sisters and protest with strikes, etc., to let management know you will not allow such divisive ploys and tactics.

White-collar workers:

1. Refuse collectively to do all the little extras that women are supposed to do for their boss: getting him coffee; making his lunch and dinner reservations; typing his son's term papers; working overtime for no pay, etc.

2. Have an office party just for women. Exclude the men in order to emphasize that you're not interested in the usual, standard socializing games.

3. Utilize a radical women's suggestion box.

4. If your office has dress codes organize one day to wear pants or dungarees, turn in your stockings and heels and deliver them to your boss.

5. Recruit your boss's wife to your ranks.

Union members:

1. Women should organize to form a caucus within the union.

2. If strong enough, they can break from the union and form their own, but this is *very* difficult and a last resort.

3. Run their own candidates for positions of shop steward and upper managerial positions.

4. Form study groups or workshops through the unions to study problems of working women.

5. Participate in strikes and other union activities not just as workers, but as women; carry your own signs, stick together.

6. Present women's demands to platform committees at national union meetings.

Professional women:

1. When confronting lack of representation in the professional organizations, organize boycotts, pickets, etc.

2. Organize a counterconvention when the organization holds its national meeting.

3. Form a women's caucus within your organization.

4. If working for institutions concerned about their public-relations image—hospitals, universities—have demonstrations, picketing, guerrilla theater actions, hold press conferences, as effective levers to disrupt business and press for specific demands.

5. On a short- or long-term basis, demand accessibility to professional institutions of training, graduate schools, and law schools, medical schools, etc. Women should band together, write to the alumni magazines, demonstrate on class days, support women's caucuses in the schools themselves.

While actions such as those listed can be effective in educating people to the demands of the movement and achieving short-range objectives, they cannot, in and of themselves, effect the deeper changes necessary to the liberation of women. Through consciousness-raising, women have built a foundation for actions. They have organized women's centers, publications, forums and conferences, child-care centers, women's studies programs; sought alternative life-styles to free themselves from stereotyped roles; fought abortion laws in the states and job discrimination in business and factories. From these activities, women have learned that the influence of feminism goes far beyond local struggles and legal reforms.

The women's strike of August 26, 1970, provided the first clear demonstration of the potential strength of feminism. In its wake, women began more active organizing around issues basic to women's liberation. Out of one of these issues —abortion law repeal—has come the first national coalition for women's rights since the suffrage movement. But it will not be the last. Women are now taking the first steps toward organizing a politically based movement which will bring significant changes in the quality and shape of their lives.

V. The Military

1. The Draft

The Selective Service provides the war machine with an unlimited supply of manpower. It does this by forcing young men into involuntary servitude, while pressuring others into enlisting.

In many ways, the draft is a gift of the U.S. government to the radical movement. Not only is it in blatant violation of constitutional provisions against slavery, but like so many other mechanisms of government, it operates decidedly in favor of the moneyed classes. Therefore, Selective Service provides an excellent issue around which to organize, serve people, and educate them as to the nature of the American political system.

I. Community Organizing Around the Draft

A. *Community draft counseling center*

The basic function of a community draft center should be sound draft counseling. Other activities, such as demonstrations and newspapers, can be coordinated from the center, but people will not relate to an organization that does not serve the people.

1. Pick a neighborhood that is ready for this kind of activity. An area where people are already politically mobilized through an existing peace group or a neighborhood action program is preferable. You will receive a better reception if you can operate as a service under the auspices of such a group, or utilize part of their office. In a working-class neighborhood where people have been fighting highway expansion or urban renewal, residents may be prepared to escalate their struggle against the status quo.

2. Publicize the nature and intent of your activity. You

can reach draft-age young men by leafleting induction centers or obtaining a list of 1-A's from the draft board. They are contained in the minutes of the draft board's meetings and are open to the public. However, the draft board will not give addresses. If you can contact the young men in no other way, you may write them through the board. They must forward mail to 1-A's.

B. *What draft counseling can offer*

1. Most people have been down so long that the idea of actively and openly trying to fight the system is a big step. Many do not know about draft counseling. For these people, a chance to achieve a medical deferment or a CO classification may literally save their lives.

2. If there are 1-A's in the neighborhood ready to refuse induction, or refuse to fight in Vietnam, a draft information center should be ready to publicize their plight and generate local support for them. Leaflet campaigns and petition drives can be coordinated from the draft center.

C. *Gain community support*

1. Leaflet community people. Find out what they want a draft information center to provide. Make the draft a public issue, relevant to more people than just young men.

2. Circulate a petition to support your right to be in the neighborhood. Emphasize the right of people to find out about the draft and alternatives.

3. Have a listed phone number which people can call for information.

4. Publish materials such as a newsletter in the language of the community.

5. Contact local organizations and leaders; seek opportunities to speak about the issues.

6. Fight alongside local people on other issues important to them.

7. Approach housewives who may have doubts about the draft, especially since it affects their children.

II. The Counseling Process

Counseling is serious business. The information that you have may save a guy's life.

A. *Who should train counselors*

Prospective counselors should be taught by those with practical experience. AFSC and WRL people and lawyers specializing in the draft make excellent teachers. Novices should sit in on actual counseling sessions and attend workshops. These should be led by resource people such as lawyers, psychiatrists, and ex-political prisoners.

B. *What training should emphasize*

1. CO claims: If this intricate process can be mastered, a draft counselor will be equipped to handle many draft problems.

2. Draft law: Knowing the mechanics of the Selective Service Law can make the difference between a deferment and induction as a delinquent. (See Bibliography–Directory.)

3. Army medical standards: Most deferments are granted because of mental or physical unfitness. Unfortunately, many potential inductees are not aware of minor ailments which may make them ineligible to kill or be killed.

C. *Lawyers*

It goes without saying that this profession provides the most effective allies in the fight against the draft.

1. Find names of lawyers experienced in draft matters. These are available from CCCO, ACLU, NAACP, WRL, AFSC, the National Lawyers Guild, and area law-school faculties. A sympathetic lawyer helps in making contacts.

2. A program for committed lawyers might be a good start: informal counseling, compilation of briefs, gathering resources, etc.

3. Try to get lawyers to commit themselves to one or more annual free draft cases. They should at least agree to charge according to the ability of the client to pay.

4. If lawyers will not commit themselves to the handling of specific draft cases, at least seek their aid to court-appointed lawyers so that the strongest possible argument in each case may be presented.

D. *The medical profession*

Sympathetic physicians and psychiatrists are invaluable in obtaining deferments. They often spot and record disabilities that army doctors tend to overlook when filling draft quotas.

III. Draft Harassment

A. *Legal methods of stopping the normal flow of business at the local board*

1. Letter-writing campaign: A group is organized to create a constant flow of letters which will keep the secretaries busy opening them and answering legitimate requests. Certified letters are even more effective, since they must be signed for.

Each member of this group should send a "letter of the day." It may ask a legitimate question, or report on a trivial change in the health or mental attitude of the writer. The writer can also request a replacement for a lost card at weekly intervals. Letters can also express opinions such as, "I have heard about the Communist plot to flood the draft board with mail; I am totally against this red plot."

2. Phone-call campaign: Call and ask the question that you have been thinking of asking and never did.

3. Walk-in appearances: Ask your questions personally.

4. The junk-in: Send items to your board. The law says that they must be filed. You may wish to add symbolic dead fish or army surplus items to your file.

5. Female registration: Women over eighteen years of age should write to their local board requesting to register. Such letters should be signed with a last name and first initial. The Selective Service must check these out.

6. Vigil of death: Station someone outside the local board during business hours. Have him dressed as a cloaked and hooded specter of death, carrying a skull and hourglass.

Recent Supreme Court decisions have ruled punitive reclassification to be unconstitutional. However, some local boards still attempt it and you may be involved in long court action.

IV. Draft Resistance

Draft counseling usually entails using Selective Service law to keep men out of the draft. The law is thus recognized and utilized fully to find deferments for as many potential inductees as possible. While sparing some individuals, effective draft counseling ultimately can only *perpetuate* the draft by helping it operate smoothly and equally.

If the draft is going to be broken it may have to be done

with extralegal action and pressure. At the same time, a national antimilitary recruitment program is needed if the whole military machine is going to be stopped.

A. *Some individual illegal acts against the draft*

1. Failure to register for the draft.
2. Arranging to flunk a physical by studying and assuming the symptoms of a mental or physical disorder.
3. Failure to report for induction.
4. Refusing induction.

B. *Collective illegal actions against the draft*

1. Draft-card turn-ins.
2. Mass refusal to register for the draft.
3. Sit-ins at local boards and induction centers.
4. Blocking buses at induction centers.
5. Riding buses to and from induction centers with inductees.
6. Disrupting physicals at the induction center.
7. Destroying draft files.

V. If You Decide to Leave for Canada

Canada has no draft, and has generally allowed American draft resisters to settle without much difficulty. However, anyone thinking of emigration to Canada must understand it is unlikely that he can ever return to the U.S. He must become a Canadian.

Many organizations, both American and Canadian, exist to help young men find sanctuary from the U.S. military. Before taking any action, it's best to write to a Canadian resistance group and include the following:

1. Your draft status and when you anticipate a change in status.
2. When you plan to come to Canada, where you hope to apply, and what means of transportation you'll be using.
3. How much money you will be bringing. And how many debts.
4. Whether you think you may fall into a prohibited class (see below).
5. Whether you have had dealings with the Canadian Immigration Department.

U.S. citizens cannot be extradited from Canada for offenses under the Selective Service laws. But political subversives, drug users, felons, prostitutes, chronic alcoholics and persons "who are . . . or are likely to become public charges" are prohibited. Immigrants can be deported for criminal offenses within Canada or for entering the country illegally.

Deserters from the American military are treated much the same as other applicants by the Canadian Immigration Department. They may enter with "visitor" status and then apply for "landed immigrant" or, in some cases, "student" status from within Canada. Application can also be made at the border, by mail from the U.S., through Canadian relatives, or at a Canadian consulate.

Any potential deserter should read *Manual of Draft-Age Immigrants to Canada* and contact a Canadian antidraft program before taking action. (See Bibliography–Directory.)

2. GIs

ORGANIZING GIs

GIs are low-ranking inducted and enlisted men in the army, navy, air force, and marines, many of whom have not reached voting age. There are several million American GIs policing the world to bolster American business interests and foreign policy abroad, and to serve as cannon fodder in Southeast Asia. Frequent challenges to the U.S. power structure have made GIs an important factor in the ability of the U.S. corporate-military establishment to dominate this country and much of the third world. The GI is becoming an uncertain, if not totally unwilling instrument of the U.S. power structure, however. Together with other constituencies discussed in this book, GIs are becoming aware of the nature and source of their oppression, and are beginning to organize against it.

GIs are much praised but little heard. They are little heard because they are also much repressed. For while they are charged with defending and upholding the Constitution and honor of the United States, GIs are denied their constitutional rights by being forced to fight in a war which has not been declared by Congress; they are also denied the First Amendment rights guaranteed them by this same Constitution.

The rank-and-file GI does the fighting, killing, and dying in Southeast Asia. He must work for less than $4 a day under an open totalitarian dictatorship where he can be court-martialed for refusing to say "Sir" or for refusing a "lawful" order, no matter how unreasonable or criminal.

Organize for What?

GIs want to come home alive and in one piece. GIs are organizing against the war, racism, and class privilege of the brass in the army. They push for an end to external aggression abroad and internal repression at home. They organize to win the rights promised them by the Constitution. They organize against the dehumanizing process that mind-fucks them in basic training and makes them into killers. The American Servicemen's Union has drawn up the following demands as points around which GIs should organize:

1. The right to refuse to obey illegal orders—like orders to fight in the illegal imperialist war in Vietnam.
2. Election of officers by vote of the men.
3. An end to saluting and sir-ing of the officers.
4. The right of black and brown-skinned servicemen to determine their own lives, free from the oppression of any racist whites. No troops to be sent into black or Spanish-speaking communities.
5. No troops to be used against anti-war demonstrators.
6. No troops to be used against workers on strike.
7. Rank-and-file control of court-martial boards.
8. The right of free political association.
9. Federal minimum wages.
10. The right of collective bargaining.

Existing GI Organizations

The American Servicemen's Union (ASU) and the Movement for a Democratic Military (MDM) are existing organizations that should be checked out and joined by all GIs interested in organizing around the issues previously mentioned. These organizations should be supported by civilians. There are also numerous underground GI papers on bases, ships, and in Nam itself, which should be supported and subscribed to.

The American Servicemen's Union, responsible for the ten-point plan listed under "Organize for What?" exists on two hundred military bases around the world, and on fifty ships at sea. It was involved in the struggle of the Fort Hood Forty-three (forty-three black GIs court-martialed for refusing riot duty in Chicago during the Democratic National Convention), and the Fort Dix Thirty-eight (a stockade rebellion), and the Fort Lewis Thirty-five (thirty-five ASU GIs arrested for holding a meeting on the base). The ASU publishes regularly a newspaper called *The Bond.* Subscriptions to *The Bond* are available free for GIs and $3.50/6 mo. to non-GIs. To subscribe write:

American Servicemen's Union
156 Fifth Ave., Rm. 538
New York, N.Y. 10010

The Movement for a Democratic Military (MDM) was formed in November 1969 by marines from Camp Pendleton and sailors from San Diego naval installations. It has spread to military bases all over California. The preamble to its list of twelve demands is a clear statement of purpose:

We are dedicated to using every means at our disposal to bring about a prompt end to the war in Vietnam, the exploitation of our brothers and sisters abroad, and the re-repression—both physical and economic—of those in our own land. We feel that by remaining silent, the American serviceman has contributed to the denial of this deepfounded right of himself and of people everywhere to live free from intimidation and oppression. We have been silent for a long time. We will be silent no longer.

Fighting racism has been a central issue for MDM. Aided by a *civilian* staff of organizers called the Green Machine, MDM has been mobilizing public sentiment outside the bases and advertising the nature and depth of the GIs' grievances. MDM has found collaboration with civiilan groups desirable as civilians have freedom to move about and immunity from military courts and harassment, and can provide important support.

Both ASU and MDM organizers assume great risks and are harassed frequently on American bases by military police, rank oppression, and life-threatening terrorism.

Another group that has gotten involved in antiwar activities and the fight for constitutional rights at Fort McClellan, Alabama; Fort Bragg, North Carolina; and Fort Jackson, South Carolina, is the GIs United Against the War in Vietnam.

The GI Civil Liberties Defense Commitee was organized

in 1968 to defend *and extend* the First Amendment rights of GIs—these include the right to freedom of speech, freedom of press, freedom of assembly and association, and the right to petition the government for a redress of grievances. The group has been involved in court cases to guarantee GIs the right to have open legal meetings on post, and to distribute GI newspapers at Fort Jackson and Fort Bragg respectively. The GI Civil Liberties Defense Committee believes GIs can win liberties around which they are willing to organize themselves, and for which they are willing to wage a serious fight. The Defense Committee solicits the support of all those who uphold the constitutional rights of American servicemen.

Racism in the Military

Racism keeps soldiers divided and unaware that black and white share common oppressions. As long as black and white soldiers are fighting each other, as they do on occasion, effective organizing against the military hierarchy will be thwarted. A military organizer must keep this problem in mind and try to overcome it. As in civilian life, black people can organize themselves as a group, and, feeling together, work with whites to solve the problems they share.

Black, brown, and yellow contingents of the services have a special beef against the war. Many have come to look at all but the white minority of the world as their brothers. They repeatedly observe and experience the oppression of people of color at the hand of the white man. Vietnam to them is merely another example of a white man's colonial war.

At this stage of the struggle, blacks have been forced to organize as a race in order to protect themselves from the racism of white GIs and the military substate.

If white organizers accomplish little else, they should at least help turn the aggressions of enslaved white GIs away from the scapegoats of race and nationality. They must come to direct their hatred where it belongs, against the military war industries and their politician pimps.

Who Will Organize?

One determined man in a company unit can initiate purposeful discussion, organize dissent and help lead it to action. *You should be that man.* Organize for your own protection. If your group is tight, all will stand up to defend one another against repression. The only power is in unity! Make five fingers a fist!!

Going In

If you are going into the service:

Read and subscribe to GI underground papers before you go in.

Get subscriptions for your family, relatives, and friends to increase their awareness of the shit you are facing. Prepare them to support your organizing efforts within.

Arrange for you and your support on the outside to keep in touch regularly. Establish a code to signal you are in trouble and need civilian intervention. Pressure on your congressman can sometimes force the military to admit what has become of you. Also the military occasionally forgets where it has put people.

Try to talk to veterans or GIs on leave, particularly GIs who have been involved with organizing or have brushed with military justice.

Enter informed of your military as well as constitutional rights. Read the GI handbook and other publications available through various GI support organizations. (See Bibliography– Directory.)

Prepare a low profile.

Talk with black vets.

Be educationally and psychologically and physically prepared for basic training so you will have stamina to survive as well as organize.

Establish contacts for getting information which may be relevant to your organizing efforts: how to get a lawyer, get to Canada, Sweden.

In the Service

Seek out the actual and potential support groups off-base. Try to get an off-base headquarters and coffeehouse established. (See "Coffeehouses.")

Get a bulk supply of GI papers which you can store off-base along with other educational material.

Keep absolutely clean of drugs. Don't let them pin an easy rap on you. Beware of attempts to *plant* drugs on you.

Establish yourself with the nearest sympathetic antimilitary lawyer.

Establish a source for printing supplies and equipment.
Discover the lay of the land.
Learn the history of previous organizing efforts on the base.
Find out who are the bastards to look out for.
BE PRAGMATIC AND CAUTIOUS.

Be a friend to everyone; don't turn your back; don't show yourself too soon. Don't associate solely with any one group but don't be a loner. Start working with people closest ideologically, but don't ignore others and don't create enemies. Try to work one to one as much as possible before proceeding to group actions. Raise doubts, questions, but don't take a firm position which will precipitate premature confrontation.

The army is composed of individuals, so a resister and organizer should seek help cautiously from all areas. He shouldn't make assumptions as to who will help and who won't. Each military installation is a small society, with its own particular weak spots. Use base politics to your advantage.

Who to Sound Out

Low-ranking specialists of all sorts who are not rewarded for their talents by the brass can be extremely helpful for organizing purposes as well as for direct-action tactics.

Inspector general is a post created as a watchdog in the army to help soldiers solve particular grievances. IGs do not have to answer to anyone in the chain of command. Therefore, they can criticize without fear of repression.

A GI who can locate an IG who takes his job seriously can occasionally reap some helpful benefits. However, in general, the IG won't help. Sending petitions to him may only get your names to the brass. If a delegation of GIs goes to the IG and they make *demands* and don't beg for sympathy, there is a possibility that he will respond to the pressure somewhat positively.

Chaplains and doctors must be sounded out individually. Some double as informants. Their job is to assist the military by blinding the conscience of murderers or by keeping the fodder alive for the cannon. An occasional doctor will help you get a medical discharge.

Remember, *workers who have had union experience* can often be excellent help for organizing.

When and where to organize:

Wherever and whenever you and your buddies are together and free of brass and leaders is the time to organize.

Barracks, latrine, stockade, KP, off-base on passes, at recreation and recuperation centers, in the hospitals, etc.—all can provide liberated areas and opportunities for short meetings. Apply pertinent graffiti when the chance presents itself.

A good bull-organizing session points up issues, creates excitement and emotion as individuals have what may be a rare opportunity to express their grievances and reservations about the military and the war. Encourage quietly a sense of participation by all. A good action, a good struggle, brings people together in solidarity.

Know examples of organizing successes to reply to pessimism.

Newspaper

Initiate your own base or ship newspaper to air grievances and stimulate discussion. Lay hold of a mimeograph machine off-base. For the large jobs where facilities can't be found, send proofs laid-out and ready to be photoed. Send to printer to be mailed back to base or ship. Or send to ASU. Write to ASU first to discuss it. Money to pay for the printing would be helpful. It can usually be raised among the men. A hundred dollars will print five thousand eight-page papers. Men with previous experience in journalism or printing are helpful. Typists are needed as well. Involve secretaries on the base to support your organizing efforts.

Reprisals Against Inside Organizers

Many an underground editor on military bases has been busted, CM'd, dishonorably discharged, or sent to the front for stirring thought among servicemen. Phony raps, frame-ups, terrorist tactics are used to suppress dissenters. It is *not* illegal to publish off base. Distribution rights should be requested as part of the GIs' fight for constitutional rights.

Include this note on any publication or leaflet which you distribute:

NOTICE—This newspaper publication is your personal property. It cannot be legally taken from you for any reason.

What to Write and Rap about

Get GIs thinking and feeling about the humiliations, risks,

and deprivations which they are being forced to undergo and the cruelties which they are forced to perpetrate for no purpose. Help them learn about the history of the war, the nature of the society and people whom American technology seeks to destroy. Show them the contradications of our foreign policy and our economy. Show who is profiting by the war and how the innocent, the GIs and the Vietnamese, are forced to suffer to support the pride, power, and wealth of the military, political, industrial elite.

Relate external aggression to repression inside the military and inside the U.S. We're all niggers; we're all Viet Cong; we're all oppressed.

Racism—a black skin is the uniform that ensures that even in civilian courts, blacks receive a summary court-martial, i.e., no justice at all. Blacks are kept as privates in civilian life by racist institutions and behavior.

The brass military-industrial complex—"who's who" games among the brass, among politicians, among corporations. Who profits from us getting killed? What are we fighting for anyway??

Labor movement—organizing for mutual protection. Army as factory, sergeants are foremen, brass are bosses, pay and food are lousy; gripes, grievance procedures, benefits; collective bargaining.

Discuss elements of the ASU ten demands; develop new demands.

Specific Actions

Institute happenings. Sit down and write letters to the inspector general or to the chaplain; or to homeless South Vietnamese; or to your congressman. Signatures are a matter of discretion. Such letters do have a tendency to end on an officer's desk near you.

Send letters, articles, cartoons, photographs of atrocities, etc., to antiwar GI organizations and publications.

Join. Start a local chapter. Get a subscription. Most antiwar GI papers are free to servicemen.

Silk-screen posters.

Have Sunday teach-ins after church.

Relate national issues to GI problems and to the townspeople.

Coordinate GI protests with antiwar civilian demonstrations. Plan them on holidays or march in traditional holiday marches—but under your own banners.

Write letters to congressman and government officials, as well as to your home-town newspapers. Have selective boycotts of PXs.

Show army films available from Newsreel. (See Bibliography–Directory.)

Play tapes available from the ASU, Radio Free Europe, etc.

Invite speakers from the ASU and MDM, and GIs United Against the War in Vietnam.

In the mess hall, collectively refuse a certain portion of all of your meal (get hamburger off-base), and then call in sick; or on base, all boycott the same meal. Go off-base for dinner and discuss issues.

Flood the sick wards with "sick of the war" cases—with accompanying psychosomatic reactions.

Stand up and begin singing peace songs before and after meals. Institute a prayer for peace before and after eating. Sing: "Come on down to Vietnam—one, two, three, four, what are we fighting for?"

Have people stand up and present themselves as GIs killed in Vietnam or imprisoned unjustly, giving short life histories followed by a prayer.

Petition against the war and racism.

In the stockade, write graffiti, sing peace songs. Organize inmates against the guards' brutality. Expose the conditions in the stockade by sneaking reports to friendly GI and peace organizations. Civilian news media are increasingly more sympathetic in many areas and dig sensational news about grotesque conditions (e.g., *Life* magazine on the condition of VA hospitals). Exposure of conditions, especially on TV, can be a tremendously effective weapon.

Circulate *The Bond* and other GI publications; send away for free subscriptions for your GI friends, and recruit membership for existing GI organizations.

See *M°A°S°H, Z, Catch-22*.

Strike; sick calls, clergy calls, mass appointments with inspector general, issue demands.

Make peace groups, movement groups beneficiaries should you be killed while in the service ($10,000 is what you are worth dead. Look how much they pay us while we're alive . . .).

Use collective punishments as an opportunity to organize

protest and discussion. People laboring under the same unjust order are likely to develop a strong solidarity given the slightest stimulus. MP chores, for example, are good times to organize, to fight back. Leave symbolic graffiti.

People's "trials" of officers, politicians, corporations, war crimes, tribunals, etc., can be done on time off (Saturday afternoon and Sunday) to raise issues, prompt thought and discussion.

Do guerrilla theater and agitprop; KP capers; quick happenings with concealed instruments and elements of costumes. Be quick, be organized. Try to divert the authorities elsewhere. (See "Guerrilla Theater.")

Study possibilities and consequences of desertion. Many GIs proceed through basic training trying to convince themselves that Nam won't be that bad. They get a short leave following completion of basic training and then receive their orders—when they are away and tasting freedom again, it strikes that it's for real. Be prepared to use leave time effectively. Visit a sympathetic lawyer. Legal studies may be possible. Transportation may be available.

If you plan to refuse orders, many members of the peace movement would be willing to arrange sanctuary in a church or liberated building. Pacifists, War Resisters League, Friends, practitioners of nonviolent civil disobedience, students, and liberal peace groups may help arrange a ceremony of breaking with the military and condemning the war and its makers.

Asylum might be attempted at appropriate neutralist embassies or at the UN, but study the legalities involved in choosing a host.

Publicity and the Public

The value of publicity for the struggle against the military from within should not be underestimated. It has the power to give other GIs courage to resist illegitimate authority, to soften court-martials, and to precipitate the exposure of corruption at the highest levels of the military—e.g., My Lai and West Point, Department of Defense slush funds and the Pentagon's attempt to discredit CBS reporting on the war.

CIVILIAN SUPPORT FROM OUTSIDE

Civilian support for activist GIs can be very effective and is important to mobilize. Civilian support can assume innumerable forms.

Far from Base

If you're located far from a base, you can be active by keeping your organization informed of GI dissent and repression.

You should get many people to subscribe to the larger GI underground papers. All the standard educational and support-raising activities can be applied to publicize the GI rights and repression issue.

Provide support to individuals from your community who have gone into the services. Help them get the contacts, information, and resources needed to do organizing.

Educate young men going into the military about GI activism.

Do "mail-order" organizing: sponsor and mail hundreds of letters with GI newspapers to random soldiers.

Participate in major demonstrations on the nearest base.

Near Base

If you live near a military base, all the usual methods of organizing can apply with special modifications.

Leaflet the base when you can achieve access.

Hold vigils, demonstrations, stall-ins, lie-downs at the entrance to the base.

Leaflet civilians coming in to work and GIs going out on passes.

Contact antiwar GIs by any means possible which will not jeopardize them. Coordinate outside and inside organizing efforts. Utilize all methods to publicize GI grievances at the base when requested. Organize in the outside community along the GI issues.

Townspeople who live near the base may be hostile toward GIs. If GIs are disruptive of the town, explain the oppressive conditions inside the base. Mobilize sympathy for GI reform and "opening up" of the military.

Organize a series of "Civilian Days" on the base along neutral topics, but which will permit organized activists to mingle with GIs on the base for people to discover contacts. Then arrange a series of "Town Days" in which GIs and townspeople meet together in workshops on military organizing issues: the war, racism, brass-industrial complex, denial of constitutional rights, etc.

Organize joint demonstrations of GIs, students, people

groups, church groups. Utilize existing forums in the community to widen the debate.

Set up a GI coffeehouse, and a GI draft counseling and information center and a travel agency.

Get a lawyer trained to handle military cases.

Investigate conditions in stockades. Find out who is imprisoned and discover his legal situation. Support victims of repression.

Assist setting up a GI paper.

Reach local unions on the issue of GI right to union recognition and collective bargaining.

Assist in sanctuaries, underground railroads, etc.

CIVILIANS WITHIN

Civilians who live or work on bases, military wives and families represent a potentially powerful and influential force for action organizing from within. Women's rights, peace and liberation organizations should make special attempts to reach wives of GIs, secretaries who work on bases, and nurses who work in VA hospitals.

Women are organizing to free women and their husbands and boys from bondage to the insensitive, chauvinistic, and inhuman armed services.

Wives and Kids

GIs' wives and children are direct victims of oppression of GIs. The draft and war destroy marriages and families at home as well as abroad. Conjugal love is deprived. Husbands very often cannot be present in cases of medical emergency, pregnancy, and birth, and other family crises and satisfactions. A wife must work to survive on her husband's meager salary without day-care facilities or equal wages. She suffers anxiety for his safety. The army may make her a widow or an unpaid nurse to an invalid for the rest of her married life.

On or near the base wives can do petitioning, leafleting, speaking, protesting, etc. Servicemen are often strongly affected by such activism by women, for much of the armed services' prowar sentiment is built on a false notion of patriotic virility. Antiwar women can help destroy the military's perversion of masculinity.

GIs' wives are a vanguard who are increasingly aware of the suffering created by the military for themselves and others. Organized, they may initiate further action among women who compose the secretarial staff on bases.

Secretaries on Base

The vast secretarial staff employed on bases can and should be organized. Most are civilian workingwomen and represent an oppressed, underpaid worker horde as well as a potentially powerful group with which an organized contingent of GIs' wives can work or vice versa. If they don't feel particularly oppressed, GIs' wives can at least appeal to them as women to women, all of whom are suffering under the gross inequities of the present system.

The secretaries have the power to close down the military administrative bureaucracy should they go on strike or all call in sick one day (sick of the war; low pay; discrimination, etc.). This type of protest, identified with the movement, would be impossible to ignore and difficult to suppress.

Male civilian workers at military installations usually have a "lifer" mentality. Even so, all civilians serving the base should be approached and organized whenever possible.

SENDING MAIL TO GIs

Mail-Order Organizing

The daily mail call is an excellent opportunity to introduce bored and lonely soldiers to GI newspapers. But if a soldier's name were written on the envelope, he could catch hell if CID or his officer investigated his mail.

Junk Mail

GIs in Vietnam often receive letters addressed to "an American Marine" or "an American serviceman." These letters are opened by any serviceman who wants to—most often someone discouraged with the war or harassment. The letters usually come from various "patriotic" groups. Many GIs wish they would come from other GIs or resistance people.

The American Deserters' Committee suggested much of the following procedure for mailing antiwar literature and GI newspapers to troops on base and in Vietnam without identifying the troops personally.

Mailing Techniques

Good techniques are as follows:

Return address: A real name and address or box number, or a phony organizational name and a real return address are suggested. However, brass are becoming more suspicious of letters from political or even patriotic-sounding names and may check them first themselves. It is better to use a personal envelope and personal return address, e.g., your grandmother's or your own. A real return address enables you to get back unopened mail if it is undelivered, or even a reply from a GI. But don't expect a reply. Just keep writing.

Warning: Use of a phony return address, while it is untraceable, could cause the newspapers to fall into the hands of the mail pigs.

Mailing name: Use such titles as "An American . . ." serviceman, soldier, enlisted man, marine, airman, sailor. Or use "Any American Fighting Man," "An American Defender of Freedom," etc. The envelope may also be addressed "Unit Mail Clerk." This is a person with little time left in the Nam and less patience. "Company Clerk" ditto on the above, a grunt with less than thirty days. "Commanding Officer"-addressed mail will be opened by the clerks in the office, not the CO himself. "Commanding Officer—Personal"—this will be opened by the lifer himself. "Police Sergeant"—another short-timer in the Nam. "Day Room"—few bases have them, but the envelope will probably be given to enlisted men. A short-timer is the person most likely to pass GI newspapers on to someone else interested: having been in Nam twelve months, his orientation lecture has worn off; he knows where it's at.

Warning: Don't use an individual's name, for the guy could catch hell just for receiving your letter or newspaper packet.

Mailing address: Give as complete a military mailing address as you can find. Check home-town newspapers. They usually run pictures and articles on local GIs and give their mailing address.

Check with the local draft board and recruiting offices for bases and basic training camp addresses; Forts Lewis, Dix, Bragg, Hood, and others. For additional addresses of units in Nam check the *Army* (or *Navy*) *Times, Sea Tiger, Stars and Stripes, Leatherneck,* and other military magazines, and the obituary columns in the newspapers. Also call the local Veterans of Foreign Wars, American Legion, etc.

A sample address would read as follows:

> An American Fighting Man
> "P" Btry 4th Bn
> 11th Mar 1st MarDiv FPO
> San Francisco, Calif. 96602

Remember: Use the zip code. It is very important to have the zip code right in order to ensure unchecked processing of mail.

What to enclose: underground newspapers, reprints, leaflets, addresses of ASU, MDM, Committee for GI Rights, AFSC, etc.; newspaper clippings, handwritten letters explaining your position, information on dissent at home or on other military installations.

Always enclose a slip of paper to EXPLAIN who you are, why you sent the paper, and ask the reader to pass it on. Explain the false address if you used one, for it would waste a GI's time or even get him in trouble for writing back, should the letter end up with a mail pig. Don't make the envelope too bulky. It wastes too much postage and printing expenses and increases risk of detection.

Mailing Procedures

Use correct postage. For overseas, send it airmail at regular rates for inside the U.S., addressed to the appropriate departure point, e.g., for Vietnam, airmail first goes to the San Francisco APO and is then flown out all the way at no additional cost. Check post office for current rates.

Mail one paper in one envelope to be dropped one to every post box per mail pickup. Never put two papers in the same mail bag, or send two papers to the same unit on the same day. This will make censorship almost impossible, or if attempted, tie down half the army from here to Nam trying to keep the other half from reading the newspaper.

Much credit to: American Deserters Committee and thanks to LNS.

3. Veterans

Veterans have had firsthand exposure to the atrocities of war, and to the racism, dehumanization, and lack of justice that characterize the military and American foreign policy. When they say "I have been there, I have seen," they cannot be challenged. They hold a warm spot in the hearts of the American people and can "bring the war home" to the uncommitted in a unique, personal way.

Vietnam Veterans Against the War, a national organization founded in 1967, and local "veterans for peace" groups want to involve veterans in the antiwar movement and in the development of new social and economic priorities. (See Bibliography–Directory.) They are trying to provide an alternative to the American Legion and Veterans of Foreign Wars, two organizations that reinforce militarism in this country through massively funded lobbying. Vietnam Veterans Against the War also wants to make hospitalized veterans more aware of the benefits for which they are eligible, and to expand existing programs to be more responsive to the needs of young veterans.

Thirty percent of all Vietnam veterans are on college campuses. Every college registrar's office has a list of veterans enrolled in the college. Ask a sympathetic dean or bursar to get you a copy of the list. Contact veterans on campus individually and let them know about veterans' peace activities in the area and nationally. Have them contact New York headquarters of Vietnam Veterans Against the War or their nearest area coordinator about setting up a chapter on their campus. Campus chapters should encourage veterans to speak, lead seminars, publish articles in campus and local newspapers, talk to uncommitted, apathetic campus and community groups, appear on radio, TV, panel shows, pulpits, at political rallies, and at any podium available; they should channel their unique talents into the mainstream of political activity on the campus and in the local community.

The idea of veterans' "complicity in war crimes" is very touchy and difficult, and should be initially avoided when organizing veterans. The attack should be focused on the government's policy, and everyone's shared responsibility for it rather than on the guilt an individual veteran should feel for having been a "war criminal."

(With thanks to Vietnam Veterans Against the War.)

VI. Labor

STUDENTS AND THE LABOR CONSTITUENCY

Contacting labor is likely to be the most difficult part of our work, requiring a decision for long-term commitment. Basic goals should be long-range: overcoming the mistrust and misunderstanding between the labor movement and the radical youth movement, establishing a dialogue, and laying the groundwork for future cooperation between labor and students. These goals, and the very process of obtaining them, have great potential significance. Working people have a long tradition of struggle and are so strategically placed in society that their actions strike immediately at the heart of the system. Simply compare the serious effects of a national student strike with the potential effects of a national labor strike (such as the one in France in May-June 1968) and this will be clear.

Workers and students share a common opponent—the capitalist power structure. Students and recent graduates go unemployed, just as the worker on the line is laid off. Workers and students hear promises of a "new economic policy" while prices and unemployment continue to rise. The lies with which the government defends its war policy are wearing thin with the American working man. A liaison of common interest can and should be forged between the labor movement and the students. This work has already begun, e.g., the Labor-University Alliance sponsored by several unions and university groups, and the solidarity of labor and students in the antiwar offensive in Washington and in San Francisco in the spring of 1971.

Class Prejudice

The first, and perhaps the most serious, problem for students in relating to a labor "constituency" is the estrangement which our society has produced between worker and student.

The bourgeois "American dream" has given rise to a tendency on the part of the nonblue-collar component of society to look down on manual labor as an occupation for those who are "backward" or lacking in cultural or academic background. Such attitudes can be rooted out by appreciation of the practical (as opposed to theoretical) experience of the workers, their long organizational struggle, their proximity to the conflicts of our society, and their lengthy struggle for social justice. Just read labor history, especially the period since 1929.

A change of attitude is most easily accomplished by simple contact with the worker and his world. This can be done through discussion, not necessarily on political and social issues, but on sports, the weather, the job, etc. Such discussion can help to establish fundamental relationships and understanding on a personal basis. One should also familiarize oneself with the information and ideas which are part of the worker's life; read union papers or the local Hearst tabloid. Students may also establish a comfortable relationship with university workers (among the most oppressed of workers). Contact them, not with slogans, rhetoric, and leaflets, but on a human level, with scrupulous courtesy and great care to make their underpaid labors as minimal as possible.

As the student attempts to overcome his own prejudices, he must also cope with the workers' deep antistudent bias. Students have been used as strikebreakers in this country for years. Workers also recall incidents in which a white "kid" with a B.A. or a few years of college has risen quickly from coworker to supervisor. Workers have, in addition, been exposed to the prejudices of seasonally or temporarily employed students, engineers, and management trainees, giving rise to understandable resentment.

In general, workers do not understand middle-class "hangups" and look with envy on financial security and the trappings of material possessions and social prestige. In attempts to relate to the worker, the student organizer should avoid debunking these aspirations, since insensitivity to the existence of such feelings may only accentuate alienation.

Respect and Consideration

The best foundation upon which to build worker-student cooperation is respect. The student should be willing to listen to workers with respect, understanding, and sensitivity. What may appear to be an offhand remark by a worker is likely to be the result of reflection on years of experience. Go home and think about it.

Above all, remember that we are in no position to coerce unions or workers. Workers will organize themselves and move in the direction of their own choosing. They are subject to tremendous pressures. A brief strike can ruin them financially. Being labeled as an "agitator" by company or union can cause them harassment, physical danger, and loss of work. Even talking to an outside agitator openly or accepting a leaflet may mean trouble, and *people resent strangers who place them in jeopardy without sharing the consequences of that jeopardy*.

Divisions in the Working Class

Labor is not a single undifferentiated group. Workers within and outside the labor movement are divided into a number of groups, based on such things as kind of industry, race, region of the country, age, and sex. Labor may be skilled or unskilled and workers may be unionized or not unionized. It is necessary to acquire a rough idea of each situation with which one comes into contact in dealing with the labor movement.

In any working-class community, of even moderate size, there is often one numerically predominant group, with its own unique set of characteristics and attitudes and its own life-style. These must be understood and appealed to. An area may contain several distinct segments, each of which must be approached on its own terms, if success is to be expected. There is no universal formula. Learn the specifics and pertinent variables before you undertake any actions.

The vast majority of organized workers are in the mass industrial unions of the CIO type, with progressive traditions and at least paper democracy. There are also smaller and less technologically advanced craft unions based on the older guild system. The average American worker belonging to the mass industrial union takes home an average of $84 per week (April 1970, Bureau of Labor Statistics) and is constantly threatened by layoffs and unemployment. On the other hand, plumbers, electrical installers, and skilled construction workers earn upward of $10 an hour and have a good deal of freedom to work where and when they see fit. Their unions are the ones which suppress dissent, often by means of coercion (e.g., the recent murders of rank-and-file dissidents among miners, painters, and merchant mariners), and are frequently in alliance with management on the basis of financial interest, ethnic ties, family ties, ties touching organized crime, and a variety of other interests. The questionable unions should be approached with extreme caution. Do not, as the newspapers always do, confuse them with the labor movement as a whole.

In forging student-worker cooperation, greatest success will probably be met in dealing with the big, integrated, more democratic unions: former CIO unions, miners' unions and the recently organized service workers (hospital workers, teachers, social workers, etc.). Here the big distinction is between union officials (or "bureaucrats," as most workers call them, but don't *you* do it) and rank-and-file. In matters of contract, the union officials are intermediaries between workers and management. They have their own interests and often a style which alienates the rank-and-file. They have often played political games, including red-baiting, in order to get and keep their jobs. They know every trick in the book and seem to speak for the unions while in reality they are just keeping the workers in line. Stewards and committeemen represent workers in the shops. They are most responsive to the rank-and-file because they work in the shops and are elected by coworkers. If the shop stewards are really respected by the ranks, they can be the most effective people in the unions.

Since the 1950s, workers have been reacting to the bureaucratization and cooptation of their labor leadership in a variety of ways. The unofficial or "wildcat" strikes and caucuses of various kinds are examples of this reaction. A prominent case in point is the 1970 postal workers' strike, which began as a wildcat strike in New York City and turned into a nationwide postal strike. Caucuses are often the "outs" fighting the "ins" of union politics, but the recent rise of black caucuses and informal caucuses has a potential for providing the leadership nuclei for a redirection of union policies.

Of course, there are some unions with a history of radical leadership and strong rank-and-file solidarity: e.g., the International Longshoremen's and Warehousemen's Union (which represents dock workers on the entire West Coast and Hawaii) and the United Electrical, Radio and Machine Workers. The Oil, Chemical and Atomic Workers is run almost entirely by rank-and-file members.

Racism

Racist attitudes are common among white workers in America. Nonwhites have long been made the scapegoats for labor's problems by racist bosses, just as southern politicians have used racism to distract poor southern whites from the real causes of their difficulties. Fear of economic competition and an encroaching ghetto only nurture the racism already engendered by misinformation.

Blacks were once excluded or ignored by organized labor and occasionally were used as strikebreakers. However, a great increase in power of the CIO was achieved in the thirties under the slogan "Black and White, Unite and Fight." Although this slogan is still enshrined in many labor halls, many unions put down black workers' demands for fair treatment as "divisive" or "racist." Construction workers, plumbers, electricians, and other such tradesmen have kept blacks out of their unions and thus out of their trades for years, because of racism and the desire to preserve available jobs for their relatives.

Black workers are still the last to be hired and the first to be fired. They tend to have the least seniority and they get fewer promotions and fewer chances to get into training programs. They are only rarely represented in the higher echelons of the labor bureaucracy. Although nonwhite workers are 11 percent of the labor force, recent statistics show that they are vastly underrepresented in managerial, clerical, sales, and skilled trades. In some industries (auto, aircraft, coal, steel, and rubber) black workers are from a fifth to a third of the workers on the line. Many blacks are active in union affairs, because they realize that they can thus have some influence as a group. While realizing that the union is not treating them equally, they still remain loyal to it. Because of this, black workers may provide a militant hard core in union activities and be sympathetic contacts in unions and factories.

Although few of the black unionists identify with the Panthers, they know all about Jim Crow courts and will be able to tell you more about why Bobby Seale couldn't get a fair trial than any radical white law student can. You will meet many black Vietnam veterans, since blacks have been the first to be drafted. Many of these veterans are bitterly antiwar and antiarmy. We can expect support from them and we can learn from them.

In each industry and community, and even in each plant, the degree of racism differs. The organizer will have to estimate the situation and decide whether to meet the problem head on, as a major educational campaign, or to deal consciously with it in the course of struggles for immediate demands. In general, the issue is difficult to handle in isolation from basic bread-and-butter questions. It can and should, however, be raised in connection with every action—not in an abstract appeal to "fair play" or to "guilt," but as a matter of the workers' most profound self-interest. The divisive tactics of the bosses must be exposed. Students should demonstrate solidarity by approaching workers in teams of black and white. White organizers should appeal to militant workers' own long history of court injunctions and frame-ups to explain the persecution of the Panthers and other political targets today.

Sex

Women also suffer from job discrimination. They are underpaid and rarely promoted and are usually consigned to service occupations. They are also underrepresented in unions. Women workers have only recently begun to unite to rectify their situation in labor and can provide another front line of activism, aimed not only at improving their job conditions and opportunities but also at improving the society in which many of them are trying to redefine their roles.

Age

Age is another factor in relating to workers. Older workers will demand a certain amount of respect for their experience, and they deserve it. Many have struggled through the depression, World War II, and the recessions of the fifties; they have been disappointed by the present struggle which has continued through recent recessions, high taxes, and inflation. Some will resent younger people who have "had it easier." Forging any basis of cooperation with older workers will require patience, tolerance, sensitivity, and understanding.

Younger workers are the people you went to school with.

They may resent your greater educational and social opportunities, since most of them had to join the army or get a
job instead of going to college. They may be shy at first. But
the young workers are for the most part still undiscouraged
by defeat and are energetic and ambitious.

METHODS FOR PRACTICAL WORK

Preparation—Organize a labor contact committee.

Gathering Information—A general historical background of
the labor movement can be obtained by exposure to literature
on the labor movement (see Bibliography–Directory) and
through workshops led by professors or students who are
familiar with the history of labor in this country. The leader
should concentrate on the period from 1929 to the present
and emphasize the point of similarity between the worker's
problems and ours (e.g., labor history is filled with more
repression than we hope we'll ever see). A filing and reference
system of information gathered at workshops should be prepared for future reference, for those who may have missed the
workshops, or for further research.

Information about local factories and unions may be
obtained from a state labor information board or other such
agency. Contacts may also be made in very large state or
social unions in which many of the stronger local unions are
nominal members. Such contacts may be taking great risks
in helping you, so never mention them as a source or contact
without specific permission. Union people are reluctant if
not positively forbidden to give out membership lists.

After you know where unions are, you need information
concerning the recent and present problems of each union
or plant you intend to tackle. This can be obtained by canvassing local labor meeting places, bars, and restaurants,
and by contact with worker friends. One object of these in-
teractions should be to determine the basic mood in a plant
or union so that the committee knows best how to approach
it if it gets the chance.

Newspapers and union papers should be examined for
information as to issues, injunction negotiations, "wildcat"
strikes, caucuses, ongoing strikes, etc., and a file should be
kept up to date with this information.

Reports should also be filed by committee members on

their experience in the field and any information gathered in direct relations with workers, unions, and companies.

Organizing from Within:

Working in a Shop—The best way to communicate with workers is to go to work. In fact, the actual accomplishment of a worker-student alliance may require that committed students spend one or two years working in a factory. Summer work can be valuable, but it is usually too short-term to be very useful in making real gains toward breaking down student-worker mistrust. Part-time or night work usually does not allow much contact with full-time day workers.

Before taking a job in a factory be sure that you are not taking a job away from a workingman who may need it. Get a job only in an industry which does not have a surplus of workers. When you do apply for a job expect a suspicious employer and a suspicious union official. If the shop you are trying to get into is a closed shop, not getting into the union will keep you from getting the job. If you are rebuffed in your attempts, apply for a job somewhere else or make a formal complaint to your state job discrimination agency.

Most workers possess an inherent sympathy and sincere regard for "struggling" students, i.e., students obviously involved in providing for their own education. Therefore, students who take jobs in plants should take rigorous care not to appear to be working as a lark, slumming, or doing political homework. They should do their best on the job, work hard, and acknowledge appreciation for the opportunity to support themselves by their own labors. It is also important to join your coworkers in agitating around local shop issues such as the election of stewards and general grievances (ventilation, production speed, safety devices, overtime hours, etc.).

If the shop you work in is not unionized, you may contact an appropriate union and offer to help organize it. Be prepared to receive flak from workers, who, through self-interest, are antiunion, and be prepared to receive a pink slip from your boss. Helping to organize workers in a nonunion shop is the best way to learn about workers and unions.

Union Membership—Union membership is an obvious advantage to the political activist. It will give you access to local meetings and local and district officers. You can initiate resolutions, take an active part in the decisions of the local, and serve on union committees. Direct involvement in union affairs allows you to come to know the attitudes of the leadership and the prospects for changing them.

In the plant, the key to the organization of the union is the steward system. Because grievances are the major continuing business of a local union, the "griever" may be a more important leader than the local president.

Organizing from Outside:

Friendly Contacts—Conversation with individual workers is probably the easiest way to find out what they feel about student activism and national issues. Meetings with workers as a group may not be so easy. It is best to begin by calling acquaintances who work in a plant and speaking with them to gauge the temperament of the workers in those plants. Then start to formulate plans for meetings of plant workers with your labor committee representatives.

Contacting Strangers—A friendly clerk in the State Labor Board, local liberals, or local unionists can provide you with information as to sympathetic union officials or locals which you can approach. This may open up the possibility of distributing leaflets at union meetings or arranging for speakers or debates. If these are successful, further steps can be outlined for meeting with other locals and their leaders.

In many areas the labor movement includes only the building trades and one large local representing the employees of a big manufacturing plant, the town's "big industry." If these locals are not interested in having a speaker or a debate about the war, racism, etc., your group should attempt to reach the workers outside their union structure. This can be done with leaflets handed out door to door in working-class neighborhoods and at plant gates.

In the Community—In almost every working-class community the organized labor movement represents less than a third of the population. This is plenty of reason for going into the working-class neighborhoods, even if you have good contact with local unions.

The problems of the working-class "ghettos" (both black and white) in the big cities are innumerable. They include poor schools, crime, debt, high rent and mortgage payments, alcoholism, inadequate health care, and inadequate care of the elderly. There are still relatively few people in working-class communities who are involved politically. But disappointment with the way things have been handled is rising, political consciousness is increasing. Community control is beginning to be the demand in white neighborhoods as it has been in black. Uniting black and white groups around common interest, even when issues clearly suggest that the two should join, may often still be difficult. The potential for community activism among the working class and cooperation with other exploited peoples increases as the conditions provoking indignation become more blatant. Now is the time to begin organizing and pushing for change.

Multiply Contacts—In addition to contacts in unions and local organizations, and friends, you can meet people in bars and restaurants that are frequented before and after shift changes. Simply by sitting in the bar for an extended period of time, you can overhear discussions about the war, blacks, conditions in the plant, inflation, etc. If questioned and identified, you should be prepared to deal with arguments. Bear in mind that you are there to establish communications and *not* to teach the workers about politics. Avoid pressing the discussion into an argument. A sympathetic worker may be a potential contact in the factory, but be careful to approach him in such a manner that he is not placed in a tenuous position with his fellow workers.

Workers tend to see students in a curious kind of love-hate attitude based, on the one hand, on a desire (especially for their own children) for college education and, on the other, on disrespect of the student's ignorance of "the way life really is." The upshot of this is that you must listen to the worker. In a real sense, *he* must educate *you*. The worst thing you can do is to go to a factory and begin telling the workers how to solve their problems. The best you can do is to go with a familiarity with their concerns and let them tell you their own personal feelings. Be honest, present your views tactfully, listen, and see what develops. *Above all, don't rush things—results, if you get them, will take a long time*.

Be sure to keep sources and contacts confidential—do not expose any of them to personal risks. Additional sources of contacts are union halls, union-taught workshops for outsiders, union information officers, and union political action groups such as the Committee on Political Education (AFL-CIO) and LIVE, Labor's Investment in Voter Education (Alliance for Labor Action). Another source of contacts is provided by volunteering to help in union organizing activities and in strike work (actual picketing, or support in providing food, transportation, family assistance, donations for the strike fund, etc.).

Appearance and Rhetoric—Long hair, unconventional dress, use of terms such as "pig," "fascist," "repression," and other bits of revolutionary rhetoric may seriously alienate workers, making it unnecessarily difficult for you to "reach" them because of first-impression biases. Don't make the worker unwilling to be seen talking to you.

Labor contacting committees should be made up of individuals who are in some way related to or representative of the workers to be contacted. Blacks, other minority group members, women, veterans, etc., should be included when the composition of a shop or union suggests that these persons are the best to establish rapport.

Leaflets—The general outline for leaflet writing (see in "Mass Education and Communication") should be followed. However, in addressing and distributing leaflets to workers certain additional steps should be taken:

1. Try to use excerpts from trade-union statements which share a similar viewpoint with you on an issue—e.g., the war, full employment, reconversion.

2. State demands clearly but not arrogantly and relate them to the workers' problems.

3. Get some of the workers you have contacted to advise you as to how to approach a particular plant and help you in revising and writing the final draft.

4. Never distribute a leaflet cold. Know the mood of the factory and have some idea of what to expect.

5. Distribute leaflets at walk-in and drive-in gates, but don't give unsympathetic workers an excuse for harassing you or having you removed because of inconvenience.

6. Leaflet early in the morning and at breaks and lunchtime, to allow discussion of the leaflet by workers during their daily routine.

7. Arrange to get feedback to the leaflet from a contact in the plant.

Warning—It bears repeating that great caution should be exercised in dealing with workers. Careless actions, rash remarks, and insensitivity to the workers' problems and aspirations may alienate the labor "constituency" so thoroughly that attempts at any further organization are defeated. Contacts and sympathizers should never be exposed without specific permission. The atmosphere in unions and factories is highly charged and you should not appear to be nosy or meddlesome. Remember at all times that workers are struggling to provide a decent life for themselves and their families. Consider all your actions in terms of the possibility of jeopardizing their struggle.

Do not expect immediate results; commit yourself to a long struggle; do not give up at the first epithet thrown at you; use all your experiences to your advantage and when results begin to become favorable do not relax in a flush of success, lest your entire effort turn against you. Above all, be yourself. If you are middle class, don't deny it—to others or to yourself. Put your privileges to the service of the mass of the people—confidently, but modestly.

ADDENDUM

There are still a large number of workers in this country who are not in unions. In the South, workers both black and white sweat for oppressive bosses—bosses who will go to great lengths to keep them out of unions. People who are interested in assisting unions in their organizing efforts, even if only for a summer, should contact district or national offices of unions involved in organizing farm, distributive, hospital, chemical, oil, cannery, and mill workers, or any other nonunion workers. Nonunion workers are treated like serfs in southern mills and textile union organizers, for example, are trying to change this. To help their organizational drives, contact the Textile Workers Union (see Bibliography-Directory: Labor).

VII. Professionals

Professional workers provide the essential skills required to make the technocratic society function. The ruling class provides the direction; and the poor, the minorities, and the lower-echelon white-collar and blue-collar workers provide the sweat, energy, and blood which propel the system; but the middle-class professionals are the linkages which connect everything together and operate the legal, technical, financial, and other machinery of the system.

For example, the power structure relies on the school system to continue repressing original thought, replacing it with conformity and jingoism ("patriotism"), teaching false history, and inculcating defeatism. If lawyers were not willing to devise clever ways of protecting corporations from the outrage of cheated consumers; if middle-level bureaucrats were not willing to enforce regulations which take from the poor and give to the rich; if accountants were not willing to find ways for corporations and millionaires to pay light taxes while workingmen pay annually increased tax; if engineers were not willing to design multibillion-dollar military boondoggles and cheap, defective, and dangerous consumer products; if doctors were not willing to treat wealthy hypochondriacs while children die of lead poisoning in the ghetto; and if professionals of all sorts were not willing to sell their skill and close their eyes to the consequences, the policy makers at the top would be unable to operate except by blatant force.

Because of their key position professionals have an importance far greater than their numbers. A relatively small fraction of them can, if radicalized, seriously change the way the structures of the society operate.

Organizing professionals is complicated by their being (except for teachers) a well-paid elite. So they cannot easily be organized on the basis of their own grievances. Moreover, to the extent that they have grown accustomed to their material benefits and elite status, their politicization is inhibited by fear of the loss of these advantages. Consequently the organizer must base his campaign on altruism and ideology, and the best procedures are "top-down" and "young-old."

The process begins by making the professionals fully aware of the biased distribution of their professional services in the society, the causes of this constriction (in terms of the interests of the power structure), and the serious social ills which result. You've got to present a strong argument, so start by choosing a target profession and researching its position in the system, its connections with the power structure, the ways in which its talents are misused, the de facto racist or sexist restrictions on its membership, the constricted channels through which its services are employed, and the reasons for the restrictions on those channels (social convention, institutional structures, etc.). The handiest tool in this research is the *NACLA Research Methodology Guide.* (See "Power Structure Research.")

Organizing professionals tends to work best "top-down." The successful and prestigious members of the profession have considerable influence with status-oriented audiences and are themselves most likely to respond to your arguments. Middle-class middle-level professionals are the most difficult to organize; involved in acquiring possessions, repaying mortgages, raising children, and straining for professional success, they are vulnerable to fear of loss of their income or status if they stick their necks out. The more prestigious professionals are less vulnerable, and after they make radical thought fashionable, the middle-level members may follow.

Organizing should also proceed "young-old." The power structure depends on an adequate number of young people entering each profession each year to keep the system functioning. (Until recently the draft was used to "channel" youth into the professions for this reason.) If large numbers of new professionals refuse to fit the old molds and instead seek alternate paths for employing their skills, they can create severe recruiting problems and thus pressure the institutions to become more socially responsible. So organizing effort must be focused in the technical schools, colleges, and graduate schools.

One of the most valuable tactics in organizing professionals is action at professional conventions, not only because of its convenience (drawing together members from every area of the country), but especially because conventions tend to attract the successful, prestigious professionals and the young activist professionals, rather than the middle-level members.

To plan convention action, examine in a college library the journals of the relevant profession. For example, meetings involving physics and the related sciences are listed months in advance in *Physics Today*. *Science*, the journal of the American Association for the Advancement of Science (AAAS), also lists major scientific conventions.

If you are unable to join the organization and hence obtain legitimate credentials for attending, you may sometimes request youth membership, a visitor's pass or observer's status. Saturate your chosen convention with literature; try to set up displays; canvass and debate with individual members; and try to arrange to speak to the convention formally. In some cases you may chose to stage demonstrations to expose the results of your research or to press for action on a specific issue. Irrational and violent tactics are not usually advisable, however, as they alienate the professional mind, even if it is sympathetic to the cause you represent.

Every professional convention should have a radical caucus which presses for reform of the organization. The caucus may be scheduled in advance of the conference or convention, or it may emerge from the floor of the meeting itself. Once formed, the caucus may chose to stay within the association and by its legitimacy utilize resources such as mailing lists, an office, newsletter, budget appropriations, and allotted speaking time. The caucus can run a slate of officers and use this opportunity to present its radical views. Caucus members can also attempt to amend the constitution of the association (toward greater decision-making power for rank-and-file members, for instance), and bring the association out front in controversial areas.

Where the caucus meets with little official tolerance, it may be worthwhile to run a counterconvention as close to and as open as possible to the convention you are dealing with. During the annual meeting of a society of microbiologists in Boston, competing sessions were held at a nearby hotel by an ad hoc group. The topic of the countermeeting was the drug industry. The alternate program was publicized through leafleting at the official meeting place.

Professional conferences are often well covered by local

and national media, so be sure to provide the press with full details of your actions.

In the following pages we discuss organizing procedures and goals for four groups of professionals only. The approaches to these four typify the methods and ideas which can and should be adapted to other professional groups as well: accountants, social workers, architects, computer programmers, advertisers and P.R. men, systems analysts, journalists, actuaries, managers, TV producers, librarians, and many others.

1. Public-School Teachers

The first purpose of organizing public-school teachers is to free them to become more effective *as teachers*. This goal is behind the increasing activism of teachers' unions. Their goals include job security (so that a teacher cannot easily be fired or demoted for unconventional appearance, beliefs, or methods); better pay (to make it economically practical for good teachers to teach); smaller class size; better physical conditions, especially in run-down ghetto schools; provision of adequate teaching materials; replacement of racist or obsolete textbooks with good ones; provision of nonteaching assistants to free the teacher for the important creative and communicative work of teaching; freedom to teach socially relevant subject matter, to use innovative teaching methods, and to alter regimented classroom patterns; and power to revise the curriculum.

Movement organizers who are not teachers can help promote these goals by providing manpower for fund raising, canvassing, leafleting, and similar tasks to help the teachers' unions, and by encouraging apathetic teachers to become active. Perhaps the most important work a nonteaching organizer can do is to organize *parents* to support teachers' demands and to put pressure on the administration or school board to cooperate with the teachers. This is vital, but it may be difficult because many parents become paranoid about teachers, suspecting them either of teaching "communism" or of causing ruinous tax increases.

The best antidote to this is effective communication between teachers and parents. Organizers may be able to aid this by, for example, promoting and distributing a newsletter (written by teachers, not by the school's P.R. man), preferably with a format which encourages parents to reply and acknowledges their replies in subsequent issues. The existence of an active avenue of two-way communication with the parents increases the likelihood that when a confrontation comes, the parents will actively support the teachers' demands in the interest of better education.

In a community where the teachers' union is not active, the organizer's task is to arouse both the teachers and the parents to demand improvement. First study the situation to determine the best rallying cause. Examine the textbooks: are they racist, or antifeminine? Do the history texts grossly distort history to indicate that the government is infallible and that the Indian, Spanish-American, and Indochina wars were heroic and good? Study the facilities: is the school a credible learning environment, or is it a repressive jailhouse? Rap with teachers, and investigate all the union target goals listed earlier. For more information and suggestions, read Jonathan Kozol's *Death at an Early Age*, John Holt's *How Children Fail*, A. S. Neill's *Summerhill*, George Dennison's *The Lives of Children*, and current high-school underground literature. Consider showing the films *High School* and *No Reason to Stay* to the local teachers and parents. (See "Mass Education and Communication: Films.")

Obtain maximum publicity for the deficiencies of the school system. The key to reforming the schools is the active support of the parents—don't forget them.

The second purpose of organizing teachers is to help them use the classroom to free the children from their ideological straitjackets, to enable them to form their own conclusions. They must develop critical and analytical ability, learn how to recognize hidden assumptions and prejudices, and form the habit of asking pointed questions and demanding real answers. Following are some useful teaching techniques:

Have students read descriptions of situations or events in *diverse news sources*—domestic, foreign, left-wing, right-wing, newspapers, TV, radio, films—to study the objectivity (or lack of it) in reporting and the difficulty of learning the whole truth from any one source.

Discuss the use of *slanted language and jargon* as hidden

persuaders. Distinguish the denotations (definitions) and connotations (emotional biases) of words and expressions. Illustrate the use of political, bureaucratic, and military jargon to suppress emotional meaning (e.g., "gathering intelligence" vs. "spying"). See George Orwell's essay "Politics and the English Language" (frequently anthologized).

Study *commercial advertising and statements by public officials*. Analyze their logic and try to measure their real factual content. Document deceptions, omissions, and non sequiturs; and make a list of common rhetorical props, logical fallacies, and ways of evading giving real answers to questions. Study *Consumer Reports* magazine for illustrations of how some capitalists deceive, endanger, and exploit consumers.

Teachers who try to increase their pupils' political awareness, or who even try to do a better job of straight teaching than the local status quo, should expect to be hassled by school officials, the school board, disturbed parents, the PTA, older teachers, and the pupils themselves. Especially in ghetto schools kids learn at an early age that teachers are jailhouse wardens, so even the best teaching may be foiled by discipline problems. Teachers who want to replace a racist or obsolete textbook may find that the school won't buy new books until the old ones are physically worn out. Teachers who want to distribute supplementary text material (ditto or mimeograph) may find no money available for stencils. Many schools won't permit you to use new teaching materials (mimeographed text, pamphlets, films, etc.), even though they may be free, unless approved in advance by the board. In the face of such obstructions the idealistic teacher will find it difficult to avoid becoming bitter, giving up, or being coopted. He needs your support.

2. Lawyers

Lawyers, more than any other single group, are the power brokers of this society. As legislators, politicians, and government officials they make the laws and enforce them. As corporation counsel they grease the wheels of businesses which exploit the people. But as private attorneys they can (if they are willing) defend the people from oppression. They can also use their inside track in government to make the laws and enforcement structures operate more to the benefit of the people than for the bureaucrats and capitalists.

To make established lawyers more aware of their social responsibilities, go to legal conventions, meetings of the bar associations, etc. Emphasize in your presentations that, as creators and protectors of the structures of the society, lawyers have a moral obligation to protect also the people whom these imperfect structures cripple, just as doctors have a basic moral obligation expressed by their Hippocratic oath.

Much of the work of organizing lawyers must be the responsibility of reform-oriented law students and freshman lawyers. Their refusal to follow standard career patterns can, over the years, force changes in the legal community as a whole. A reform trend has already begun, and there are currently five major alternatives for reformist or radical lawyers:

1. As top law students have chosen careers in civil rights, constitutional, or poverty law, *establishment law firms* have faced recruiting problems and some are responding by making pro bono publico work ("for the benefit of the people") part of the job. In this position a lawyer can use his high salary to support the movement while doing socially constructive work, and can learn the inside track in the power structure. But he is only a part-time activist, runs the risk of being coopted, and could find his public-service work in conflict with his fee-paying clients.

2. Of the various *legal resource groups,* the American Civil Liberties Union (with chapters in every state) is best known. ACLU lawyers concentrate on defending political and civil rights rather than attempting to change power relationships or alter social conditions. The National Lawyers Guild consists of lawyers who make their skills directly available to movement groups or individuals. They give courses on the rights of tenants, debtors, and defendants, and attend demonstrations to observe (see "Legal Protection") and to provide legal defense for those arrested. Another resource group is the legal staff of the NAACP. Several legal support groups have grown out of the GI antiwar movement, such as the U.S. Serviceman's Fund, the Southern Legal Action Movement, and the Northwest Military Law Project.

3. *Public-interest law firms,* such as the Nader Center for

Responsive Law, function as researchers and advocates for disenfranchised groups such as consumers or the public as it is victimized by pollution, poor housing, monopolistic institutions, etc. They investigate and expose hidden relationships and the evils of bad business and bad government; they push for the correction of abuses both through public pressure and through the legal system.

4. *Legal Aid offices* under the OEO (federal Office of Economic Opportunity) exist throughout the country. They concentrate on poverty case law—landlord/tenant, domestic relations, consumer protection, welfare cases, etc. One limitation is that the great need for routine legal services among the poor (such as divorce cases) tends to swallow up all of one's time, leaving little opportunity to work for large-scale changes in the legal system itself. Another limitation is that Legal Aid lawyers usually cannot undertake criminal work, or fee-generating work in general, (such as a personal-injury suit against a landlord), because of monopoly practices of local bar associations.

5. *Law communes* (such as the New York Law Commune) are legal collectives dedicated to defending radical community, labor, and political groups such as the Black Panther party and GI organizers. They are committed to radical social change rather than just increasing representation of disenfranchised groups inside the system, and think of themselves as radicals first and lawyers second. This view is reflected in communal living, with democratic decision making and need-based pay distribution.

Which of these paths a lawyer chooses will reflect the nature and degree of his commitment to the movement. The distinction is between one whose career is dedicated to building a movement for a radically reformed and restructured society and one whose basic career goal is personal or financial success but who wants constructive involvement with society.

3. Scientists and Engineers

Introduction. Creative scientists and engineers tend to be idealistic. Their basic motivations are in many ways similar to those of other creative people. This fact has often been obscured by the antitechnological bias of many members of the movement, because of a fuzzy distinction between creative science and big-business technology. It is important because the creative scientists and engineers are usually those who gain prestige within the professional community, recognition by the press and public, and influence in government circles. Organization of the scientific community therefore rests on appealing to, and reinforcing, the latent high motivations of the creative members of the profession.

This *must* be followed, however, by a thoroughly rational analysis of the issue in question, because a really competent scientist or engineer will be convinced only by a rational argument supported by demonstrable facts. It must not be supposed that masses of scientists can be induced to go trooping off to Washington mouthing vaguely emotional phrases about the bomb, the war, repression, etc. The value of organizing the scientific community consists in using their technical expertise, inside knowledge, and influence to change government or management policies.

Identifying specific issues and targets. Tactically, it is important to single out from the broad issues of the movement those specific issues to which the sciences are relevant. Appropriate examples are ABM, prison reform, and military domination of university research. Next, identify the specific branch of science which is to be the focus of action. For example, ABM involves physicists, programmers, and electronic engineers; prison reform involves sociologists and psychologists; and military domination of research affects the physical and medical sciences.

Researching the issues. In order to stimulate the scientist's commitment you must establish with facts and with solid moral and logical arguments that the issue really deserves active concern. (In-depth immersion in the technical details is not necessary at this stage, though.) On the ABM issue, for example, it was necessary to argue at the outset that ABM would increase the likelihood of thermonuclear war, that its cost would cripple social programs, and that its technical workability was doubtful. Similarly in the case of prison reform one might show (from data available in the press and from almanacs) that our prisons create rather than cure career criminals and that backward prisons are thus a major cause of the rising crime rate.

You will need to search out good sources of information relevant to major policy-making decisions. For instance, on the issue of military domination of research, much data on the awarding of research and development (R and D) contracts is published in military-interest magazines such as *Aviation Week & Space Technology*, available in libraries or by subscription; and on a local basis, government contracts to colleges or industries are almost invariably announced in press releases, so seek out a contact at the local newspaper. The *NACLA Research Methodology Guide* contains an outstanding bibliography on military research and the military-industrial-university complex.

Converting the first few. Having assembled a basically strong argument from the nontechnical and semitechnical information available to the general public, and having selected a relevant branch of the profession as a focus for action, bring the two together vigorously and repeatedly through the media, public demonstrations, and action at conventions. The approach depends on the nature of the issue; thus a reprehensible research contract at a local lab might be approached with maximum media publicity and/or picketing, followed by pressure on the individual faculty. In a national issue, however, action at professional conventions is by far the most valuable approach.

Converting other scientists. Some scientists will be converted to the cause by the above steps. Other activist scientists may already be working on it when you become involved. In either case, those committed scientists will then (on their own) investigate the arguments in detail, and proceed to create presentations which are far superior in technical content and logical persuasiveness to those based only on information available to the general public. They will present their detailed arguments and data in scientific journals, semi-popular scientific magazines such as *Scientific American*, congressional testimony, and public speeches.

The task at this stage is to *ensure that these presentations receive the widest possible dissemination within the scientific community. This is the most important single contribution*

*that the movement can make in organizing scientists and
engineers.* Reprints of the presentations should be distributed
at colleges, at industrial labs, and at conventions. This should
be followed by demonstrations and canvassing, both at conventions and at the scientists' homes, colleges, or labs, to
induce them to use their influence to change policy.

4. Health Professionals

Organizing in the health professions should proceed through
a combination of political education and activist projects
which expose professionals both to the failures of the present
health care nonsystem and to the social and economic causes
of disease. Action on specific health issues is an effective
tactic because health professionals often find it much easier
to get involved in direct service to people than to identify
with a political view. Such action projects, if well chosen,
will demonstrate that much disease and human wreckage is
the product of the inadequate health care system and the
people-destructive priorities of our industry, government,
and society.

For a thorough discussion of the biased distribution of medical care in this country, see *Health Care in America* (hearings
before the Senate Subcommittee on Executive Reorganization,
April 1968). Two excellent monthly publications are the
Health-PAC Bulletin and *Health Rights News*. (See Bibliography–Directory for addresses and for names of activist medical groups.)

The following suggestions for actions should be supplemented on the basis of your study of local conditions:

—Train community workers to do door-to-door health surveys
  and screenings to determine the health needs of the community and the failings of the system. Use the information
  to press for the establishment of a free community medical
  clinic. (See "Alternate Structures: Medical Clinics.")
—Provide free health and nutrition courses in the ghetto,
  advise welfare mothers on creating nutritional low-budget
  diets, expose medical frauds and quacks who flourish among

people who cannot afford doctors, make available (free or wholesale) basic home medical items such as thermometers and first-aid kits, and teach first-aid.

—Identify patient populations which are not receiving any health care from the system: Indians, migrant workers, rural poor (as in Appalachia), chronic alcoholics and addicts, etc. Reinforce public vaccination programs to prevent epidemics, which usually hit hardest in inner-city areas.

—Organize coordinated medical attacks on the problems of rats and lead-paint poisoning in the ghetto. Investigate the public-health departments that haven't been doing their job.

—Study the major individual and group insurance programs. Learn what fraction of their income is paid back in benefits. Identify population groups which have no insurance, and analyze the causes and effects of that lack.

—Support twenty-four-hour drug counseling groups, residencies, trouble pads, and telephone services. (See "Alternate Structures.") Make walk-in psychiatric clinics available in the inner city.

—Reform the medical-school curriculum: include study of social causes of illness and the needed correctives; study minority medicine—problems peculiar to nonwhites; require competent sex education; train community people as paraprofessionals and establish continuing education programs for them; and establish free health career education programs for disadvantaged youth who cannot now consider health careers because of the training cost and upper-class orientation.

VIII. Other Groups

1. Organizing Your Family

How to Approach Parents

Find out who your parents are.

Listen to them; ask their opinion on national issues; find out where they stand.

Analyze their point of view logically; understand both the rational and the emotional roots of their argument.

Talk with each individually and frequently. Find out what their adolescence was like. Find out what they thought about the New Deal, the Fair Deal, or any other appropriate deal.

Devise the most effective strategy for gaining their support. This may include taking out the garbage without being asked, or combing your hair.

Show them your love, save them from involutional depression.

Concentrate on your most sympathetic parent. Divide and conquer. Exercise your maturity and maintain your cool.

Sacrifice. Have patience.

Bring the Oppression Home

Relate the oppression abroad to the oppression at home.

For metaphoric purposes become a nudist at home. Chances are you will be oppressed, suppressed, and force-dressed. Relate this to the less startling demands of oppressed peoples around the world.

Show your parents figures on the current inflation, recession, and defense spending. Compare your family income for one year with the cost of the Indochina war for one day.

Explain how the war is largely responsible for higher taxes, the recession, climbing interest rates, and the high cost of education.

Analyze your family's individual financial difficulties and relate them to the war.

Visit your local supermarket; ask how much prices have been raised in the past few years.

If all else fails, appeal to their parental instincts for love of their children and the children of others. Tell them you wish to live beyond draft age or that you do not wish to be a Vietnam widow, or both. Discuss alternatives to the draft.

ORGANIZE POLITICAL DISCUSSION

Use the dinner table as a center of political discussion but don't forget to eat and finish every bit of your green vegetable—it will make your mother happy.

Comment on the six o'clock (seven Central and Pacific) news.

Criticize biased news coverage.

Criticize Walter Cronkite's tie.

Go to your friends' homes and talk to their parents.

If your family does not have some kind of minority group identity, invent one.

Attend all family gatherings and discuss involvement in Southeast Asia, Pentagon power, university complicity, inflation and the war, the Panthers, the Chicago Eight, United Fruit, the legal system, and reconversion of the economy.

If your expertise is questioned say that you just finished a year course in the appropriate field, even if you haven't.

Request apologies and corrections for racist remarks.

POLITICIZE YOUR SIBLINGS

Bring them to rallies.

Tell them revolutionary bedtime stories; decorate them in buttons.

Let them help you leaflet, write signs.

Get them to donate a nickel a week of their allowance to the cause; put it in a revolutionary "antipiggy" bank.

Donate *your* allowance, birthday, and graduation money to the movement.

FLOOD YOUR PARENTS WITH LITERATURE

Put them on movement mailing lists: Another Mother for Peace, Clergy and Laymen Concerned About Vietnam,

SANE, American Friends Service Committee, etc. (See Bibliography–Directory.)

Give gift subscriptions to: *Village Voice, New Republic, Harper's, L.A. Free Press*, the *Black Panther, I. F. Stone's Newsletter*, etc.

Send your school newspaper home or paste appropriate literature or posters on the bathroom wall.

Start a revolutionary library in your hometown, in your home, in your parents' bedroom.

LIBERATE YOUR HOME

Take full advantages of your resources. Use the telephone —lots.

Use your home as a youth hostel, underground railroad station, revolutionary headquarters, political sanctuary.

Hold showing of revolutionary flicks.

Whistle "The Times They Are a-Changing" around the house.

Play antiwar recordings.

Use the family car for shipping leaflets, literature, canvassers.

Take advantage of your father's job or business contacts, and office supplies.

WHAT PARENTS CAN DO

Give money.

Raise money: flower sale by mothers for peace, cocktail parties and dinners for the movement, hit the churches for a weekly peace collection.

Organize their neighborhood and set up discussions and action groups.

Go to the PTA—ask for education for all (parents, teachers, students) on the issues.

Write to their senators, congressmen, and newspapers telling them their views.

Pass out leaflets at the supermarket, job, train station.

Join whatever organizations they feel comfortable in as a start to involvement.

Refuse to pay the phone tax, or income taxes corresponding to defense (sic) spending.

Picket your local draft board.

WHEN YOUR FOLKS GET ANGRY (they will get angry)

Do not get angry back.

Do not get baited.

Tell them they look young when they are angry.

Be silent until they exhaust themselves.

Know when to retreat like a guerrilla to await another attritional skirmish. Planting the seeds of doubt may be enough for today.

Do not risk forced exile. If they won't let you operate aboveboard, go underground and work behind their backs until they come around. Just because they support you economically doesn't mean that they have bought your mind or conscience. It is not hypocrisy to maintain a truce with conservative parents.

Don't ever concede that it is hopeless to convert them. Just don't waste too much effort trying.

2. The Elderly

The elderly, persons over sixty-five, make up 10 percent of the American population. As a group they are one of the most—perhaps the most—alienated and neglected minorities. A large percentage of the elderly live on incomes which are below or at the poverty line. Living on fixed incomes they are severely affected by wartime inflation. To a great extent, they are inadequately sheltered and fed and are the victims of the "ageism" of the general public. They are relegated to segregated housing for the elderly or exploited by the new "growth industry" of the nursing homes. The irony of their position is that they gave rise, both physically and historically, to the very power structure which in many ways denies them the right to run their own lives with dignity.

Myths about the elderly

There are many myths about the aged which contribute to the disregard if not disdain with which the elderly are treated by an "ageist" society. Some of these myths are:

1. *The elderly are all sick.* While 80 percent of the aged are victims of chronic diseases, these present virtually no

impairment of function for a vast majority, except for the psychological impairment stemming from the societal opinion that they are sick and that their problem is unsolvable. In fact, less than 10 percent of the total elderly population is seriously ill in any given year.

2. *The elderly are all senile.* The characteristic symptoms of senility are not to any significant extent more prevalent among the elderly than among other segments of our society. In fact, recent research has shown that in terms of the accepted standards of psychological impairment students are more "senile" as a group than the elderly. The latter have been found to be at no significant disadvantage in work-retraining programs, although the programs offered are minimal.

3. *Most of the elderly live in cozy community projects for the aged* or in retirement "fun cities" in Florida. In fact, most live in urban blight or its rural counterpart, and cozy is not the best description for most segregated old-age housing. Only 5 percent of the aged live in institutions.

4. *The elderly can live satisfactorily on social security, pensions, and welfare.* Such sources of income are totally inadequate. A number of the aged live on $60 a month: $2 a day to live on forces many to sustain themselves on a diet of canned dog food and beans and to steal such "luxuries" as soap and toilet paper from public facilities.

5. *The elderly are reactionary.* Some of them do cling to the status quo as a lifesaver while they live off annuities or clog the arteries of Congress. But many of the elderly are fed up with inadequate housing, being told they are useless, sick, and senile, and being stripped of their human dignity. They are also becoming sick of war, oppression, racism, imperialism, and the repetition of all the evils which they saw over and over again in their long lives. They are beginning to organize to demand change.

Potentials of the "aged constituency"

The elderly can be an asset for any movement. They have time, experience, demands of their own, a taste of class oppression, 15 percent of the national electoral strength, and the need to overcome the despair, depression, and futility which society has conditioned them to accept as a part of age. They are immediately affected by urban blight, rural poverty, war inflation, and recession. In clear realization of their own mentality, they tend to be more responsive to the general problems of society as well as their own just demands, and in that certain wisdom of experience tend to have a real or potential desire to leave the world a little better off for their existence.

Organizing the elderly

One of the main tasks of the organizer is to provide information enabling the old to implement their own solutions. Efforts should be made to provide a resource so that they can address their powers in the most efficient manner. Information on Social Security, welfare programs, low-cost food and housing can be provided in addition to footwork, transportation, repair work, communications, medical assistance, and general supportive aid. Alliances can be forged with tenants' unions, welfare rights groups, and minority-group organizations. Work can be carried out through established organizations such as the National Council of Senior Citizens and local "golden age" groups and elders' councils. There are volunteer groups in many cities which are set up to telephone elderly persons daily to check on their well-being. Volunteers are also needed in high-crime areas to escort the elderly to and from banks so that they can cash their social security and welfare checks.

Listen to the old. They can best point out social and community problems that need solving. Meetings of elderly groups welcome visitors who show an interest in their activities and problems or who have something new to tell them. Such groups are among the most responsive, interested, and discerning audiences available. The elderly usually are more than willing to talk with concerned visitors, especially the young.

Through direct assistance and discussion with informal groups of the aged or existing organizations, cooperative assistance programs can be established. Care should be taken to assist the elderly—not to control, make assumptions, or act for them. Work among the elderly should have to be only in a resource role, not a leadership role. Most importantly, be very certain that any activities undertaken with the elderly are carried to completion. If there is one thing they don't need, it's more disappointed expectations.

Once certain demands are achieved, problems faced by the aged can be related to the larger system. The aged are a significant segment of the population. Their dissatisfaction and disappointment can be channeled from their immediate problems to the root causes. The elderly and the youth movement, at the extremes of the age range whose middle controls the power structure, are natural allies in the fight against the oppression which they produced and have been produced from.

3. Welfare Recipients

Welfare recipients are among the most victimized members of our economic system. They not only need organizing for immediate demands, but new leadership with which to fight for long-range changes in their lives. They are kept alienated in their homes, tied to children because of inadequate day-care facilities. They are intimidated and made to feel powerless by the authoritarian and moralistic stance and procedures of most welfare agencies. Their households are controlled by a system that employs social workers as omniscient, benevolent paternalists who know nothing of the life of their "charges."

Among the groups fighting for reform is the national Welfare Rights Organization (WRO) with branches in many cities and states. It wishes to unionize welfare recipients and seek:

1. Sole bargaining power for all the welfare recipients in a state.

2. The power (through membership and electoral voting pressure) to negotiate on equal terms with welfare departments.

3. A democratic organization to extend a sense of power and responsibility to all their members. To create a constituency with electoral power.

4. To get all the money they can directed into welfare.

5. A guaranteed annual income for all people.

It is important to work to meet the immediate needs of the welfare recipients, while at the same time making certain these "victories" are evaluated in the light of their "real" gains.

To organize welfare recipients:

1. Obtain a list of those on welfare rolls either through

proper channels, or if refused, through a friendly social worker; it can be helpful in many ways.

2. Conduct a door-to-door canvassing campaign to meet welfare recipients and discuss issues.

3. Early, find five to ten recipients to help you canvass and set up an office.

4. Call a meeting after several weeks of canvassing and getting word passed through the gossip grapevine.

5. Set specific goals, their goals, and determine these through informal sessions. Organize committees to research the problems and the authority you must fight. Committees are important because they encourage involvement and a sense of worth.

6. Be aware of neighborhood rivalries and the groups' friendship affiliations. Try to eliminate "back stabbing" about privileges from the welfare department by educating the group to the fact that this is just what the enemy wants, to keep them separated and arguing about petty benefits.

7. Attempt to enlist welfare workers to your group's aid. The administrators are usually patronage appointments, but the lower-echelon people are easier to reach. If the workers for the bureaucracy desert it, it will collapse. Encourage the workers to strike in conjunction with the recipients' demands. In Massachusetts, social workers unionized and struck against the state, not for salary issues, but because the state hindered them in doing their job, i.e., raising the living standard of those on welfare.

8. Listen to your group and to those sympathetic to it inside the welfare department. Together these two groups have a potential understanding of the whole system—its causes and effects.

The main actions of WRO have been to keep pressure on the welfare departments through all avenues open to them. Demonstrations and rallies have been two main actions they have utilized. Organize your group to show up on check day at the welfare offices to demonstrate for more money for particular needs that welfare doesn't respond to even when prices and expenses go up. This is a good way to recruit new members. You are visible on a day when welfare mothers get a check too small for their needs. You are there to channel their anger into constructive actions. Use picketing and leafleting. You can also hold rallies to educate people to particular issues. In New York, rallies are being held in communities on the issue of education. The New York group is trying to get Title I funds to be administered through the welfare department to be channeled into better community education.

In addition, campaigns can be mounted around the particular issues of food, furniture, and utility expenses not sufficiently covered by welfare checks. Many local groups have also worked to start free medical clinics and day-care centers. On the latter issue many groups have made alliances with women's liberation groups to discuss the issues of the matriarchally run home of most welfare recipients.

Other actions involve internal self-education—workshops and seminars on skills, consumer protection, buying techniques, landlord problems, etc. You might consider expanding the group to form food cooperatives, tenants' unions, and other related alternative structures.

In all these actions related to short-term needs it is important never to forget the long-range goals of returning full control of their lives to all the people.

4. Religious Institutions

Organized religion tends to be conservative and to provide support for established structures and secular values. Businessmen and professionals, who hold prime positions in the power structure, sit on church boards and get special consideration for their large donations. Most churches in America sanctify the private ownership of property. On army bases and on the battlefield chaplains in uniform pray for "victory." American missionaries bring Christ and capitalism to the people of the third world. Churches are ghetto landlords. They make heavy investments in corporations producing the machinery of war and helping to support fascist and racist governments. The religious leader influences the opinions of his congregation, who look to him for guidance. Often he fails to confront issues from the pulpit, speaks around them—not to them.

But, like many institutions today the churches are going through a process of examination and reform. While still serving the individual spiritual needs of their members, they are beginning to concern themselves with the basic needs of the oppressed, impoverished peoples of the world. There are now an increasing number of clergymen who are determined to make their churches viable forces for providing services and effecting social change. The churches are becoming more involved in civil rights, the antiwar movement, etc. Black affairs councils are being formed in many churches to stimulate programs run by the black community. On many campuses chaplains are allying with students on issues, offering their homes or offices as meeting places, and organizing within their own sects. Church-affiliated universities and other religious institutions have been used to aid war and draft resisters and provide draft counseling. Churches are reexamining their investment portfolios and are putting more of their money into community public-service projects and grants for other organizations. The national Episcopal hierarchy responded to the "Black Manifesto" issued by James Foreman which demanded reparations for four hundred years of the oppression of blacks, to be used to institute a communications network, a black studies progam, and a black university.

Some religious leaders have even become involved in radical activity. Fr. Daniel Berrigan has been imprisoned for acts stemming from his opposition to the Indochina war. William Sloan Coffin, Jr., at Yale University has supported student demands and has been harassed by the establishment legal structure for his antiwar stand. Jesse Jackson and other black ministers of the urban ghettos are continuing their efforts for the liberation of their communities.

A relatively neutral church or temple may prove to be the most accessible or easily approached. The greatest potential for organizing lies with the youth. Most religious institutions have youth groups. Contact the youth adviser. Get to know him and his politics. He is probably on some executive board of the church or organization.

Attend youth group meetings. Note their procedure and intergroup relations. Determine their level of political awareness and involvement. What conflicts are there? What actions has the group taken in the past? Once you become familiar, raise issues by conducting discussions, study groups, and workshops. These should involve their relation to world and national problems, their political development, and the social and political role of religion. The ideal is for the group to create its own experience through relevant group action and planning. The group may eventually use the pulpit during a service to present their own message. With the cooperation of the clergyman they may help to create a new service.

A religious youth group organized around social issues rather than social activities can help to raise the political consciousness of the entire congregation. If the preacher of a sermon takes a conservative or reactionary line they can challenge him and engage him in discussion. They can suggest that pledges be donated to worthwhile community activities, such as the Panther breakfast program. They can start a newspaper or newsletter to publicize key events. As congregants themselves, the activist youth can act as a liaison between the congregation and the women's liberation movement, the black community, other religious institutions, etc.

The following is a list of several organizations associated with organized religions and some of their activities. (See also Bibliography–Directory.)

Clergy and Laymen Concerned About Vietnam
—Fact-finding survey of Indochina and the war.
—Fund raising for deserters in Canada.
—Teach-ins on Southeast Asia.
—Has twenty-four paid field staff members and about a hundred local and national organizers.
—Strategy aimed at working with church-affiliated groups and using the church as a viable force in organizing political activity.

Arlington Street Church (Boston)
—Sanctuary for draft resisters.
—Draft counseling service.
—Runs coffeehouses.
—Church made available as a meeting place for many groups.

Judson Memorial Church (New York City)
—Mobile medical clinic.
—Drug and runaway counseling.

Thoughts for a New Printing: Prisons

If this were a new edition instead of a reprint, the O.M. Collective could now incorporate all the valuable additions and corrections that have come from our readers. As things stand, we are limited to minor corrections. One revision cannot wait—a new section on prisoners' rights and the reform/abolition of the present penal system: (See also Bibliography-Directory.)

As Kent State ushered in a more deeply serious stage of the movement against the system of repression and poverty, so Attica signalized the extension of the struggle by and for the prisoners of that system—the minorities and the poor. Those who seek fundamental change in our society will have to challenge the philosophy, the practice, the very existence of our penal institutions. The work begins in organization of support for prisoners' rights and has three distinct, though interrelated, aspects: (1) education of the public to an understanding of its stake in prison reform; (2) organization of pressure on legislatures and public officials; (3) aid and support to prisoners, parolees, and their families.

Since the demands you raise must come from the inmates of particular prisons, you must inform yourself about the institutions in your area. Conditions such as those in Attica thrive on secrecy: it is not easy to gain access to a prison or, even if you do, to discover the true state of affairs. If you have a friend who is doing time, try to visit him. Approach citizens' groups in your area, or write to the National Council on Crime and Delinquency for contacts. Confer with any public official who stands for prison reforms. Establish connections with local prisons and parole boards through a university law school or sociology department. There are organizations of ex-convicts, like the Fortune Society in New York, and clearinghouse groups like the Massachusetts Council on Crime and Correction in Boston, that will send speakers to your meetings and inform you of specific local problems. The Black Muslims and the Black Panthers organize extensively within the prisons.

You will need full and precise information on the following conditions in and around the prisons (federal, state, county, or city) of your area:

1. state of the buildings; work and pay schedules; censorship (be careful with letters!); rules and discipline.

2. education and counseling programs; health care.

3. prisoners' civil rights; access to the media; grievance procedures; community monitoring, etc.

4. racial, sexual, social composition of particular prisons.

5. major laws governing penal institutions and parole; pending reform legislation.

6. the state (or county, etc.) budget for "correction"; how it is arrived at and administered.

7. special institutions or programs for youth, women, the psychologically disturbed, etc.

8. the status of work-release programs, "halfway" houses, or other arrangements for parolees in which community people can be involved.

Some prisons have "rehabilitation" programs—on paper, at least. (Only 5% of correctional budgets go for rehabilitation, so don't expect too much.) If there is a prison in your area where community or university groups can participate in debates, classes, sports, theatricals, social events, etc., this provides your best opportunity for getting acquainted "inside" —*if* you are prepared to make a steady, long-term commitment. Stick to the announced activity (debate, game, seminar, etc.) and prepare to do your best. Obey prison rules of dress and behavior, no matter how stupid. (The inmates, not you, will suffer if you don't.) Don't come on radical until you assess the situation; convicts are wary of rhetoric and suspicious of betrayal. Let your group reflect the composition of the prison population if possible—i.e., this activity is usually best led by black, Puerto Rican, and Chicano students or community people. Never promise to write, to return, or to do *anything* unless you *do* it. Never be late; a prisoner's time is less "free" than yours. Act natural; if you are nervous or in doubt, admit it, and ask questions; argue if you must (many convicts are far from radical). Above all, never condescend. Prisoners are not caged animals, children, or mental cripples, though prisons encourage that self-image.

Where possible, meet with prisoners' committees as a "community monitor" and try to persuade the media to cover conditions in the local prisons. Much of your work will consist in legislative lobbying, publicity, and education. Other "outside" support can be organized around employment and housing assistance for parolees, help to prisoners' families (providing rides on visiting days, etc.), and legal aid programs for inmates before and after release. A school or community drive to build up a prison library or provide a projector can upgrade education in the typical understaffed, undersupplied institution.

Bibliography-Directory

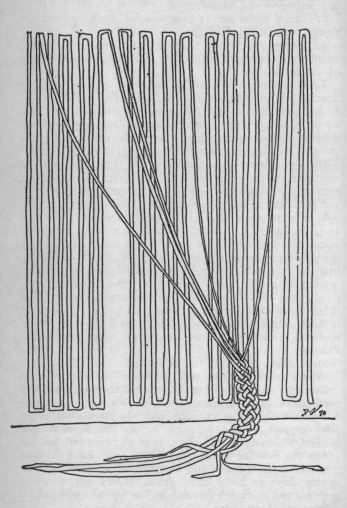

[The Bibliography–Directory does not claim to be exhaustive. Rather, the Bibliography represents works that have proved useful to various members of the Collective and their friends, and the Directory attempts, in a constantly changing situation, to guide readers to those groups and sources where they can obtain further information and organizational help.]

Principles

Organizing and Fund Raising

Applied Imagination: Principles and Problems of Creative Problem Solving, Alex Osborn, Scribner, 1963, $4.95. On brainstorming.

The Community Activist's Handbook: A Guide to Organizing, Financing and Publicizing Community Campaigns, John Huenefeld, Beacon Press, 1970.

Don't Mourn, Organize: SDS Guide to Community Organizing, The Movement Press, 345 Franklin St., San Francisco, Calif. 94102.

Foundation Directory, published for the Foundation Library Center, 444 Madison Ave., New York, N.Y. 10022, by Russell Sage Foundation; published irregularly, latest in 1967, $12.

Foundation News, published for the Foundation Library Center, bimonthly, $3/yr. Write Subscription Dept., 428 E. Preston St., Baltimore, Md. 21202.

Fund Raising (brochure), Student Mobilization Committee, 1029 Vermont Ave., NW, Washington, D.C. 20005, $2 for 100.

Guide to Conducting Meetings, J. E. Baird, Abingdon, 1965, 75¢.

Handbook on Community Foundations in the United States and Canada, and *Report on Status, Community Foundations in the United States and Canada*, Council on Foundations, 345 E. 46th St., New York, N.Y. 10017.

Lowndes County Freedom Organization, Jack Minnis, Southern Conference Education Fund, 3210 W. Broadway, Louisville, Ky. 40211, 50¢.

Modern Rules of Order, L. S. Cushing, Fawcett World, 1969, 75¢.

The Movement, Movement Press, 345 Franklin St., basement, San Francisco, Calif. 94102, monthly, $2.50/yr. Deals primarily with organizing issues.

"The Myth of Saul Alinsky," Frank Reisman, *Dissent*, July–August 1967.

"Of Means and Ends," Saul Alinsky, *Union Seminary Quarterly Review*, January 1967.

The Organizer's Library Series, available from Southern Conference Education Fund (SCEF), 3210 W. Broadway, Louisville, Ky. 40211. Pamphlets by Alan McSurely including: *Common Group Problems*, 50¢; *Getting and Keeping People Together*, 25¢; *Hang-Ups—Common Problems of People Who Organize Other People into Communities*, 50¢; *How to Negotiate*, 25¢.

Organizing the YSA (pamphlet), Young Socialist Alliance, P.O. Box 471, Cooper Sta., New York, N.Y. 10003, 1970, 40¢.

Successful Conference and Discussion Techniques, H. P. Zelko, McGraw-Hill, 1957, $2.75.

A Training Plan for Campus-Community Organizing, Pam Dickson Senterfitt and Allen Toothaker, United States Student Association, 1969, $2.00.

Where It's At: A Research Guide for Community Organizing, Jill Hamberg et al., New England Free Press, 1967, $1.00.

Self-Education

Political Self-Education

Anarchism, Daniel Guerin, Monthly Review Press, 1970, $6.00.

The Anarchists, ed. Irving L. Horowitz, Dell Laurel, 1964, 95¢.

Anatomy of Anti-Communism, Peace Education Division of American Friends Service Committee, Hill & Wang, 1969, $1.50.

The Campaigner, National Caucus of Labor Committee, P.O. Box 49, Washington Bridge Sta., New York, N.Y. 10033, monthly, $4/yr., $2.50/6 issues. Socialist theory and practice.

Capital, Karl Marx, International Publishers, 3 vols., 1967, $22.50. Marx on the "basic laws of motion of capitalism."

Capitalism as a System, Oliver J. Cox, Monthly Review Press, 1964, $3.95. A sociological and systemic analysis of international capitalism.

The Civil War in the United States, Karl Marx, International Publishers, 1937, $2.25.

Communist Manifesto, Karl Marx and Frederick Engels, International Publishers, 1948, 40¢.

Containment and Change, Carl Oglesby and Richard Schaull, Macmillan, 1967, $1.45.

Contours of American History, William Appleman Williams, Quadrangle Books, 1966, $2.95.

Culture Against Man, Jules Henry, Random House Vintage, 1963, $2.95. Contemporary American culture.

The Daily World, 205 W. 19th St., New York, N.Y. 10011; or P.O. Box 544, Old Chelsea Sta., New York, N.Y. 10011, $15/yr. Marxist daily (CP-USA).

Dissent, 509 Fifth Ave., New York, N.Y. 10017, bimonthly, $5/yr., $2/yr. to students. Journal devoted to radical ideas and the values of socialism and democracy.

Divided We Stand, Editors of *Ramparts,* Harper & Row, 1970, $3.95. Selection of articles from *Ramparts,*

Do It! Jerry Rubin, Simon & Schuster, 1969, $2.45.

Documents on SDS and the Split (packet of seven articles), New England Free Press, 791 Tremont St., Boston, Mass. 02118, 65¢.

Economics: Mainstream Readings and Radical Critiques, ed. David Mermelstein, Random House, 1970, $5.95. An anthology of essays and articles organized as a radical textbook on economics.

Essay on Liberation, Herbert Marcuse, Beacon Press, 1969, $1.95.

Four Essays in Philosophy, Mao Tse-tung, China Books and Periodicals, 1966, 60¢; $1.00 hardback. Essays include "On Contradiction"; "On Practice," Mao's statement on the interaction between political practice and theoretical knowledge; "Where Do Correct Ideas Come From?" and "On the Correct Handling of Contradictions Among the People."

Government Publications and Their Use, L. F. Schmeckebier and R. B. Eastin, Brookings Institution, 1961 (rev. ed. 1969), $6.00.

The Great Speckled Bird, Atlanta Cooperative News Service, P.O. Box 54495, Atlanta, Ga. 30308, $6/yr., $3.50/yr. to students and GIs, 10 issues free to GIs.

The Greening of America: The Coming of a New Consciousness and the Rebuilding of the Future, C. A. Reich, Random House, 1970, $6.95.

The Guardian, 197 E. 4th St., New York, N.Y. 10009, weekly, $10/yr., $5/yr. to students, $1/yr. to GIs. The closest thing to a national movement paper.

Guerrilla Warfare and Marxism, W. J. Pomeroy, International Publishers, 1969, $2.95.

Hard Times, P.O. Box 3573, Washington, D.C. 20007, weekly, 25¢/issue, $8.50/yr., $6/yr. to students.

The Haunted Fifties, I. F. Stone, Random House Vintage, 1969, $2.45. Collection of articles from Stone's weekly.

How to Find Out: A Guide to Sources of Information for All, G. Chander, Pergamon, 1968, $2.95.

Human Nature: The Marxian View, Vernon Venable, World Meridian, 1966, $1.95.

"I Have a Dream," the Quotations of Martin Luther King, compiled and ed. Lotte Hoskins, Grosset & Dunlap, 1968, $1.00.

Imperialism, the Highest Stage of Capitalism, V. I. Lenin, International Publishers, 1969, $1.50. Describes the development of capitalism to its later imperialist stage; why and how.

In a Time of Torment, I. F. Stone, Random House Vintage, 1968, $1.95. Essays from his newsletter, dealing with the early to mid-sixties.

Internal War, H. Eckstein, Free Press, 1964, $7.95. An in-depth analysis on the proper use of terror and aspects of guerrilla war.

International Socialist Review, 873 Broadway, New York, N.Y. 10003, monthly (except August), $5/yr., $6/foreign.

An Introduction to Marxist Economic Theory, Ernest Mandel, Pathfinder Press, 1967, $1.00.

Karl Marx: His Life and Environment, Isaiah Berlin, Oxford Galaxy, 1963, $1.50.

The KUDZU, P.O. Box 22502, Jackson, Miss. 39205, periodical, 25¢/issue.

Left-Wing Communism, an Infantile Disorder, V. I. Lenin, International Publishers, 1940, 95¢. Lenin's attack on loosely organized, "left-wing" factions within and outside of the party.

Leninism or Marxism, Rosa Luxemburg, University of Michigan Press, 1961, $1.65. A critique of Leninist party elitism, centralism, and rigidity, and an exposition of what Marxism, in her view, ought to be.

Leviathan, 968 Valencia St., San Francisco, Calif. 94110, ten issues per year, $5/yr., $5.50/yr. in Canada, $6.50/yr. overseas. Revolutionary politics and culture.

Liberated Guardian, c/o Jill Bostcey, 533 E. 12th St., Apt. 6R, New York, N.Y. 10009, weekly, $10/yr. By former *Guardian* staffers who split to set up their own paper.

Life Against Death: Psychoanalytical Meaning of History, Norman O. Brown, Wesleyan University Press, 1959, $1.95.

The Little Red, White and Blue Book—Revolutionary Quotations by Great Americans, ed. Johnny Rosen, Grove Press, 1969, $1.00.

Los Angeles Free Press, 7813 Beverly Blvd., Los Angeles, Calif. 90036, weekly, $6/yr.

The Making of a Counter-Culture, Theodore Roszak, Doubleday Anchor, 1969, $1.95.

Marxism: An Introduction, Mike Goodfield, Radical Education Project Study Guide Series, 10¢. Annotated bibliography.

Marx's Concept of Man, Erich Fromm, Ungar, $2.25.

The Militant, Militant Publishing Arm, 873 Broadway, New York, N.Y. 10003, weekly, $4/yr.

The Modern Prince and Other Writings, Antonio Gramsci (ed. and trans. Lois Marks), International Publishers, $1.85.

Monopoly Capital, Paul A. Baran and Paul M. Sweezy, Monthly Review Press, 1968, $3.95. An essay on the American economic and social order from a Marxist viewpoint.

Monthly Review, 333 Sixth Ave., New York, N.Y. 10014, $6/yr. Independent Socialist magazine.

Movement History and Perspectives (packet of sixteen articles), New England Free Press, 719 Tremont St., Boston, Mass. 02118, $2.00.

Mutual Aid, Peter Kropotkin, Porter Sargent, 1955, $2.00.

The Nation, 333 Sixth Ave., New York, N.Y. 10014, weekly, $10/yr., $18/2 yrs. Political reporting and commentary.

New America, 1182 Broadway, New York, N.Y. 10001, biweekly, $5/yr., $2/yr. to students. Newspaper of the Socialist party.

The New Left, ed. Priscilla Long, Porter Sargent, 1969, $3.00. History and theory of the new left; essays.

New Left Notes, SDS, 173A Massachusetts Ave., Boston, Mass. 02115, $5/yr. to members, $10/yr. otherwise.

The New Left Reader, ed. Carl Oglesby, Grove Press, 1969, $1.50.

New Left Review, 7 Carlisle St., London W1, England, periodical, $7.50/yr.

New Politics, 507 Fifth Ave., New York, N.Y. 10017, periodical, 90¢/copy, $3.50/yr., $4/yr. foreign. Independent Socialist journal.

The New Radicals: A Report with Documents, Paul Jacobs and Saul Landau, Random House Vintage, 1966, $1.95. Excellent movement history and collection of documents up to 1966.

New York Review of Books, 250 W. 57th St., New York, N.Y. 10019, 50¢/issue, $10/yr.

News and Letters, 415 Brainard St., Detroit, Mich. 48201, monthly, $1/yr.

Obsolete Communism: The Left-Wing Alternative, Daniel and Gabriel Cohn-Bendit, McGraw-Hill, 1968, $1.95.

On Coalition Government, Mao Tse-tung, China Books and Periodicals, 1960, 75¢.

On the Origins of the Family, Private Property, and the State, Frederick Engels, International Publishers, 1942, $1.85.

One Dimensional Man, Herbert Marcuse, Beacon Press, 1964, $2.25.

The Other America, Michael Harrington, Penguin, 1962, 95¢.

The Palestine Problem, and Israel and Imperialism, Members of Israeli Socialist Organization, New England Free Press, 20¢.

Patterns of Anarchy, Leonard Krimerman and Lewis Perry, Doubleday Anchor, 1966, $1.95. Anthology of anarchist writings.

People's War, Mao Tse-tung, China Books and Periodicals, 1967, 40¢.

Pittsburgh Peace and Freedom News, periodical, 618 S. Millvale Ave., Pittsburgh, Pa. 15224, contributions.

Points of Rebellion, William O. Douglas, Random House Vintage, 1970, $1.95.

Political Economy of Growth, Paul A. Baran, Monthly Review Press, 2d ed., 1968.

Political Philosophy of Bakunin, M. A. Bakunin, Free Press, 1964, $2.95.

Poverty: Views from the Left, eds. Jeremy Larner and Irving Howe, Apollo, 1968, $1.95.

The Professional Radical: Conversations with Saul Alinsky, Marian K. Sanders, Harper & Row, 1970, 95¢.

The Progressive, 408 W. Corham St., Madison, Wis. 53703, monthly, $6/yr., $11/2 yrs., $15/3 yrs.

Progressive Labor, Progressive Labor Party, P.O. Box 808, Brooklyn, N.Y. 11202, bimonthly, $2.50/yr.

The Pursuit of Loneliness, Philip E. Slater, Beacon Press, 1970, $7.50.

Quotations from Chairman Mao (Red Book), Mao Tse-tung, China Books and Periodicals, 1966, 60¢.

Radical America, 1237 Spaight St., Madison, Wis. 53705, periodical, $5/yr., $10/yr. with pamphlets. Ten issues.

Ramparts, 1606 Union St., San Francisco, Calif. 94123, monthly, $8.50/yr., $15/2 yrs., $9.50/yr. foreign.

Reason and Revolution: Hegel and the Rise of Social Theory, Herbert Marcuse, Beacon Press, 1960, $2.45.

The Red Papers (pamphlet), Bay Area Revolutionary Union, P.O. Box 219, 1230 Grant Ave., San Francisco, Calif. 94133, 25¢ each (5 @ 15¢, 25 @ 10¢). A collection of statements and a bibliography on Marxism-Leninism.

Report from Iron Mountain on the Possibility and Desirability of Peace, Leonard Lewin, Dial Press, 1967, $5.00.

The Review of Radical Political Economics, Union of Radical Political Economists, P.O. Box 287, Cambridge, Mass. 02138, quarterly, $15/yr. to nonmembers.

Revolution for the Hell of It, Free (Abbie Hoffman), Dial, 1968, $1.95.

The Sane Society, Erich Fromm, Fawcett World, 1955, 95¢.

SANE World, SANE, 318 Park Ave. S., New York, N.Y. 10016, periodical, $10/yr., $2/yr. to students.

The Selling of the President 1968, Joe McGinniss, Trident Press, 1969, $5.95. How Richard M. Nixon was sold to the nation.

"The Slum That Saved Itself," Elinor Richey, *The Progressive*, October 1963.

Social Origins of Dictatorship and Democracy, Barrington Moore, Beacon Press, 1967, $2.95.

Social Policy, International Arts and Science Press, 901 N. Broadway, White Plains, N.Y. 20613, periodical, $1.50/issue, $6/yr., $8/2 yrs. Magazine of debate, analysis, and theory devoted to major movements for social change.

Socialism and Man, Che Guevara, Pathfinder Press, 1968, 35¢.

Socialism in America, ed. Albert Fried, Doubleday Anchor, 1970, $3.95. A documentary history.

Socialism: Utopian and Scientific, Frederick Engels, International Publishers, 1935, $1.50.

Socialist Humanism: An International Symposium, Erich Fromm, Doubleday Anchor, $1.75.

Socialist Revolution, Agenda Publishing Co., 1445 Stockton St., San Francisco, Calif. 04133, bimonthly, $6/yr. Marxist; successor to *Studies on the Left*.

The Southern Patriot, Southern Conference Education Fund, 3210 W. Broadway, Louisville, Ky. 40211, monthly (except July, August), 30¢/copy, $3/yr.

Soviet Marxism, Herbert Marcuse, Random House Vintage, 1st ed., 1958, $1.95.

State and Revolution, V. I. Lenin, International Publishers, 1932, $1.00. Lenin analyzes the role of the state in capitalist societies.

Still Hungry in America, Robert Coles, World Publishing, 1969, $2.95.

The Superstructure (packet of seventeen articles), New England Free Press, $2.17.

Teach-Ins, U.S.A.: Reports, Opinions, Documents, L. Menashe and R. Radosh, Praeger, 1967, $1.95.

Telos, Dept. of Philosophy, SUNY at Buffalo, 4224 Ridge Lea Rd., Amherst, N.Y. 14226, periodical, $1/issue, $2/yr. A journal of radical philosophy.

Terror and Resistance: A Study of Political Violence, E. V. Walter, Oxford University Press, 1969, $8.50.

Tooth and Nail, 452 60th St., Oakland, Calif. 94609, periodical, $5/yr.

Toward a Democratic Left, Michael Harrington, Pelican-Penguin, 1965, $1.25.

Toward a Marxist Humanism, Leszek Kolakowski, Grove Press, 1968, $1.95.

Toward a New Past, ed. Barton J. Berstein, Random House Vintage, 1967, $1.95. Dissenting essays in American history.

Trans-Action, Box A, Rutgers—The State University, New Brunswick, N.J. 08903, monthly, $8.50/yr.

Urban Underground, Movement for a Democratic Society, 210 W. 82d St., New York, N.Y. 10024, monthly, $2/yr.

Vietnam: The Logic of Withdrawal, Howard Zinn, Beacon Press, 1967, $1.25.

War/Peace Report, 218 E. 18th St., New York, N.Y. 10003, $5/yr., $3.50/to students.

Washington Monthly, 1150 Connecticut Ave., NW, Washington, D.C. 20036, $8/yr., $15/2 yrs., $21/3 yrs.

What Is to Be Done? V. I. Lenin, International Publishers, 1967, $1.65. On party organization.

Win Magazine, 339 Lafayette St., New York, N.Y. 10012, monthly, $5/yr., $3/six-month trial.

World Revolution, Progressive Labor Party, P.O. Box 808, Brooklyn, N.Y. 11202, quarterly, $2/yr.

Why We Need Socialism in America (pamphlet), Michael Harrington, The Norman Thomas Fund, 112 E. 19th St., New York, N.Y. 10003, $1.25.

Zionism: A Political Critique, Tabitha Petran, New England Free Press, 20¢.

Zionism and the Israeli State, Larry Hochman, New England Free Press, 20¢.

Power Structure Research

American Power and the New Mandarins, Noam Chomsky, Random House Vintage, 1969, $2.45.

The Care and Feeding of Power Structures, Jack Minnis, New England Free Press, 50¢.

The Case Against Congress: A Compelling Indictment of Corruption on Capitol Hill, Drew Pearson and Jack Anderson, Simon & Schuster, 1968; Pocket Books, 1969, 95¢.

Chemical and Biological Warfare: America's Hidden Arsenal, Seymour M. Hersch, Doubleday, 1969, $1.95.

Corporations and the Cold War, ed. David Horowitz, Monthly Review Press, 1969, $6.00 hardback.

Due to Circumstances Beyond Our Control, Fred W. Friendly, Random House Vintage, 1967, $1.65. How the television corporate structure manages the news.

Gothic Politics in the Deep South, Robert Sherrill, Ballantine, 1968, 95¢. An exposé.

In a Few Hands: Monopoly Power in America, Estes Kefauver, Pelican-Penguin, 1965, $1.25.

Mass Communications and American Empire, Herbert I. Schiller, Augustus M. Kelley, 1969, $9.00. The overseas empire of the U.S. media corporations.

The Military Industrial Complex, Sidney Lens, Pilgrim Press, 1970, $2.95.

NACLA Research Methodology Guide, North American Congress on Latin America, 25¢.

Pentagon Capitalism, Seymour Melman, McGraw-Hill, 1970, $8.00.

The Power Elite, C. Wright Mills, Oxford Galaxy, 1961, $2.25.

The Power Structure: Political Process in American Society, Rose Arnold, Oxford University Press, 1967, $2.95.

Researching the Ruling Class of America, William Domhoff, New England Free Press, 10¢.

The Rich and the Super-Rich, Ferdinand Lundberg, Bantam, 1968, $1.95.

SANE Publications:
  "Military-Industrial Complex," $1.00, Lit. List No. 318.
  "Arms Industry Conversion," $1.00, Lit. List No. 1000.
  "Chemical-Biological Warfare," 50¢, Lit. List No. 611.

Television: A World View, Wilson P. Dizard, Syracuse University Press, 1966, $7.95. About the communication empire of the three major TV networks.

Television Today: The End of Communication and the Death of the Community, Ralph Stavins, Institute for Policy Studies, 1540 New Hampshire Ave., NW, Washington, D.C. 20036, 1969, $10.00.

United States Government Organization Manual for 1970–1971 (Catalog G.S.4.109:970), available from U.S. Government Printing Office, Division of Public Documents, Washington, D.C. 20402. Includes information on government agencies and their functions; creation and division of authority; descriptions of quasi-official agencies; and other research material.

Wealth and Power in America: An Analysis of Social Class and Income Distribution, Gabriel Kolko, Praeger, $2.25.

Who Rules America? G. William Domhoff, Prentice-Hall Spectrum, 1967, $2.45. America's power elite.

SELF-EDUCATION: ORGANIZATIONS

Agit Prop Information, 160 N. Gower St., London, NW 1, England. Source of anti-imperialist information and data on an international basis.

American Institute for Marxist Studies, 20 E. 30th St., New York, N.Y. 10016.

Armadillo Press, 802 W. 28th St., Austin, Tex. 78705.

Bay Area Institute, 9 Sutter St., Suite 300, San Francisco, Calif. 94104. Nonprofit educational center, concerned with war in Indochina, political economy of California, ecology. A newsletter available for a contribution.

Bay Area Radical Education Project, 491 Guerrero St., San Francisco, Calif. 94110. Variety of topics published; regular reviews of literature.

Center for the Study of Democratic Institutions, P.O. Box 4068, Santa Barbara, Calif. 93103.

Central Committee of Correspondence, P.O. Box 307, Pennington, N.J. 08534. Semiannual list of movement groups.

China Books and Periodicals, 2929 24th St., San Francisco, Calif. 94110. The source for printed material from China; also carries many of the standard Marxist material and miscellaneous items.

Citizens' Advocate Center, 1211 Connectivut Ave., NW, Washington, D.C. 20036. Concerned with federal programs that affect the poor; acts on citizen complaints; does research exposés (*Hunger, U.S.A.; Our Brothers' Keeper: The Indian in White America*).

Committee of Concerned Asian Scholars (CCAS), Phillips Brooks House, 3d fl., Cambridge, Mass. 02138. Publishes Factsheet series on Asia, *Bulletin of Concerned Asian Scholars;* speakers' bureau; briefing seminars.

Council on Economic Priorities, 1028 Connecticut Ave., NW, Washington, D.C. 20036. Does research into pollution, military industry, discrimination, economic imperialism, and other aspects of the industrial state; publishes *Economic Priorities Report*, $25 for subscription.

Institute for Policy Studies, 1520 New Hampshire Ave., NW, Washington, D.C. 20036.

International Publishers, 381 Park Ave. S., New York, N.Y. 10016. Publishers of the American Communist party; good list of the older Marxist works.

I.S. Book Service, 874 Broadway, Rm. 1005, New York, N.Y. 10003. Posters, pamphlets, buttons, etc.

National Action/Research on the Military-Industrial Complex (NARMIC), 160 N. 15th St., Philadelphia, Pa. 19102. Designs methodology for local military-industrial research; movement-oriented.

National Committee for the Repeal of the McCarran Act, 434 S. Dearborn St., Suite 318, Chicago, Ill. 60605.

National Committe to Abolish HUAC/HISC, P.O. Box 74757, Los Angeles, Calif. 90004.

New England Free Press (NEFP), 791 Tremont St., Boston, Mass. 02138. Excellent list of inexpensive radical literature. Printshop for movement groups.

North American Congress on Latin America (NACLA), P.O. Box 57, Cathedral Sta., New York, N.Y. 10025. Publishes *Research Methodology Guide; The University-Military Complex: Directory and Related Documents.*

Pathfinder Press (formerly Merit Publishers), 873 Broadway, New York, N.Y. 10003. Associated with Socialist Workers party and Young Socialist Alliance; publishes Malcolm X and Trotsky along with other Socialist writings.

Peace Action Research Institute, Phillips Brooks House, 3d fl., Cambridge, Mass. 02138. Issues reports on economics and the war, welfare, repression, medical care, etc.; has radio tapes on Cambodian invasion and medical care, with further radio taping and possible television programming in the works.

People's Press, 968 Valencia St., San Francisco, Calif. 94110. Small list now, but expanding.

Radical Clearinghouse, 293 Illini Union, Urbana, Ill. 61801. Handles original research and literature; tapes, speakers, and literature from national sources.

Radical Education Project (REP), P.O. Box 625, Ann Arbor, Mich. 42107.

Radical Research Center, Carleton College, Northfield, Minn. 55057. Publishes *Alternative Press Index.*

Mass Education and Communication

Publications and Publicity

Alternative Press Index, Radical Research Center, Carleton College, Northfield, Minn. 55057, quarterly, $30/yr., $10/yr. to movement. Index of articles and publications by movement people; listed by subject.

Complete Book of Silk Screen Printing and Production, J. I. Biegeleisen and J. A. Cohn, Dover, 1963, $2.75.

Creative News Editing, Alfred A. Crowell, W. C. Brown, 1969, $6.50.

Editing Small Newspapers; A Handbook for Young Journalists, Walter Rae, M. S. Mill Co., Inc., 1943.

Grassroots Press, John Sim, Iowa State University Press, 1969, $7.50.

How to Put Out Community Newspapers, Alan McSurely, Southern Conference Education Fund, 25¢.

How to Use the Telephone Effectively, Prentice-Hall Editorial Staff, Prentice-Hall, 1967, $2.25.

Introduction to Fundamentals of Layout for Newspaper and Magazine Advertising, for Page Design of Publications and for Brochures, Franz Hermann Wills (trans. Kenneth T. Dutfield), Sterling, 1965.

Lettering, Harry B. Wright, Pitman, 1962, $1.00.

Modern Newspaper Design, Edmund C. Arnold, Harper & Row, 1969, $10.95.

Newspaper Organization and Management, Frank W. Rucker and Herbert L. Williams, Iowa State University Press, 1969, $10.50.

Notes on Left Propaganda and How to Spread the Word, Leo Huberman, New England Free Press, 10¢.

Office Machines Course, P. L. Agnew and N. J. Cornelia, S. W. Publishing, 3d ed., 1963, $1.88.

Photography from A to Z, D. Daniels, Chilton, 1968, $4.95.

Poster Ideas and Bulletin Board Techniques, Kate Coplan and others, Oceana, 1962, $9.00.

Posters, Edward Boughner, Pitman, 2d ed., 1962, $1.00.

Student Journalist; A Handbook for Staff and Advisor, Edmund C. Arnold and Hillier Krieghbaum, New York University Press, 1963, $6.95.

Typography: Basic Principles, J. Lewis, Van Nostrand-Reinhold, 1964, $2.45.

Workbook for Lead Writing and News Editing, Arthur Wimer and Dale Brix, W. C. Brown, 1966, $5.50.

Speakers' Bureaus

Chairman and Speaker's Role Made Easy, David and Ruth Belson, Citadel, 1968, $1.95.

Complete Art of Public Speaking, J. M. Braude, Bantam, 1969, 95¢.

Preparing for Platform or Pulpit, John E. Baird, Abingdon, 1968, $4.50.

Public Speaking Made Easy, R. C. Forman, Revell, 1967, $3.95.

Film

Contemporary Cinema, Penelope Houston, Pelican-Penguin, 1963, $1.45.

Elements of Film, Lee Bobker, Harcourt, Brace, 1969, $4.50.

Film Book 2: Films of Peace and War, ed. R. Hughes, Grove Evergreen, 1962, $2.45.

Film-Makers on Film-Making, ed. H. M. Geduld, Indiana University Press, 1969, $1.95.

Guide to Film Making, E. Pincus, Signet NAL, $1.50.

How to Shoot a Movie Story, A. L. Gaskill and D. A. Englander, Morgan-Morgan, 1960, $1.95.

Independent Film Makers' Handbook, Leonard Lipton, Harper & Row, 1969, $3.95.

International Film Guide, ed. P. Cowie, A. S. Barnes, vols. 3–5, 1966–68, vol. 6, 1969, vol. 7, 1970, $2.95 each.

Introduction to American Underground Film, Sheldon Renan, E. P. Dutton, 1967, $2.25.

Introduction to the Art of the Movies, Lewis Jacobs, Farrar, Straus & Giroux, 1960, $1.95.

Guerrilla Theater

Anthology of German Expressionist Drama, ed. Walter Sokel, Doubleday Anchor, 1969, $1.75.

Brecht on Theatre, ed. J. Willett, Hill & Wang, 1964, $2.45.

Commedia dell'Arte, G. Oreglia, Hill & Wang, 1968, $1.95.

Complete Plays and Prose, Georg Büchner (trans. C. R. Mueller), Hill & Wang, 1963, $1.75.

Eyes on Mime: Language without Speech, Katherine Walker, Day, 1969, $4.95.

Guerrilla Theatre Essay (pamphlet), San Francisco Mime Troupe, Dept. R., 450 Alabama St., San Francisco, Calif. 94110.

Happenings: An Illustrated Anthology, ed. M. Kirby, E. P. Dutton, 1965, $1.95.

Improvisation: Discovery and Creativity in Drama, J. Hodgson and E. Richards, Barnes & Noble, 1966, $2.25.

Modern French Drama: The Avant Garde, Dada and Surrealism, M. Benedikt and G. E. Wellwarth, E. P. Dutton, 1964, $2.75.

New Underground Theatre, ed. R. J. Schroeder, Bantam, 1969, $1.25.

Organizing a Community Theatre, S. Seldon, Theatre Arts Books, $1.75.

"Politics of Performance," *The Drama Review*, and most issues of this quarterly since 1968. *TDR*, New York University, 32 Washington Pl., New York, N.Y. 10003; $5/yr.

Radical Theatre Festival, San Francisco Mime Troupe, Dept. R., 450 Alabama St., San Francisco, Calif. 94110, $1.50. Discussion of the nature and practice of radical theater.

Stagecraft for Non-Professionals, F. A. Buerki, University of Wisconsin Press, 1955, $1.50.

Toward a Poor Theatre, J. Grotowski, Clarion, 1969, $2.45.

Ubu Plays, Albert Jarry, Grove Evergreen, 1960, $1.95.

MASS EDUCATION AND COMMUNICATION: ORGANIZATIONS

American Documentary Films, 336 W. 84th St., New York, N.Y. 10024; or 376 Bay St., San Francisco, Calif. 94133. Produces and distributes films documenting liberation struggles.

Artworkers' Coalition, P.O. Box 553, Chelsea Sta., New York, N.Y. 10011.

Atlantis Distributing Co. (attn. J.F.), 1030 Annunciation St., New Orleans, La. 70130. Will help anyone start a distributing service for alternative publications in their city.

Citizen's Communication Center, 1816 Jefferson Pl., NW, Suite 103, Washington, D.C. 20036.

Community Radio, 1006 Constant Ave., Peekskill, N.Y. 10566. Will teach the electronics needed to set up a carrier current radio station (for small areas; can be operated without a license).

Film Industry for Peace, 817 Broadway, Rm. 1506, New York, N.Y. 10003.

G.I. Coffeehouse Project, 339 Lafayette St., New York, N.Y. 10012. Resource people for helping set up GI coffeehouses.

Inter-Tribal News Service, P.O. Box 26, Village Sta., New York, N.Y. 10027. For underground and hip radio stations.

Liberation News Service (LNS), 160 Claremont Ave., New York, N.Y. 10027. Serves a large number of underground newspapers; semiweekly information packets with a radical perspective. Also has a Radical Media Bulletin Board which carries news about underground papers.

Liberation News Service Print Shops, 160 Claremont Ave., New York, N.Y. 10027. Helps movement print shops to get set up.

Movement Speakers Bureau, 333 E. 5th St., New York, N.Y. 10003.

New People's Media Project, P.O. Box 4356, Sather Gate Sta., Berkeley, Calif. 94704.

Newsreel, 162 N. Clinton St., Rm. 204, Chicago, Ill. 60606; 322 Seventh Ave., New York, N.Y. 10001; 451 Cortland St., San Francisco, Calif. 94110; 595 Massachusetts Ave., Cambridge, Mass.

02139; P.O. Box 5432, E. Sta., Atlanta, Ga. 30307. Nationwide organization of activist filmers; arranges screenings; mails films to interested groups.

Puppet Theater, 1034 Bancroft Way, Berkeley, Calif. 94701. Teaches the use of puppets for political education; construction and use of puppets; and how to make up skits.

Radical Theater Repertory, 32 Washington Pl., New York, N.Y. 10003. Serves radical theater groups around the country in a variety of ways, e.g., arrangements of bookings.

Radio Free People, 133 Mercer St., New York, N.Y. 10012. Distributes tapes for broadcast and organizing; provides recording facilities for radical groups around New York City; advice on low-power community radio stations.

Student Communications Network, 418 S. Division St., Ann Arbor, Mich. 48104.

Underground Press Syndicate (UPS), P.O. Box 26, Village Sta., New York, N.Y. 10014. Serves underground newspapers by arranging collective subscriptions, advertising contracts, assistance and advice to new papers. Catalog of members $2.00.

Alternate Structures

Alternate Life-Styles

Alternative Society, 113 Queen St., St. Catharines, Ont., Canada, bimonthly.

Alternatives! Foundation, 1526 Gravenstein Hwy., Sebastopol, Calif. 97455, membership $10, publications include: *Directory of Personal Growth; Directory of Social Change; Free Goods; The Modern Utopian* (quarterly, $4/yr. to nonmembers); *Vision* (the best of the underground/alternative press).

Be Your Own Carpenter, Carlson Wade, Key Books, $2.95.

Be Your Own Plumber, Carlson Wade, Key Books, $2.95.

Commune, Salene Community, Bryn Villa Farmers, Llandwrda, Sir Gaerfyrddin, Wales, U.K.

"Communes: Why and How They Are Formed; Which Are Likely to Make It and Why," Rosabeth Moss Kanter, *Psychology Today*, July 1970.

The Green Revolution, Heathcote Community, Rt. 1, Box 129, Freeland, Md. 21503. Periodical published by and for communes; free sample.

How to Stay Alive in the Woods (*Living Off the Country*), B. Angier, Macmillan, 1966, 95¢.

How to Use Hand and Power Tools, G. Daniels, Popular Science, 1964, $1.95.

How to Work with Concrete and Masonry, D. Huff, Popular Science, 1968, $1.95.

The Mother Earth News, P.O. Box 38, Madison, Ohio 44057. Newsletter; comparable to *Whole Earth Catalog.*

1,001 Ways to Live Without Working, T. Kupferberg, Grove, 75¢.

One Thousand and One Valuable Things You Can Get Free, No. 2, M. Weisinger, Bantam, 75¢.

VSC Newsletter, Vocations for Social Change, Canyon, Calif. 94516, bimonthly, $6 contribution. News on alternate life-styles, jobs and training from around the country.

Whole Earth Catalog, Portola Institute, 558 Santa Cruz Ave., Menlo Park, Calif. 94125, 1970, $3.00. The universal reference book for people who want to do things for themselves.

Community Health, Education, and Counseling Centers

Action on the Streets: A Handbook for Inner City Youth Work, F. J. Carney, Association Press, 1969, $2.75.

The Addict and the Law, A. R. Linesmith, Random House Vintage, 1965, $1.95.

Birth Control, Abortion and VD, Linda Thurston, Boston University Student Union, 755 Commonwealth Ave., Boston, Mass. 02115, 1969, 25¢.

Birth Control Handbook, Student Society of McGill University, 3480 McTavish St., Montreal, Que., Canada, 1970, individual copies free, $35 for 1,000.

Dear Dr. Hip Pocrates, Eugene Schoenfeld, Grove Press, $1.25.

Drug Awareness, eds. R. E. Horman and A. M. Fox, Avon, 1970, $1.45.

Free School Movement in America: Contacts, Leads, Addresses, Jonathan Kozol, c/o Storefront Learning Center, 90 W. Brookline St., Boston, Mass. 02118, $2.00.

Handbook of Prescription Drugs, R. Burack, Pantheon, 1967, $1.95.

"Low Income and Barriers to Use of Health Services," *New England Journal of Medicine,* 1968.

The Marihuana Papers, ed. David Soloman, Signet NAL, 1968, $1.50.

Medical Cadre, International Liberation School, 1925 S. Grove St., Berkeley, Calif. 94704, 25¢.

"Medical Ghettos," Anselm Strauss, *Trans-Action,* May 1967.

Medicine in the Ghetto, ed. J. C. Norman, Appleton-Century, 1969.

9226 Kercheval: The Storefront That Did Not Burn, Nancy Milio, University of Michigan Press, 1970. Case study: the organization, funding, and administrative hassles of a community-run health and day-care center in a Detroit ghetto neighborhood.

San Francisco Switchboard, 1830 Fell St., San Francisco, Calif. 94117. Lists of switchboards around the country; switchboard operating manual.

Consumer and Tenant Organizing

"The Advent of the Right to Housing," Frank Michaelman, *Harvard Civil Rights—Civil Liberties Review,* vol. 5.

"The Berkeley Tenants Union," Jack Nichols, *Berkeley Tribe,* March 1970.

Buyer Beware! Fred Trump, Abingdon, 1965, $3.50. Consumer guide to hoaxes and hucksters.

Buyer's Guide to Nearly Everything, R. Burg, Macfadden, 60¢.

Consumer Information Price List, available from Superintendent of Documents, U.S. Government Printing Office, Washington, D.C. 20402, free.

Consumer Protection and Poverty Law Reports, Commerce Clearing House, 420 Lexington Ave., New York, N.Y. 10017, 1968. A legal outline.

Consumer Reports Buying Guide 1969, Consumers Union, Doubleday, 1969, $1.95.

Consumer's Voice, Connecticut Consumer Association, P.O. Box 404, Storrs, Conn. 06268, monthly.

Directory of Government Agencies Safeguarding Consumers and Environment, Serina Press, 1963.

Guide to Federal Consumer Services, President's Committee on Consumer Interests, Government Printing Office No. 0–282–461, 1967.

The Ill-Housed, Urban America, Inc., League of Women Voters, 1730 M St., NW, Washington, D.C. 20036, $1.25. Excerpts of recent writings and reports on national housing policy, and comparative listings of selected recommendations from Douglass Commission and Kaiser Committee reports.

The Innocent Consumer vs. the Exploiters, Project on Social Welfare, Law Supplement No. 2, New York University School of Law, 1968. Legal problems and solutions; bibliography references.

Legal Protection for the Consumer, Paul Crown, Oceana, 1963, $3.00. Places to turn for help with consumer problems.

A Manual of Basic Co-op Management, Co-op League, 1012 14th St., NW, Washington, D.C. 20005.

The Most for Their Money, President's Committee on Consumer Interest, Government Printing Office, 1965, 40¢. How to approach consumers; projects and techniques; resources and bibliography.

Poor Housing Almanac, John Marcy, Boston University Student Union, 755 Commonwealth Ave., Boston, Mass. 02115, 1970, 25¢/copy.

Tenant Organizing (packet), Emergency Tenants' Council, South End Tenants' Council and Boston Area Congress for Tenants' Rights, 45 Rutland St., Boston, Mass. 02118. (212) 536-6107, 1970.

Tenants' Rights: Legal Tools for Better Housing (pamphlet), Government Printing Office, 25¢.

Tenants Rising, Berkeley Tenants Union Organizing Collective, The People's Office, 1925 Grove St., Berkeley, Calif. 94704, periodical, 25¢/issue.

The Thumb on the Scale or the Supermarket Shell Game, A. Q. Mowbray, J. B. Lippincott, 1967, $4.95. Examples and problems with truth in packaging.

Ecology and Environment

America the Raped, Gene Marine, Avon Discus, 1969, $1.25.

The Book of Survival: Everyman's Guide to Staying Alive in the City, the Suburbs, and the Wild Lands Beyond, A. Greenbank, Harper & Row, 1967, $5.95; New American Library, 1970, 95¢.

The Chemical Feast, James S. Turner, Grossman, 1970.

Crisis in Our Cities, Lewis Herber, Prentice-Hall, 1965, $5.95.

Curious Naturalist, Niko Tinbergen, Doubleday Anchor, 1968, $1.75.

The Diligent Destroyers, George Laycock, Doubleday, 1969.

Do It Yourself Ecology, Environmental Action, 2000 P St., NW, Washington, D.C. 20036, 25¢.

The Earth Belongs to the People: Ecology and Power, New England Free Press, 791 Tremont St., Boston, Mass. 02118, 50¢.

Earth House Hold, Gary Snyder, New Directions, 1969, $1.95.

Earth Times, 625 3d St., San Francisco, Calif. 94107, monthly, $5/yr.

Ecology, E. P. Odum, Holt, Rinehart & Winston, 1963, $3.25. Basic ecology text.

Ecology: Pollution Means Profit, SDS, 173A Massachusetts Ave., 2d fl., Boston, Mass. 02115, 1970, 15¢.

Ecotactics: The Sierra Club Handbook for Environment Activists, Pocket Books, 1970, 95¢.

Environmental Action, Environmental Action, 2000 P St., NW, Washington, D.C. 20036, semimonthly, $4/yr.

The Environmental Handbook, ed. Garrett DeBell, Ballantine, 1970, $1.25. Organization information,

The Herring Gull's World, Niko Tinbergen, Doubleday Anchor, 1963, $1.75. Ecological psychology.

How to Kill a Golden State, William Bronson, Doubleday, 1968, $6.95.

The Living Earth, Peter Farb, Harper & Row, 1969, $1.60.

The Making of a Pollution-Industrial Complex (pamphlet), Martin Gellin, New England Free Press, 791 Tremont St., Boston, Mass. 02118, 10¢.

"People's Park, 270' x 450' of Confrontation," W. Griffith, *New York Times Magazine,* June 29, 1969.

The Politics of Ecology (pamphlet), Barry Weisberg, New England Free Press, 5¢.

Silent Spring, Rachel Carson, Fawcett Crest, 1969, 95¢.

The Subversive Science: Essays Toward an Ecology of Man, ed. P. Shepard and D. McKinley, Houghton Mifflin, 1969, $8.95. Anthology of writings on ecology.

Survival Book, P. Nesbitt et al., Funk & Wagnalls, 1969, $1.95.

Water Resources Background Package, League of Women Voters, 1730 M St., NW, Washington, D.C. 20036. Seven publications on water pollution and what can be done about it.

ALTERNATE STRUCTURES: ORGANIZATIONS

Alternatives! 1526 Gravenstein Hwy. N., Sebastopol, Calif. 95472, membership $10. A nonprofit educational program for people exploring alternative life-styles; a host of publications and directories comes with membership.

Berkeley Ecology Action, 3029 Benvenue Ave., Berkeley, Calif. 94705.

Boston Area Ecology Action, 925 Massachusetts Ave., Cambridge, Mass. 02139. Guerrilla theater, public-school education, use of power and land resources, supermarket resistance.

Carleton Collective Communities Clearinghouse, Carleton College, Northfield, Minn. 55057. Information and list of communities available.

The Committee for Environmental Information, 438 N. Skinker Blvd., St. Louis, Mo. 63130. Provides scientific information relevant to political and social issues; publishes *Environment.*

Committee for the People's Medical Clinic, P.O. Box 3205, Stanford, Calif. 94305.

Co-op League, 1012 14th St., NW, Washington, D.C. 20005.

Cooperative Action, 492-A 41st St., Oakland, Calif. 94609. Will assist in starting a cooperative.

Cooperative Services, Inc., 7404 Woodward St., Detroit, Mich. 48202. Cooperative service organization; helps start co-ops.

Ecology Action East, c/o Alternate University, 69 W. 14th St., New York, N.Y. 10011.

Ecology Center, 2179 Allston Way, Berkeley, Calif. 94704. Ecology service center and bookstore; extensive reprints, information packets, switchboard, speakers' bureau, and research facilities.

Environmental Action, 2000 P St., NW, Washington, D.C. 20036. Publishes *Environmental Action* and other literature.

Foundation for Co-operative Housing, 1012 14th St., NW, Washington, D.C. 20005.

International Institute for Independence, RFD 1, Box 1978, Voluntown, Conn. 06384. Research on alternatives to capitalism.

Metropolitan Urban Service Training, 235 E. 49th St., New York, N.Y. 10017. Publishes directory of institutes which train people for inner-city work.

National Association for Community Development, 1424 16th St., NW, Washington, D.C. 20036.

National Consumers' League, 1029 Vermont Ave., NW, Washington, D.C. 20005.

The National Free Clinic Counsel, P.O. Box 27278, San Francisco, Calif. 94127. Publishes *The Free Clinic Journal* (annual) with articles on setting up and running free clinics.

National Institute for Education in Law and Poverty, Northwestern School of Law, 25 W. Chicago Ave., Suite 800, Chicago, Ill. 60610. Publishes two-volume handbook on housing law.

National Tenants' Organization, 711 14th St., NW, Washington, D.C. 20004. A national organization of activists seeking decent low-income housing for the poor.

New Schools Exchange, 2840 Hidden Valley La., Santa Barbara, Calif. 93103. Publishes a biweekly newsletter on free school/experimental education; has comprehensive directory. Subscription rates $5/5 months, $10/yr.

Poverty Rights Action Group, 1419 H St., Washington, D.C. 20005.

Project Place, 37 Rutland St., Boston, Mass. 02118. Preparing a list of reliable counseling places.

United Cooperative Industries, Rt. 1, Box 3150, San Marcos, Calif. 92069. Information on cooperatives.

VISTA-USA, College Campus, Schenectady, N.Y. 12308. Free information by mail on community projects, e.g., sinking a well, simple bookkeeping.

Vocations for Social Change, Canyon, Calif. 94516. Information clearinghouse for paying jobs that help people.

Taking Action

Armies of the Night, Norman Mailer, Signet NAL, 1968, $1.25.

Civilian Resistance as a National Defense, Adam Roberts, War Resisters League, $1.65.

French Student Revolt: The Leaders Speak, Daniel Cohn-Bendit and Others, Hervé Bourges (trans. B. R. Brewster), Hill & Wang, 1968, $1.50.

Gandhi on Non-Violence: Selected Texts from Gandhi's Non-Violence in Peace and War, Mohandas Gandhi, ed. T. Merton, New Directions, $1.50.

Handbook on Non-Payment of War Taxes, War Resisters League, 50¢.

How Industrial Unionism Was Won: The Great Flint Strike Against GM, 1936–37, Walter Linder, New England Free Press, 25¢.

Manual for Direct Action, M. Oppenheimer and G. Lakey, Quadrangle, 1965, $1.75.

Miami and the Siege of Chicago: An Informal History of the Republican and Democratic Conventions of 1968, Norman Mailer, Signet NAL, 1968, 95¢.

Non-Violent Resistance, Mohandas Gandhi, ed. B. Kumarappa, Schocken, 1961, $1.95.

Sing Out: The Folk Song Magazine, 595 Broadway, New York, N.Y. 10012.

SNCC: The New Abolitionists, Howard Zinn, Beacon Press, 1964, $1.95.

Stride Toward Freedom: The Montgomery Story, Martin Luther King, Jr., Harper & Row, 95¢.

Up Against the Ivy Wall: A History of the Columbia Crisis, J. Avorn et al., Atheneum, 1968, $3.25.

The Vietnam Songbook, eds. Barbara Dane and Irwin Silber, The Guardian, 197 E. 4th St. New York, N.Y. 10009, 1969, $3.95.

War Tax Resistance: Individual Witness of Community Movement, Ted Webster, War Resisters League, 50¢.

ORGANIZATIONS

War Tax Resistance, 339 Lafayette St., New York, N.Y. 10012. (212) 228-0450.

Defense

Legal Protection

The Bust Book (*What to Do Until the Lawyer Comes*), K. Boudin et al., Grove Evergreen, 1969, $1.25.

"Censorship and Student Rights," *College Law Bulletin*, 1970.

Civil Liberties, American Civil Liberties Union, 156 Fifth Ave., New York, N.Y. 10010, bimonthly, subscription by membership of $3, $6, $10, $15, $25, $50, $100, and up, of which 50¢ is for one year of *Civil Liberties*.

"From Protest to Resistance," Tom Hayden, *Ramparts*, July 1970. An account of the Chicago Seven trial.

Rights, National Emergency Civil Liberties Committee, 25 E. 26th St., New York, N.Y. 10010, $5/yr.

The Tales of Hoffman, Bantam, 1970, $1.50. Excerpts from the trial of the Chicago Seven.

Trials of the Resistance, Random House Vintage, 1970, $2.95. Collection of essays from the *New York Review of Books* on political trials.

Up Against the Law: The Legal Rights of People Under 21, Jean Strause, Signet, 1970, 95¢. A comprehensive handbook covering matters such as contracts, employment, sex, as well as student rights, drugs, draft, etc.

When in Court, Defend Yourself, Larry Lockshin, New England Free Press.

Medical Aid

"First Aid in the Streets," Linda Winklestern, Richard Winklestern, and John Johansson, supplement in *Broadside*, Broadside Publications, 1970.

First Aid Textbook, American National Red Cross, Doubleday, 1957, 75¢.

Medical Cadre, International Liberation School, 1925 S. Grove St., Berkeley, Calif. 94704, 25¢.

Patching Up the Movement: First Aid Manual, Linda Borenstein, John Johansson, and Richard Winklestern, New England Free Press, 10¢.

Self-Defense

Anti-Riot Control Training, National Guard Organizing Committee, 1737 Garden St., San Luis Obispo, Calif. 93401. Use of riot control training as a weapon against communities and trainees themselves; cost of training; who profits.

Complete Book of Self Defense, B. Tegner, Bantam, $1.00.

Firearms and Self Defense: A Handbook for Radicals, Revolutionaries and Easy Riders, International Liberation, c/o People's Office, 1925 Grove St., Berkeley, Calif. 94704.

Innovator, P.O. Box 34718, Los Angeles, Calif. 90034, $4/yr. Offers practical information on two strategies of survival if national affairs get funny: (1) hiding, (2) running.

Judo-Karate for Law Officers: Defense and Control, Bruce Tegner, Thor, 1962, $1.95.

Plainclothesman, Frederick Egan, Arco, 1952, $4.00.

Police Guide to Search and Seizure, Interrogation, and Confession, Arlen Specter and Marvin Katz, Chilton, 1967, 95¢.

Police Selection, Richard Blum, Thomas, 1964, $7.50.

Police Training in the U.S., Allen Gammage, Thomas, 1963, $12.75.

A Radical Defense Handbook, International Liberation School, c/o People's Office, 1925 Grove St., Berkeley, Calif. 94704, 50¢. Moral: Don't get caught, but if you're busted, ORGANIZE! !

DEFENSE: ORGANIZATIONS

American Civil Liberties Union, 156 Fifth Ave., New York, N.Y. 10010 (affiliates in every state).

American Civil Liberties Union of Northern California, 503 Market St., San Francisco, Calif. 94105.

Citizens Committee for Constitutional Liberties, 22 E. 17th St., Rm. 1525, New York, N.Y. 10003. Fights police state laws.

Coalitions to Fight Political Repression, 19 Brookline St., Cambridge, Mass. 02138.

Committee United for Political Prisoners, 701 Fillmore St., San Francisco, Calif. 94117. Funds for legal defense.

Law Center for Constitutional Rights, 116 Market St., Newark, N.J. 07102.

Massachusetts Defense League, (212) 962–5441. Defends political prisoners and handles bail in New York, Connecticut, New England area.

Movement Lawyers: *Massachusetts:* (617) 742–0450, 742–4256, 566–7877; *New York City:* 1 Hudson St., (212) 227–1038; *Los Angeles:* 3175 W. 6th St., (213) DU5–6111; *San Francisco:* 341 Market St., (415) EX2–1320; *Denver:* 5650 Evans St., (303) 757–5641; *Detroit:* 19195 Griggs Ave., (313) 965–0050; *Philadelphia:* 1421 Fox Bldg., (215) LO3–8825; *Tucson:* 45 W. Pennington St., Suite 407, (602) 622–6755.

NAACP Legal Defense Fund, Inc., 10 Columbus Circle, New York, N.Y. 10019.

National Emergency Civil Liberties Committee, 25 E. 26th St., New York, N.Y. 10010.

National Lawyers Guild, P.O. Box 673, Berkeley, Calif. 94701; 5 Beekman St., New York, N.Y. 10038.

Prisoners Information and Support Service, P.O. Box 387, BU Sta., Boston, Mass. 02215. Helps local prisoners support programs; provides speakers and counselors; publishes a newsletter.

Southern Legal Assistance Movement, 1133 Fern St., New Orleans, La. 70118.

Using Establishment Structures

The Mass Media

How to Announce for Radio and TV, W. I. Kaufman, Hastings, $2.95.

Mass Communications: A Research Bibliography, D. A. Hansen and J. H. Parsons, Glendessary, 1968, $2.95.

Mass Media: Reporting, Writing, Editing, William Rivers, Harper, 1964, $7.95.

North American Radio-TV Station Guide, V. A. Jones, Howard W. Sams Co., 5th ed., 1968, $2.95.

"Peace and the News Media," Literature List No. 1100, available from SANE, 318 Massachusetts Ave., NE, Washington, D.C. 20002, 50¢.

Practical Publicity: A Handbook for Public and Private Workers, Herbert Jacobs, McGraw-Hill, 1964, $6.50.

Political Structures

Cooperative Lobbying: The Power of Pressure, D. R. Hall, University of Arizona Press, 1969, $8.50.

The Electoral Process, ed. M. K. Jennings and L. H. Zeigler, Prentice-Hall, 1966.

Government Publications and Their Use, Laurence F. Schmeckelier and Roy B. Eastin, Brookings Institution, 1775 Massachusetts Ave., NW, Washington, D.C. 20036, 1961, $6.00.

How Organizations Are Represented in Washington, L. A. Dexter, Bobbs-Merrill, 1969, $2.95.

How to Win an Election: The Art of Political Victory, S. C. Shadegg, Taplinger, 1964, $5.00.

Interest Groups and Lobbying, A. Holtzman, Macmillan, 1966, $1.65.

Kennedy Campaigning: The System and the Style as Practiced by Senator Edward Kennedy, Murray B. Levin, Beacon Press, 1966, $5.95.

Legislators and the Lobbyists, Congressional Quarterly Service, 1968, $2.95.

Lobbying and the Law: State Regulation of Lobbying, Edgar Lane, University of California Press, 1964, $6.50.

The Lobbyists: The Art and Business of Influencing Law-Makers, Karl Schriftgiesser, Little, Brown, 1951.

Politics, Parties and Pressure Groups, Valdimer Orlando Key, Crowell, 5th ed., 1968, $9.00.

Politics and Voters, Hugh A. Bone and A. Ranney, McGraw-Hill, 2d ed., 1967, $1.95.

The Power of the Unknown Citizen, Paul Kresh, Lippincott, 1969, $4.95.

Step by Step, Registration of Voters, Douglas Dowd and M. Nichols, Norton, 1965, $1.45.

A Student Guide to Campaign Politics, D. G. Herzberg and J. W. Peltason, McGraw-Hill, 1970, $1.95.

Student Politics, ed. Seymour M. Lipset, Basic Books, 1967, $8.95.

Theory of Voting, Robin Farquharson, Yale University Press, 1969, $5.00.

Vote Power: The Official Activist Campaign Handbook, by the Movement for a New Congress, Prentice-Hall, 1970, $1.50.

Voting and Election Laws, C. E. Smith, Oceana, 1960, $1.50.

Voting Is People's Power: Registration and Voting Manual for Inner City Drives, League of Women Voters, Education Fund, 1200 17th St., NW, Washington, D.C. 20036, 1967, 25¢.

Using Establishment Structures: Organizations

League of Women Voters. National office: 1730 M St., NW, Washington, D.C. 20036. Local offices in most cities.

National Committee for an Effective Congress (NCEC), 10 E. 39th St., New York, N.Y. 10016.

New York Media Project, P.O. Box 266, Village Sta., New York, N.Y. 10014. Organizes workers in the nation's media; publishes newspaper on the systematic distortion in "reliable" news media.

Strike News Service, Coffman Memorial Union, Rm. 213, University of Minnesota, Minneapolis, Minn. 55455. (612) 373–2414, 5, 6. Will publish this fall a book of dos and don'ts on relating to establishment media.

Constituencies

General Movement Organizations

American Friends Service Committee (AFSC). National office: 160 N. 15th St., Philadephia, Pa. 19102. Other offices in major cities. Pacifist service organization; does antidraft work among other things.

Center for the Study of Democratic Institutions (CSDI), P.O. Box 4546, Santa Barbara, Calif. 93103.

Communist Party, U.S.A., 23 W. 26th St., New York, N.Y. 10010.

International Socialists, 874 Broadway, Rm. 1005, New York, N.Y. 10003. Formerly Independent Socialist Clubs of America. Offices in major cities.

Movement for a Democratic Society, 210 W. 82d St., New York, N.Y. 10024.

National Caucus of Labor Committees, P.O. Box 49, Washington Bridge Sta., New York, N.Y. 10033.

New Democratic Party, 301 Metcalf St., Ottawa, Ont., Canada. Labor party; two million members.

New Democratic Youth, 11½ Spadina Rd., Toronto, Ont., Canada. Youth wing of labor party; more radical.

Peace and Freedom Party, 1727 W. Washington Blvd., Venice, Calif. 90291. Ran Eldridge Cleaver for president in 1968, but party politics varies from locality to locality.

People Against Racism, 5705 Woodward Ave., Detroit, Mich. 48202.

Progressive Labor Party, G.P.O. Box 808, Brooklyn, N.Y. 11202. Claim to be Marxist-Leninist-Maoist Communist party.

Socialist Labor Party, P.O. Box 200, Brooklyn, N.Y. 11202.

Socialist Party USA, 1182 Broadway, New York, N.Y. 10001.

Socialist Workers Party, 873 Broadway, New York, N.Y. 10003. Trotskyites.

Southern Conference Education Fund (SCEF), 3210 W. Broadway, Louisville, Ky. 40211. Organizes whites in the deep South, Appalachians, Kentucky; peace, draft, antipoverty, antiracist, antirepression.

Students for a Democratic Society (SDS), 173A Massachusetts Ave., Boston, Mass. 02115. SDS is now much splintered, while the national office is primarily Progressive Labor-oriented, the politics vary from campus to campus.

White Panther Party, 1520 Hill St., Ann Arbor, Mich. 48104. "Mother country" white radical organization styled after the Black Panther party.

Young Communist League, 24 Cecil St., Toronto, Ont., Canada.

Young People's Socialist League, 1182 Broadway, Rm. 402, New York, N.Y. 10001. Youth group of Socialist party.

Young Socialist Alliance (YSA), P.O. Box 471, Cooper Sta., New York, N.Y. 10003. Youth group of Socialist Workers party; Trotskyite.

Antiwar Organizations

Canadian Peace Congress, 232 Wynchwood St., Toronto, Ont., Canada. Liberal peace group.

Canadian Peace Research Institute, Clarkson, Ont., Canada.

Coalition on National Priorities and Military Policy, 100 Maryland Ave., NE, Washington, D.C. 20002.

The Fellowship of Reconciliation, P.O. Box 271, Nyack, N.Y. 10906. Pacifist group.

Individuals Against the Crime of Silence. Promotion of a "Declaration to Our Fellow Citizens of the United States, to the Peoples of the World, and to Future Generations," which is sent to the UN. P.O. Box 69960, Los Angeles, Calif. 90069.

Massachusetts Political Action for Peace (Mass Pax), 44 Brattle St., Cambridge, Mass. 02138.

New England Committee for Nonviolent Action, RFD 1, Box 1979, Voluntown, Conn. 06384.

New Mobilization Committee to End the War in Vietnam, 1029 Vermont Ave., NW, Washington, D.C. 20005.

Peace Action Coalition, 2102 Euclid Ave., Cleveland, Ohio 44115. A national antiwar coalition.

SANE, 381 Park Ave. S., New York, N.Y. 10016. Old ban-the-bomb people.

Student Mobilization Committee (SMC), 1029 Vermont Ave., NW, Washington, D.C. 20035.

Vietnam Mobilization Committee, 241 Victoria St., Toronto 2, Ont., Canada. Central coordinating place of much radical activity; also information-distribution center.

War Resisters League (WRL), 339 Lafayette St., New York, N.Y. 10012.

Washington D.C. Labor for Peace, 6005 Greentree Rd., Bethesda, Md. 20034.

Women Strike for Peace, 799 Broadway, New York, N.Y. 10003.

Women's International League for Peace and Freedom, 2006 Walnut St., Philadelphia, Pa. 19103.

Gay Liberation Organizations

Chicago Gay Liberation, 667 W. Barry Ave., Chicago, Ill. 60657.

Committee for Homosexual Freedom, 330 Ellis St., San Francisco, Calif. 94102.

Daughters of Bilitis, 141 Prince St., New York, N.Y. 10012.

Gay Activist Alliance, 99 Wooster St., New York, N.Y. 10012.

Gay Liberation Front, 2398 Bancroft Way, Berkeley, Calif. 94704; also 79 Devine St., San Jose, Calif. 95110; also P.O. Box 642, Old Chelsea Sta., New York, N.Y. 10001.

Homosexual Information Center, 3473½ Cahuenga Blvd., Hollywood, Calif. 90028.

Institute for Homosexual Liberation, 15 Beaver St., San Francisco, Calif. 94114.

Mattachine Society, 243 West End Ave., New York, N.Y. 10023.

New York City Gay Community Center, 130 W. 3rd St., New York, N.Y. 10012.

Student Homophile League, 33 Bowdoin St., Boston, Mass. 02114.

Students for Gay Power, 2389 Bancroft Way, Berkeley, Calif. 94704.

High Schools (see also Professionals: Public-School Teachers)

Coming of Age in America, Edgar Z. Friedenburg, Random House Vintage, 1965, $1.95. Education and adolescence.

Compulsory Miseducation, Paul Goodman, Random House Vintage, 1962, $1.95.

Education and Revolution, Eldridge Cleaver, New England Free Press, 25¢.

Growing Up Absurd, Paul Goodman, Random House Vintage, 1956, $1.45.

Hassling: Two Years in a Suburban High School, Sylvia Berry Williams, Little, Brown, 1970, $2.95.

The High School Bill of Rights and Its Use (leaflet), Student Mobilization Committee, $2 for 100.

The High School Revolutionaries, eds. Marc Liberle and Tom Seligson, 1970, Vintage, $1.95. Writings by students.

Highschool Journalism Today, Gene Gilmore, Interstate, 1967, $2.50.

How to Start a High School Underground, available from 530 N. Brainards St., Naperville, Ill. 60540.

Our Time Is Now: Notes from the High School Underground, ed. John Birmingham, Bantam, 1970, 95¢.

The Soft Revolution: A Student Handbook for Turning Schools Around, Neil Postman and Charles Weingartner, Delta, 1971, $1.95.

ORGANIZATIONS

Cooperative High School Independent Press Service (CHIPS), 530 N. Brainards St., Naperville, Ill. 60540. Has directory of high-school newspapers.

High School Student Union, 208 W. 85th St., New York, N.Y. 10024.

High School Students Against the War, P.O. Box 484, Bronx, N.Y. 10471.

National Federation of High School Undergrounds, 530 N. Brainards St., Naperville, Ill. 60540.

Universities (see also Professionals: Public-School Teachers)

"Black Panthers and White Radicals: Notes from New Haven," P. Starr, *Commonweal*, June 12, 1970.

Campus Scene, Calvin B. T. Lee, McKay, 1970, $7.95.

The Closed Corporation, James Ridgeway, Ballantine, 1968, 95¢.

Directory of Free Schools, extensive listings of free universities, experimental colleges. Available from Alternatives! Foundation, 1526 Gravenstein Hwy., Sebastopol, Calif. 97455.

Education and the Barricades, ed. Charles Frankel, Norton, 1969, $1.50.

"The European Student Movements," John Ehrenreich and Barbara Ehrenreich, *Monthly Review*, September 1968, on Germany, Italy, France, and England.

"Festival in Berlin." J. Maguire, *Saturday Review*, November 11, 1967.

Free Universities Catalog, Union for Research and Experimentation in Higher Education, Antioch College, Yellow Springs, Ohio 45387.

"How to Wreck a Campus: Violence at San Francisco State College," D. Swanston, *Nation*, January 8, 1968, an indictment of Hayakawa.

Manual for Trustees of Colleges and Universities, Iowa State University Press, 1951, $1.00.

"Mexico: Why the Students Rioted," James N. Goodell, *Current History*, January 1969.

The Middle of the Country, ed. Bill Warren, Avon, 1970, $1.25. Kent State people tell it like it was.

"The New French Revolution: May 1968," D. A. Leith, *Queens Quarterly*, Spring 1969.

New Prospects for the Small Liberal Arts College, Sidney Letter, Teachers College Press, 1968, $3.75.

The New Student Left, M. Cohen and D. Hale, Beacon Press, Boston, 1966, $1.95.

"On Strike: Shut It Down. The Crisis at San Francisco State College," T. MacEvoy and A. Miller, *Trans-Action*, March 1969.

"One, Two, Three . . . Many S.D.S.'s" (a symposium), *Ramparts*, September 1969.

"One Week in Paris," *Ramparts*, June 29, 1968.

"Out of the Blue" (French student strike), *Nation*, June 3, 1968.

Overlive: Power, Poverty and the University, William M. Birenbaum, Dell, 1969, $1.95.

Plate-Glass Universities, Michael Beloff, Fairleigh Dickinson University Press, $6.00.

Political Science Quarterly, June 1969. Special issue on student rebellion worldwide.

"Political Thrust Motivating Campus Turmoil," S. M. Lipset, *Saturday Review*, March 1, 1969.

Protest! Student Activism in America, J. Foster and D. Long, Morrow, 1970. $2.95.

"Protest and Reaction: Students and Society in Conflict," A. L. Gleason, *North American Review*, Summer 1969.

Publications of the United States National Student Association, USNSA, 2115 S St., NW, Washington, D.C. 20008, free.

"The Revolution on the Campus," *The American Scholar*, Autumn 1969.

Search for Relevance: The Campus in Crisis, J. Axelrod et al., Jossey-Bass, 1969, $7.75.

The Silent Revolution, Dynamic Leadership in the Student Council, by Kent M. Keith, Harvard Student Agencies, 2 Trowbridge St., Cambridge, Mass. 02138, $1.50.

State of the University: Authority and Change, Carlos E. Kruytbosch and Sheldon L. Messinger, Sage Publications, 1969, $3.95.

The Student as Nigger, Jerry Farber, Contact Press, 1969, $2.95.

"Student Power: A Symposium," Charles Frankel et al., *The Humanist,* May/June 1969.

"Student Power and the Business of Intellectuals," interview with D. Cohn-Bendit, *Ramparts,* June 29, 1968.

"Student Power in Berkeley," Nathan Glazer, *University Quarterly,* September 1968.

"The Student Protest Movement in West Berlin," Richard L. Merritt, *Comparative Politics,* July 1969.

"Student Radicalism in Japan: A Cultural Revolution?" Tuomasa Fuss, *Comparative Education Research,* October 1969.

"Student Revolt Italian Style," M. L. Stein and J. V. Ricapito, *Saturday Review,* February 21, 1970.

"Student Unrest in the U.A.R.," Amnon Kapeliuk, *New Outlook,* January 1969.

"Students Against the World: Student Movement on Three Continents: Symposium," *Saturday Review,* August 17, 1968.

The Uncommitted: Alienated Youth in American Society, Kenneth Keniston, Delta Dell, 1967, $2.45.

"Unexpected Revolution," J. J. Kaplow, *Nation,* January 13, 1969. The French student strike.

The University (packet of seven articles), New England Free Press, 791 Tremont St., Boston, Mass. 02118. (617) 536–9219, $1.20.

The University-Military Complex, A Directory and Related Documents, North American Congress on Latin America (NACLA), $1.00.

Up Against the Ivy Wall: A Handbook of Campus Complicity, Student Mobilization Committee, 25¢.

"When if Ever Do You Call in the Cops?" a symposium, *New York Times Magazine,* May 4, 1969.

"Who Killed the Student Revolution?" R. Nisbet, *Encounter,* February 1970.

"Who Rules the University?" (special issue), *Saturday Review,* January 1970.

The Young Radicals: Notes on Committed Youth, Kenneth Keniston, Harcourt, Brace & World Harvest, 1968, $2.45.

"Youth Liberates America" (a symposium with editorial comment), *America,* April 25, 1970.

ORGANIZATIONS

American Commuter Campus Association, P.O. Box 51, University Center, Kansas City, Mo. 64110. A research organization trying to collect information relevant to people interested in forming projects on commuter campuses.

Canadian University Press, 45 Rideau St., Suite 106, Ottawa 2, Ont., Canada.

College Press Service, 1779 Church St., NW, Washington, D.C. 20036. Issues biweekly press reports of interest to students.

National Student Association, 2115 S St., NW, Washington, D.C. 20008.

New Schools Exchange, 2840 Hidden Valley La., Santa Barbara, Calif. 93103. Free school development and experimental education.

New University Conference, 622 W. Diversey Pkwy., Chicago, Ill. 60614. A Socialist organization primarily of professors and graduate students.

Radical Student Union, 7105 Hayvenhurst Ave., Van Nuys, Calif. 91406. For the Los Angeles area.

Southern Student Organizing Committee, P.O. Box 6043, Nashville, Tenn. 37212.

Union for Research and Experimentation in Higher Education, Antioch College, Yellow Springs, Ohio 45387.

Ethnic and Racial Groups

Blacks

Afro Six, H. Lopez, Dell, 75¢.

Amistad, ed. J. A. Williams, Vintage, $1.95.

Amsterdam News, 2340 Eighth Ave., New York, N.Y. 10033, daily.

The Autobiography of Malcolm X, Malcolm X, ed. A. Haley, Grove Press, 1964, $1.25.

Bay State Banner, 25 Ruggles St., Roxbury, Mass. 02119.

Black Fire: An Anthology of Afro-American Writings, eds. Larry Neal and LeRoi Jones, Apollo, 1969, $3.95.

Black Music, LeRoi Jones, Apollo, 1968, $1.95.

Black Nationalism, E. U. Essien-Udom, Dell, 1962, 75¢.

The Black Panther, Black Panther Party, 3106 Shattuck Ave., Berkeley, Calif. 94705, weekly.

Black Power and Urban Unrest, Nathan Wright, Jr., Hawthorn, 1967, $1.95.

Black Power Revolt, ed. Floyd Barbour, Porter Sargent, 1968, $2.95, Crowell Collier and Macmillan, 1969, $1.95; $5.95 hardback.

Black Rage, W. H. Grier and P. M. Cobbs, Bantam, 1968, 95¢.

Black Reconstruction, W. E. B. Du Bois, Atheneum, 1969, $4.95.

The Black Seventies, ed. Floyd Barbour, Porter Sargent, 1970.

Black Skin—White Masks: The Experience of Black Man in a White World, Frantz Fanon, Grove Press, 1968, $1.95.

The Black Solution, Journal of Black Students vs. Research, P.O. Box 908, Sausalito, Calif. 94965.

Black Voices from Prison, Etheridge Knight, Pathfinder Press, 1970, $2.45; $5.95 hardback.

Conversation with Eldridge Cleaver—Algiers, Lee Lockwood, Dell Delta, 1970, $1.95.

The Crisis of the Negro Intellectual, Harold Cruse, Apollo, 1967, $3.50.

The Dark Ghetto: Dilemmas of Social Power, Kenneth B. Clark, Harper & Row Torchbook, 1965, $1.75.

Dialectics of Black Power, Robert I. Allan, Guardian, 35¢.

Frederick Douglass: Selections, ed. P. S. Foner, International Publishers, 75¢.

From Slavery to Freedom: A History of Negro Americans, John Hope Franklin, Random House Vintage, $3.45.

Home: Social Essays, LeRoi Jones, Apollo, 1967, $1.95.

Impossible Revolution: Black Power and the American Dream, L. M. Killian, Random House, $2.45.

Invisible Man, Ralph Ellison, Signet NAL, 1963, $1.25.

The Los Angeles Sentinel, 1117 E. 43d St., Los Angeles, Calif. 90011.

The Man That Cried I Am, J. A. Williams, Signet NAL, 95¢.

Native Son, Richard Wright, Harper & Row, 1969, 95¢.

Negro in America: A Bibliography, Elizabeth W. Miller, Harvard University Press, 1966, $2.95.

Negro in the United States: A Research Guide, E. K. Welsch, Indiana University Press, 1965, $1.85.

Negro in the U.S.: A List of Significant Books, 9th rev. ed., New York Public Library, $1.00.

Negro Press International, 5708 S. State St. Chicago, Ill. 60637.

Negroes with Guns, Robert Williams, Marzani and Munsell, 1962.

Pinktoes, Chester Himes, Dell, 75¢.

Post-Prison Speeches and Writings of Eldridge Cleaver, ed. Robert Sheer, Random House Vintage, 1969, $1.95.

Prelude to Riot: A View of America from the Bottom, Paul Jacobs, Random House Vintage, 1968, $1.95.

Racism (packet of nineteen items), New England Free Press, $2.45.

Revolutionary Notes, Julius Lester, Baron, $5.95.

Rivers of Blood, Years of Darkness, Robert Conot, Bantam, 1967, 95¢.

Seize the Time, Bobby Seale, Random House, 1970, $6.95.

Soledad Brother, the Prison Letters of George Jackson, Bantam, 1970, $1.50.

Soul on Ice, Eldridge Cleaver, Dell Delta Books, 1968, $1.95.

Souls of Black Folk, W. E. B. Du Bois, Signet NAL, 1969, $1.25.

Up from Slavery, Booker T. Washington, Bantam, 60¢.

Washington Afro-American, 800 11th St., NW, Washington, D.C. 20001.

Where Do We Go from Here: Chaos or Community, Dr. Martin Luther King, Jr., Bantam, 1967, 95¢.

Why We Can't Wait, Dr. Martin Luther King, Jr., Signet NAL, 75¢.

ORGANIZATIONS

Ball and Chain, P.O. Box 9001, Berkeley, Calif. 94719. An organization of black journalists.

Black Panther Community News Service, 35 Sylvan Ave., New Haven, Conn. 06519.

Black Panther Party, 3106 Shattuck Ave., Berkeley, Calif. 94705. National headquarters.

Black Political Party, 300 Ninth Ave., New York, N.Y. 10034.

Committee to Defend the Panthers (Bobby Seale Legal Defense Fund), P.O. Box 628, New York, N.Y. 10025.

Congress of Racial Equality (CORE), 200 W. 135th St., New York, N.Y. 10030. One of the oldest militant civil rights organizations.

Muhammad's Nation of Islam (Black Muslims), 436 E. 79th St., Chicago, Ill. 60609.

National Association for the Advancement of Colored People (NAACP), 20 W. 40th St., New York, N.Y. 10018.

National Urban League, 55 E. 52d St., New York, N.Y. 10022.

Southern Christian Leadership Conference (SCLC), 322 Auburn Ave., NE, Atlanta, Ga. 30303.

Student National Coordinating Committee (SNCC), 300 Ninth Ave., New York, N.Y. 10034.

Mexican Americans

Forgotten People: A Study of New Mexicans, George I. Sanchez, University of New Mexico Press, 1940, and C. Horn, 1967, $5.95.

Decision at Delano (about the grape strike), available from La Causa, 1560 37th Ave., Oakland, Calif. 94601. A film.

Huelga (about the grape strike), available from McGraw-Hill Text-Film Division, 330 W. 42d St., New York, N.Y. 10017. Fifty-minute color film. Rental fee: $30.00.

I Am Joaquin (the best film to date on Mexican Americans), 22 minutes, with Luis Valdez of the Teatro Campesino. Available from Canyon Cinema Coop, Industrial Center Bldg., Rm. 220, Sausalito, Calif. 94967; or Canyon Cinema Coop, P.O. Box 2302, Fresno, Calif. 93720. Rental fee: $40.00.

I Am Joaquin: An Epic Poem, Rodolfo "Corky" Gonzales, Crusade for Justice, 1567 Downing St., Denver, Colo. 80218.

The Invisible Minority, available from the Crusade for Justice, 1567 Downing St., Denver, Colo. 80218.

La Raza: The Mexican Americans, Stan Steiner, Harper & Row, 1970, $8.50.

Labyrinth of Solitude, Octavio Paz, Grove Press, 1962, $1.95.

Mexican-American History: A Critical Selected Bibliography, Mexican-American Historical Society, Santa Barbara, Calif., 1970.

Mexican-American Youth: Forgotten Youth at the Crossroads, Celia Heller, Random House, 1966, $1.95.

Profiles of Man and Culture in Mexico, Samuel Ramos, University of Texas Press, 1962, $5.50. Mexican history.

Sal Si Puedes—Escape if You Can: Cesar Chavez and the New American Revolution, Peter Matthiessen, Random House, 1969, $6.95 hardback.

ORGANIZATIONS

Crusade for Justice, 1567 Downing St., Denver, Colo. 80218.

La Raza Unida, 100 E. 27th St., Austin, Tex. 78705. President: Ben Canales.

Mexican-American Political Association (MAPA), 2415 Whittier Blvd., Los Angeles, Calif. 90023. President Abe Papia. Also chapters on various university campuses.

Mexican-American Youth Association (MAYA), 959 S.W. 38th St., San Antonio, Tex. 78235. President: Mario Compian.

Movimiento Estudiantil Chicano de Aztlan (MECHA), Campbell Hall, 405 Hilgard Ave., Los Angeles, Calif. 90024. Chapters on various university campuses.

Puerto Ricans

"The Adjustment of Puerto Ricans to New York City," Joseph P. Fitzpatrick, in *Minorities in a Changing World,* ed. Milton and Barron, Knopf, 1967, $5.50; also in *Journal of Intergroup Relations* (Winter 1959–60).

Background and General Information on Puerto Rico and the Puerto Rican Migrant, Commonwealth of Puerto Rico, Dept. of Labor, Migrant Division (available at Migrant Division offices or public libraries).

Claridad (Movimiento para Independencia), Casa Puerto Rico, 106 E. 14th St., New York, N.Y. 10003.

Down These Mean Streets, Piri Thomas, Knopf, 1967, NAL Signet, 95¢.

El Diario, La Prensa, 181 Hudson St., New York, N.Y. 10013, daily. The major Spanish newspaper in the city.

Emotional Adjustment of Problems of the Puerto Rican Migrant, Petroamerica Pagen de Colon, Commonwealth of Puerto Rico, Dept. of Labor, Migrant Division.

La Vida: A Puerto Rican Family in the Culture of Poverty, Oscar Lewis, Random House Vintage, 1966, $2.95.

Latino, P.O. Box 621, Peter Stuyvesant Sta., New York, N.Y. 10009, $1/yr. A new monthly in English and Spanish.

Palante, 1678 Madison Ave., New York, N.Y. 10029. The newspaper of the Young Lords. Also 834 Armitage St., Chicago, Ill. 60614.

Party Politics in Puerto Rico, Robert W. Anderson, Stanford University Press, 1965, $6.75.

"Portrait of Gabriel: Puerto Rican Family in San Juan and New York," *Harper's,* January 1966.

Puerto Rico: A Colony of the United States, Puerto Rican Youth Movement, New England Free Press, 1964, rev. ed. 1969.

"Report from Spanish Harlem: Troitus," Richard Hamer, *New York Times Magazine,* January 5, 1964.

ORGANIZATIONS

Aspira of America, Inc., 254 Fifth Ave., New York, N.Y. 10001. (212) 683–6054. Scholarships and student social services.

Bronx Multiservice Community Corporation, 661 Cauldwell Ave., Bronx, N.Y. 10455. Organization of Puerto Ricans and blacks.

Committee of Solidarity with Puerto Rican Liberation, 120 Howard St., Apt. 4, Cambridge, Mass. 02138. (617) 547–8877.

El Grito del Barrio, 1799 Lexington Ave., New York, N.Y. 10029. (212) 876–7475.

En la Brecha, 12 Leston St., Mattapan, Mass. 02126. (617) 296–1375.

Huntspoint Community Corporation, 1464 Southern Blvd., Bronx, N.Y. 10460.

Las Americas, 152 E. 23d St., New York, N.Y. 10010. Publishing company; does books on Puerto Rican history.

Metro North Association, Inc., 309 E. 104th St., New York, N.Y. 10029. (212) 722–0061. Puerto Rican, black, Italian, Jewish community coordinating group.

Movimiento Para Independencia, c/o Casa Puerto Rico, 106 E. 14th St., New York, N.Y. 10003. (212) 743–9764. Independence movement and Culebra and Vieques.

P.O.D.E.R., Norton Hole Box 13, State University of New York, Buffalo, N.Y. 14214.

Puerto Rican Community Development Corporation, 310 W. 50th St., New York, N.Y. 10019. (212) 234–4221.

Puerto Rican Family Institute, 116 W. 14th St., New York, N.Y. 10003. (212) 924–6320.

Puerto Rican Forum, Inc., 296 Fifth Ave., New York, N.Y. 10001. (212) 244–1110. Deals with business and industry.

Union Estudiantil Boricua, 440 E. 138th St., Bronx, N.Y. 10454. Working for open admissions of Puerto Ricans to schools and for Puerto Rican studies programs.

Young Lords, 834 Armitage St., Chicago, Ill. 60614. (312) 549–8505. New York: 1678 Madison Ave., New York, N.Y. 10029. (212) 427–7745.

American Indians

ABC (American Before Columbus), National Indian Youth Council, P.O. Box 118, Schurz, Nev. 89427.

Akwesasne Notes, Antioch-Putney Graduate School of Education, Putney, Vt. 05346. Newspaper.

"Angry American Indians: Starting Down the Protest Trail," *Time*, February 9, 1970.

Black Elk Speaks: Being the Life Story of a Holy Man of the Ogalala Sioux, J. G. Neihardt, University of Nebraska Press Bison, $1.50.

Custer Died for Your Sins: An Indian Manifesto, Vine Deloria, Jr., Avon, 1970, $1.25.

"Day on Alcatraz with the Indians," K. Boyle, *New Republic*, January 17, 1970.

Fort Apache Scout, P.O. Box 898, Whiteriver, Ariz. 85941. Newspaper.

House Made of Dawn, N. Scott Momaday, NAL Signet, 1968, 95¢.

The Indian: America's Unfinished Business, eds. William A. Brophy and Sophie D. Aberle, Report of the Commission on the Rights and Liberties and Responsibilities of American Indians, University of Oklahoma Press, 1966, $5.95.

The Indian and the White Man, ed. Wilcomb E. Washburn, Documents in American Civilization Series, Doubleday Anchor, 1964, $1.95.

The Indian Heritage of America, Alvin M. Josephy, Jr., Bantam, 1969, $1.65. Archaeology, ethnology, and history.

Indian Voices, University of Chicago, 1126 E. 59th Pl., Chicago, Ill. 60637. Periodical.

Indians of the United States, Clark Wissler, Doubleday Anchor, 1966, $1.95.

Little Big Man, Thomas Berger, Fawcett Crest, 1964, 95¢.

The Navajo Times, P.O. Box 428, Window Rock, Ariz. 86515.

The New Indians, Stan Steiner, Dell Delta, $2.45.

Our Brother's Keeper: The Indian in White America, ed. Edgar S. Cahn, Citizens' Advocate Center, 1211 Connecticut Ave., NW, Washington, D.C. 20036.

"Our Most Silent Minority," P. Nabokov, *Nation,* January 26, 1970.

"Red Man's Burden," P. Collier, *Ramparts,* February 1970.

The Sentinel, National Congress of American Indians, 1346 Connecticut Ave., NW, Washington, D.C. 20036.

Stay Away Joe, Daniel Cushman, from Stay Away, Joe Publishers, P.O. Box 2054, Great Falls, Mont. 59401, 4th ed., 1968, $4.90.

Tundra Times, P.O. Box 1287, Fairbanks, Alas. 99701.

"War Between the Redskins and the Feds," Vine Deloria, Jr., *New York Times Magazine,* December 7, 1969.

We Talk, You Listen: New Tribes, New Turf, Vine Deloria, Jr., Macmillan, 1970, $5.95.

ORGANIZATIONS

Albuquerque Indian School Canteen; 907 Indian School Rd., NW, Albuquerque, N.M. 87107. An urban Indian center.

Boston Indian Community Center, 249 E. Berkeley St., Boston, Mass. 12116.

Gallup Indian Community Center, 200 W. Maxwell St., Gallup, N.M. 87301.

Indian Rights Association, 1505 Race St., Philadelphia, Pa. 19102. White Indian-support group.

Indian-Eskimo Association of Canada, 277 Victoria St., Toronto 2, Ont., Canada. Native alliance for red power.

John F. Kennedy Center, Devils Lake, N.D. 58301. The Sioux tribal headquarters.

National Congress of American Indians, 1346 Connecticut Ave., NW, Washington, D.C. 20036. The only national private membership association of Indians, made up of Indians from ninety tribes representing 300,000 Indians.

National Indian Youth Council, P.O. Box 118, Schurz, Nev. 89427. An action group of young Indian students.

Native Alliance for Red Power, P.O. Box 6152, Vancouver 8, B.C., Canada.

North American Indian Correspondence Council, 306 W. State St., Centerville, Iowa 52544.

Organization of Native American Students, c/o Michael Benson, Dartmouth College, Hanover, N.H. 03755.

Phoenix Urban Indian Project, 376 N. First Ave., Phoenix, Ariz. 85003.

Tucson Indian Center, 120 W. 29th St., Tucson, Ariz. 85713.

United American Indians, Inc., P.O. Box 26149, San Francisco, Calif. 94126.

United Indians of All Tribes, Inc., Indian Studies Program, University of California, Berkeley, Calif. 94720. Group which occupied Alcatraz.

United Sioux Tribes, Rosebud, S.D. 57570. Formed to correct the present image of the Indian and to promote Indian solidarity.

Asian Americans

Asian American Research Bibliography, available from Asian American Concern, University of California, Davis, Calif. 95616. A comprehensive list of all available resources.

Asians in America (pamphlet), from Asian American Concern, University of California, Davis, Calif. 95616. Good brief summaries of different Asian groups in this country.

Between Two Worlds: Policy, Press, and Public Opinion in Asian-American Relations, John Hohenberg, Praeger, 1967, $8.95.

Chinatown Study Report, Chinatown Study Group, c/o School of Architecture, Columbia University, New York, N.Y. 10027.

Health, Welfare and Social Organizations in Chinatown, Community Services Society of New York, 105 E. 22d St., New York, N.Y. 10010.

The Politics of Prejudice: The Anti-Japanese Movement in California and the Struggle for Japanese Exclusion, University of California Press, 1962; reprinted Atheneum, 1968, $1.95.

The Spoilage: Japanese-American Evacuation and Resettlement, Richard S. Nishimoto and Dorothy S. Thomas, University of California Press, 1946 (reprinted 1968), $1.95.

ORGANIZATIONS

Asian American Concern (AAC), University of California, Davis, Calif. 95616.

Asian American Political Alliance (AAPA). Chapters: University of California, Berkeley, Calif. 94720; Columbia University, New York, N.Y. 10027; c/o Jean Ishibashi, 125 S. Franklin St., Madison, Wis. 53703.

Asian Americans for Action, 545 W. 126th St., Apt. B, New York, N.Y. 10027.

Asian Political Alliance, c/o Louis Gsen, 610 Blaine St., Detroit, Mich. 48202.

Asian Radical Coalition, c/o Terry DoFoo and Steve Louie, 30 Bigelow St., Cambridge, Mass. 02139.

Asian Society, 112 E. 64th St., New York, N.Y. 10021.

Center for Social Action, University of Southern California, Los Angeles, Calif. 90007.

Common Bond, c/o Stephanie Wong, 16 Oxford St., Boston, Mass. 02111. Chinese, black, Puerto Rican group.

GIDRA, 3222 Jefferson Blvd., Los Angeles, Calif. 90016. Publishes monthly newspaper and serves as clearinghouse for Asian-American organizations.

Japanese American Citizen's League (Yellow Brotherhood Chapter), c/o Warren Furatani, 125 Weller St., Rm. 310, Los Angeles, Calif. 90012.

Japanese American Community Service, 125 Weller St., Los Angeles, Calif. 90012.

Japanese American Student Council, c/o Sasha Hohri, 4427 N. Clark St., Chicago, Ill. 60640.

Third World

African Encounter: A Selected Bibliography of Books, Films and Other Materials, American Library Association, $1.50.

After Pinkville, Noam Chomsky, reprinted from *New York Review of Books* (January 1, 1970) by Student Mobilization Committee.

Against the Crime of Silence: Proceedings of the Russell International War Crimes Tribunal, O'Hare, 1968, $5.75 flexicloth, $8.50 hardback. Evidence and reports on American war crimes in Vietnam.

Agrarian Problems and Peasant Movements in Latin America, ed. Rodolfo Stavenhagen, Doubleday Anchor, 1970, $2.45.

American Atrocities in Vietnam, Eric Norden, Student Mobilization Committee, 25¢.

American Economic Imperialism: A Survey of the Literature, William Caspary, Radical Education Project, 1968, 20¢.

Armed Struggle in Africa, Gerard Challiand, Monthly Review Press, 1969, $5.50.

Autobiography of Kim Il Sung, Kim Il Sung. Available from New England Free Press, 32 W. 22d St., New York, N.Y. 10010.

China (packet of sixteen items), New England Free Press, 791 Tremont St., Boston, Mass. 02118. (617) 536–9219, $1.90.

The China Reader, Franz Schurman and Orville Schell, Random House Vintage, 1967, vol. 1, *Imperial China,* $1.95; vol. 2, *Republican China,* $1.95; vol. 3, *Communist China,* $2.45. A good general history.

Chinese Foreign Policy in an Age of Transition, Ishwer C. Ojha, Beacon Press, 1969, $5.95. Excellent introduction.

The Colonizer and the Colonized, Albert Memmi, Beacon Press, 1967, $1.95.

David and Goliath (pamphlet), available from New England Free Press, 791 Tremont St., Boston, Mass. 02118. (617) 536–9219.

The Diary of Che Guevara, ed. Robert Scheer, Bantam, $1.45. In English and Spanish.

Fanshen, William Hinton, Random House Vintage, 1966, $2.95. A documentary of revolution in a Chinese village.

Fidel Castro Speaks, eds. Martin Kenner and James Petras, Grove Press, 1968, $1.45. Speeches by Fidel.

The Great Fear in Latin America, John Gerassi, Collier Books, 1968, $1.50.

The Growth of the Modern West Indies, Gordon K. Lewis, Monthly Review Press, 1968, $4.50. Capitalism and the Caribbean.

Guerilla Warfare, Che Guevara, Random House Vintage, 1962, $1.65.

Guerrilla War, ed., trans. William McNaughton, Crane Press, 1970, 50¢. Mao, Che, and classic Chinese sources on the subject.

The Hidden History of the Korean War, I. F. Stone, Monthly Review Press, 1952 (reprinted 1969), $7.50 hardback.

Ideology and Organization in Communist China, Franz Schurman, University of California Press, 1969, $4.95; $12.95 hardback.

Imperialism (packet of eleven articles), New England Free Press, 791 Tremont St., Boston, Mass. 02118. (617) 536–9219, $1.70.

In the Fist of the Revolution, Jose Yglesias, Random House Vintage, 1969, $1.95.

The Indochina Story, Committee of Concerned Asian Scholars, Bantam, 1970, $1.25.

International Dependency in the 70's (pamphlet), Africa Research Group, $1.00 in the Empire; 50¢ to the movement. From NACLA, P.O. Box 57, Cathedral Sta., New York, N.Y. 10025.

The Israel-Arab Reader, ed. Walter Laqueur, Bantam, 1970, $1.65.

Juche (pamphlet), Kim Il Sung, available from the *Guardian,* 32 W. 22d St., New York, N.Y. 10010, 25¢/copy, $1 for 100.

Karl Marx on Colonialism and Modernization, ed. Shlomo Aviberi, Doubleday, 1969, $1.95.

Latin America (packet of sixteen items), New England Free Press, 791 Tremont St., Boston, Mass. 02118. (617) 536–9219, $3.50.

Latin American Development: A Selected Bibliography, 1950–1967, ed. J. L. Weaver, from American Bibliographical Center–Clio Press, Riviera Campus, 2010 Alameda Padre Serra, Santa Barbara, Calif. 93103, 1969, $7.25.

Latin American Radicalism: A Documentary Report on Left and Nationalist Movements, eds. Horowitz, de Castro, and Gerassi, Random House Vintage, 1969, $2.45.

Long Live the Victory of the People's War (pamphlet), Lin Piao, Peking English Language Press, 1966.

The Military Half, Jonathan Schell, Random House Vintage, 1968, $1.65.

Mylai 4, Seymour Hersh, Random House, 1970, $1.95; $5.95 hardback.

Neo-Colonialism: The Last Stage of Imperialism, Kwame Nkrumah, International Publishing Company, $2.95.

On the National and Colonial Question, China Books and Periodicals, 1967, 35¢.

The Peasants of North Vietnam, Gerard Challiana, Penguin, 1969, $1.65.

Peking Review, P.O. Box 399, Peking, China, Mail Order Dept., GUOZI SHUDIAN, Foreign Language Press.

Pentagonism, Juan Bosch, Grove Press, 1969, $5.00.

The Pillage of the Third World, Pierre Jalée, Monthly Review Press, 1968, $1.75; $6.00 hardback. Statistical study.

Puerto Rico: A Colony of the United States, Puerto Rican Youth Movement, New England Free Press, 1964, rev. ed. 1969.

Puerto Rico Libre, Apartado 2492, San Juan, P.R. 00903, $2.50/yr. Spanish-language weekly.

Red Star over China, Edgar Snow, Grove Press, rev. ed., 1968, $1.75.

Report from a Chinese Village, Jan Myrdal, NAL Signet, 1966, 95¢.

Revolution in the Revolution: Armed Struggle and Political Struggle in Latin America, Regis Debray, Monthly Review Press, 1969, $5.95.

Southeast Asia (packet of eleven articles), New England Free Press, 791 Tremont St., Boston, Mass. 02118. (617) 536–9219, $1.90.

Statistical Bulletin for Latin America, United Nations, New York, N.Y. 10017, biennial, $3.00.

Studies in Dying Colonialism, Frantz Fanon, Grove Press, 1967, $1.95. Essays on the Algerian revolution by its leading spokesman.

The Third World in the World Economy, Pierre Jalée, Monthly Review Press, 1969, $6.50. Statistical data based on UN reports.

Third World Liberation and the Fight Against the War (leaflet), Student Mobilization Committee, $2.00/10 copies.

Three Documents on the National Liberation Front, intro. Gabriel Kolko, Beacon, 1970, 95¢.

Towards the African Revolution, Frantz Fanon, Grove Press, 1968, $1.95.

Vietcong, Douglas Pike, MIT Press, 1966, $2.95. Pro-U.S. bias; organizational study of the NLF.

Vietnam: A Thousand Years of Struggle, People's Press, 50¢ (less in bulk).

Wretched of the Earth, Frantz Fanon, Grove Press, 1963, $1.25. Revolutionary violence in ex-colonial countries.

ORGANIZATIONS

Africa Research Group, P.O. Box 213, Cambridge, Mass. 02138. Radical research and educational organization; publishes *Organizer's Guide to Southern Africa; How Harvard Rules; Radical Study Guide to Africa*.

National Information Network on Latin America (NINOLA), P.O. Box 548, Cathedral Sta., New York, N.Y. 10025. Education for action; publishes newsletter, directory, reprint packet.

Pacific Studies Center, 1963 University Ave., East Palo Alto, Calif. 94303. Publishes the *Pacific Research and World Empire Telegram*, monthly, political economy of Pacific; assists research projects for that area.

Southern Africa Committee, 475 Riverside Drive, Rm. 752, New York, N.Y. 10027. Publishes the *Southern Africa Newsletter*.

Third World Coalition, c/o Susan Kakesako, Antioch College Union, Yellow Springs, Ohio 45387.

Tri-Continental Information Center, 1133 Broadway, New York, N.Y. 10010. Aids in third-world research.

Venceremos Brigade, P.O. Box 643, Cathedral Sta., New York, N.Y. 10025. Organizes people to go to Cuba to help with the sugar harvest.

Women

Abortion Rap, Florynce Kennedy and Diane Schulder, McGraw-Hill, 1971, $3.95.

Ain't I a Woman, WLF Publications Collective, 301 Jefferson Bldg., Iowa City, Iowa 52240, $1/issue, $4/yr.

The American Woman: Who Was She? ed. Anne Firor Scott, Prentice-Hall, 1971, $2.45. Letters, diaries, articles covering 120 years of feminism.

American Women and the Radical Movement, Freedom Socialist Publications, 3117 E. Thomas St., Seattle, Wash. 98102, 1968.

"Angry Notes From A Black Feminist," Doris Wright, c/o FEM, Box 454, Lenox Hill Sta., New York, N.Y. 10021, 50¢ (enclose stamped self-addressed envelope).

Aphra, P.O. Box 322, Springtown, Pa. 18081, $3.50/4 issues. A women's literary magazine.

Birth Control Handbook, McGill Student Association, New England Free Press, 791 Tremont St., Boston, Mass. 02118.

The Black Woman: An Anthology, ed. Toni Cade, Signet (NAL), 1970, 95¢.

The Blue Collar Marriage, Mirra Komarovsky, Random House, Vintage, 1964, $1.95.

Born Female, Caroline Bird, Pocket Books, 1970, 95¢. Job discrimination.

Century of Struggle, Eleanor Flexner, Atheneum, 1968, $3.45.

Current Women's Liberation Material Newsletter, c/o Laura X, 2325 Oak St., Berkeley, Calif. 94708. List of women in world history, $1.50; Bibliography of items in newsletter, $1.00; Packet of action project ideas, periodicals, papers, book reviews, $5.00.

Day Care: How to Plan, Develop and Operate a Day Care Center, E. Belle Evans, Beth Shub, Marlene Weinstein, Beacon Press, 1971, $6.95.

The Dialectic of Sex: The Case for Feminist Revolution, Shulamith Firestone, Bantam, 1971, $1.25.

The Diary of Anais Nin, ed. Gunther Stuhlmann, Harcourt, Brace, 1966-1971, Vols. 1-3, $2.85 each (paperback); Vol. 4, $7.95 (hardcover).

Everywoman, 1046 B.W. Washington Blvd., Venice, California 90291, $6/26 issues.

The Family, a Bread and Roses publication, 1151 Massachusetts Ave., Cambridge, Mass. 02138.

Female Liberation and the Sexual Caste System (packet of twenty-nine items), New England Free Press, 791 Tremont St., Boston, Mass. 02118, $5.00.

The Feminine Mystique, Betty Friedan, Dell, 1963, 95¢.

Good-Bye to All That, 120 Brooks Ave., San Diego, Calif. 92103, $5/26 issues.

The Legal Rights of Women, Brian R. Boyland, Award Books, 1971, 95¢.

Lilith: Journal of Women's Liberation, Women's Majority Union, P.O. Box 1895, Seattle, Wash. 98111.

Male and Female: A Study of Sexes in a Changing World, Margaret Mead, Dell, 1970, 95¢.

A Marxist Approach: Problems of Women's Liberation, Evelyn Reed, Pathfinder Press, 14 Charles Lane, New York, N.Y., 95¢.

A Matter of Simple Justice: The Report of the President's Task Force on Women's Rights and Responsibilities, available free from the Women's Bureau, Dept. of Labor, Washington, D.C. 20210.

The Mothers: The Matriarchal Theory of Social Organization, Robert Briffault, Humanities Press, 1931, $7.00.

New Broom, Box 341 Prudential Center Sta., Boston, Mass. 02143, $1/issue. Monthly legislative newsletter.

The New Feminism, Lucy Komisar, Franklin Watts, 1971, $5.95. For junior high and high school.

No More Fun and Games, Cell 16, 16 Lexington Ave., Cambridge, Mass. 02138, $1/issue. Publishes erratically.

Notes from the First Year, New York Radical Women, 799 Broadway, Rm. 412, New York, N.Y. 10003, 1968, $1.00. Collection of papers from early women's liberation groups.

Notes from the Second Year, P.O. Box AA, Old Chelsea Sta., New York, N.Y. 10011, 1969, $1.50. Radical feminist articles.

Off Our Backs, P.O. Box 4859, Cleveland Park Sta., Washington, D.C. 20008, $6/yr., $6.50 in Canada. Biweekly except August.

Patterns of Culture, Ruth Benedict, Houghton Mifflin Sentry, 1959, $1.95.

The Pedestal, Vancouver Women's Caucus, 511 Carroll St., Vancouver, B.C., Canada, $2/yr. in Canada, $2.50/yr. elsewhere.

The Place of American Women (economic exploitation of women), Joan Jordan, New England Free Press, 791 Tremont St., Boston, Mass. 02118, 15¢.

Prisoner of Sex, Norman Mailer, Little, Brown, 1971, $5.95, or *Harper's Magazine*, March 1971.

RAT, 241 E. 14th St., New York, N.Y. 10003, $6/yr.

The Second Sex, Simone de Beauvoir, Bantam, 1953, $1.25.

The Second Wave, A Magazine of the New Feminism, Box 303 Kenmore Sq. Sta., Boston, Mass. 02215, $3/4 issues, 75¢/issue. Feminist politics, fiction, poetry, etc.

Sexual Politics, Kate Millet, Avon, 1971, $2.95.

Sisterhood Is Powerful, ed. Robin Morgan, Vintage, 1970, $2.45.

Southern Journal of Women's Liberation, Box 30087 Lafayette Sq. Sta., New Orleans, La. 70130.

The Spokeswoman, 5464 South Shore Drive, Chicago, Ill. 60615, $7/yr. A monthly information service.

Up From Under, 339 Lafayette St., New York, N.Y. 10012, $3/5 issues, 60¢/issue.

A Vindication of the Rights of Women, Mary Wollstonecraft, Norton, 1967, $1.75. A feminist classic, originally published in 1791.

Voices from Women's Liberation, ed. Leslie B. Tanner, Signet (NAL), 1970, $1.50.

The Woman Question, International Publishers, $1.00. Marx, Engels, Lenin, and Stalin on women.

Woman Worker, P.O. Box 26605, Los Angeles, Calif. 90026, 15¢/copy, $1/subscription. Primarily for working women not in the movement.

Women: A Bibliography, c/o Lucinda Cisler, 102 W. 80th St., New York, N.Y. 10024, 50¢/copy; $4.50/10 copies; $12/30 copies.

Women: A Journal of Liberation, 3028 Greenmont Ave., Baltimore, Md. 31218, $1.00/issue, $4.00/yr.

Women and Their Bodies, Boston Women's Health Collective, 791 Tremont St., Boston, Mass. 02118, 1970, 90¢.

Women and the Law: The Unfinished Revolution, Leo Kanowitz, University of New Mexico Press, 1969, $3.95.

"Women in American Society," *Radical America* (Vol. 4), 1237 Spraight St., Madison, Wis. 53703, $1/single copy, discounts for quantity.

Women's Rights Law Reporter, 119 Fifth Ave., New York, N.Y. 10003, $12/year, lawyers $18/year, $3/issue. Review of legal problems and issues relating to women.

Working Women, the Forgotten Third of the Working Class, Ilene Winkler, International Socialists, P.O. Box 910, Berkeley, Calif. 94701.

ORGANIZATIONS

Black Women's Liberation Committee, 300 Ninth Ave., New York, N.Y. 10001.

Bread and Roses, 1151 Massachusetts Ave., Cambridge, Mass. 02138. Socialist women's liberation organization.

Center for Women's Studies, San Diego State College, San Diego, Calif. 92115. Good women's studies program; Bibliography of Women Writers (International), 50¢.

Chicago Women's Liberation Center, 5406 S. Dorchester Ave., Chicago, Ill. 60615.

Everywoman Bookstore and Publishing Co., 6516 83rd St., Los Angeles, Calif. 90045.

Federally Employed Women (FEW), c/o Daisy Fields, National Press Bldg., Suite 487, Washington, D.C. 20004.

Female Liberation, 303 Kenmore Sq. Sta., Boston, Mass. 02215.

National Association for Repeal of Abortion Laws (NARAL), 250 W. 57th St., Rm. 2428, New York, N.Y. 10019.

National Organization for Women (NOW), 146 W. 68th St., New York, N.Y. 10023; also 9601 Wilshire Blvd., No. 22, Beverly Hills, Calif. 90210. Chapters in major U.S. cities.

New Feminist Bookstore, 1525 E. 53rd St., Rm. 503, Chicago, Ill. 60615.

New York Strike Coalition, 118 E. 28th St., Rm. 405, New York, N.Y. 10016.

New York Women's Center, 36 W. 22nd St., New York, N.Y. 10010.

Redstockings, Box 748, Stuyvesant Sta., New York, N.Y. 10009.

Women's Center, 1027 S. Crenshaw Blvd., Los Angeles, Calif. 90019.

Women's History Research Center, 2325 Oak St., Berkeley,

Calif. 94708. One of the best sources of feminist literature and information; includes research, lending, corresponding, selling library of books, periodicals, bibliographies, articles, tapes, pictures; catalogs, course outlines, term papers, theses from women's studies courses around the country. $12 for first 2 years.

Women's Liberation, 2398 Bancroft Way, Berkeley, Calif. 94704.

Women's Liberation Distribution Center, 1945 Calvert St., NW, Washington, D.C. 20009.

The Military

The Draft

Amex (*The American Expatriate in Canada*), P.O. Box 187, Sta. D, Toronto 165, Ont., Canada, 35¢/issue, $1/3 issues, $3/9 issues, $5/16 issues.

Emigration to Canada: Legal Notes for Draft-Age Men, CCCO, 2016 Walnut St., Philadelphia, Pa. 19103, free. Emigration and American law.

Exiled: Handbook for the Draft-Age Emigrant, Daniel Finnerty and Charles Funnell, Philadelphia Resistance, 2006 Walnut St., Philadelphia, Pa. 19103. Information on immigration requirements for some two dozen countries.

Face to Face with Your Draft Board: A Guide to Personal Appearances, Allan Blackman, War Resisters League, 1969, 95¢. For COs.

Guide to the Draft, Arlo Tatum and Joseph Tuchinsky, War Resisters League, 1969, $1.95. Quite thorough discussion of alternatives to the draft including emigration to Canada and prison. Also includes long list of draft counseling and legal aid organizations.

Handbook for Conscientious Objectors, ed. Arlo Tatum, Central Committee for Conscientious Objectors, $1.00. *The* book for COs.

Immigration to Canada and Its Relation to the Draft and the Military, Montreal Council to Aid War Resisters, free.

In the Service of Their Country: War Resisters in Prison. Willard Gaylin, Grosset and Dunlap, 1970, $1.95.

IV-F: A Guide to Draft Exemption, David Suttler, Grove Press, 1970, $1.50.

Mastering the Draft: A Comprehensive Easy-Reference Guide to Solving Draft Problems, A. O. Shapiro and J. M. Striker, Avon, 1971, $3.95.

New Canada, Canadian Liberation Publishers, Box 6106, Station A, Toronto, Ont., Canada, monthly, $2/year, 15¢/sample copy.

New Draft Law Manual, ed. Ann Fagan Ginger, National Lawyers Guild Publications, 1970, $6.00. Complete reference text for lawyers, draft counselors, registrants, and draftees.

The New Exiles: American War Resisters in Canada, Roger N. Williams, Liveright, 1971, $2.95.

The Resister, Philadelphia Resisters, 928 Chestnut St., Philadelphia, Pa. 19107. Monthly, available for a contribution.

Selective Service Regulations, U.S. Government Printing Office, $5.00 for an indefinite period. (Published irregularly.) Catalogue #Y3.Se4:7. A morass of details, but essential for lifesaving loopholes.

ORGANIZATIONS

Calgary Committee on War Immigrants, P.O. Box 3234, Calgary, Alta., Canada.

CCCO—Western Region, 437 Market St., San Francisco, Calif. 94105. Counseling Montana, Wyoming, Colorado, New Mexico, and west; consultants to counselors.

Central Committee for Conscientious Objectors (CCCO), 2016 Walnut St., Philadelphia, Pa. 19103. Counseling, advice and information to counselors; publishes newsletter, CO handbook ($1).

Charlottesville Pledge, 128 Chancellor St., Charlottesville, Va. 22903. Circulates petitions pledging noncooperation with the draft.

Chicago Area Draft Resisters (CADRE), 519 W. North Ave., Chicago, Ill. 60610.

Committee to Assist War Objectors, 250 York St., Winnipeg, Man., Canada.

Draft Information Center of New Jersey, c/o Rutgers Draft Information Center, R.P.O. 5513, New Brunswick, N.J. 08903.

Draft Information Service, American Friends Service Committee, P.O. Box 247, Cambridge, Mass. 02138.

Immigration and Refugee Aid Society, 2101 Lansdowne Ave., Saskatoon, Sask., Canada.

Logos, P.O. Box 782, Montreal 101, Que., Canada. For help in moving to Canada.

Montreal Council to Aid War Resisters, Case Postale 5, Succ. Wsmt., Montreal 215, Que., Canada. (514) 843-3132.

Nova Scotia Committee to Aid American War Objectors, P.O. Box 19, Armdale (Halifax), N.S., Canada.

Red, White and Black, 44 St. George St., Toronto 5, Ont., Canada. Multi-issue exile group of draft resisters.

Resist, 763 Massachusetts Ave., Cambridge, Mass. 02139. Support for draft resistance: money; organization of national actions and programs; newsletter and other material.

Riverside Association for Selective Service Avoidance (RASSA), RASSA News Service, University of California, Riverside, Calif. 92507. Would like information on all draft actions; setting up mailing list and communications network.

St. John Anti-Draft Programme, 11 Prince William St., Apt. 3, St. John, N.B., Canada.

Toronto Anti-Draft Program, 2347 Yonge St., Rm. 14, Toronto 14, Ont., Canada. Gets people into Canada; central coordinating group for draft counseling and information.

Union for National Draft Opposition, 226 Palmer, Princeton University, Princeton, N.J. 08504. Coordinates draft turn-ins; organizing public support to end the draft.

Vancouver Committee to Aid American War Objectors, P.O. Box 4231, Vancouver 9, B.C., Canada.

Vietnam Mobilization Committee, 241 Victoria, Toronto, Ont., Canada. (416) 863-0494. Contact for affiliates in other Canadian cities.

GIs and Veterans

The Bond, 150 Fifth Ave., New York, N.Y. 10011, $3 for nonservicemen. A serviceman's newspaper, published by American Servicemen's Union.

Fatigue Press, P.O. Box 388, Killeen, Tex. 76541. By and for GIs at Fort Hood.

GI Rights and Army Justice: The Draftee's Guide to Military Life and Law, Robert S. Rivkin, Grove Press, 1970, $1.75. How to protect your rights under the Constitution and the Uniform Code of Military Justice.

GIs and the Fight Against the War (leaflet), Student Mobilization Committee, $2 for 100.

The GIs Handbook on Military Injustice, PFC F. O. Richardson, American Servicemen's Union, 10¢ for GIs, 25¢ for civilians. How military justice works against the rank-and-file GI, and what we can do about it.

Potemkin, American Servicemen's Union, free to servicemen.

The Unlawful Concert, Fred Gardner, Viking Compass, 1970, $1.25. An account of the Presidio mutiny case.

Up Against the Brass, Andy Stapp, Simon & Schuster, 1970, $4.95. Stapp's experiences trying to organize within the army and the founding of the American Servicemen's Union.

ORGANIZATIONS

American Deserters Committee, 75 Huntley St., Toronto, Ont., Canada; 102 Villeneuve E., Montreal 151, Que., Canada; 1326 Hamilton St., Regina, Sask., Canada; Unga Philosophers, 13 Drottningatan, Stockholm, Sweden; P.O. Box 3822, Sta. D., Vancouver, B.C., Canada.

American Servicemen's Union, 156 Fifth Ave., Rm. 538, New York, N.Y. 10010.

Committee of Returned Volunteers, P.O. Box 380, Cooper Sta., New York, N.Y. 10003.

GI Alliance, P.O. Box 9087, Washington, D.C. 20003. Information clearinghouse for GI affairs.

GI Civil Liberties Defense Fund, 41 Union Sq. W., New York, N.Y. 10003.

GI Counseling Services, 339 Lafayette St., New York, N.Y. 10012. Counseling by mail or in person; trains counselors.

GI-Civilian Solidarity Committee, c/o American Serviceman's Union, 156 Fifth Ave., New York, N.Y. 10010.

G.I.'s Against the War, 3400 N. Sheffield Ave., Chicago, Ill. 60657.

GI's United Against the War in Vietnam, P.O. Box 543, Columbia, S.C. 29202.

Link, the Servicemans' Link to Peace, 1029 Vermont Ave., NW, Rm. 200, Washington, D.C. 20005. Clearinghouse for information on GI antiwar activities.

Movement for a Democratic Military, 429 J St., San Diego, Calif. 94704. A press service for GI papers; information on military counseling and legal aid; GI organizing.

Reservists and National Guardsmen Against the War, c/o Penn Comment, Houston Hall, 3417 Spruce St., University of Pennsylvania, Philadelphia, Pa. 19104.

Reservists Committee to Stop the War, P.O. Box 4398, Berkeley, Calif. 94704.

United States Serviceman's Fund, P.O. Box 3061, Oakland, Calif. 94608. Active on GI rights and antiwar movement; organizes and supports coffeehouses.

Vietnam Veterans Against the War, 156 Fifth Ave., New York, N.Y. 10010. Branches in most major cities, plus sixteen area coordinators around the country. Contact central office for names and addresses.

Labor

The American Worker in the Twentieth Century: A History Through Autobiographies, E. Ginzberg and H. Berman, Free Press of Glencoe, 1963, $8.95.

Blue Ridge: The History of Our Struggle (pamphlet), Brenda Mull, New England Free Press.

Booklet of Labor Statistics, Victoria Bonnell and Michael Reich, New England Free Press.

Brother Bill McKie: Building the Union at Ford, International Publishers.

Catholic Worker, 36 E. 1st St., New York, N.Y. 10003, 25¢/mo.

Challenge/Desafio, Progressive Labor Party, $2.00/yr.

Farm Labor Organizing, 1905–1967, New England Free Press, 50¢.

Forty Acres, Mark Day, intro. by Cesar Chavez, Praeger, 1971, $6.95.

History of the Labor Movement in the United States, Philip Foner, International Publishers, 4 volumes, 1947–1965, Vols. I-III, $7.50 each; Vol. IV, $8.50.

John L. Lewis: An Unauthorized Biography, Saul Alinsky, Putnam, 1949.

Labor in the South: Black Workers Set Against White, Strike Broken (pamphlet), Robert Analavage, Radical Education Project.

Labor Today, 343 S. Dearborn St., Rm. 600, Chicago, Ill. 60604, $3.50/yr., 50¢/copy, 5 or more @ 30¢.

Labor's Story as Reported by the American Labor Press, ed. G. H. Cole, Glen Cove Community Press, 1961.

Labor's Untold Story, Richard Boyer and Herbert Morais, UE, 11 E. 51st St., New York, N.Y. 10022, $2.50. Classic.

News and Letters, 415 Brainard St., Detroit, Mich. 48201.

Organize! My Life as a Union Man, Wyndham Mortimer, Beacon, 1971, $9.95.

Organizing and the Law, S. I. Schlossberg and F. E. Sherman, BNA Books, 1967 (2nd. ed.), $5.50.

Strategy for Labor: A Radical Proposal, André Gorz, Beacon Press, 1967, $1.95.

The Wobblies, Patrick Renshaw, Doubleday Anchor, 1968, $1.45.

The Working Class (packet of twenty-six articles), New England Free Press, $4.85.

ORGANIZATIONS

A. Phillip Randolph Institute, 217 W. 125th St., New York, N.Y. 10027.

AFL-CIO, 815 16th St., NW, Washington, D.C. 20006. Source for addresses of individual unions.

Alliance for Labor Action (ALA), 810 Rhode Island Ave., NE, Washington, D.C. 20018.

Catholic Worker Movement, 36 E. 1st St., New York, N.Y. 10003.

Environmental Health Programs, Inc., 1411 K St., NW, Washington, D.C. 20005. Organizing for occupational safety and health.

Industrial Workers of the World, 2422 N. Halsted St., Chicago, Ill. 60614; also 607 Queens Ave., New Westminster, B.C., Canada.

International Longshoremen's and Warehousemen's Union (ILWU), 150 Golden Gate Ave., San Francisco, Calif. 94102. Long-time radical tradition.

Labor Research Association, 80 E. 11th St., New York, N.Y., 10003.

Labor-University Alliance. For information contact district offices of the ILWU and UE.

League for Industrial Democracy, 112 E. 19th St., New York, N.Y. 10003.

National Advisory Committee on Farm Labor, 112 E. 19th St., New York, N.Y. 10003.

National Caucus, SDS Labor Committee, 647 W. 184th St., New York, N.Y. 10033.

Textile Workers Union of America, 99 University Place, New York, N.Y., 10003. Contact: A. Gordon, General Counsel. Information and assistance in combating racial or sex discrimination, consumer fraud, working in the South as a union organizer.

United Auto Workers, 8000 E. Jefferson St., Detroit, Mich. 48214.

United Electrical, Radio and Machine Workers of America (UE), 11 E. 51st St., New York, N.Y. 10022.

United Farm Workers Organization, P.O. Box 130, Delano, Calif. 93215; also 4520 Colerain Ave., Cincinnati, Ohio 45223.

Wildcat Action Group, P.O. Box 253, New York, N.Y. 10009.

Worker's League, 243 E. 10th St., Rm. 8, New York, N.Y. 10003.

Workingman's Circle, 175 E. Broadway, New York, N.Y. 10002.

Professionals

Public-School Teachers (see also High Schools; Universities)

The Challenge of Youth, Erik Erikson, Anchor Doubleday, 1963, $1.95.

Childhood and Society, Erik Erikson, Norton, rev. ed., 1964, $2.95.

Death at an Early Age, Jonathan Kozol, Bantam, 1968, 95¢.

Early Socialization (packet of twelve articles), New England Free Press, 791 Tremont St., Boston, Mass. 02118. (617) 536–9219, $2.20.

Edcentric, Center for Educational Reform, 2115 S St., NW, Washington, D.C. 20008. 8 issues/yr. free.

Education and Ecstasy, George Leonard, Dell Delta, 1969, $2.25.

Free School Movement in America, Jonathan Kozol, c/o Storefront Learning Center, 90 W. Brookline St., Boston, Mass. 02118, $2.00. Contacts, leads, addresses.

How Children Fail, John Holt, Dell, 1970, 95¢.

How Children Learn, John Holt, Pitman, 1967, $2.25.

The Lives of Children, George Dennison, Random House, 1969, $6.95.

Open Classroom, Herbert Kohl, Random House Vintage, $1.65.

Summerhill: A Radical Approach to Child Rearing, A. S. Neill, Hart, 1960, $1.95.

Teacher, Sylvia Ashton Warner, Bantam, 1964, 95¢.

Teaching as a Subversive Activity, Neil Postman and Charles Weingartner, Delacorte, 1969, $5.95.

36 Children, Herbert Kohl, Signet NAL, 1968, 95¢.

This Magazine Is About Schools, 56 Esplanade St., Suite 301, Toronto 1, Ont., Canada, $1.15/issue, $3.50/yr. Experimental schools and teaching innovations.

Turning on the System: War in the Philadelphia Public Schools, Henry Resnick, Pantheon, 1970, $6.95.

Vietnam Curriculum, New York Review of Books published with Boston Area Teaching Project, New York Review of Books, 250 W. 57th St., New York, N.Y. 10019, 4 vols., looseleaf.

ORGANIZATIONS

American Federation of Teachers, 716 N. Rush St., Chicago, Ill. 60611.

New Schools Exchange, 2840 Hidden Valley La., Santa Barbara, Calif. 93103. Publishes biweekly newsletter on free school/experimental education, and comprehensive directory; subscriptions $5/5 mos., $10/yr.

Summerhill Society, 6063 Harges St., Los Angeles, Calif. 90034; also 339 Lafayette St., New York, N.Y. 10012; or 5 Beekman St., New York, N.Y. 10038.

Lawyers, Scientists, and Health Professionals

The Body Politic, Medical Committee for Human Rights, 1520 Naudain St., Philadelphia, Pa. 19146.

Bulletin of Atomic Scientists, Education Foundation for Nuclear Science, 935 60th St., Chicago, Ill. 60637, $10/yr.

The College Law Bulletin, U.S. National Student Association, 2115 S St., NW, Washington, D.C. 20008, monthly.

The Coming Revolution in Medicine, David Rutstein, MIT Press, 1967, $4.95.

Community Psychiatry: Epidemiological and Social Themes, Mervyn Susser, Random House, 1968, $8.95. Textbook.

"The Doctor-Nurse Game," Leonard Stein, *American Journal of Nursing,* January 1968. Effects of hierarchies; powerlessness of nurses and effect on patient care.

Doctors, Martin Gross, Dell, 1967, $1.25.

Doctors, Patients and Health Insurance, H. M. and A. R. Somers, Brookings Institution, 1961, $7.50.

Getting By with a Little Help from Our Friends, Barbara and Al Haber, Radical Education Project, P.O. Box 625, Ann Arbor, Mich. 48107. Summary of the Radical in the Professions Conference, Ann Arbor, 1967.

Health Care in America, hearings before Senate Subcommittee on Executive Reorganization, April 1968.

Health PAC Bulletin, Health Policy Advisory Center, 17 Murray St., New York, N.Y. 10007, 25¢/issue, $5/yr. to students, $7/yr. regular. Articles include "The Malfeasance of Health," March 1970; "Medical Empire: Who Controls?" December 1968, April 1969; "The Medical-Industrial Complex," November 1969; "Medicine and the Military," Howard Levy, April 1970; "Mental Health for the Masses," May 1969.

Medical Cadre, International Liberation School, 1925 S. Grove St., Berkeley, Calif. 94704, 25¢.

"The Medical Student," Kenneth Keniston, *New Physician,* October 1968.

The Myth of Mental Illness, Thomas Szasz, Dell Delta, 1967, $2.25.

Professional Power and American Medicine, E. Rayack, World Publishing, 1967, $7.25.

The Radical Therapist, P.O. Box 1215, Minot, N.D. 58701, periodical, $6/yr. (for 6 or 9 issues).

Sickness and Society, Raymond S. Duff and August B. Hollingshead, Harper & Row, 1968, $12.50.

So Human an Animal, René Dubos, Scribner, 1968, $2.45. A humanistic approach to science and technology; how they can benefit man.

ORGANIZATIONS

Academic and Professional Lobby for a Responsible Congress, 3041 Broadway, New York, N.Y. 10027. Coordinates lobbying efforts in Congress; sets up briefings for professional groups wishing to talk with congressmen.

The Action Caucus for Social Change and World Peace, c/o Dwight Arnold, 310 Education Bldg., Kent State University, Kent, Ohio 44240.

Alliance for Radical Change, 11 Norris St., Cambridge, Mass. 02140. Professional organizing.

American Civil Liberties Union (ACLU), 156 Fifth Ave., New York, N.Y. 10010.

American Civil Liberties Union of Northern California, 503 Market St., San Francisco, Calif. 94105. Not a legal defense organization, but will take precedent-setting cases.

Association of Scientist-Engineers for a Reorientation of Technology (ASSERT), Swarthmore College, Swarthmore, Pa. 19081.

Federation of American Scientists, 2025 I St., NW, Washington, D.C. 20006.

Health Education Project, 2024 N. Halsted St., Chicago, Ill. 60614. Affiliated with the Student Health Organization; publishes monthly newsletter for activist health students.

Health Policy Advisory Center, Inc., 17 Murray St., New York, N.Y. 10007. Research on health care problems.

Law Commune, 156 Fifth Ave., New York, N.Y. 10010.

Law Students Civil Rights Research Council, 156 Fifth Ave., New York, N.Y. 10010.

Lawyers Committee for Effective Action to End the War, 74 Trinity Pl., 24th fl., New York, N.Y. 10006.

Lawyers Committee on American Policy Towards Vietnam, 38 Park Row, New York, N.Y. 10038.

Medical Committee for Human Rights, 1520 Naudain St., Philadelphia, Pa. 19146. Local chapters in many cities. An action organization for health professionals; handles medical crises, physical exams for the draft, references to friendly doctors.

Medical Resistance Union, P.O. Box 382, Prudential Sta., Boston, Mass. 02199.

National Lawyers Guild, 1 Hudson St., New York, N.Y. 10038. An organization of lawyers and law students which provides legal support for the movement; chapters in most major cities.

National Lawyers Guild Publications, P.O. Box 673a, Berkeley, Calif. 94701.

Physicians' Forum, Inc., 510 Madison Ave., New York, N.Y. 10017.

Psychologists for a Democratic Society, P.O. Box 427, Peter Stuyvesant Sta., New York, N.Y. 10009.

Radical Caucus of the American Psychiatric Association, Tom Harper, 2 Greenwich Ave., White Plains, N.Y. 10605.

Science Action Coordinating Committee, MIT, Rm. 50–316, Cambridge, Mass. 02139.

Science Action Group, 400 Osborne Memorial Laboratory, Prospect St., New Haven, Conn. 06520.

Society for Social Responsibility in the Sciences, Rock Hill Rd., Bala Cynwyd, Pa. 19004.

Student Health Organization, 1613 E. 53d St., Chicago, Ill. 60615. National organization of activist students.

Union of Concerned Scientists, P.O. Box 289, MIT Branch Sta., Cambridge, Mass. 02139.

Union of Radical Sociologists, c/o Irwin Sherber, Dept. of Sociology, University of California, Berkeley, Calif. 94720; or Carol Brown, Sociology Dept., Hunter College, New York, N.Y. 10012.

Other Groups

Activities for the Aged and Infirm: A Handbook for the Untrained Worker, Toni Merrill, Thomas, 1967, $12.75.

Adult Health: Services for the Chronically Ill and Aged, Frank W. Reynolds and P. C. Barsam, Macmillan, 1967, $8.25.

Aging and Society, Matilda Riley, Russell Sage, 1968, $25.00. Inventory of research findings.

Elderly Patient: Mental Patients in Nursing Homes, Bernard Stotsky, Grune, 1968, $5.75.

Employment, Income and Retirement Problems of the Aged, Juanita Kreps, Duke University Press, 1963, $7.50.

Group Work with the Aged, Susan H. Kubie and Gertrude Landau, International Universities Press, 1969, $1.95.

How Churches Fight Poverty: Sixty Successful Local Projects,
E. Greenwood, Friends Press, $1.95.

*Individual and Group Service in the Mobilization for Youth
Experience,* H. H. Weissman, Association Press, 1969, $2.50.

Medicare and Hospitals, Herman M. and Anne R. Somers, Brookings Institution, 1967, $2.50.

Medicare and Social Security Explained, Commerce Clearing
House, 1968, $3.50.

Medicare and You, W. Adler and S. Ross, Signet NAL, 1966,
60¢.

A Modern Priest Looks at His Outdated Church, J. Kavanaugh,
Pocket Books, 1967, 95¢.

Motive Magazine, P.O. Box 871, Nashville, Tenn. 57202, $5/yr.
Religious activist magazine.

Problems of Aging, Herman J. Loetner, Dickenson, 1967, $2.95.

Religion in the United States, B. Y. Landis, Barnes & Noble,
1965, $1.25.

*The Religious Factor, a Sociological Study of Religion's Impact
on Politics, Economics and Family Life,* George Lensky, Doubleday, 1961, $1.95.

Relocation in Urban Planning: From Obstacle to Opportunity,
Paul L. Niebanck and Mark P. Yessian, University of Pennsylvania
Press, 1968, $4.95.

Social and Medical Problems of the Elderly, Kenneth Hazell,
Thomas, 1966, $10.50.

Social Welfare of the Aging, J. Kaplan and G. Aldridge, Columbia University Press, 1962, $10.00.

38th Annual Yearbook of American Churches, ed. C. H. Jacquet,
Council Press, 1970.

WELFARE RECIPIENTS: ORGANIZATIONS

National Welfare Rights Organization, 1419 H St., NW, Washington, D.C. 20005. National organization of local welfare recipients' groups; resource for information, leadership training, and
other services; coordinates nation's welfare rights actions.

Poverty Rights Action Center, 1419 H St., NW, Washington,
D.C. 20005.

Welfare Rights Organization, 2631 Woodward Ave., Detroit,
Mich. 48201.

RELIGIOUS INSTITUTIONS: ORGANIZATIONS

Arlington Street Church, Arlington St., Boston, Mass. 02116.
Unitarian-Universalist; a base of much radical activity in Boston;

runs a coffeehouse and continual draft counseling; has given sanctuary to draft resisters; offers facilities to many radical groups.

Catholic Central Union, 3835 Westminster Pl., St. Louis, Mo. 63108.

Catholic Peace Fellowship, 3619 12th St., NE, Washington, D.C. 20017; also 339 Lafayette St., New York, N.Y. 10012.

Clergy and Laymen Concerned About Vietnam, 475 Riverside Dr., Rm. 510, New York, N.Y. 10027.

Council for Christian Social Action, 289 Park Ave. S., New York, N.Y. 10010.

Fellowship of Reconciliation, 60 Lowther St., Toronto, Ont., Canada.

The Havurat Shalom, 113 College Ave., Somerville, Mass. 02144; also a group in New York City. A collective of young Jews, who study and organize outside the religious institution; work toward social change.

Jewish Liberation Project, 150 Fifth Ave., Rm. 700, New York, N.Y. 10011.

The Jewish Radical Coalition, 150 Fifth Ave., Rm. 700, New York, N.Y. 10011.

Judson Memorial Church, 55 Washington Sq. S., New York, N.Y. 10012. Offers many community services: youth counseling, drug programs, free mobile clinic in Lower East Side.

Ministry of Urban Concern, 1313 Clarkson St., Denver, Colo. 80218.

National Federation of Temple Youth (NFTY), 838 Fifth Ave., New York, N.Y. 10021. An organization of high-school-aged Reform Jews; organized on local, regional, and national level; sponsors educational conferences, leadership institutes, and community action projects for youth. Has liaisons with European youth movements.

Program in Appalachia Through Christian Effort, P.O. Box 273, Allen, Ky. 41601.

Quaker Resistance, 3611 Powellton Ave., Philadelphia, Pa. 19104.

Society of Friends, 60 Lowther St., Toronto 5, Ont., Canada.

Society of Priests for a Free Ministry, 86 Linda Ave., No. 204, Oakland, Calif. 94611.

Student Christian Movement, Hart House, University of Toronto, Toronto 5, Ont., Canada.

Union of American Hebrew Congregations (UAHC), 838 Fifth Ave., New York, N.Y. 10021 (Commission on Social Action).

Unitarian Universalist Association, 25 Beacon St., Boston, Mass. 02108.

University Christian Movement, 1145 Massachusetts Ave., Cambridge, Mass. 02138; also 475 Riverside Dr., New York, N.Y. 10027. A regional organization of activists; does organizing and funding.

World Council of Churches, 475 Riverside Dr., New York, N.Y. 10027. Represents mainline Protestant, Anglican, and Orthodox churches throughout the world.

Prisoners (see also Legal Protection; Ethnic and Racial Groups)

Accomplices to the Crime: The Arkansas Prison Scandal, Thomas Murton and Joe Hyams, Grove Press, 1970, $1.45.

Attorney for the Damned, ed. Arthur Weinberg, Simon & Schuster, 1961, $2.45.

Brief Against Death, Edgar Smith, Avon, 1968, $1.25.

Children in Trouble: A National Scandal, Howard James, Pocket Books, 1970, 95¢.

Conversations with the Dead, Danny Lyon, Holt, Rinehart & Winston, 1970, $6.95.

Crime in America, Ramsey Clark, Pocket Books, 1971, $1.50.

The Crime of Martin Sostre, Vincent Copeland, McGraw-Hill, 1970, $1.50.

The Crime of Punishment, Dr. Karl Menninger, Viking, 1969, $1.95.

Crimes without Victims—Deviant Behavior and Public Policy: Abortion, Homosexuality, Drug Addiction, Edwin Schur, Spectrum, 1965, $2.45.

Criminal Law Reporter, 1231 25th St., NW, Washington, D.C.

The Death Penalty in America: An Anthology, ed. Hugo Adam Bedau, Anchor, 1968, $2.45.

An Eye for an Eye: Four Inmates on the Crime of American Prisons Today, H. J. Griswold et al., Holt, Rinehart & Winston, 1970, $6.95.

The Felon, John Irwin, Spectrum, $2.45.

Fortune and Men's Eyes, John Herbert, Grove Press, 1968, $1.95. A play.

Fortune News, 333 Avenue of the Americas, New York, N.Y. 10014. Monthly. Contribution to the Fortune Society requested.

Maximum Security: Letters from Prison, eds. Eve Pell and the Prison Law Project, Dutton, 1972 (Jan.), $5.95.

Minorities and the Police, David H. Bagley and Harold Mendelsohn, Free Press, 1968, $2.45.

Miracle of the Rose, Jean Genet, Grove Press, 1968, $1.25.

On the Yard, Malcolm Braly, Fawcett, 1967, 75¢.

Our Criminal Society: The Social and Legal Sources of Crime in America, E. M. Schur, Spectrum, 1969, $2.95.

Penal Digest International, Box 89, Iowa City, Iowa 52240, monthly, $6/year.

The People vs. Baby, Gertrude Samuels, Avon, 95¢.

Prison Action News, c/o Linda Taylor, 103 Quinn Road, Rochester, N.Y. 14623. Newsletter on how relatives and friends are organizing to aid inmates.

Prison Community, Donald Clemmer, Holt, Rinehart & Winston, $6.95.

"Prison Discipline and Inmate Rights," *Harvard Civil Rights, Civil Liberties Law Review*, 1970, Harvard University Law School.

Prison Notes, Barbara Deming, Beacon Press, 1970, $1.95.

Prison within Society: A Reader in Penology, ed. Laurence Hazelrigg, Anchor, 1969, $1.95.

The Professional Thief, ed. E. H. Sutherland, Phoenix, 1937, $1.95. A classic.

Prostitution and Society, Fernando Henriques, Grove Press, 1966, 95¢.

"The Role of the Eighth Amendment in Prison Reform," *University of Chicago Law Review*, 1971.

The Society of Captives: A Study of a Maximum Security Prison, Gresham M. Sykes, Princeton U. Press, 1958, $1.95.

Tattoo the Wicked Cross, Floyd Salas, Grove Press, 1968, $1.25.

The Violent Gang, Lewis Yablonsky, Penguin, $1.95.

ORGANIZATIONS

Chicago Connections, 21 E. Van Buren, Rm. 605, Chicago, Ill. 60605. Inmate families organizing.

Committee for the Advancement of Criminal Justice, 3 Joy St., Boston, Mass. 02108. Penal reform lobbying organization composed of representatives of citizens' groups, professional correction officers, and experts in penology.

Fortune Society, 1545 Broadway, Suite 603, New York, N.Y. 10036. (212) 265-5644. Pioneer ex-convict organization for education of the public to an awareness of the problems of the prison system.

LIBRA, 1145 Massachusetts Ave., Cambridge, Mass. 02138, (617) 661-1966. Jobs and homes for men and women on their release from prison.

Massachusetts Council on Crime and Correction, 3 Joy St., Boston, Mass. 02108. (617) 523-5527. Clearinghouse for activities in prisons and among the public.

NAACP Legal Defense and Educational Fund, 1776 Broadway,

Suite 1900, New York, N.Y. 10019. Fighting to end capital punishment.

National Council on Crime and Delinquency, 44 E. 23rd, New York, N.Y. 10010. (212) 254-7110. Research Center, Paramus, N.J. 07652. (201) 262-7300.

Prison Law Project, 5406 Claremont Ave., Oakland, Calif. 94618. Group of lawyers and others working for prisoners' rights in California.

Self-Development Group, 3 Joy St., Boston, Mass. 02108. (617) 523-3580. Organization of former convicts working within prisons and with released men.

TO OUR READERS

The O.M. Collective would like to hear your suggestions, experiences, corrections, or ideas for revising this book. Write to us at:

O.M. Collective
211 Bay State Road
Boston, Mass. 02215

The O.M. Collective is not able to fill orders. Please order additional copies from your local book outlet or: Bantam Books, Inc., Dept. CS 31, 666 Fifth Avenue, New York, N.Y. 10019. (Send check or money order—no currency or COD's, please. If less than 6 books, add 10¢ per book for postage and handling. There is no postage or handling charge for orders of 6 or more books. Allow 4 weeks for delivery.)